MONEY,
BANKING,
and the
UNITED STATES
ECONOMY

Harry D. Hutchinson

UNIVERSITY
OF
DELAWARE

MONEY, BANKING, and the UNITED STATES ECONOMY

NEW YORK

Appleton-Century-Crofts

DIVISION OF MEREDITH PUBLISHING COMPANY

To my wonderful family

PREFACE

This book is designed primarily for use in undergraduate money and banking courses, normally taken by students with a background of at least one introductory economics course. It was written with a one-semester course in mind but could be used in a two-semester course if supplemented generously with some of the excellent paperback readings books now available in the money area.

In many ways the text is conventional. Like many others it approaches the subject in four parts. First, the institutional material needed for understanding the monetary structure and the determinants of the money supply are discussed; second, the analytical material required to extend the student's grasp of macroeconomic theory and the role of money in it, to a usable and, hopefully, enlightening level, is introduced; third, the institutional and theoretical requirements for understanding problems of the balance of payments and international finance are explained; finally, all the preceding are employed in a discussion of economic policy. Also, like many other money and banking books, the emphasis is on the *economics* of money with institutional and historical material being included as means, necessary for putting meat on the analytical bones, rather than as ends in themselves.

But every textbook writer hopes he has done some things that are different, and some that are better than those in books already in existence. My objective was to write a book that would carry the gifted, motivated student just as far along the road to understanding the murky jungles of monetary economics as do contemporary undergraduate texts, while providing the average student with as logical and nontechnical a discussion of the subject as was possible.

The text does develop a full, simplified macroeconomic model and illustrates its use. In this respect the theory treatment carries the student as far, if not further than many others. The economics major, for example, should be prepared to go immediately into an intermediate macroeconomic theory course after his money and banking course, with a rather well-defined notion of what macroeconomics is all about. One of the prime objectives of this text is to accomplish this.

For the student who does not now plan to do further work in economics, however, it is my feeling that a text should offer a basic, understandable framework with as many of the technical "tools of the trade" omitted from the main body of discussion as is possible. With the latter student in mind the text relegates to separate appendixes or to detailed footnotes such widely discussed, but often confusing, technical matters as the *ex post-ex ante* distinction, the complete source and use of member-bank reserves table, the development of L-M and I-S curves, and the exact formula for the marginal efficiency of investment. In addition, because it has been the author's experience that the average student forgets much that he has learned in his introductory course, a complete review of what is usually principles-level macrotheory is included.

Such a treatment provides greater flexibility for the instructor who, after all, is the only one who knows the backgrounds and objectives of his students. For those, for example, who will not pursue economics further, the basic text material, which develops all of the pieces of the macro-model and puts them together, may be sufficient—without taking the final step (and risking the possible confusion) of collapsing all this into the neat geometrical constructs popularly called L-M and I-S curves. For the economics major, however, since I-S and L-M curves are by now an integral part of the technical apparatus of the profession, this final step —carried out in an appendix—may be quite necessary.

Whether or not this book achieves its objectives, my debt to my teachers, students, colleagues, and family is great. To those at the University of Michigan who kindled my interest in money and banking, macroeconomic theory, and the exposition of both to undergraduates— such fine teachers as Professors Warren Smith, Richard Musgrave, Gardner Ackley, Shorey Peterson, and last, but far from least, Professor Emeritus Leonard Watkins—I owe much. To Professor Murray E. Polakoff of New York University, who carefully reviewed the entire manuscript and offered many helpful and thoughtful suggestions, my sincere thanks. To my students at the University of Delaware who have suffered through preliminary drafts of the manuscript in my money and banking classes and who have many times prodded me to a clearer expression of ideas, my obligation is especially weighty. Most of all, I am indebted to my wife, who not only cheerfully assembled, pasted, cut, and typed the entire manuscript in her "spare time," but provided both the reason and the moral support to get the job done.

To all the above I am extremely grateful. It goes without saying that they deserve much of the credit for whatever is worthwhile in the book. Much as I wish they could also be held responsible for the errors, I shall have to absolve them and accept that burden myself.

H.D.H.

CONTENTS

II. MONETARY AND INCOME THEORY

Quiz (handwritten annotation)

IV. THE ROLE OF POLICY

Contents

FIGURES

TABLES

MONEY,
BANKING,
and the
UNITED STATES
ECONOMY

Introduction

The story of money and the history of modern man are virtually inseparable; of all the vital institutions involved in the economic development of society, none has played a more fundamental role than money itself.

THE NEED FOR MONEY

The use of money in modern society has evolved naturally from pressing need—the need to overcome the crippling obstacles to exchange inherent in a barter society. It became a necessary institution because its absence—in a pure barter society—was almost totally inconsistent with economic development.

The disadvantages of barter are elementary and obvious. Without money to serve as a unit of account, a measuring rod for comparing the value of different goods and services, comparative values would have to be calculated by direct exchange ratios between different goods. The value of product A, for example, would have to be expressed in terms of so many units of B, so many of C, so many of D, and so forth, instead of in terms of so many dollars. The difficulty with such an arrangement is apparent when it is recognized that 499,500 exchange ratios would be required to express the comparative values of 1,000 products. Such a system would be an accountant's nightmare, to put it mildly!

But that is not all there is to it. The most fundamental function of money is to facilitate exchange in a specialized economy. If Mr. Jones produces pogo sticks he cannot live on them alone. He must find some means of exchanging the bulk of his output for the food, clothing, and other amenities he finds necessary and desirable. In a money economy this

1

is a simple operation. All he need do is sell his pogo sticks for money—and then use the money to purchase the other things he wants. In a barter economy, however, the task of exchange is much more formidable. It is not enough simply to find someone who wants his pogo sticks; if he must trade, his trading partner must not only want what he has, but have what he wants! Barred from the simple exchange of his product for a generally acceptable money substance, he must locate a seller of food who wants pogo sticks in exchange, a seller of clothing who wants pogo sticks in exchange, and so forth. In such circumstances our Mr. Jones is likely to spend a majority of his time trying to market his output.

It has become traditional to refer to the services provided by money in overcoming these obstacles of barter as the *functions* of money. Money's function as a *unit of account*—as a numeraire or yardstick—in terms of which the values of all goods and services can be conveniently expressed and compared—is fundamental. Crucial also is its function as a *medium of exchange*—facilitating the exchanges so vital to a highly specialized economy. In addition money also serves, though it is neither unique nor always well behaved in this role, as a *store of value*—a medium in which those who are not yet ready to commit themselves to specific goods, may hold generalized purchasing power.

More fruitful than the memorization of a list of functions of money, however, is an appreciation of the ways in which an efficiently operating money system promotes economic development.

Two of the essential ingredients of economic development are specialization and capital formation. Both depend on a money system.

Specialization, an essential for high-level production, is the antithesis of self-sufficiency. It makes each specialist dependent, not only upon all other specialists, but upon the system for exchanging products with them. If specialization is to be carried very far, a barter system is impossible. Money is a necessity.

Capital formation, the process whereby new capital goods are produced, also depends heavily on a money system. For in a fundamental sense capital formation requires saving to release productive resources from the production of consumer goods, and transference of those released resources to the building of plants, equipment, and other capital goods. All this could, conceptually, be done without money but it would be extremely difficult.

In a barter system the savers would then be required to accumulate stocks of consumer goods and somehow make them available to investors who, in turn, would use them to "pay" the workers who are building the capital goods. It could be done, but hardly extensively. How much simpler it is for the savers to save money income and lend *that* to the investors!

THE DEFINITION OF MONEY AND THE U.S. MONEY SUPPLY

"Money is what money does" is one of the oldest adages in economics. The point, of course, is that money is defined according to the function it performs rather than according to the material it is made of, the identity of the issuer, or other such criteria. For our purposes, money will be defined as *anything that is generally accepted as a medium of exchange.* IN DISCHARGE OF A CONTRCT TO PAY

For the United States of the 1960's this would include all the currency and coins in circulation, plus the demand deposits at commercial banks. Many other claims, of course, fulfill the store of value function and are quickly and easily convertible into cash. Savings accounts, savings and loan shares, and U.S. Savings Bonds, to name a few, are all highly liquid claims that can be very readily exchanged for money. But, since they cannot be spent in their present form, they are only "near moneys."

While, in general, currency, coins, and demand deposits fit the definition of money, we need to be somewhat more specific when we use the term money *supply*. It has become usual to use this term to refer to the amount of money in the hands of the spending public. As such, it would include all currency and coins, except those held by the U.S. Treasury or those in bank vaults, plus all demand deposits at commercial banks except those owned by the U.S. Treasury, commercial banks, or foreigners.

THE U.S. MONEY SUPPLY IN THE MID-SIXTIES

As of April 1966, the U.S. money supply totaled just over $170 billion, $37 billion of which was currency and coins and the rest, demand deposits. Over 85 percent of the currency and coin total was in the form of Federal Reserve Notes and about 8 percent in fractional coins. The remaining amount included about $1 billion of silver dollars and silver certificates, and less than half a billion in the forms of U.S. Notes, National Bank Notes, Treasury Notes of 1890, and Federal Reserve Bank Notes. Most of the latter are in process of being retired so that the dominance of Federal Reserve Notes and fractional coins in the total will undoubtedly be increased as the years pass.

THE PLAN OF THE BOOK

In Part I we shall embark upon a description of the nation's financial machinery with heavy emphasis on the activities of commercial banks and their chief regulators, the Federal Reserve System.

In Part II, we shall delve into some of the intricacies of macroeconomic theory. For the student who is well grounded in the principles of economics much of the early material in this section will be a review of the basic fundamentals, which is necessary, however, to provide a sound basis for the more complicated material covered in the concluding chapters.

In Part III, we depart from the assumption of a closed economy to consider some of the institutional and theoretical issues in international finance. Heavy stress is placed upon recent U.S. balance of payments deficits and the efforts to deal with them.

Finally, in Part IV, we shall turn to consideration of a number of aspects of monetary and other types of stabilization policy as well as some suggestions for the reform of our monetary mechanism.

I

FINANCIAL INSTITUTIONS AND THE MECHANICS OF THE MONEY SUPPLY

1

The Role of Financial Institutions

One of the characteristic features of a highly developed and productive economy is the diversion of more and more workers out of those industries directly engaged in "making things" and into those that more indirectly support the productive process. Such a trend is merely a reflection of the increased specialization and more intensive use of capital goods in the "goods making" industries.

In the United States, for example, whereas almost 60 percent of our work force was tied up in agriculture, mining, manufacturing, and construction in 1929, only about 40 percent were similarly employed in 1965. While these industries were increasing their employment only from 23.7 million to 26.4 million, as Table 1-1 reveals, retail and wholesale trade and the finance industries were more than doubling their work forces while the services and the government were tripling theirs.

Certainly there can be no doubt that this massive shift of workers, out of what have sometimes been called the primary and secondary industries into the supportive tertiary and service industries, has paid off in terms of rising production. For, in real terms, our Gross National Product (GNP) has almost exactly tripled in that same 1929-1965 period. In the aggregate, it is clearly evident that the benefits from added specialization and capitalistic production have far outweighed the costs of using up much of our labor force in the "tertiary" industries.

Our chief concern here, however, is with the approximately 2.5 million workers tied up in the finance industry.[1] In what sense do they con-

---

[1] Approximately 500,000 of the workers included in the "Finance, Insurance, and Real Estate" category in Table 1-1 are in real estate. See *Employment and Earnings*, Vol. 12, No. 10 (U.S. Department of Labor, April, 1966).

TABLE 1-1   Employment by Industry, 1929 and 1965 (thousands)ᵃ

Industry	1929	1965
Agriculture	10,450	4,585
Mining	1,087	628
Construction	1,497	3,211
Manufacturing	10,702	17,984
Transportation and Public Utilities	3,916	4,031
Wholesale and Retail Trade	6,123	12,588
Finance, Insurance, and Real Estate	1,509	3,044
Government	3,065	10,051
Services and Miscellaneous	3,440	8,907
Totals	41,789	65,029

ᵃ Totals exclude self-employed in nonagricultural work force.

SOURCE: *Employment and Earnings*, Vol. 12, No. 10 (U.S. Department of Labor, April, 1966).

tribute to the fuller realization of the nation's economic goals? After all, this represents three times as many workers as the automobile industry employs, about three times as many as the basic steel industry and nearly twice as many as are directly involved in the manufacture of clothing. Such a major commitment of manpower to an activity only indirectly related to production requires justification. What is the basic economic function performed by our vast network of financial enterprises?

THE ECONOMIC FUNCTION OF FINANCIAL INSTITUTIONS

The Capital Formation Process

In the highly artificial Robinson Crusoe-type economy often visualized for the purpose of simplifying or throwing into sharp relief, some basic theoretical ideas, there is no financial mechanism to complicate the issue. Indeed one of the main purposes of such abstractions is to sweep aside the "veil" with which money and a financial system seem to distort and conceal the "real" economic developments underneath.

In the Crusoe-type economy where there is no money, the capital formation process is a very simple one. If Crusoe and Friday desire to raise their production of fish, they may consider it worthwhile to take several days off from actually fishing to produce a fishing net (a capital good). Before doing so, however, they realize that they must continue eating while they construct the net. Consequently, they must produce an excess of con-

sumer goods (fish, cocoanuts) to have available to sustain them while working on their net. The act of building up this reserve stock of food is, in
the purest sense, an act of *saving*—consuming less than the full amount of
their income. It is this abstention from consumption which permits them
to devote several days of their scarce labor supply to the construction of
their net—an act of *investment*.

The fundamental "real" effect of saving, then, is the release of productive resources from the production of consumer goods. Investment, on the
other hand, is the use of those released resources to produce a new capital
good. In the Crusoe case there is no money or financial structure to "muddy
up the water" or obscure our vision of what goes on. The saving consists
of stocking up real consumer goods and the investment consists of building
the capital good while living off this previously saved excess.

In a money-using economy, however, things are more complicated. Suppose we have an economy in which many people are specializing, so that
exchange—and therefore money—is essential. In such a case saving takes
the form of people not spending all their money income to buy consumer
goods. To keep it simple let us assume there are still no banks, so that each
saver amasses, at least temporarily, a pile of cash.

Does this kind of saving have the same real effects as that of Crusoe?
Of course. People who do not spend all their money incomes to purchase
consumer goods thereby release some productive resources, which they
could have tied up producing more consumer goods, for other purposes.
Now if the money savings are lent to business firms who desire to purchase
more capital goods, they may spend them to hire these released resources
to build them. On the monetary level, money is saved, lent to investors and
they spend it to purchase capital goods. On the real level, productive resources are released by the savers' act of abstention, but they are rehired by
the investors' act of investing.[2]

Now, as far as it goes, the above is all perfectly correct. But it slides
over one major problem that cannot legitimately be ignored. Note that in
the preceding paragraph we have glibly stated ". . . if the money savings are
lent to business firms . . ." all will be well. The extent to which, the ease
with which, and the manner in which savings are made available to investors
has to do largely with the development of the financial system.

The Need for Financial Institutions

If savers and investors were always the same people, as in the
Crusoe case, there would be no problem and no need for a middleman to
provide facilities for bringing them together. In a modern developed econ-

[2] We shall, for the moment, ignore the possibility of unemployment and assume
that there is always enough investment spending to absorb the resources released
by saving.

omy, however, those units that have a surplus available to be borrowed—the savers—are normally groups other than those willing to operate at a deficit by borrowing—the investors. And some means of getting them together is essential.

Of course even this would create no problem—no need for an intricate financial system—if the savers were willing freely to accept the IOU's of the investors. But therein lies the rub.

The bulk of the investors—the dominant deficit units—are business firms; the prime surplus units—the savers—on the other hand, are households. Business firms desiring funds to finance investment spending can and do borow some of what they need directly from savers by selling them stocks and bonds; but many savers are unwilling to lend their money directly to business in exchange for these types of financial claims. It is clear that in such a situation some intermediary is needed to provide a means of bringing the deficit and surplus units together. This is the prime economic role of the financial institution.

In the words of two authorities, financial institutions exist primarily in order to ". . . issue debt of their own, *indirect* debt, in soliciting loanable funds from surplus spending units, and to allocate these loanable funds among deficit units whose direct debt they absorb."[3]

That is, the financial institution, recognizing the reluctance of savers to accept stocks and bonds in return for directly financing investors, offer them claims that are more to their liking. Then, having obtained the loanable funds of the savers, the financial institution turns around and makes them available to investors by purchasing the stocks, bonds, or other claims that savers have found unacceptable.[4]

How, it may be asked, can financial intermediaries entice savers to make their loanable funds available to them, when they were unwilling to deal directly with the investors? The answer is that the intermediaries offer savers financial claims that have features not possessed by the usual stocks and bonds of investors.

A prime consideration for a saver is liquidity—the ability to obtain his funds in a hurry, if need be, with little risk of loss. Many are quite willing to forego the potentially higher return of stocks and bonds in order to obtain the much greater degree of liquidity offered by the financial institutions in the form of such claims as savings deposits and shares.

Then, too, savers often save for the specific purpose of protecting themselves against risk. The risk of leaving a family unprotected in case of the untimely death of the breadwinner motivates many to put their savings into the form of life insurance. The reverse risk, that of living too long after

---

[3] J. G. Gurley and E. S. Shaw, "Financial Aspects of Economic Development," *American Economic Review*, Vol. XLV, No. 4, p. 515.

[4] These statements abstract from the fact that, as we shall soon see, commercial banks can lend a multiple of the amount savers make available to them.

retirement, leads many to purchase annuities or to participate in contributory pension plans.

Finally, there are many savers who consider themselves inadequately informed for direct participation in the corporate securities market. They know about and understand savings accounts or perhaps U.S. Savings Bonds, and, despite possible interest differentials, prefer to use these more familiar methods.

For all these reasons and others, claims against financial intermediaries are often more attractive to savers than the direct obligations of investors. So the financial institutions (1) provide utility to savers by offering them a wide variety of claims suited to their needs and (2) channel these savings to the investors by buying their obligations, thereby facilitating the allocation of resources and the capital formation process. There is little doubt that the absence of *any* financial intermediaries to perform this vital function would mean that many savers would prefer to hold idle cash rather than lend out their savings—a decision that would surely markedly reduce our rate of capital formation.

Some Flow of Funds Data for 1965

It was mentioned above that households normally are net savers, having excess funds available for loan, while the nonfinancial business sectors are usually net borrowers. Let us take a more detailed look at some of the facts for 1965.

The Household Sector

During 1965 households received an after-tax income totaling $471.8 billion.[5] Of this total $367.1 billion was spent on consumer outlays, leaving gross saving as $104.7 billion.[6]

Saving is thus defined, as is conventional in economics, negatively. It is simply the amount of income received which is *not* spent on consumption, or $471.8 billion minus $367.1 billion. We do not have to know what households *do* with this $104.7 billion in order to call it saving. All we know is that—since saving is defined as income minus consumption—$104.7 billion is *not* spent on consumption.

[5] This figure, as all others used in this section, is derived from Flow of Funds data as reported in the *Federal Reserve Bulletin* for May, 1966, pp. 724-735. Actually, household Disposable Income was $465.3 billion but the Flow of Funds Accounts include an imputation of $6.5 billion, which is primarily to account for the growth of government life insurance and pension reserves accruing to households.

[6] Once again, this is not the consumer outlay figure reported by the National Income Division. The Flow of Funds Accounts treat purchases of consumer durable goods as capital expenditures, and therefore a part of saving. This accounts for the bulk of the difference in the two figures.

However, it would be instructive to know something about the ways in which households *do* use their saving. Fortunately, Flow of Funds data provides us with just this sort of information. In 1965, $88.8 billion of it was used for the purchase of capital goods, most of it to purchase homes and consumer durables. Another $3.6 billion was spent to purchase stocks and bonds issued by corporations and governments.[7] In addition, householders chose to increase their holdings of cash and demand deposits by the extremely large figure of $10.7 billion. On the other side of the ledger, some $4.4 billion of *dis*investment in noncorporate business occurred during the year. The remainder, a net amount of $12.4 billion, was made available to the financial intermediaries.[8] These data, are shown in greater detail in Table 1-2.

TABLE 1-2   Disposition of Household Saving, 1965 (billions of dollars)

A. Purchase of Capital Goods		88.8
1. Housing	19.6	
2. Consumer Durables	65.0	
3. Plant and Equipment for Nonprofit Organizations	4.2	
B. Investment in Noncorporate Business		−4.4
C. Net Purchase of Corporate and Government Stocks and Bonds		3.6
D. Net Increase in Demand Deposits and Currency Held		10.7
E. Net Purchase of Obligations of Financial Institutions		12.4
1. Gross Increase in Claims on Financial Institutions	41.2	
a. Savings Accounts	24.6	
b. Life Insurance Reserves	4.1	
c. Pension Fund Reserves	12.5	
2. Gross Borrowing from Financial Institutions	28.8	
a. Mortgages	16.3	
b. Consumer Credit	9.2	
c. Other	3.3	

SOURCE: Flow of Funds, *Federal Reserve Bulletin*, May, 1966.

[7] Actually during 1965 households were net *sellers* of corporate securities. They purchased government obligations in the amount of $6.7 billion and sold $3.1 billion of corporate securities.

[8] It is evident that the above does not really add up. Households had only $104.7 billion to dispose of and we have listed a total of $111.1 billion used. The difference is a statistical discrepancy in the Flow of Funds data.

The Nonfinancial Business Sector

The nonfinancial business sector purchased $81 billion of capital goods and increased its ownership of financial assets (gross) in the amount of $24.8 billion during 1965. A large part of the funds required to do this—some $69.8 billion—was raised internally via the firms' own depreciation allowances and retained earnings. The rest, however, a total of $41 billion, was borrowed from other sectors, most of it from the financial intermediaries.[9] A summary of this sector's activities appears in Table 1-3.

TABLE 1-3 Sources and Uses of Funds for Nonfinancial Business Sector, 1965 (billions of dollars)

A. Gross Capital Expenditures		81.0
B. Gross Increase in Financial Assets		24.8
1. Demand Deposits and Currency	−3.3	
2. Time Deposits	5.5	
3. U.S. Securities	−2.1	
4. Trade Credit	13.5	
5. All Other	11.7	
C. Internal Financing		69.8
1. Depreciation	49.4	
2. Retained Earnings	20.4	
D. Gross External Finance		41.0
1. Mortgage Loans	9.3	
2. Other Bank Loans	12.6	
3. Trade Debt	8.3	
4. Corporate Bonds	5.4	
5. Corporate Stock	.3	
6. All Other	5.2	
E. Statistical Discrepancy		5.0[a]

[a] Difference from Flow of Funds data represents rounding difference.

SOURCE: Flow of Funds, *Federal Reserve Bulletin*, May, 1966.

The Government Sector

In 1965, the federal, state, and local governments were also net borrowers. Although all three levels of government combined acquired financial assets totaling $13.7 billion, they increased their liabilities out-

[9] Once again, a statistical discrepancy of about $5 billion, this time in the other direction, shows up in the Flow of Funds data.

standing by some $4 billion more than that figure. The detail of these activities is presented in Table 1-4.

TABLE 1-4   Financial Investment of Government, 1965 (billions of dollars)

A. Net Acquisition of Financial Assets		13.7
1. Demand Deposits and Currency	−1.9	
2. Time Deposits	3.0	
3. Loans Made	4.5	
4. U.S. Securities (State and Local)	2.3	
5. All Other	5.8	
B. Net Increase in Liabilities		17.7
1. Life Insurance and Retirement Reserves	5.6	
2. U.S. Securities	4.1	
3. State and Local Securities	7.4	
4. All Other	.6	

SOURCE: Flow of Funds, *Federal Reserve Bulletin*, May, 1966.

Summary—1965 Flow of Funds Data

There is, of course, much complication in the detail of the Flow of Funds in a highly developed economy such as the United States. It may therefore be useful to see what can be said, in more simplified form, about the overall picture and particularly, the place of financial institutions therein.

On balance the household sector found itself to be a net supplier of loanable funds to the rest of the economy, in an amount exceeding $12 billion. *Within* the sector many households were net borrowers from financial institutions—to finance home and durable consumer goods purchase—of almost $29 billion. However, other households accumulated increased claims on financial intermediaries totaling $41 billion, so that the sector as a whole supplied $12 billion in excess of what it used. It should be noted, however, that financial institutions were involved in a total of $70 billion of transactions with households.[10]

The nonfinancial business sector found itself in need of funds from outside to finance its investment spending in the amount of almost $16 billion. Some of this was raised via direct sale of securities to households but most of it came from the financial intermediaries. Once again, however, the intermediaries played a bigger role than the net figures reveal. Nonfinancial

---

[10] These figures exclude another $10 billion of financial asset accumulation, in the form of currency and deposits, most of which was undoubtedly on deposit at commercial banks.

business actually borrowed about $41 billion from them but lent $25 billion, at the same time.

Finally, the government sector, on balance, had to borrow some $4 billion. The difference between the household sectors surplus and the deficits incurred by both business and government is made up partly by the financial sector itself and partly by the fact that the household sector had $10.7 billion in demand deposits and currency (most of which commercial banks can lend on), which our $12 billion figure for that sector did not include. It should be clear from all this that the role of the financial intermediaries in bringing savers and investors together in the U.S. economy is a major one.

THE GROWTH OF FINANCIAL INSTITUTION ASSETS

In terms of value of assets and, indeed, in terms of economic significance, commercial banks have always been the most important of the financial institutions. This is still true. However, as Table 1-5 clearly indicates, other competing financial intermediaries have made rapid inroads on commercial bank domination since World War II.

TABLE 1-5   Total Assets of Selected Financial Institutions, 1940-1964 (millions of dollars)

Year	Commer- cial Banks	Mutual Savings Banks	Savings and Loan Associa- tions	Life In- surance Com- panies	Private Pension Plans[a]	Credit Unions	Invest- ment Com- panies[b]
1940	67,807	11,925	5,733	30,802	2,400	253	2,500[c]
1945	146,245	15,924	8,747	44,797	5,400	435	3,250
1950	156,914	22,252	16,893	64,020	12,100	1,005	4,700
1955	199,244	30,382	37,656	90,432	27,500	2,743	12,000
1960	242,526	39,598	71,476	119,576	52,000	5,658	23,500
1964	346,921	54,239	119,295	149,470	77,200	9,359	41,600
			Percent Growth				
1945- 1964	140	241	1,271	234	1,330	2,051	1,180

[a] Data are Pension Plan reserves.
[b] Data are for end of fiscal year rather than December 31.
[c] Figure is for 1941 rather than 1940.

SOURCE: Data for Commercial Banks, Mutual Savings Banks, Savings and Loan Associations, and Life Insurance Companies from *Federal Reserve Bulletin*. Those for Private Pension Plans and Credit Unions are from *Social Security Bulletin*. Investment Company data are from the *Annual Report of the Securities and Exchange Commission*.

Whereas commercial banks possessed about 60 percent of the total assets owned by these seven financial institutions in 1945, their share had fallen to about 43 percent by 1964. And the trend appears to be continuing.

This is not to say that the giants of the financial sector have been withering away in any absolute sense. As Table 1-5 reveals quite the reverse is the case. Commercial banks have increased their total assets by 140 percent since 1945 and by well over 400 percent since prewar 1940. But when it is recognized that the nation's GNP rose by almost 200 percent between 1945 and 1964 and by over 500 percent between 1940 and 1964, the absolute growth in the value of commercial bank assets does not look so impressive.

On the other hand the growth in the assets of the other major financial intermediaries has, in all cases, exceeded that of our GNP, and has, in some cases, been phenomenal. Mutual savings banks and life insurance companies each had well over three times as many assets in 1964 as in 1945. But despite this impressive growth, they too are among the laggards in a relative sense.

The other four institutions reported in Table 1-5 have grown at truly phenomenal rates. By 1964 investment companies, for example, had over twelve times their 1945 assets; savings and loan associations had over thirteen times as many; private pension plans, over fourteen times as many; and very small credit unions had multiplied their assets by an incredible twenty-one times since World War II! Small wonder the commercial banks have been looking over their shoulder in recent years.

CHARACTERISTICS OF SOME LEADING FINANCIAL INSTITUTIONS

Categorizing financial institutions is a hazardous occupation. There are so many different types and they are so diverse in function that cross-classification and sometimes outright omission are probably inevitable. Nonetheless the effort seems worth making.

In the list below, a number of the more important financial intermediaries are classified, largely according to the type of service provided the creditor. It is by no means an exhaustive list as we shall point out shortly.

Types of Financial Institutions

A. Those Providing Depositors Perfect Liquidity, but No Income
    1. Commercial Bank Checking Departments
B. Savings and Thrift Institutions Providing Near-perfect Liquidity Plus Income
    1. Commercial Bank Savings Departments
    2. Mutual Savings Banks
    3. Savings and Loan Associations
    4. Credit Unions
    5. Postal Savings System

C. Institutions Providing Some Liquidity, but Primarily Risk Protection
   1. Life Insurance Companies
   2. Private Pension Plans
D. Institutions Offering Equities and Longer-term, Less-liquid Securities
   1. Investment Companies
   2. Investment Bankers
   3. Securities Exchanges
E. Institutions that Raise Some of Their Funds from Other Financial Institutions
   1. Small Loan Companies
   2. Consumer Finance Companies

The distinguishing characteristic of commercial banks is the fact that, in their checking departments, creditors are offered assets of perfect liquidity—money itself. In the Savings and Thrift Institution Category, all offer depositors (or "share owners" or "members") assets of very high liquidity which, in practice if not in law, are withdrawable on demand. In Category C both institutions offer participants liquidity but the major attraction is probably protection against risk; in the case of life insurance companies, against the risk of dying too soon and in the pension plans, against the risk of living too long.[11] Category D includes three intermediaries that vary widely but which have in common, the sale of much less liquid stocks and bonds to their customers. The final group includes financial institutions that borrow some of their funds from other intermediaries and then lend them to the public—pretty much a reversal of direction from the others.

Excluded from the list above is a host of very important governmental institutions, such as the Housing and Home Finance Agency, the Farm Credit Administration, the Federal Reserve banks, the U.S. Treasury, and others, as well as such specialized private institutions as mortgage companies, over the counter securities dealers, and commercial bank trust departments. Some of these are of major importance and will be discussed later.[12]

We shall turn now to a brief description of some of the chief characteristics of a few of the more important financial institutions. Because a number of later chapters are devoted to commercial banks, we shall by-pass them at this point.

Mutual Savings Banks

The first of the purely savings institutions, mutual savings banks, first appeared on the American scene in 1816. Fulfilling a need for a thrift institution aimed primarily at the small saver which the

---

[11] It should be noted that, especially in the case of the sale of variable annuities, life insurance companies also offer protection against the latter risk.

[12] For those who may be interested in reading about the institutions we do not cover in this book, or those who desire a more detailed account of the ones we do cover, a number of excellent texts on financial institutions are available.

then-existing commercial banks had not met, savings banks were an early success and spread rapidly. By 1875 there were 674 mutual savings banks serving over two million depositors.

In a rapidly developing industrial power one might well have expected a mushrooming growth of savings banks after 1875. In fact quite the reverse was the case. Faced with developing competition from savings and loan associations and from commercial banks, both of which were better able to expand in the newer, developing sections of the nation, mutual savings bank expansion stopped right there and the succeeding years have seen a steady decline in the number of banks until by mid-1966, only 505 were still in existence. Of these only 36 began business in the twentieth century and fully 80 percent were established prior to 1875!

Mutual savings banks have lost ground, relative to the other savings institutions, for a number of reasons. Chief among these has been their inability to expand, along with competing institutions, into the newer, more rapidly growing areas of the nation. They are concentrated almost entirely in New England and the Middle Atlantic States and do not exist at all in thirty-three of the fifty states. In fact, as of 1960, 75 percent of their assets were concentrated in banks in New York and Massachusetts alone.

Mutual savings banks, as the term "mutual" indicates, are run for the mutual benefit of the depositors, with policy determined by a Board of Trustees, which generally serves without pay. All are state-chartered institutions and, although since 1933 they have been eligible to belong to the

TABLE 1-6   Distribution of Mutual Savings Bank Assets, December 31, 1960 (billions of dollars)

State	Amount of Assets	Percent of Total Assets	State	Amount of Assets	Percent of Total Assets
Connecticut	2.8	6.9	New York	23.9	58.9
Maine	.5	1.2	Pennsylvania	2.3	5.6
Massachusetts	6.5	16.1	Indiana	.06	.2
New Hampshire	.6	1.5	Minnesota	.3	.9
Rhode Island	.6	1.4	Ohio	.03	.1
Vermont	.1	.3	Wisconsin	.03	.1
Delaware	.2	.4	Oregon	.05	.1
Maryland	.6	1.5	Washington	.4	1.0
New Jersey	1.5	3.7			

SOURCE: National Association of Mutual Savings Banks, Commission on Money and Credit, *Mutual Savings Banking:* Basic Characteristics and Role in the National Economy, © 1962. Reprinted by permission of Prentice Hall, Inc., Englewood Cliffs, N.J.

Federal Reserve System, no more than three have ever chosen to join it. The accounts of depositors are insured by the Federal Deposit Insurance Corporation at approximately two-thirds of the banks.

As thrift institutions, almost all their funds come from their depositors, outstanding deposits and reserve accounts making up about 98 percent of their liabilities in 1965. As with most savings accounts, legally depositors may be required to wait thirty to sixty days to withdraw funds but, in practice, this is seldom enforced.

Portfolio practices pretty well reflect the nature of the business. Slightly over 10 percent of their assets were in liquid form in the mid-sixties, about three-quarters in mortgages, and most of the rest in high grade corporate securities.

All but two of the seventeen mutual savings bank states have passed a *legal list* of assets to which mutual savings banks must restrict themselves. In general these permit the purchase of any government securities, certain high-grade corporate securities and mortgages. The legal restrictions imposed on savings banks are generally less restrictive than those imposed on savings and loan associations, but considerably more so than for life insurance companies and commercial banks.[13]

Some indication of the effects of legal restrictions as well as the requirements of their respective businesses can be obtained from a comparison of the relative proportions of assets held in different forms. Such a comparison is provided in Table 1-7.

TABLE 1-7   Percentage Distribution of Assets of Four Savings Institutions, December 31, 1965

	Mutual Savings Banks	Savings and Loan Associations	Life Insurance Companies	Commercial Banks
Cash	1.7	3.1	0.9	16.1
U.S. Securities	8.9	5.7	3.2	15.8
State and Local Government Securities	0.5	—	2.1	10.3
Corporate and Other Securities	9.5	—	43.5	1.6
Mortgages	76.3	85.2	37.8	13.1
Other Loans	1.6	—	4.9	39.8
Other Assets	1.6	6.1	7.6	3.3

SOURCE: Computed from data from *Federal Reserve Bulletin.*

[13] See *Mutual Savings Banking: Basic Characteristic and Role in the National Economy*, a monograph prepared for the Commission on Money and Credit (Englewood Cliffs, N.J., Prentice-Hall, Inc., 1962), p. 3.

Mutual savings banks and savings and loan associations, as can be observed readily, lean heavily toward mortgages. Life insurance companies have a much wider dispersion of assets. Commercial banks are noteworthy since a very large percent of their assets are kept in the most liquid of forms—cash and U.S. securities. We shall have more to say about this at a later point.

TABLE 1-8   Consolidated Balance Sheet of All Mutual
Savings Banks, March, 1966 (millions of dollars)

Assets		Liabilities and Reserve Accounts	
Cash	896	Deposits	53,286
U.S. Securities	5,352	Other Liabilities	1,228
State and Local		Reserve Accounts	4,742
Government Securities	317		
Corporate and Other			
Securities	5,600		
Mortgages	45,180		
Other Loans	913		
All Other	998		
Total	59,256	Total	59,256

SOURCE: Computed from data from *Federal Reserve Bulletin*.

Savings and Loan Associations

Savings and loan associations and mutual savings banks are alike in many ways. Both collect savings and both use the preponderant amount of it to finance home construction. There are, however, a number of not insignificant differences. In the words of one savings and loan official:

Savings and loan associations differ from other deposit-type savings institutions in one very important respect. The other deposit-type institutions have as one of their primary objectives the mobilizing of funds (savings) and the providing of a return to depositors and shareholders. They are thrift institutions first and they hold themselves to be simply that. The attitudes of such institutions toward diversification in risk assets, liquidity, borrowing from reserve pools of credit, such as the Federal Home Loan Bank System and the Federal Reserve, are a reflection of their concern for depositors and shareholders and for the safety of their investments. In contrast, savings and loan associations, as specialized institutions, hold quite different attitudes toward diversification of risk assets and borrowing from central credit pools. Although they, too, are concerned about the welfare of savers, their concern is prompted by the need to secure funds to support home financing and home ownership in this nation. Simply, if the home financing

element were eliminated from savings and loan activity and the general investment market were made its province, there probably would not be so great an
economic and social justification for the existence of these associations. Savers and
thrift could be served readily by any of a number of other institutions.[14]

In other words a first concern of the savings and loan association is
the financing of home construction while, at least in the opinion of this
spokesman, mutual savings banks are primarily concerned with the en-
couragement of thrift.

Savings and loan associations first appeared in the United States in
1831 and were, for many years, truly voluntary associations devoted to the
financing of home building. As they prospered, their numbers grew, and
their operations formalized over the years, they came under regulations
and controls set up, first by the states, and then later, starting in 1933, by
the federal government. Today there are over 6,200 savings and loan associations located, unlike mutual savings banks, in every state in the union.
About two-thirds of the associations are chartered and regulated by the
state in which they are located. The rest, chartered by the federal government, are subject to the supervision of the Federal Home Loan Bank
Board. As Table 1-10 indicates, the federal associations, though smaller in
number, are larger in terms of assets.

TABLE 1-9   Composition of Savings and Loan Industry,
1964

	Number of Associations	Value of Assets (millions of dollars)
Federally Chartered	1,981	61,642
State-chartered	4,267	57,653
Total	6,248	119,295

SOURCE: *1965 Savings and Loan Fact Book*, U.S. Savings and
Loan League.

Like the mutual savings banks, most savings and loan associations are
mutual institutions, "owned" by their depositors or shareholders. At the
end of 1964, only 785 of the associations were of the capital stock type and
they held about 21 percent of the assets.[15]

[14] Leon T. Kendall for the United States Savings and Loan League, Commission on
Money and Credit, *The Savings and Loan Business:* Its Purposes, Functions, and Economic Justification, © 1962. Reprinted by permission of Prentice-Hall, Inc., Englewood
Cliffs, N.J.
[15] *1965 Savings and Loan Fact Book*, U.S. Savings and Loan League.

Some indication of the tremendous growth of the associations since World War II can be obtained from Table 1-10, which shows savings held in different forms by the American public from 1945 to 1964.

TABLE 1-10   Savings Held in Different Media, 1945-1964
(billions of dollars)

Year	Savings and Loan Associations	Mutual Savings Banks	Commercial Bank Time Deposits	Credit Unions	U.S. Savings Bonds	Postal Savings	Total
1945	7.4	15.3	29.9	0.4	42.9	3.0	98.9
1950	14.0	20.0	35.2	0.9	49.6	3.0	122.7
1955	32.1	28.1	46.3	2.4	50.2	2.0	161.1
1960	62.1	36.3	67.1	5.0	45.7	0.8	217.0
1964	101.8	48.8	113.2	8.3	49.0	0.4	321.5

Percent of Total Held in Each Media

1945	7.5	15.5	30.2	0.4	43.4	3.0	100.0
1950	11.4	16.3	28.7	0.7	40.4	2.5	100.0
1955	20.0	17.4	28.7	1.5	31.1	1.3	100.0
1960	28.7	16.7	31.1	2.3	20.8	0.4	100.0
1964	31.7	15.2	35.2	2.6	15.2	1.0	100.0

SOURCE: *1965 Savings and Loan Fact Book.*

Generally speaking, savings and loan associations are restricted to investing in home mortgages, U.S. securities, Federal Home Loan Bank debentures and, in some states, municipal bonds, property improvement loans, and mortgages on some commercial property.

Because of the mutual character of most savings and loan associations, they are required by law to build up *reserves* over time, out of retained earnings, until they equal 5 percent of the savings deposited with them. These reserves, of course, are intended to provide a "cushion" to protect savers in case of losses in the association's portfolio. Liquidity requirements are met through holdings of cash and U.S. securities, which, in early 1966, averaged about 10 percent of their outstanding deposits.[16]

[16] Technically speaking savers hold "shares" rather than deposits at savings and loan associations. The difference, however, is primarily legal and not of great importance.

TABLE 1-11   Consolidated Balance Sheet of All Savings and
Loan Associations, March, 1966 (millions of dollars)

Assets		Liabilities and Reserves	
Cash	3,249	Savings Deposits	111,560
U.S. Securities	7,850	Borrowing	6,070
Mortgages	112,001	Loans in Process	2,223
Other	8,018	Other	2,544
	131,118	Reserves and Undivided Profits	8,721
			131,118

SOURCE: *Federal Reserve Bulletin.*

Life Insurance Companies

Life Insurance companies, which in the United States date
all the way back to 1759, sell substantially more than liquidity and an
income on savings. It seems safe to argue that the vast majority of the
savers who channel large portions of their incomes each year to life insurance premium payments do so more for risk protection than for direct
income or liquidity.

To the policyholder, life insurance represents a type of protection,
especially in the early years of family formation, which savings accounts
normally cannot provide. His savings, sent to the insurance company in
the form of premium payments, do provide some liquidity for emergencies in the form of the policy's accumulated cash value or policy loans
against it. But there is little doubt that the prime motivating factor is the
much greater face value of the policy available for the policyholder's de-
pendents in the case of his untimely death.

This fact, plus the contractual nature of most of the premium payments and the substantially more liberal regulatory legislation, permits
the insurance company portfolio manager a great deal more discretion
than his counterpart in a mutual savings bank or savings and loan
association.

Liquidity is a much less restraining influence. This is due partly to
the fact that policyholders do not formally look upon their accumulated
cash value as liquid savings to be drawn upon except in the direst of emergencies; partly to the fact that the annual inflow of funds to an insurance
company is largely in the form of contractual premium payments, totaling, in the mid-1960's, almost $25 billion—an inflow that can be depended

on much more confidently than an inflow of savings deposits in other savings institutions. And finally, it is because the obligations of insurance companies are long run and, with the aid of the law of large numbers, reasonably confidently predictable.

In recognition of all this, regulatory legislation permits a much wider range of discretion to the life insurance company portfolio manager. For example, as of 1960, the state of New York permits investment, with some quantitative limitations, in any of the instruments listed below.[17]

Types of Investment Permitted by New York Insurance Law

1. U.S. Government Obligations
2. State and Local Government Obligations
3. U.S. Corporate Obligations
   a. Secured by Adequate Collateral
   b. Qualified by Earnings Test
4. Preferred and Guaranteed Stocks
5. Common Stocks
6. Trustee's or Receiver's Obligations
7. Equipment Trust Obligations
8. Acceptances and Bills of Exchange
9. Mortgage Loans
10. Real Estate
    a. For Own Use
    b. Foreclosed
    c. Housing Projects
    d. Income-producing
11. Foreign Investments
12. Policy Loans
13. Collateral Loans
14. Miscellaneous
    a. Certain Federal Agency Issues
    b. Obligations of World Bank
    c. Savings and Loan Association Shares
15. "Leeway" (2 Percent of Assets in Forms not Expressly Permitted)[18]

Of the 1,500-plus life insurance companies in the United States, about 90 percent are owned by stockholders; the other 10 percent are mutuals, "owned" by the policyholders. The mutuals, however, are the larger com-

[17] New York law is highly strategic in shaping life insurance regulatory legislation, since companies representing about 80 percent of total life insurance assets have licenses to do business in that state, and therefore, must comply with its laws.

[18] Life Assurance Association of America, Commission on Money and Credit, *Life Insurance Companies as Financial Institutions,* © 1962. Reprinted by permission of Prentice-Hall, Inc., Englewood Cliffs, N.J.

panies and, as of the mid-sixties, they owned about 70 percent of the industry's total assets.

Life insurance companies are heavy purchasers of corporation bonds, with almost one quarter of their total assets being committed to industrial bonds alone. An additional 14 percent is invested in railroad and public utility bonds. Over 35 percent of their assets are mortgages, with somewhat over half financing the purchase of residential properties for from one to four families, the rest being mortgages on apartment buildings, commercial properties, and farms. Insurance companies hold more mortgages than mutual savings banks and more than half as many as savings and loan associations.

TABLE 1-12   Distribution of Assets of All Life Insurance Companies, March, 1966 (millions of dollars)

1.	U.S. Government Securities	5,031
2.	State and Local Government Securities	3,375
3.	Foreign Government Securities	3,018
4.	Corporate Bonds	59,558
5.	Corporate Stocks	7,269
6.	Mortgages	61,288
7.	Real Estate	4,725
8.	Policy Loans	7,849
9.	All Other Assets	8,685
	Total Assets	160,798

SOURCE: *Federal Reserve Bulletin*, June, 1966.

Private Pension Plans

Another very rapidly growing financial intermediary in the post-World War II era has been the private pension plan. As of the end of 1964, their reserves totaled an impressive $77 billion, of which some $25 billion were included in pension plans insured by life insurance companies. To that degree there is duplication in the figures, since the assets of life insurance companies given in Table 1-14 include those covering the pension plans they insure.

The income of these pension funds, of course, comes primarily from regular payments made by the employees covered and their employers. Between 1950 and 1964 these contributions have totaled $65.6 billion and benefit payments have aggregated $19.3 billion. In addition, over this 14-year period, the funds have earned some $18.8 billion in investment income. Total reserves have thus risen by over $65 billion.

The noninsured private pension funds, as of the end of 1964 possessed assets with a book value of about $52 billion. These funds were invested primarily in corporate securities, with about $21 billion each committed to bonds and to stocks.[19] Some $3 billion each in U.S. securities and in mortgages accounted for most of the rest.

TABLE 1-13　Distribution of Assets of Private Noninsured Pension Funds, 1964 (millions of dollars)

1. Cash and Deposits	892
2. U.S. Government Securities	3,069
3. Corporation Bonds	21,206
4. Preferred Stock	654
5. Common Stock	20,836
6. Mortgages	2,746
7. Other Assets	2,509
Total Assets	51,912

SOURCE: *Statistical Bulletin*, Securities and Exchange Commission, June, 1965.

It is interesting to note that the assets of private pension funds exceed even the huge accumulations built up under federal, state, and local government pension programs. As of the end of 1964, the government funds, invested primarily in government securities, totaled about $70 billion.

TABLE 1-14　Assets of All Public and Private Pension Funds, 1964 (billions of dollars)

Private Funds	
Insured Pension Reserves	25.2
Noninsured Corporate Funds	47.3
Other Noninsured Funds	4.6
Total Private Funds	77.2
Government Funds	
Railroad Retirement	3.8
Civil Service	15.0
State and Local	29.0
Federal Old Age and Survivors	19.1
Federal Disability Insurance	2.0
Total Government Funds	69.2
Total—All Pension Funds	147.1

SOURCE: *Statistical Bulletin*, Securities and Exchange Commission, June, 1965.

[19] If market value figures are used, however, total assets equal $63 billion, of which over $33 billion is in stocks and about $21 billion in bonds.

Credit Unions

Credit unions are governmentally chartered organizations aimed at collecting savings from their members and making consumer loans, at moderate interest rates, to those members. Credit unions are generally open to all members of a specified group—usually all employees of a particular firm. Members deposit their savings with the union, receive an interest return roughly comparable to that of competing savings institutions, and are eligible to borrow, when necessary, from them.

They are mutuals in the sense that they are owned by their depositors. Indeed, they are also run by representatives of these depositors, many of whom serve without compensation. This feature, plus certain favorable tax provisions, give them a competitive advantage over some of their rival institutions.

Credit unions, though essentially voluntary associations, are not without governmental regulation. Since 1934, when the Federal Credit Union Act was passed, credit unions have been able to choose between federal and state charters. Those who operate under federal charters come under the supervision and control of the Bureau of Federal Credit Unions. Those who obtain state charters are regulated, of course, by the state issuing the charter. As of the end of 1965 there were 11,560 federal credit unions, with 8,625,000 members and $5,129,000,000 of assets as compared with 10,580 state-chartered unions, with just over 8,000,000 members and $5,339,000,000 of assets. Most credit unions are small, with less than $250,000 of assets but over 200 of them possess assets in excess of $5 million.[20]

As of the end of 1965, just over $8 million of the total credit union assets of $10,464,000 were committed to loans to members.[21] The bulk of their remaining assets were held in such highly liquid forms as cash, U.S. securities, and savings and loan shares. Their liabilities are principally the shares owned by their depositors, plus sizable reserve and undivided earnings accounts.

Investment Companies   *Do not create Debt*

For those savers who are willing to run a somewhat greater risk in return for the opportunity of receiving a greater return, investment companies have become a major attraction. An investment company is a corporation that sells its own stock to savers and uses the proceeds to purchase securities issued by a wide variety of operating companies. The com-

[20] Robert M. Gardner, "State-Chartered Credit Unions in 1964," *Social Security Bulletin*, November, 1965.

[21] *Social Security Bulletin*, April, 1966.

mon stock of the investment company then "reflects" the income from, and market price of, the securities it has purchased.

Investment company stock occupies a middle ground between savings accounts on the one hand and direct purchase of operating company stock on the other. In comparison with the somewhat more liquid, somewhat safer alternative of a savings account, investment company stock offers not only an income from dividends but an excellent hedge against inflation, as well as a chance to obtain even greater rewards in the form of capital gains arising from increases in the market value of the stock. As opposed to direct purchase of operating company stock, investment company stock offers the twin advantages of a diversification of risk, which the small saver could hardly obtain on his own, plus the experienced market knowledge of a specialized management that makes the basic investment decisions.

There are two kinds of investment companies—closed end and open end. A closed-end company generally issues only a certain fixed amount of its own common stock and uses this, plus whatever additional capital is raised by borrowing, to purchase operating company shares. Its common stock is then bought and sold on the stock exchange and the individual saver, who wants to purchase more of it, must do so from somebody else on the Exchange. Similarly, a present owner of a share of a closed-end investment company can only "get his money out" by selling it to someone else on the Exchange.

An open-end investment company, on the other hand, will issue new shares of its own stock to anyone who desires to purchase them. Consequently, the total assets of a successful open-end company tends to grow at the discretion of savers in contrast to the closed-end company, which maintains only a fixed amount of stock outstanding. A second major difference is that owners of open-end stocks may redeem them for cash at any time by turning them in to the company. The amount paid in redemption depends upon the market value of the company's portfolio of securities at the time, which may, unlike the more liquid savings account, be greater than or less than the amount originally paid in.

The growth of investment company assets in recent years has been remarkable, especially in the case of open-end companies. In the stock market boom of the 1920's, closed-end companies pretty nearly dominated the scene and just before the 1929 market crash their assets had reached about the $3 billion level. The crash and its aftermath came very close to sounding the death knell for investment companies, some of which had gotten deeply involved in some rather highly speculative practices during the 1920's.

Careful governmental investigation during the 1930's led finally to the passage of the Investment Company Act of 1940, a federal regulatory act that provided the foundation for the reemergence of these companies as a significant segment of the financial community. Since that time, investment company assets have risen from $2.5 billion in 1941 to $44.6 billion in 1965, with most of the increase occurring among open-end companies.

There seems little doubt that action taken in the 1940's to increase the appeal of open-end investment companies to small savers played an important role in their meteoric rise. At that time the companies instituted the present practice of allowing amounts as small as $25 per month to be contributed; these amounts were held in trust by the investment company until they had accumulated to a level equal to the purchase price of a share. Recent surveys indicate that almost one-third of the total assets of these companies were accumulated in this manner.

Investment companies also appeal to investors with special investment desires. The majority invest their assets in a diversified selection of common stock of operating companies, therefore, providing perhaps the greatest opportunity of growth. A significant number, sometimes called "balanced" funds, however, reduce the risk by investing in bonds and preferred stock, as well as common stock. For those who are willing to devote all their equity capital to one field that appears particularly promising— such as electronics, for example—there are a number of specialized investment companies that concentrate only on the stock of a particular industry.

Federal regulation of investment companies is contained largely in the provisions of the Investment Company Act of 1940, which, in the words of one expert in the field, aims to:

1. Provide investors with complete and accurate information concerning the character of investment company securities and the circumstances, policies, and financial responsibility of investment companies and their management;
2. Assure that investment companies are organized and operated in the interest of all shareholders rather than in the interest of officers, directors, investment advisers, or other special groups or persons;
3. Prevent inequitable provisions in investment company securities and protect the preferences and privileges of outstanding securities;
4. Prevent undue concentration of control through pyramiding or other devices, and discourage management by irresponsible persons;
5. Assure sound accounting methods;
6. Prevent major changes in organization or business without the consent of shareholders;
7. Require adequate assets or reserves for the conduct of business.[22]

[22] Arthur Wiesenberger, *Investment Companies, 1964* (New York, Arthur Wiesenberger & Company, 1964), pp. 35-36.

Investment Banks, Securities Exchanges, and the Over-the-counter Market

In one sense, none of the financial intermediaries discussed to this point is a pure middleman. Each of the institutions we have thus far considered uses the funds collected from savers to purchase the obligations of investors *for their own account*. One could argue that a pure middleman does not buy for his own account. Rather he simply provides facilities, or a market, for bringing the ultimate buyer and seller together.

Although even they sometimes purchase securities for their own account for inventory purposes, much of the activity of investment bankers and the broker-dealer firms that participate on the securities exchanges and the over-the-counter market are of the "pure" middleman variety, providing a market wherein buyers and sellers can come together.

The function of investment bankers is quite different from that popularly associated with the term banker. Investment banking houses exist primarily for the purpose of marketing, for a corporation or government, a new issue of securities.

The initial distribution of a block of new securities is a highly specialized business requiring sales outlets, capital and expertise not normally possessed by the issuing organization. The result, as in any business, is to call in a specialist to do the selling—the investment banker.

The investment banker acts as adviser to the security issuer as well as its retailer. At the outset he solicits business by going directly to those who need new capital and suggesting means of raising it, as well as negotiating for the right to handle the account. The firm or syndicate of firms which obtains the privilege of distributing the borrower's securities will usually "underwrite" the sale of the entire issue, assuring the issuer of the funds he seeks. When underwriting an issue, the investment banker purchases it outright, relying on his ability to resell the securities promptly to individuals and other financial institutions at a price high enough to cover his full original cost plus a return for his services. If the borrower is new, or if for other reasons the resale of all the securities appears to be in some doubt, the investment banker may refuse to underwrite, agreeing instead to make the "best effort" to find buyers for the securities, but not purchasing them himself or making any guarantee of disposing of all of them.

Success for an investment banking concern thus depends heavily upon two factors—the strength of its sales force and the extent of its access to short term capital to enable it to "carry" a large issue until it is finally distributed.

The industry includes a large number of firms that specialize in the investment banking business, plus a sizable number of the larger commercial banks that, in addition to their other activities, operate investment banking departments. The latter have some advantage in the matter of short-term capital support, but are forbidden to underwrite corporate securities or state and local government revenue bonds.[23]

The willingness of lenders to purchase new securities depends, in large measure, on the facilities available for selling them to someone else should the need arise. Providing these facilities, and thereby indirectly promoting the raising of new capital is the function of over six thousand broker-dealer firms who participate on the securities exchanges and the over-the-counter market. Investment bankers help raise new capital for firms and governments. The securities exchanges and over-the-counter markets provide a market place wherein "old" securities may readily change hands.

Fundamentally, securities exchanges differ from the over-the-counter market only in the fact that trading in securities listed on the exchange is carried out at auction in one geographical location, whereas over-the-counter deals, primarily sales of the many securities that are not listed on the exchange, take place through brokers and dealers scattered throughout the nation.

A transaction on the floor of the exchange is initiated by an investor who, desiring to buy (or sell), contacts his broker. If his broker's firm is one of the almost 1,400 members of the exchange, the order is wired or telephoned in to the firm's representative on the floor. The representative then goes to the "post" on the floor, where securities are continuously being auctioned off between buyers and sellers, and carries out the purchase (or sale). If the broker is not a member of the exchange, the actual transaction must be carried out through a firm that is.

Over-the-counter transactions are often facilitated by the dealer's practice of carrying, on his own account, inventories of securities for sale, at a price, to the public. A few of the larger broker-dealer firms, primarily in New York City, act as "wholesalers" of over-the-counter securities, making continuous markets by standing ready to buy or sell at any time.[24]

CONCLUSION

The financial "industry" is so vast that we can only scratch the surface in a textbook with the objectives of this one. This chapter then is merely an introduction to the topic and, as mentioned earlier, no attempt has been made to consider all financial institutions.

We shall be making some additional later references to the effects of the financial institutions mentioned, but our prime emphasis in succeeding chapters will be on the largest of all financial institutions and the only private institution with the power to create money—the commercial bank.

[23] As of late 1966, the legality of commercial bank purchase of revenue bonds is being tested in the courts.
[24] For a worthwhile account of securities markets see *The Investment Business*, by John W. Hazard and Milton Christie (New York, Harper & Row Co., 1964).

2

The Commercial Bank and the Banking System

The commercial bank has often been referred to as the "department store" of finance. And it is an apt title. The typical commercial bank is far more than a mere safekeeper of liquid funds for its customers. Indeed it often performs the functions of *several* of the financial institutions discussed in the last chapter in addition to its own unique activities.

For example, if it has a savings department, it performs, to that extent, not substantially different functions from a mutual savings bank or savings and loan association. If it operates a trust department, it acts in a fiduciary capacity to administer the portfolio of wealthy individuals in a manner not too different from the operations of an investment company. If it is one of the larger commercial banks, it may operate an investment banking business along with its other responsibilities. And, if it is close enough to a financial center to do so effectively, it may be a foreign exchange dealer, offering to buy or sell foreign money to all comers.

But despite its complexities, despite its many similarities to other financial institutions, despite the fact that it, too, is primarily a middleman between savers and investors, the commercial bank is, in one essential respect, unique. It is the only financial institution that issues as a prime obligation, money itself, in the form of demand deposits. And more than that, the commercial bank alone, among privately owned financial institutions, possesses the power to expand or contract the size of that crucial economic variable we call the money supply.

It is because of this key role in the determination of the money supply, rather than simply because of the commercial banking sector's overwhelming size, that we choose to concentrate so heavily on this segment of the financial structure. Indeed, in what follows we shall all but ignore the many other hats worn by the commercial banker in order to focus as completely as possible on his central role as a money creator.

THE BALANCE SHEET OF A TYPICAL COMMERCIAL BANK

In Table 2-1, a consolidated balance sheet for all commercial banks in the United States as of December 31, 1965, is shown. We shall use this picture of the entire banking system to get some idea of the relative importance of the various assets and liabilities to an "average" or "typical" commercial bank in this country.

A number of general observations regarding the normal operations of commercial banks can be made on the basis of this statement. To begin with, the average commercial bank, as revealed by this picture of all of them, is able to get by with cash in vault which is only a very small percentage of its outstanding demand liabilities. At the end of 1965, cash on hand totaled less than 3 percent of demand deposits. As we shall see shortly, it is a part of the art of commercial banking to keep the non-income-earning cash account as low as is consistent with safety.

The "deposits at other banks" includes checking accounts held at Federal Reserve banks by those commercial banks that are members of the Federal Reserve System, plus demand deposits owned by some commercial banks in others. Since, for any one bank, all of these deposits are readily available to meet emergency situations, they, plus cash, are often termed *primary reserves* of commercial banks. At the end of 1965, banks held primary reserves equal to just over one-fifth of their outstanding demand deposits.

Commercial banks, being private business concerns in a free enterprise economy, are operated with a view to making a profit. Consequently, a bank's loans and securities, often referred to as its *earning assets,* are of central importance. As can be seen clearly in Table 2-1, commercial banks, unlike many of the other financial institutions, consider the granting of loans to be their most important activity. Within the loan category, short-term credit to finance local, commercial, and industrial business ventures is still, as has been for many years, the leader with over $70 billion. However, mortgage loans with $49 billion and a rapidly developing consumer loan business totaling $45 billion are the most important runners-up in the use of bank loan funds.

Commercial banks, committed though they are to serving the loan requirements of their local communities, also find it possible to earn sizable amounts of income from an imposing portfolio of securities. U.S.

TABLE 2-1 Consolidated Balance Sheet of All Commercial Banks, December 31, 1965 (millions of dollars)

ASSETS

Currency and Coin		4,851
Deposits at Other Banks		33,292
Loans and Discounts		
Commercial and Industrial	71,437	
Real Estate Loans (Mortgages)	49,300	
Consumer Loans	45,468	
Loans to Financial Institutions	15,449	
Loans to Brokers, Dealers, and Others for Security Purchase	8,489	
Agricultural Loans	8,212	
All Other[a]	1,200	
Total Net Loans		199,555
Securities		
U.S. Government Obligations	59,547	
State and Local Government Obligations	38,655	
Other Securities	6,201	
Total Securities		104,403
All Other Assets		35,163
Total Assets		377,264

LIABILITIES AND CAPITAL ACCOUNTS

Demand Deposits		
Individuals, Business, and All Other	165,970	
U.S. Government	5,525	
State and Local Governments	14,244	
Total Demand Deposits		185,739
Time and Savings Deposits		146,697
Borrowings		5,610
Other Liabilities		8,946
Capital Accounts		30,272
Total Liabilities and Capital Accounts		377,264

a Includes adjustment for valuation reserves.

SOURCE: *Federal Reserve Bulletin.*

securities, totaling almost $60 billion in 1965, have the happy facility of fulfilling a double requirement for the banks. Not only do they provide a secure interest return but, being highly liquid and virtually riskless, they serve as a supplement to the defense against emergencies which the primary reserves provide. As such, U.S. securities make up the bulk of what are often referred to as the banks' *secondary reserves*.

The $39 billion worth of securities of state and local governments, while not nearly so liquid as U.S. securities, have their own special attractions for commercial banks. Not only do they permit the banks to pursue more fully their objectives of financing the credit needs of their local communities but they have the attractive feature of being free of federal taxes. This latter quality is of special importance to commercial banks because they are virtually the only institutions within the financial community which are subject to the full bite of the federal corporate income tax.

It is, of course, the nature of the liabilities of commercial banks which plays the main role in determining the composition of their assets. Unlike all other financial institutions, commercial banks are obligated to be prepared, if need be, to pay cash *on demand* to the majority of their creditors —the holders of $186 billion of checking accounts. In addition, they have almost $147 billion of savings accounts outstanding, a figure that places them above all saving institutions except life insurance companies. We shall have more to say about these liabilities.

THE USE OF THE T-ACCOUNT

One all but indispensable tool in the study of commercial banks is the T-account and, since we shall rely upon it heavily in future chapters, the student should take pains to see that he understands it thoroughly.

A T-account is intended to reflect the change in a bank's (or in the banking system's) balance sheet as a result of a single transaction. It is, of course, not the only way to show this. One could, by depicting a full balance sheet before, and a full balance sheet after a transaction, accomplish the same purpose. And we shall, in some cases, use this more time consuming method. But in the vast majority of situations the T-account is preferable and we shall employ it extensively in this section.

A few examples should make clear the nature of this important tool. Suppose that Bank A, initially, is in the position reflected below:

Initial Balance Sheet of Bank A (thousands of dollars)

Cash	100	Demand Deposits	4,000
Deposits at		Time Deposits	2,100
Other Banks	1,000		
Loans	3,000		
Securities	2,000		

Now we are concerned with showing the effects on Bank A's balance sheet, of a single transaction. Suppose, for example, that a depositor places $100 cash in his checking account. We could reflect of this transaction in either of two ways—by laboriously making up an entirely new balance sheet, to incorporate the changes caused by the deposit or by using a T-account.

If we take the long way around, we would construct a balance sheet like that below:

Balance Sheet of Bank A After $100 Cash Deposit (thousands of dollars)

Cash	200	Demand Deposits	4,100
Deposits at Other Banks	1,000	Time Deposits	2,100
Loans	3,000		
Securities	2,000		

If we want to show the same thing in the simpler form of a T-account, however, we have simply:

Bank A

Cash + $100	Demand Deposits + $100

Here, we need only write down the accounts that are changed by the transaction itself in addition to a positive or negative sign to indicate whether an increase or decrease is involved.

In order to solidify the idea of the T-account and to provide some practice for the reader before we get to some more complicated uses, the following additional examples may be of some benefit.

1. Depositor withdraws $100 cash from his checking account in Bank A.

Bank A

Cash — $100	Demand Deposits — $100

2. Bank A purchases a $100 U.S. security, paying the seller in cash.

Bank A

Cash — $100	
U.S. Securities + $100	

3. Bank A makes a $100 loan to a borrower, granting the proceeds in the form of an addition to his checking account.

Bank A

Loans + $100	Demand Deposits + $100

4. A depositor at Bank A writes a $100 check on his checking account and deposits it in his saving account at Bank A.

Bank A

	Demand Deposits — $100
	Time Deposits + $100

5. Bank A borrows $100 of reserves from its Federal Reserve bank.

Bank A

Deposits at Federal Reserve Bank + $100	Borrowings (Notes Payable) + $100

6. A borrower from Bank A pays back a $100 loan from the bank by writing a check on his account there.

Bank A

Loans — $100	Demand Deposits — $100

THE BUSINESS OF COMMERCIAL BANKING

Much of our ensuing consideration of commercial banks will center on the activities and control of the banking system as a whole since this more "global" approach seems the relevant one for our purposes. We would, however, be remiss if we should turn directly to the subject of the control of the banking system without at least some preliminary coverage of the banking business, as such, from the individual banker's vantage point.

Commercial banking, more so than many businesses, is an art that requires a peculiar blend of experience, insight, intelligence, and prudence. It is an exacting profession that requires the successful practitioner to satisfy not only his own stockholders and depositors but also an imposing network of governmental regulatory agencies, as well as a general public that often looks with jaundiced eye upon the caretaker of "other people's money." In no other business is a public image of integrity and prudence of greater importance.

At the risk of oversimplifying the problems confronting the banker, his main task might be said to be maintaining a careful balance between solvency, liquidity, and profitability. This is a task of no small proportions since, as is so often the case, there are inherent conflicts among the three objectives.

A bank is *solvent*, if given time, it can convert its assets into sufficient cash to meet at least all its outstanding liabilities. *Liquidity*, however, requires that it be able to pay cash *immediately*, when called upon to do so, for all of its demand liabilities. Now it is this latter requirement that forces the commercial banker into a pattern of portfolio management, which is notably different from that of the other financial institutions. While other institutions often *do* pay on demand, only commercial banks are faced with a preponderance of liabilities that are *legally* payable on the demand of the holder.

It should be made clear that a bank may be perfectly solvent without being sufficiently liquid. Given several weeks or months to dispose of its assets in an orderly fashion, it may be able to raise more than enough cash to meet all its liabilities. But the liquidity problem is a different kind of constraint. Claims for cash by its demand depositors must be met in full immediately, not within several weeks or months. And a bank that is perfectly solvent in the sense that it could in time pay off all claimants, could easily be forced to close its doors because of illiquidity—inability to honor its promise to pay cash on demand to any checking account owner.

The third requirement, profitability, introduces new complications. Presumably a bank can maintain its solvency by purchasing only the safest of financial assets. At the same time it must be certain that a sufficient number of these safe assets are liquid enough, that is, quickly convertible into a fairly fixed amount of cash, to meet the likely demand for cash. But it is precisely these assets, the safest and most liquid, which will earn them the lowest rates of return. After all, the safest, most liquid asset of all is cash, but a bank that held a portfolio composed entirely of cash would earn no income whatever and would quickly disappear from the scene.

The commercial banker, therefore, must walk a narrow line. He must balance his investment portfolio in such a way as to satisfy all three basic requirements. This is the skill, the knowledge, the central art of banking.

But he cannot even put himself to this test until he has funds to employ. And, therefore, if the tasks of the commercial banker were being listed in chronological order, it should be pointed out that step number one is the attraction of depositors to the bank. This is accomplished with the aid of the conventional sales techniques—advertising, a record of service, an image of integrity, etc.—all matters of unquestioned importance but into which we shall not delve.

What does require mention here is the difference between the outlook of the single commercial banker in this respect and that of the banking system as a whole. For the single banker, it is the attraction of the liability of deposits which gives rise to the opportunity of purchasing earning assets. And, therefore, he must devote himself first to attracting deposits. As we shall see later, however, when one takes the viewpoint of the banking system as a whole, things are largely the other way around; the acquisition of assets gives birth to the bulk of deposit liabilities. We shall have more to say about this seeming contradiction at a later point. For the moment it is sufficient to make clear that, for the individual banker, deposits give rise to assets.[1]

Once the funds are raised, the task of properly dispersing them begins. A certain portion must be retained in cash form, either as vault cash or as deposits in other banks. This, of course, is needed to meet liquidity requirements and the amount so held is determined partly by the judgment of the banker and partly by the force of legal reserve requirements—a topic we shall soon discuss. These funds, as noted earlier, are the bank's primary reserves.

But primary reserves are not normally sufficient to provide the margin of safety required by most bankers. Consequently a second line of defense is thrown up in the form of secondary reserves. These usually take the form of U.S. securities—a safe investment, highly liquid with a modest interest return. These secondary reserves are kept at hand, partly to meet virtually certain future liquidity needs as a result of seasonal economic variations and partly to counter unexpected withdrawals such as might occur in a bank "run" or a cyclical downturn.

Once an adequate level of safety has been achieved via primary and secondary reserves, the bank is free to pursue more vigorously what it considers its main function, meeting the demand for loans from its local community.

The proportion of commercial bank assets committed to loans has varied widely over the years. In the late 1920's loans were almost five times as large as securities. By 1945, however, heavily influenced by the large government debt built up during World War II and the relative

[1] For an illuminating discussion on this point, see the excellent book by Roland I. Robinson, *The Management of Bank Funds*, 2nd ed. (New York, McGraw-Hill Book Company, Inc., 1962), especially Chapter 1.

scarcity of loan demand, this situation had reversed itself; securities owned were almost four times the volume of loans. But, by the end of 1965, loans once again exceeded securities by almost two to one.

There is probably no "normal" loan-to-security ratio that can be expected to reassert itself again and again in the long run. Conditions vary and as they do, so will bank portfolios. But it can be said with some confidence that, barring the disturbing influence of war, commercial banks prefer, after meeting liquidity needs, a preponderance of loans.

For if commercial banks are unique among financial intermediaries in providing checking accounts for their depositors, they are almost equally unique in their suitability for serving the local loan market. Most commercial banks are one-office, local institutions. They, better than almost any other lender, are in a position of knowing the credit needs of their locality. They, perhaps more so than any other lenders, feel it their purview, indeed, their responsibility, to fill those needs.

So, after liquidity needs are met, the commercial banker will seek to commit as many of his remaining funds as is possible and prudent to the granting of commercial, industrial, real estate, and consumer loans. In so doing he is not only fulfilling what he looks upon as his main function, but he is also enhancing his bank's profit, since the interest rate on loans is generally somewhat higher than that available on securities.

Finally, to the extent that primary and secondary reserves and loans do not exhaust the banker's available funds, he will generally place those remaining into other securities such as tax-free municipals, some corporates, and some longer-term U.S. securities. How much is available for these purposes is largely a function of the loan demand. A bank in a growing area, with a thriving business community will probably encounter a vigorous loan demand and, consequently, devote little beyond that needed for liquidity to security purchase. In the case, on the other hand, of a bank located in a declining area, or of banks generally during periods of severe economic recession, a substantially larger proportion of assets may be held in security form.[2]

THE U.S. COMMERCIAL BANKING SYSTEM

So much for the main problems of the individual commercial banker. We turn now to the U.S. banking system as a whole, with an attempt at a descriptive overview.

[2] Much of the preceding owes a heavy debt to the discussion of this topic by R. I. Robinson, *ibid.*

A Unit-banking System

There were, as of mid-1966, about 13,800 commercial banking companies operating in the United States. Compared with most other countries this is a tremendous number. England, for example, has fewer than two dozen banks and, of them, five do the vast majority of the banking business. Canada, our closest neighbor, operates with a total of nine chartered banks to serve the entire dominion.

Why the tremendous difference in the number of banks? The answer is simple. In England and Canada a fully developed, nationwide branch-banking system is the rule, whereas in the United States, the vast majority of banks are single units, without branches. The "average" bank in England and Canada operates literally hundreds of branch offices throughout their countries whereas the average bank in the United States as of the mid-1960's had one branch. The United States, it is often said, depends heavily on a *unit-* rather than a *branch-*banking system.

All this, as might be expected, came about largely as a result of legal restrictions on branch banking in the United States which continue to this day. As of 1964 nationwide branch banking is prohibited; statewide branch banking is permitted in seventeen states; seventeen states permit only limited branch banking, such as within the same city or county; and sixteen limit branch banking so severely as to virtually forbid it.[3] In an attempt partially to evade the restrictions on branch banking, the techniques of *group banking,* wherein a holding company controls the policies of a number of otherwise separate banks, has been developed. This, however, is also regulated and, as of the beginning of 1965, only 460 banks with about 8 percent of total deposits were included.[4]

This legislative antipathy to the development of branch banking in the United States is rooted in our national heritage. Decentralization has long been considered a major virtue in economic life, for good or ill, and no potential concentration of power has been more feared by the American people and their representatives than that of the financial community—the "money lenders."

Our efforts to maintain a unit banking system and whatever virtues of decentralization accompany it, however, have not come without a cost. Our history has been replete with shoddy banking practices and the outright failure of an inordinate number of small, unit banks. There were, for example, over 30,000 banks in this country in 1921. The sharp decline,

[3] See *The Banking Structure in Evaluation,* 102nd Annual Report of the Comptroller of the Currency.

[4] Another, even less-widespread technique, is chain banking whereby an individual gains control over more than one bank via majority stock ownership.

since that time, to the present 13,500 is a result of two factors; an appalling number of failures and a tacit recognition of the advantages of branch banking as evidenced by a strong merger movement.

The decline in the number of U.S. banks started in the 1920's and continues to the present. A severe agricultural depression in the early 1920's led to the failure of many banks and an additional large number, especially in the second half of the decade, disappeared through merger with other banks. In the period from July 1, 1920, to June 30, 1929, 4,925 banks closed their doors leaving about 25,000 to enter the Great Depression.

The 1929-1933 period was, of course, catastrophic for commercial banks. By the end of 1933, the 25,000 banks that entered the period had dwindled, largely because of failure, to 14,624, a loss of over 10,000 banks in four years!

The downward trend in the number of banks has continued since that date, although in greatly reduced numbers and for vastly different reasons. Major banking legislation in the thirties plus a vastly healthier national economy have since combined to virtually eliminate bank failure in the United States but the post-World War II period has seen a major reemergence of the merger movement of the 1920's. Consequently, the number of commercial banking companies has continued to decline.

The reduction in the number of banks, however, does not tell the whole story. From December 31, 1945, to December 31, 1965, while the number of *banks* has been falling from 14,011 to 13,804, the number of banking *offices,* including branches, has risen from under 18,000 to about 29,000. The number of branches alone has gone up from less than 4,000 just after the war to over 15,400 at the end of 1965.

There appears, then, to be a clear cut trend toward greater use of branch banking in the United States despite the restrictions placed upon it. The alleged advantages of branch operation over a one-unit bank are rather obvious. By allowing the bank to become larger, it can obtain certain economies of scale in its operation.[5] In addition, through branches, some banking services can be offered to small communities, which self-sufficient unit banks could not afford. Finally, diversification permitted by branching, it is argued, enhances the safety of the bank.

It is not possible to settle the issue of branch versus unit banks here. Certainly our experience with the failure rate of very small unit banks argues persuasively for "large" banks. But the advantages of size, as such, and of a branch structure must be distinguished. We face here the same

---

[5] The quantitative importance of these advantages at least for very large banks is doubted by some. In addition, it is argued that the branch bank structure, as distinct from size itself, has certain offsetting disadvantages. See Paul M. Horvitz, "Economies of Scale in Banking," in *Private Financial Institutions* (Englewood Cliffs, N.J., Prentice-Hall, Inc., 1963).

type of dilemma as is faced by our antitrust authorities—how far should we go in sacrificing the advantages of size and diversity in order to combat the disadvantages of concentration? In any case for what it is worth, it seems evident that most experts, would look favorably upon a further extension of branch banking.

Two things seem certain. On the one hand, the recent strong trend toward an expansion in branch operations will continue. On the other, unless and until we decide to rescind the present prohibition over interstate branch banking, the U.S. system will never approach the degree of concentration present in many other countries.

The student should not, however, be misled into visualizing the U.S. banking system as a homogeneous group of very many, relatively small banks. Our system, it is true, is still dominated by the one-unit bank. Almost 11,000 have no branches at all. And it is also true that the vast majority of these are small banks in terms both of assets and deposits. But some of our largest banks are giants that rival any in the world. And, as must be apparent when a decreasing number of banks is serving a growing economy, the average size of all of them is rising notably.

For example, the 14,011 commercial banks existing in 1945 held deposits aggregating $150,227 million, an average of about $11 million each. In mid-1966, 13,801 banks held $323,770 million in deposits, or over $23 million each. As of the end of 1963, ten banks out of the entire system held almost 25 percent of the total deposits. The three largest, the Bank of America, Chase Manhattan, and the First National City Bank had total deposits of over $34 billion, or well over 10 percent of the total for the entire nation.

There is no doubt that, branch-banking restrictions notwithstanding, there is a great deal of concentration in the U.S. banking system. For example, almost half the total assets are owned by the 100 largest banks. And it has been estimated that 11,000 communities in the United States, containing 40 million people, are served by a single commercial bank without direct competition.

Such figures might well cause some alarm regarding the effectiveness of competition in this most vital of industries. What are the facts on this? As is usual, there is no clear-cut proof. However there is some evidence[6] to indicate that in recent years the degree of concentration has been declining rather than increasing. And no definitive evidence exists, despite a number of studies, of abuse of the market power by the behemoths of our system. One thing is assured. This is an industry that will continue to operate under the closest of surveillance.

[6] See D. Carson and P. H. Cootner, "The Structure of Competition in Commercial Banking in the United States," *Private Financial Institutions* (Englewood Cliffs, N.J., Prentice-Hall, Inc., 1963).

A Dual Banking System

Another important characteristic of our banking system is its duality. As of the end of 1965, some 8,989 of our banks were *state* banks, having obtained their charters to do business from a state, while the remaining 4,815 were *national* banks, with a charter issued by the Comptroller of the Currency of the federal government.

The *dual* chartering system has come down to us from history. In the earliest days of the republic, in the 1780's, states began to charter banking companies. At that time, the federal government provided no paper currency, so the early banks did a flourishing business of granting the proceeds of their loans in the form of bank notes—IOU's of the issuing banks. These notes made up, at the time, our only paper money.

In 1791 the federal government chartered our first truly national bank—the Bank of the United States. It dominated the banking scene from 1791 to 1811, when its charter failed of renewal, and its successor, the Second Bank of the United States took over the same role from 1816 to 1836. Mismanagement, coupled with political difficulties, led to the revocation of the Second Bank's charter in 1836 and from that date until the National Bank Act of 1863, the United States had only state-chartered banks.

The period from 1836 to 1863, often referred to as the "era of state banking," was, from the viewpoint of sound banking principles, a disastrous one. Despite some constructive steps at the beginning of the period, the general character of banking quickly degenerated to perhaps the lowest level in our history. On the good side of the ledger were the introduction of the *free banking* principle plus the first attempts at state regulation of banks beyond a fixed limitation on the quantity of bank notes issued. In 1837, the state of Michigan became the first to permit the organization of a bank by any who could meet certain specified conditions. Previously a special act of the state legislature had been required for the chartering of any bank, a process obviously subject to the abuses of favoritism and political intrigue. The free banking principle soon spread throughout all the states and, along with it, came some of the first, faltering efforts at control and supervision of bank activities.

These two progressive steps, however, had too much mismanagement, corruption, and just plain bad banking to contend with and our banking system sunk to new depths. Banks with insufficient capital, overly speculative loans and inadequate management were commonplace. Bank notes, promising to pay specie on demand, were often all but impossible to redeem as unscrupulous operators located "redemption centers" deep in the wilderness. As a consequence, such notes circulated at substantial and varying discounts; and the failure rate was abysmally high.

This was the chaotic condition of banking in the United States until 1863 when the Congress passed the National Bank Act, authorizing for the first time, the *free* establishment of national banks. Such banks were required to obtain their charters from the Comptroller of the Currency, to meet certain minimum requirements, and to be subject to continuing supervision by the Comptroller's Office.

The requirements for national banks, while hardly severe by today's standards, were in most cases substantially more rigorous than those of the states, and it was all too apparent to the Congress that the more lenient standards of the states would place nationally chartered banks at a serious competitive disadvantage. Consequently, it was decided to counter the threat of state banks by means of a 10 percent tax on their bank notes.

It has been argued that the real intent of the Congress was the elimination of state banks, as such, because the issuance of their bank notes, as the proceeds of loans granted, was a main source of income. And a 10 percent tax made further issuance virtually prohibitive. Indeed, state bank notes did quickly disappear from circulation.

But the state banks themselves were saved from extinction, if that indeed was intended, by a fortunate quirk of circumstances. Whereas, in earlier years, borrowers from banks had often insisted on currency and had received it in the form of bank notes, by the time the National Bank Act was passed the advantages of deposits over currency had taken firm hold in the public's mind. And state banks found that they could continue to earn income by lending out *deposits,* rather than the bank notes that the new law virtually forbade. As a result a large number of state banks managed to continue to operate alongside the growing number of national banks.

The astonishingly rapid spread of the deposit banking habit among the American public in the latter 19th century is clearly revealed in Table 2-2.

TABLE 2-2   Quantities of Bank Notes and Bank Deposits in Circulation, Selected Years (millions of dollars)

Year	Bank Notes	Deposits
1834	95	76
1849	115	91
1855	187	190
1861	202	257
1870	336	775
1890	126	4,576

SOURCE: *The Story of American Banking* (New York, The American Bankers Association, 1963).

The National Bank Act did, therefore, succeed in consolidating control over the circulating currency exclusively in federal hands for the first time, but it left us with a dual system of banks—state and national banks—subject to different controlling agencies. And as the years went by the number of supervisory agencies multiplied.

When the Federal Reserve Act was passed in 1913, all national banks were required to become members while state banks were permitted to do as they wished—to join the system or to remain outside of it. This meant that national banks became subject to the supervisory control of both the Comptroller of the Currency and the Federal Reserve authorities; state member banks were subject to their own state regulatory authorities and the Federal Reserve, and nonmember state banks were regulated only by state authorities.

Nor was this the end of the confusion in supervision. In the 1930's, when the Federal Deposit Insurance Corporation (F.D.I.C.) was set up to insure deposits, a fourth group of supervisors entered the banking scene. And since practically all commercial banks have since become insured, almost all are subject to the regulations of the F.D.I.C. examiners, too.

This maze of supervisory authorities accomplishes, despite occasional confusion and sometimes outright conflict, a satisfyingly effective regulatory job. For national banks it is probably accurate to say that the Comptroller of the Currency and the F.D.I.C. concentrates on seeing to bank safety while Federal Reserve authorities specialize in controlling the quantity of credit issued.[7] Insured state banks that are members of the Federal Reserve System are controlled by the Federal Reserve, the F.D.I.C. and their state regulatory agencies, but nonmember state banks are free of, at least, the direct control of the Federal Reserve authorities. And this fact has led to some concern among students of our banking system.

With respect to bank *safety* there is, happily, not much difference between the regulations applied to state banks and those applied to national banks. For almost all banks today subscribe to the F.D.I.C. and, therefore, almost all, state and national alike, are subject to the common, careful supervision of that agency. With respect to control over the *quantity* of bank credit, however, there is a substantial difference. National and state member banks are effectively limited in this respect by the Federal Reserve System. But state nonmember banks, though subject to reserve requirements set by their states, are not, as a group, equally circumscribed. Indeed, in the words of one authority: "In the case of

---

[7] See Clark Warburton, "Nonmember Banks and the Effectiveness of Monetary Policy," *Monetary Management* (Englewood Cliffs, N.J., Prentice-Hall, Inc., 1963).

nonmember banks, reserve requirements have become of negligible importance as a limitation on expansion."[8]

The point behind the above statement is not that state reserve ratios are especially low. Indeed, as Table 2-3 makes clear, they are in many cases higher than those of the Federal Reserve System. The real difference lies in the type of asset that constitutes legal reserves. For the Federal Reserve System, up until late 1959, only deposits at a Federal Reserve bank were legal reserves. Today the F.R.S. permits both Federal Reserve deposits and vault cash to be counted. Most states, on the other hand, permit cash and deposits at *any* other bank to be counted, and some even allow reserves to be held in the form of government securities. Table 2-3 presents the details as of January 1, 1959, a date on which Federal Reserve reserve requirements for demand deposits ranged from 11 percent to 18 percent for three different classes of banks.

Note that three states require no reserves at all, in the form of cash or deposits, and that nine permit the fulfillment of part of their requirements by holding government securities. The figures given in Table 2-3 are requirements in effect as of January 1, 1959, but twenty-three states possess the power to alter the ratios at their discretion. Most states (all but five) also had reserve requirements behind savings deposits.

The important point to note about these state reserve requirements is that they are inadequate to perform the main function of reserve requirements in today's world. They do not provide adequate control over the expansion of bank credit by these banks as a group. This is because, almost without exception, state nonmember banks may satisfy their requirements by holding deposits at *other commercial banks*. This situation is far different from that of member banks. They must keep reserves either in cash or in deposits at Federal Reserve banks; and the Federal Reserve authorities have almost complete control over the amount of reserves they can obtain in these forms. State authorities, however, have no real control over the total of nonmember bank reserves. To take an extreme illustration, it would be possible for two nonmember banks to exchange reciprocal deposits with one another for $10 million, and thereby expand total bank reserves by $20 million.

Some concern over the status of nonmember state banks does exist, especially with respect to their relative freedom from credit restraint.[9] However, the degree of concern is tempered by the fact that, taken as a group, these banks are relatively unimportant. As of mid-1966 nonmember banks, while they accounted for over 55 percent of the total number of commercial banks, held only about 17 percent of the deposits and 17 percent of the total assets of all commercial banks. Consequently,

8 *Ibid.*, p. 328.
9 On this see Clark Warburton's excellent essay, *ibid.*

TABLE 2-3   Reserve Requirements for Nonmember State Banks as of January 1, 1959

State	Reserves Required (as a Percentage of Demand Deposits)	Form in Which Reserves May Be Held		
		Vault Cash	Cash or Deposits at Any Other Bank	Government Securities, Deposits at Other Banks, or Cash
Alabama	15%	0%	15%	0%
Alaska	20	0	20	0
Arizona	10	0	10	0
Arkansas	15	0	15	0
California	12	6	6	0
Colorado	15	0	0	15
Connecticut	12	2	8	2
Delaware	11	0	11	0
Florida	20	0	0	20
Georgia	15	0	15	0
Idaho	15	0	10	5
Illinois	0	0	0	0
Indiana	12.5	0	12.5	0
Iowa	7	1.05	5.95	0
Kansas	12.5	0	12.5	0
Kentucky	7	2.33	4.67	0
Louisiana	20	0	20	0
Maine	11	0	11	0
Maryland	15	0	15	0
Massachusetts	15	3	6	6
Michigan	12	0	12	0
Minnesota	12	0	12	0
Mississippi	15	0	15	0
Missouri	15	0	15	0
Montana	10	0	10	0
Nebraska	15	0	12	3
Nevada	15	0	15	0
New Hampshire	15	0	15	0
New Jersey	11	0	11	0
New Mexico	12	0	12	0
New York	11	0	11	0
North Carolina	15	0	15	0
North Dakota	10	0	10	0
Ohio	15	0	15	0
Oklahoma	15	0	15	0

| | | Form in Which Reserves May Be Held | | |
State	Reserves Required (as a Percentage of Demand Deposits)	Vault Cash	Cash or Deposits at Any Other Bank	Government Securities, Deposits at Other Banks, or Cash
Oregon	15%	0%	15%	0%
Pennsylvania	14	0	8.4	5.6
Rhode Island	15	6	9	0
South Carolina	7	0	7	0
South Dakota	17.5	0	7	10.5
Tennessee	10	0	10	0
Texas	15	0	15	0
Utah	15	1.88	13.12	0
Vermont	30	0	12	18
Virginia	10	0	10	0
Washington	15	0	15	0
West Virginia	10	2	8	0
Wisconsin	12	0	8	4
Wyoming	20	0	20	0

SOURCE: Member Bank Reserve Requirements, Committee on Banking and Currency, U.S. Senate, 86th Congress, 1st session, March 23-24, 1959.

their ability to evade effective quantitative credit control is not now an issue of great moment. They are simply too small.

There is no guarantee, however, that they will, forever, stay that way. Indeed, after declining for many years in number, deposits, and assets, as a percentage of the total, they appear to have reached "bottom" in about 1950 and have shown steady, if unspectacular relative rises ever since. In 1951, they composed 51.5 percent of the banks, and controlled 14.8 percent and 14.9 percent of the deposits and assets respectively. Today they make up 55 percent of the banks and possess, as mentioned, 17 percent of the deposits and assets. They are still too small to be a serious concern. But the trend will be worth watching.

SUMMARY—THE PRESENT STRUCTURE OF THE COMMERCIAL BANKING SYSTEM

Perhaps the simplest way to summarize this discussion of the commercial banking system's structure is by means of a table such as Table 2-4. There are, it is clear, more state banks than national banks and

TABLE 2-4   Structure of U.S. Commercial Banking System, December 31, 1965

	Deposits (billions of dollars)	Percentage of Total Commercial Bank Deposits	Assets (billions of dollars)	Percentage of Total Commercial Bank Assets	Number of Banks	Percentage of Banks
State Banks	138.6	42	157.5	42	8,989	65
National Banks	193.9	58	219.7	58	4,815	35
Member Banks	275.5	83	313.4	83	6,221	45
Nonmember Banks	56.9	17	63.9	17	7,583	55
Insured Banks	330.3	99+	374.1	99+	13,540	98+
Noninsured Banks	2.1	1—	3.2	1—	263	2—
Total—All Commercial Banks	332.4	100	377.3	100	13,804	100

SOURCE: *Federal Reserve Bulletin.*

more nonmember than member banks. But, measured in terms of assets or deposits it is even clearer that banks that are members of the Federal Reserve System dominate the structure.

We shall make use of this fact to simplify greatly the following chapters. Recognizing that nonmember banks do only a small fraction of the total banking business, we shall henceforth confine our discussion to member banks and, except where specific reference to nonmember banks is made, talk "as if" the entire commercial banking system is made up of member banks. It is hoped that the damage done to the facts by this approach will be more than made up for by the added clarity that over-simplification permits. We turn now, in the next chapter, to a consideration of the development and structure of the Federal Reserve System itself.

3

The Development, Structure, and Functions of the Federal Reserve System

BACKGROUND TO THE FEDERAL RESERVE ACT

The National Bank Act of 1863 solved some of our monetary problems but, as is so often the case, it led to still others. On the positive side it did provide for the development of a more carefully controlled system of national banks and it did, for the first time, concentrate control over the circulating currency in federal hands. And these were truly significant improvements.

But, as the nineteenth century drew to a close, it was clear that serious monetary problems remained, some of them directly attributable to the Act itself. The deplorable situation that had been created by the widespread overissue of State Bank Notes was effectively eliminated by the 10 percent issue tax but it was not long before it became clear that the provisions for the issuance of National Bank Notes were, themselves, not entirely adequate.

The bank note problem under the National Bank Act, unlike the earlier years, was not a matter of overissue. If anything it was the other way around. National banks issuing notes were required to purchase and deposit with the Comptroller of the Currency, U.S. government securities as "backing" for their outstanding notes. They were permitted to issue notes up to an amount equaling 90 percent of the par or market value (whichever was lower) of U.S. securities so deposited.

This requirement provided admirably for the safety of National Bank Notes. However, by tying the quantity that could be issued directly to U.S. securities it overlooked the necessity of providing a currency supply that could expand and contract as the "needs of trade" required. When a bigger currency supply was needed but no more U.S. securities were available, the economy's requirements could not be met.

And that is just about what happened. The value of U.S. securities outstanding fell from about $2.8 billion in 1866 to about $1.6 billion in 1890 as the federal government steadily reduced its debt during the period. Consequently, the "base" on which more national bank notes could be issued was steadily declining at a time when the nation's economy was growing by leaps and bounds. In addition, during much of the period, U.S. securities were selling at substantial premiums and, hence, were not particularly desirable for bank purchase. The number of National Bank Notes, which had totaled about $300 million in 1870, fell precipitously during the next twenty years.[1]

Nor was the long run decline in the absolute volume of notes the only problem. A properly functioning currency supply should also expand and contract in volume in response to seasonal, cyclical, and panic-induced demands by the public. To employ the word that was popular then, the currency supply should be "elastic" with respect to the public's demands for it. Based as it was on U.S. securities, the supply of national bank notes was, unfortunately, highly inelastic. In the words of the Comptroller of the Currency in 1914:

> Under the conditions existing, and which have existed for years past, the currency of the country under our national banking system has been entirely lacking in the element of elasticity which is so necessary to meet the requirements of business and the periodical demands for money and currency which come, especially in the great agricultural sections of the West and South.[2]

In addition to the currency-issue problems, reserve requirements for deposits under the National Bank Act were the source of considerable trouble. The Act divided banks into three groups: central reserve city banks, those banks located in New York, Chicago, and St. Louis; reserve city banks, those located in approximately fifty other large cities; and country banks, all other national banks. Country banks were required to keep a 15 percent reserve behind deposits, of which three-fifths could be kept as a deposit in reserve city or central reserve city banks and two-fifths in cash. Reserve city banks had a 25 percent requirement, half of which could be kept on deposit in central reserve city banks and the other half in cash. Central reserve city banks were required to maintain their 25 percent reserve entirely in cash.

[1] It should be noted that the rapid switch in public taste from notes to deposits during the same period kept this decline in currency supply from creating the havoc it might otherwise have caused.

[2] *Annual Report of the Comptroller of the Currency, 1914*, p. 9.

The problem these reserve arrangements created is perhaps best put in the words of the Comptroller of the Currency at the time of the passage of the Federal Reserve Act:

A further weakness of the system which developed—and, with the expansion of our trade and industries, had become more evident and threatening—was the imperfect, inefficient, and unscientific method of handling our bank reserves. Under the national banking system the banks throughout the country have been accustomed to accumulate their reserve balances in the central reserve cities of New York, Chicago, and St. Louis, where the national banks usually have allowed interest at the rate of 2 per cent per annum, and sometimes more, to their correspondent national banks. To avoid loss from idle funds, these depository banks employed to a large extent the balances thus kept with them by putting the money out in call loans on bond and stock collateral. . . .

When the banks throughout the country found it necessary to draw on their reserves in the large cities to meet the recurring seasonal demands of business, these large city banks, in turn, were forced to call in the broker's call loans, these calls resulting frequently in high money rates and declining security values, and sometimes in serious stringency, disturbance and panic, or alarm.[3]

Thus, short-sighted reserve requirement arrangements contributed mightily to periodic financial panics. Ordinary seasonal demands for credit in the agricultural interior led to pressure on large city banks, especially in New York City, which, in turn, created pressure on the stock market and all too often degenerated into an all-out financial panic.

Finally, to complete the picture, banks, under intense pressure compounded by U.S. currency-issue and reserve requirement arrangements, had no place to go, other than to other banks under equivalent pressure, to obtain help in periods of crisis. There was no "lender of last resort"—no central bank to absorb the shock and facilitate a return to order.

It took the severe financial panic of 1907 to stir the nation to positive steps toward fundamental reform. That experience led to a stopgap measure in 1908, the Aldrich-Vreeland Act, which set up, in turn, an important study group, the National Monetary Commission. Five years later, after much debate, the deliberations of the Commission provided the basis for the Federal Reserve Act.

THE ORIGINAL FEDERAL RESERVE ACT

The Federal Reserve System, which started operations in the fall of 1914, was a far cry from our present system, both in structure and philosophy. It was, in every way, a compromise. The need for a

3 *Ibid.*, pp. 9-10.

central bank was widely recognized, but the concentration of power that would have been involved in a single authority, such as the Bank of England had been for many years, was apparently too much for the American Congress of 1913 to accept. So it settled for a unique system wherein twelve district Federal Reserve banks with considerable autonomy were established, with a fairly weak seven-man coordinating group, the Federal Reserve Board, in Washington, D.C. As we shall see, time and bitter experience have since shifted the locus of power largely out of the hands of the individual Federal Reserve banks and into those of the Board.

More remarkable than the changes in structure, however, has been the evolution of the philosophy and objectives of the System. Whereas we now take for granted the goals of full employment, economic growth, and stable prices as almost the sine qua non of monetary policy, the framers of the original Federal Reserve Act made no mention of any of them. The Act was intended, in its own words, ". . . to furnish an elastic currency, to afford means of rediscounting commercial paper, to establish a more effective supervision of banking in the United States, and for other purposes."[4] It seems clear from this statement that the Act was aimed primarily at the specific weaknesses that had cropped up under the national banking system rather than the creation of a powerful new agency to stabilize the economy.

It is perhaps a measure of the strength of the Federal Reserve Act that it has been able to weather successfully the test of time and evolve to handle ideas and objectives not even conceived fifty years ago. And it is truly amazing to consider the changes that those years have brought about.

There is, of course, no doubt that the creators of our new central bank were aware that their brainchild would, in some general sense, affect the entire economy. But they were far from prepared to set it directly to the task of the maintenance of full employment and price stability. In the first place, few were yet ready to grant that the federal government *had* any real responsibility for maintaining full employment. And as for price stability, the following comment by Benjamin Strong, first Governor of the Federal Reserve Bank of New York, to a Congressional committee in 1921 is illuminating: "I shall ask the commission to bear in mind that our theory is that our function as a Federal Reserve System is to deal with credit and not with prices."[5]

It is probably fair to say that the framers of the Federal Reserve Act considered the task of the System to be much simpler than the one we

---

4 "Preamble," Federal Reserve Act.

5 *Interpretations of Federal Reserve Policy*, W. Randolph Burgess, ed. (New York, Harper & Row Publishers, 1930).

assign to it today. Much of the basis for this optimistic view lies in their implicit faith in what has come to be called the *commercial loan theory*.

The Commercial Loan Theory

The commercial loan theory centered on the thought that both the quantity and the quality of bank credit could be satisfactorily controlled if the basic legislation encouraged banks to restrict themselves largely to short-term (90 days in the general case) loans to business for the purpose of purchasing inventories. Such legislation, it was felt, would guarantee that banks would lend only for *productive* rather than speculative purposes and that an expansion in the quantity of bank credit would only occur when such an increase was needed to finance expanded trade. It was a soothing theory. Not only could we insure that bank loans were *sound* and that bank credit would not expand to an inflationary level but we could do so by law, thereby avoiding any heavy reliance on the discretion of policy makers.

The original Federal Reserve Act set out to implement the commercial loan theory in several respects. It required member banks that needed to borrow from their Federal Reserve bank to present *eligible* paper to be *rediscounted*. Not surprisingly, eligible paper consisted of the IOU's resulting from short term inventory loans to business. The hope was, of course, that added reserves obtained through the discount window would be restricted to those member banks who desired to make "proper," productive, noninflationary loans.

In addition, the provisions for issuance of Federal Reserve Notes were generously influenced by the same ideas. Federal Reserve banks were originally empowered to issue such currency only if they could back it with 40 percent in gold plus 100 percent collateral in the form of eligible paper.[6] The currency supply, then, could only expand along with rediscounting, which, in turn, could only rise as the volume of production rose. It would indeed have been wonderful if the perils and indecisions of discretion in monetary policy could have been avoided by such automatic legislative devices. But the early high hopes were soon to be dashed with the cold water of reality.

It follows, of course, from the logic of the commercial loan theory that, if the proper basic legislation is achieved, not much in the way of discretionary policy tools is needed. And that, indeed was the outlook of the original Act. It did provide the power to alter discount rates as one specific credit control weapon. But the more powerful tools with which we are so familiar today, open-market operation and variable reserve requirements, were all but overlooked.

---

[6] Presumably obtained by the Federal Reserve bank from its discounting activities.

The Original Monetary Policy Weapons

The original Act did grant the Federal Reserve System the authority to buy and sell U.S. securities but it seems clear that there was, at the time, little recognition of the fact that this represented the most effective of all credit control weapons. The power seems to have been included largely to provide a means of earning income for Federal Reserve banks, although there is evidence that some legislators had a slight awareness of its credit control potential. At that time the discount rate was considered the prime credit control weapon but it was popular to refer to the Federal Reserve banks selling securities "to make the discount rate effective." Presumably this meant the removal of excess reserves so that member banks would be forced to borrow from their district Federal Reserve bank. It is clear, however, that some years elapsed before open market operations were looked upon as independent and very powerful tools in their own right.

The reserve requirement provisions constituted a vast improvement over those of the old national banking system but, here too, there is evidence of an early misunderstanding of their full significance. The three-group structure inherited from the National Bank Act was retained but reserves now had to be carried entirely on deposit at Federal Reserve banks.[7] The required ratio behind demand deposits for central reserve city banks was set at 13 percent, that for reserve city banks at 10 percent, and that for country banks at 7 percent.

In the original Act, however, there was no provision for altering these percentages. And even more fundamentally there appears to have been widespread misunderstanding regarding the main function of required reserves. Today we consider the reserve requirement most important as a fulcrum to the control of the quantity of money and credit outstanding, with the function of enforcing bank liquidity for the protection of depositors distinctly secondary. In 1913, it seems clear, emphasis was the other way around. Required reserves were looked upon as primarily providing liquidity and the credit control function was often overlooked entirely.

MAJOR CHANGES IN FEDERAL RESERVE STRUCTURE AND OBJECTIVES

It has been a full half-century since the Federal Reserve System began operations. We have, in that time, endured three wars, a serious bank panic, a devastating depression, powerful postwar inflation, and

[7] After a 1917 amendment. Before that date ratios were about 5 percent higher and vault cash could be counted.

a near-revolution in economic thinking. Small wonder that the Federal Reserve System has undergone significant change!

Among the first things that had to be abandoned was the commercial loan theory and its attendant dependence on eligible paper to regulate discounts and currency issue. In 1917, partly to aid in financing World War I, member banks were given permission to use U.S. securities, as well as short-term inventory loans, as collateral for loans from the Federal Reserve. Then, in 1932, confronted with a serious bank panic and an alarmingly high bank failure rate, the discount window was further opened by authorizing member bank borrowing on the basis of "any asset acceptable to the Federal Reserve." The tie-up of the discount mechanism to the commercial loan theory was clearly broken.[8]

Essentially the same thing happened to the link between Federal Reserve Notes and eligible paper. First, during World War I, the amount of eligible paper required as collateral behind Notes issued was reduced from 100 percent to 60 percent (along with the 40 percent gold certificate requirement.) Then, during the 1930's a much more significant relaxation in requirements permitted Federal Reserve banks to use government securities as collateral behind their notes.

The Weaknesses of the Commercial Loan Theory

Although it was the exigency of World War I which prompted the initial legislative retreats from the commercial loan theory, it is clear that the doctrine would have had to have been abandoned sooner or later in any case; the commercial loan theory or "real bills" doctrine, as it is sometimes called, was basically unsound.

Its claim, for example, that restricting bank assets to short-term *inventory* loans would insure the liquidity of banks because of the *self-liquidating* character of loans secured by a firm's inventories, was surely shortsighted. The idea was that a firm which borrowed to finance the purchase of its stock-in-trade would be in a position to repay the bank as soon as it had turned over that portion of its inventory. What was forgotten in the argument was the possibility of an economy-wide collapse of economic activity which would make it difficult or impossible for the borrower to sell his goods. In such a situation, short-term inventory loans derive their liquidity only from the fact that they can be discounted at the central bank—not through any inherently self-liquidating features.

Even more seriously misleading was the argument that tying discounts and note issue to short-term inventory loans would guarantee that

---

[8] A remnant of it remained, nevertheless, in the form of a requirement that a discount rate of 1/2 percent higher be charged on loans secured only by assets other than "eligible" paper or government securities.

the money supply could not be excessive. Commercial loan advocates argued that as long as access to the discount facility and to note issue was limited to banks possessing *productive* short-term inventory loans, bank reserves and the money supply could only increase as the volume of physical production itself increased. Inflation, then, need not be a matter of concern.

But this, of course, misses the very essence of inflation. Once full employment is reached, firms bid against one another to obtain a larger share of the fixed supply of productive resource. Since no more is to be had, the bidding simply forces prices up. As prices rise, the *dollar value* of each inventory acquisition necessarily rises. Firms, then, come to banks for ever larger amounts of credit and bank portfolios become stocked with more and more short-term commercial paper "eligible" for discount. The flaw in the commercial loan idea, of course, is the fact that the quantity of short-term commercial loans does not only rise when real production rises; it also increases when the money value of production rises via inflationary price increases. And when this happens, far from preventing inflation, the commercial loan theory provisions actually feed it.

Other Significant Changes in the 1930's

The changes in discount and note issue regulations which occurred during the Federal Reserve's first twenty years, moreover, represented more than a simple disavowal of the commercial loan theory. They reflected profound changes, as a result of bitter experience, in our attitude toward bank panics. It is clear today that what is needed to halt a "run" on the banks—a mass withdrawal of cash— is not banking regulations that *restrict* banks' access to the discount window and *impede* their ability to pay out the currency demanded but precisely the reverse. A bank panic is founded on, and is fed by—fear; fear on the part of depositors that the bank will be unable to convert their deposits into cash. The liberalization of discount and note issue regulations in the 1930's are based squarely on the distinctly rational and almost routinely obvious premise that the correct way to deal with such fear is to make it easy for banks to accommodate their depositors, thereby striking at the very heart of the problem. If the problem exists because of fear that banks cannot meet demands for cash, it can be snuffed out by a clear-cut demonstration that they can. These changes, coupled with the establishment of the Federal Deposit Insurance Corporation, appear to provide us today with almost impregnable defenses against future panics.

The 1930's also saw several other highly significant changes. The Board of Governors was given, for the first time, the power to alter required reserve ratios. It also received authority to set margin requirements on the purchase of securities, its first selective credit control tool. In general, the on-going process whereby authority was centralized more in the hands of the Board of Governors and less in those of the individual Federal Reserve banks was accelerated. It was, indeed, a very different Federal Reserve System that emerged from the Great Depression.

STRUCTURE OF THE FEDERAL RESERVE SYSTEM TODAY

The Member Banks

The base of the Federal Reserve System is composed of the member banks, consisting today of some 4,815 national banks, which are required to belong, plus another 1,406 of the larger state banks that have voluntarily chosen to join. The member bank undertakes certain responsibilities in return for the privileges of membership.

It is required to subscribe to stock in the Federal Reserve bank of its district in an amount equal to 6 percent of its own capital and surplus although, to date, only half that amount must be paid in. The rest is subject to call. It must abide by a list of System regulations regarding its capital structure, its loans and investments, its branch operations, its holding company operations, and the activities of its directors. It must submit, at the discretion of the System, to supervision and examination by Federal Reserve authorities. Finally, it must observe the reserve requirements set by the Federal Reserve for member banks in the city in which it is located.

In return for these obligations, the member bank enjoys certain privileges. Its ownership of Federal Reserve bank stock entitles it to participate in the selection of six of the nine members of the Board of Directors of its Federal Reserve bank. In addition, it receives a safe 6 percent dividend on such stock owned. It is eligible, as a member of the system, to avail itself of loans of reserves, called discounts and advances, from its Federal Reserve bank whenever the need arises. It has available to it the extensive check clearing and collection facilities of the system. And finally, a matter of some importance in the financial world, it enjoys the considerable prestige that accompanies membership.

The Federal Reserve Banks

The twelve Federal Reserve banks themselves are often refered to as "quasi-public" institutions. This phrase has reference to the fact that while they are entirely privately owned, they are operated with a view to public objectives.

All the stock issued by a Federal Reserve bank is owned by the member banks of its district. In addition, as pointed out above, six of the nine members of each bank's Board of Directors are selected by their member bank owners. But despite this 100 percent private ownership and seemingly effective private control of a majority of their Directors, Federal Reserve banks today are, in most important respects, subject almost completely to the dictates of a strictly governmental agency, the Board of Governors in Washington.

The Board of Governors, for example, appoints the three remaining members of each Federal Reserve bank's Board of Directors, one of whom is selected to be Chairman of the Board. In addition, the individual Reserve Bank's directors have little direct say about such important matters as the setting of their own discount rates or the determination of the composition of their own security portfolios. Discount rates, for example, while *set* by the individual Reserve bank, are subject to *review and determination* by the Board of Governors. In actual practice this results in the Board of Governors rather than individual Federal Reserve banks determining the rate. Similarly, the purchase and sale of U.S. securities, which make up nearly the whole of Federal Reserve bank earning assets, is subject to the complete control of the Open Market Committee, a group dominatd by the Board of Governors. As a result, the private owners and their six representatives on their Reserve bank's Board of Directors have little control over fundamental policy matters.

The public status of Federal Reserve banks is further reflected in their attitude towards, and disposition of, profits. Unlike other privately owned institutions, the Federal Reserve banks view the making of a profit on their operations as an objective that is distinctly secondary to the goal of carrying out their public function. As governmentally oriented organizations, profit making is looked upon as an incidental result of their operations rather than as a goal to be achieved.

They do, however, make substantial profits, primarily as a result of interest earned on loans to member banks and on U.S. government securities, as shown in Table 3-1, which contains data for 1965.

As can be seen, virtually all the income of the System results from income on assets acquired in the process of carrying out monetary policy, specifically from the *rediscount* mechanism and open-market purchases. The reason for acquiring these assets is *not* to earn income but to exert desired influence on the cost and availability of credit in the economy. Thus, the *profit* earned is purely a side effect of measures taken primarily for other purposes.

It is interesting, also, to note the disposition of Federal Reserve earnings. After expenses of the Federal Reserve banks and the Board are met, a 6 percent dividend is paid to member-bank stockholders, and a specified

TABLE 3-1   Sources and Disposition of Federal
Reserve Bank Earnings, 1965 (millions of dollars)

Income, by Source	
Discounts and Advances	19.8
U.S. Securities	1,522.0
All Other	18.7
Gross Income	1,560.5
Net Expenses	204.3
Net Earnings	1,356.2
Disposition of Net Income	
Dividends to Member Banks	32.4
Transferred to Surplus	27.1
Paid to U.S. Treasury	1,296.8

SOURCE: *Federal Reserve Bulletin.*

amount is set aside for surplus, the remaining earnings are turned over to
the Treasury. This is a further indication of the fact that the System's
profits are not an important factor in determining its policy. They are not
permitted to keep them in any case.

Perhaps the easiest way to visualize the role of Federal Reserve banks
is via their balance sheets.

TABLE 3-2   Consolidated Balance Sheet of All Federal
Reserve Banks, May, 1966 (billions of dollars)

Assets		*Liabilities and Capital Accounts*	
Gold Certificates	13.1	Federal Reserve Notes Out-	
Currency (Bank notes)	.2	standing	36.8
Discounts and Advances	.4	Demand Deposits—	
U.S. Securities	41.1	Member Banks	17.7
Uncollected Cash Items	6.4	Demand Deposits—	
All Other Assets	.9	U.S. Treasury	.7
		Demand Deposits—Other	.6
		Deferred Availability Cash	
		Items	4.9
		Other Liabilities	.1
		Capital Accounts	1.3
Total	62.1	Total	62.1

SOURCE: *Federal Reserve Bulletin.*

The predominant asset of Federal Reserve banks is their large port-folio of *U.S. securities*. These are, of course, initially issued by the Trea-sury and are acquired by the Federal Reserve banks via their open-market operations. It should be evident that almost all the income earned by the System comes in the form of interest on these securities.

Because the second largest asset, gold certificates, constitutes an espe-cially strategic item into which we shall delve at somewhat greater length, we shall bypass it for the moment. The *currency* account includes all cur-rency and coin held by Federal Reserve banks but issued by the Treasury as well as Federal Reserve Notes that have been issued by one Federal Reserve bank but are now held by another. *Discounts and advances* are predominantly IOU's signed by member banks who have borrowed re-serves from their Federal Reserve bank via the so-called rediscount mech-anism. The asset entitled *uncollected cash items* arises out of the process of collecting checks written on member banks. We shall discuss it more fully in the next chapter; for the moment, therefore, we shall merely point out that this asset represents the value of checks that have not yet been delivered to the member banks on which they are written.

On the liability and net worth side, the $36.8 billion of *Federal Re-serve Notes outstanding* represent the majority of the nation's currency supply. It is a liability of the Federal Reserve banks, of course, because they are the issuing agents.

Among the demand deposits outstanding, those owed to the member banks constitute the bulk of the legal reserves that they, in turn, use to "back up" the demand and time deposits of their customers. The *U.S. Treasury demand deposit* is the checking account on which the Treasury writes virtually all the checks with which it makes payment for the goods and services it purchases. Although it may seem absurdly small for such a purpose, it is, as we shall see later, constantly replenished when the Treasury needs to use it. The *other demand deposits* liability includes, among others, deposits held in Federal Reserve banks by foreign trea-suries and central banks.

The *deferred availability cash items is,* like Uncollected Cash Items on the asset side, a temporary account that arises in the process of check clear-ing and collection. We shall deal with it shortly. Finally, the capital accounts represent the equity that the member-bank owners have built up in their Federal Reserve banks, by virtue of the requirement that they purchase stock in them.

The Significance of Gold Certificates

Let us return now to the asset side for a more complete dis-cussion of one of the Reserve banks' most strategic assets, *gold certificates*. All gold certificates are obligations of the Treasury, which is empowered by law to issue a $1.00 gold certificate for every $1.00 worth of gold that it holds in its gold depositories. They are, in short, no more than "warehouse receipts" for the gold that the Treasury possesses.

When the Treasury acquires more gold (which it stands ready to buy at a fixed $35 per ounce price from anyone) it normally prints up an equivalent amount of gold certificates, and deposits them in a Federal Reserve bank. In payment for the gold certificates, the Federal Reserve bank increases the Treasury's checking account by that amount. Conversely, when the Treasury sells some of its gold stock (as, under present arrangements, it does to foreign monetary authorities and others who are licensed as legitimate gold users), it must write a check on its checking account at the Federal Reserve, specifying that payment must be in the form of gold certificates.

To the Federal Reserve banks, gold certificates have a special significance. They are, in fact, the "legal reserves" of the Federal Reserve banks. Until early 1965, Federal Reserve banks had been required to maintain gold certificates as legal reserves behind both their outstanding Federal Reserve Notes and deposit liabilities, in an amount not less than 25 percent of the combined value of both. In the balance sheet above for May, 1966, the $36.8 billion of Federal Reserve Notes and the $19 billion of outstanding deposits would have required a "backing" in gold certificates of 25 percent of $54.8 billion, or $13.7 billion. But at that time the Federal Reserve possessed only $13.1 billion in gold certificates. To meet the requirements of the law before 1965, it would have been required to use its monetary policy weapons to cut member-bank reserves by $600 million, no matter what the economic conditions.

It was in order to avoid just such a situation that the Congress acted in March of 1965 to change the law specifying gold-certificate reserves. In the belief that the informed judgment of our policy makers, arrived at in light of economic conditions, is a better means of determining the money supply than the size of our gold stock, Congress eliminated the 25 percent gold-certificate requirement behind deposits at the Federal Reserve banks. Today only Federal Reserve Notes outstanding have a 25 percent gold-certificate reserve so that only $9.2 billion of the $13.1 billion of gold-certificates possessed by the System in mid-1966 were required.[9] The result is that, while the bulk of our currency supply still retains a relationship to the gold in Fort Knox, that far larger portion of the money supply composed of checking accounts does not.

This most recent action by Congress to loosen still further the connection between gold and our money supply meets, it seems fair to say, with the enthusiastic approval of the majority of economists. Under current

[9] This statement ignores the fact that the small amount of U.S. Notes still in circulation have a specific required gold backing.

conditions, unless one distrusts the wisdom or objectives of our monetary and fiscal policy makers, there is no real reason to permit our gold supply to place even an outside limit on our domestic money supply. Indeed, many would argue that the Congress would have done better to have gone all the way by eliminating the gold-certificate reserve behind Federal Reserve Notes too, thereby severing completely any legal ties between gold and the money supply.

Gold Supply Does Not, in Fact, Limit Money Supply

It has been partly a consequence of good fortune and partly a product of good management that, since the nation assumed its present modified gold bullion standard in 1934, our money supply has not, in fact, been held down by our gold supply. For during most of this period, the nation has possessed far more than enough gold (and therefore, gold certificates) to support whatever money supply was considered appropriate. Only twice has the gold-certificate requirements come close to actually limiting the money supply and both times Congress has acted to change the requirement. The first occasion was in 1945 when the booming war economy was rapidly accelerating the nation's money supply needs. At that time the gold-certificate requirement behind Federal Reserve Notes was 40 percent and that behind deposits at the Federal Reserve, 35 percent. When it became apparent that these limits would soon be reached, Congress, for the eminently sound reason that it did not desire the money supply to be held down to a level that would impede war production, cut both requirements to 25 percent.

The second change, of course, was the 1965 action, brought to a head by a sharp cut in the nation's gold supply as a result of balance of payments difficulties, by which the gold-certificate requirement behind Federal Reserve deposits was eliminated altogether. In the immediate future there appears no need for further action on this requirement, but should a change in conditions elevate the remaining requirement for a 25 percent gold-certificate reserve behind Federal Reserve Notes to a practically effective limit, there seems little doubt that it, too, will be (and should be) removed.

The Board of Governors

At the top the Federal Reserve System is controlled by the Board of Governors, a seven-man group appointed by the President to fourteen-year terms.

These seven men are the top monetary authorities in the United States. It is they who set reserve requirements for member banks. It is they who "review and determine" discount rates set by the Federal Reserve banks. It is they who set margin requirements on the purchase of securities. And it is they who compose a majority of the Open Market Committee, which determines the extent and direction of open market operations. In the final analysis it is the seven members of the Board of Governors who determine the size of the money supply and the cost and availability of credit in the United States.

The Board of Governors is a strictly governmental agency concerned solely with the public interest. It does, however, maintain a somewhat unique status among governmental agencies in that it is, to a degree, insulated from some of the direct control from the executive and the legislature to which other agencies are subject.

The fourteen-year terms, for example, guarantee any member a tenure in office of longer duration than the President who appoints him. Consequently, in case of a difference in policy views, the Board of Governors, unlike most other appointed officials, can pursue a monetary policy to which the President may be opposed, without being replaced. In addition the System, while ultimately responsible to Congress, earns its own income with which it pays its own expenses, thereby freeing it from the constraint implicit in the process of requesting appropriations from Congress.

The justification for this unusual degree of "independence" is a subject of some dispute. On the one hand, it is argued that some such independence is needed to insure that monetary policy and the public interest in a stable dollar is not dominated by the political interests of the executive departments, especially the Treasury. On the other hand, it is stressed that a sound governmental approach to cyclical and growth problems requires a degree of coordination among the various policy agencies, which the Federal Reserve System's "independence" does not always permit. Those who would reduce this "independence" argue that a democratic society requires that all elements of government entrusted with the determination of basic policy should be made directly responsible to the electorate or elected officials, rather than insulated from such responsibility. We shall dig deeper into this controversy in a later chapter.

The Open Market Committee

If there is any one location within which the basic decisions of monetary policy are made it is in the twelve-member Open Market Committee. Its membership consists of the seven members of the Board of Governors plus five presidents of Federal Reserve banks. The president of the New York Federal Reserve bank is a permanent member and the four remaining positions are rotated among the presidents of the other Federal Reserve banks.

The Open Market Committee has sole responsibility for determining the direction and extent of the System's open-market operations. After carefully considering the economy's needs, it decides upon the type and scale of operations and its decisions are binding on all Federal Reserve banks. If the Open Market Committee decides to sell, each Federal Reserve bank is *required* to make available for sale[10] its proportionate share of the securities. Conversely, if the Committee decides to buy, each Federal Reserve bank is required to make payment for its proportionate share of the total purchase.

We shall delve more deeply into the mechanics of open-market operations later. For the moment it should simply be recognized that, since the one dominant tool of monetary policy is open-market operations, the Open Market Committee is an extremely important group.

The Federal Advisory Council

Of substantially lesser importance in terms of the actual determination of basic policy is the twelve-member Federal Advisory Council. It consists of one representative from each Federal Reserve district, usually a commercial banker. It meets quarterly in, as its name indicates, a purely advisory capacity. It is intended to provide the Board of Governors direct access to the viewpoints of representative private bankers from around the country.

FUNCTIONS AND OBJECTIVES OF THE FEDERAL RESERVE SYSTEM

The privilege of working toward one single objective is a luxury that few large governmental agencies enjoy. The Federal Reserve System is no exception.

Its functions might most usefully be categorized into three groups. First, it carries out a variety of activities aimed at maintenance of a sound and effectively functioning money supply and commercial banking industry. Second, it acts as *fiscal agent* for the U.S. Treasury, aiding in the handling of Treasury cash balances, the collection of taxes, the sale of bonds, and the expenditure of funds. Finally, and by all odds of greatest importance, it uses its arsenal of monetary policy weapons to directly pursue the basic social, but sadly, often-conflicting objectives of full employment, price stability, rapid economic growth, and balance of payments equilibrium.

---

[10] As we shall see later a sale is actually carried out in New York by a System employee called the System Account Manager.

Promoting Efficient Banking System and Effective Exchange Media

Included in the group of activities aimed at facilitating the effective operation of banks and the money supply are the following:

1. *Clearing and Collecting Checks.* The vast majority of checks that are not strictly local in character are collected via the Federal Reserve banks, which not only provide the facilities for collection but also bear the expense. The result is a highly efficient mechanism that greatly enhances the effectiveness of our main payments media. In addition to carrying out the bulk of the actual check collecting chores, the System has also added immeasurably to the acceptability of demand deposits by requiring that all checks collected through its facilities be remitted at par by the bank on which they are written. This requirement has markedly reduced the number of banks that, when a check written on them is received through the mails, remit not the full amount of the check but that amount *less* a specified fee called an *exchange charge.*

In the next chapter we shall consider check-collection procedures in some detail. For the moment it is sufficient to point out that the primary vehicles used by the Federal Reserve in the collection procedure are the member banks' reserve accounts. The bank in which a check is deposited sends it in to its Federal Reserve bank, which completes the collection process by adding the amount of the check to that bank's reserve account, subtracting an equal amount from the reserve account of the bank on which it is written, and mailing the check on to that bank.

2. *Providing an Outside Source for Borrowing Additional Reserves.* One of the prime functions of a central bank is the provision of a source from which individual commercial banks in need can borrow additional reserves without, at the same time, reducing the reserves of some other commercial bank. The Federal Reserve's facilities for discounts and advances, popularly called the "discount window," provide such a source.

Now that the restrictive notions involved in the commercial loan theory have been abandoned, a member bank can borrow additional reserves from the Federal Reserve by offering virtually any sound asset it possesses as collateral. This is especially helpful to individual banks or groups of banks in particular areas that may be under some temporary but extreme pressure, as for example a bank panic. It also provides banks that may have some difficulties immediately meeting changed conditions in the economy or in the Federal Reserve's own regulations to make, with time, an orderly transition to the new circumstances.[11]

[11] It should be noted that we are referring here only to the discount window itself, rather than the alteration in discount *rates,* a credit control weapon to be discussed later.

3. *Issuance of an "Elastic" Currency—the Federal Reserve Note.* The Federal Reserve banks, as we have seen, provide the overwhelming majority of the nation's currency supply in the form of Federal Reserve Notes. In doing so, they respond in an almost completely passive manner to the desires of the public for currency. That is to say, the quantity of Federal Reserve Notes issued by the System tends to expand and contract as the public's desire for currency rises and falls.

A note of caution is in order here. The Federal Reserve System is by no means passive with respect to the total supply of *money*. Indeed its main mission is to actively control this strategic quantity. If it passively permitted the total supply of money to expand and contract according to public desire it would be defaulting on its primary task of regulation.

It can, however, passively permit an expansion in the supply of Federal Reserve Notes whenever the public desires to hold more currency *and less demand deposits*, without in any way abandoning its control over the total size of the money supply. And this is precisely what present law regulating the issuance of Federal Reserve Notes permits.

When, as is true during the Christmas season, the public develops a need for relatively more currency, checks are written at commercial banks for cash. The currency paid out, primarily Federal Reserve Notes, comes, of course, directly from the vaults of commercial banks. These banks, however, must now replenish their vault cash in order to be prepared for further cash withdrawals. They do so, if they are member banks, by going to their district Reserve bank.

The member banks obtain their needed supplies of currency by writing checks, themselves, for cash on their reserve accounts. If they possess sufficient excess reserves to do so without reducing their reserve accounts below prescribed levels, that is the end of the matter. If they do not have an adequate amount of excess reserves, however, they may, by pledging an "acceptable" asset as collateral, borrow the needed amount through the Federal Reserve's discount window.

From the Federal Reserve's point of view, this request from the member banks for more currency is easily accommodated. Since they are the issuers of Federal Reserve Notes, all that is necessary is to have more of them printed. It is true that, since Federal Reserve Notes still carry a gold certificate reserve but member-bank deposits do not, there is a theoretical limit to the issuance of the former which does not apply to the latter, but the "excess" gold certificates now possessed by the System appear adequate for any present eventuality.

Conversely, when the public's desire for currency abates, such as normally occurs after the Christmas season, the reverse process occurs. The public deposits the unwanted currency in checking accounts at member banks and the member banks, in turn, send the plethora of Federal Reserve

Notes back to the Federal Reserve banks in exchange for an increase in their reserve accounts there.

This high degree of elasticity of our currency supply represents a marked improvement over the stringent note-issue restrictions existing under the National Banking System and is one of the major accomplishments of the Federal Reserve Act.

4. *Supervision and Inspection of Member Banks.* In addition to concerning itself with *the quantity* of member-bank assets, a concern through which it controls the quantity of money, the Federal Reserve System must also consider the *quality* of these assets. It must be concerned not only with the extent of bank operations but with their soundness and prudence.

In carrying out this portion of its responsibilities, the Federal Reserve System joins a whole network of supervisory agencies whose task is to regularly visit commercial banks, audit their books, investigate their lending practices and generally determine whether "other people's money" is being handled with propriety. Also operating in the same area are the Comptroller of the Currency, concerned with national banks, the Federal Deposit Insurance Corporation, concerned with the over 98 percent of commercial banks which subscribe to deposit insurance, and the fifty state agencies that are charged with regulating the activities of state banks. Duplication of effort by the various supervisory agencies is minimized by agreements whereby only one of two agencies charged with supervising the same banks actually inspects, with the other agency accepting its report. In practice, the Federal Reserve directly inspects only state member banks, accepting the report on national banks of the Comptroller of the Currency.

Aiding the Treasury

A somewhat different hat is worn by the Federal Reserve in its role as "fiscal agent" for the Treasury Department. In this capacity the System performs many direct services for the Treasury, as well as aiding it in a more substantive manner when it offers a new issue of U.S. securities.

The services performed for the Treasury are many. The Federal Reserve banks hold Treasury checking accounts out of which most of the government's bills are paid. In addition, they supervise the *tax and loan accounts* that are additional Treasury checking accounts, held at a large number of commercial banks throughout the country. When the Treasury offers a new block of securities for sale, the Federal Reserve banks "receive the applications of banks, dealers and others who wish to buy, make allotments of securities in accordance with instructions from the Treasury, deliver the securities to the purchasers, receive payment for them, and credit the amounts received to Treasury accounts."[12] When government securities mature, Federal Reserve banks redeem them. When U.S. Savings Bonds are issued, it is the Federal Reserve banks that do the job, and when they are cashed in, the Reserve banks handle the necessary transaction. It is evident that these direct services to the Treasury make up, in and of themselves, a formidable task.

But that is not the whole of the Federal Reserve System's responsibility vis-à-vis the Treasury Department. In addition to the above list of essentially administrative tasks, the System also undertakes to facilitate, in a more substantive way, the flotation of new Treasury securities. Specifically, it is its job to see to it that a new Treasury securities issue "succeeds" in the sense that there are sufficient buyers to take up the entire issue.

This is a responsibility that is extremely difficult to spell out specifically. Generally, it has required that the Federal Reserve act to maintain "orderly conditions" in the government bond market when new borrowing is under way. The meaning of "orderly conditions" is vague at best. The Federal Reserve usually offers a partial and temporary "support" to the government bond market at such times, perhaps involving the purchase of enough old U.S. securities to keep prices from being forced down sharply by the new issue.

The very vagueness of this commitment to orderly conditions in the government bond market has, however, led to disagreement and friction between the two agencies that, in at least one famous incident, grew into a full-fledged public dispute. We shall have more to say about this potential conflict area in a later chapter.

Monetary Policy and Credit Control

Important as the other two groups of functions are, they are decidedly less important, in a relative sense, than the credit control function. When one thinks of monetary policy one thinks not so much of *serving* the banking system as of controlling it. Here is the real raison d'être of the Federal Reserve System. This is its major function.

To put it all into one sentence, the primary function of the Federal Reserve System is to control the supply of money and credit, and thereby regulate the cost of credit (the interest rate) in a manner that will affect aggregate demand in a direction that will contribute to the achievement of full employment, stable prices, and rapid economic growth. A secondary goal, which in times of difficulties in international payments sometimes assumes greater significance, is manipulation of the supply and cost of credit in a way that also contributes to balance of payments equilibrium.

The means available to System authorities for the pursuance of these

12 *The Federal Reserve System, Purposes and Functions* (1954), p. 160.

goals are, of course, the traditional tools of monetary policy. They include such general credit control weapons as the power to alter required reserve ratios, and discount rates, as well as the authority to engage in open market sale or purchase of U.S. securities. In addition, selective control over the use of credit for the purchase of stocks in the form of margin requirements is available, as well as the somewhat vague and ill-defined policy popularly called *moral suasion*.

We shall postpone detailed consideration of these monetary policy tools to a later point. To provide a more thorough grounding for this task, let us turn once again to a discussion of some of the more technical aspects of commercial bank operations.

4 | Check Collection, Reserve Requirements, and Commercial Bank Money Creation

Before we can profitably proceed with further description or evaluation of the credit control powers of the Federal Reserve System, we must learn a great deal more about the origin of that credit at the commercial bank level. This, in turn, requires familiarity with check collection procedures and the specifics of member bank reserve requirements.

Accordingly, this chapter will be aimed at covering (1) the mechanisms of check collections, (2) present Federal Reserve reserve requirement regulations, (3) the means by which commercial banks create money, and (4) the maximum possible expansion of the money supply under varying conditions.

CHECK COLLECTION

The simplest check collection procedure, of course, is the case of a check that is written on, and deposited in, the same bank. In this case all that is necessary is for the single bank involved to increase the account of the check depositor and decrease that of the check writer. No mechanism or collection agency is required since only one bank is involved. In the majority of cases, however, wherein the check writer keeps his account at one bank while the check depositor banks at another, two different banks are involved, and some procedures for settling the debt that arises between them become necessary.

We turn now to consider, in turn, the means used to collect checks (1) written on one bank and deposited in a different bank in the same city; (2) written on one member bank and deposited in a different member bank in the same Federal Reserve district; (3) written on one member bank and deposited in a different member bank located in a different Federal Reserve district; (4) written on a member bank and deposited in a nonmember bank.

Check Collection Between Banks Located in the Same City—The Local Clearinghouse

Purely local checks, written on accounts at one bank and deposited in a different bank located in the same city, are collected daily via the local clearinghouse.

A local clearinghouse is a voluntary organization of all the commercial banks in a particular community which is set up for the express purpose of facilitating the clearance and collection of such purely local checks.

Its method of operation is quite simple. Each day at an agreed-upon hour, each local bank sends a messenger, armed with all checks written on other local banks but deposited in his bank, to the clearinghouse. Physically, the clearinghouse may be simply an office in one of the more conveniently located banks or, in the case of larger cities, a separate facility. Each bank messenger turns his checks over to the manager of the clearinghouse whose function it is to make up a statement on the basis of which most of these interbank claims are cancelled out.

Suppose, for example, in a three-bank town the messenger from Bank X presents checks written on other local banks totaling $10,000, $7,000 of which are written on Bank Y and $3,000 of which are written on Bank Z; the messenger from Bank Y presents $4,000 of checks drawn on Bank X and $2,000 on Bank Z; and the messenger from Bank Z brings $5,000 worth of claims on Bank X and $3,000 on Bank Y.

The clearinghouse manager would then make up a clearing statement resembling Table 4-1 below.

In this situation, as can be readily observed, Bank X has $10,000 of claims on other local banks while other local banks have $9,000 on Bank X. Bank X is therefore said to have a *favorable clearing balance* amounting to $1,000. Similarly, Bank Z, which presents $8,000 of claims on the other two banks but has only $5,000 presented against it, has a $3,000 favorable clearing balance. Bank Y, on the other hand, presents claims on Banks X and Z totaling $6,000 but is, in its turn, confronted with

TABLE 4-1   Local Clearinghouse Statement

| | Checks Written on: | | | Total Checks |
	Bank X	Bank Y	Bank Z	Brought by
Bank X Brings	—	$ 7,000	$3,000	$10,000
Bank Y Brings	$4,000	—	2,000	6,000
Bank Z Brings	5,000	3,000	—	8,000
Total Checks Written on	$9,000	$10,000	$5,000	$24,000

claims on it of $10,000. Bank Y, therefore, has an *unfavorable* clearing balance totaling $4,000.

Note that $24,000 of local checks are involved here but that a payment of $4,000 from Bank Y—$1,000 to Bank X and $3,000 to Bank Z—will be sufficient to settle accounts. The rest disappears through the simple process of cancellation.

The $4,000 payment can be made quite simply if all three banks are members of the Federal Reserve System, by a telephone call to the Federal Reserve bank requesting an increase in Bank X's reserve account by $1,000, an increase in Bank Z's by $3,000, and an offsetting decrease in Bank Y's by $4,000.[1]

Collection of a Check Between Two Member Banks in Different Cities, but the Same Federal Reserve District

Only local checks can be collected through a local clearinghouse. When banks in different cities are involved, a different collection agency is required. For member banks, the prime collection agency is their district Reserve bank.

Suppose Mr. Jones writes a $100 check on his account in a Reading, Pennsylvania, member bank, payable to Firm X, which banks at a Philadelphia member bank. How is this check collected?[2]

The check, deposited by Firm X in its Philadelphia member bank, is sent by that bank to the Philadelphia Federal Reserve bank, which

[1] It is not much more difficult if nonmember banks are involved. If, for example, Bank Y is a nonmember bank, it will have to write checks on its account at its correspondent bank in the proper amounts, giving Banks X and Z increased deposits there.

[2] The process to be described in this section is an oversimplified version of the actual process that, despite its oversimplification, we shall use as the basis for future examples that involve check collections. For a more complete discussion of the actual process involved in such a case, see below.

serves both it and the Reading member bank. The Philadelphia Federal Reserve bank *collects* the check by increasing the reserve account of the Philadelphia member bank by $100 and decreasing the reserve account of the Reading bank by a similar amount. The check is then sent to the Reading bank, which completes the collection process by marking down Mr. Jones' checking account by $100 and, at the end of the month, sending him the cancelled check along with his monthly statement.

In terms of T-accounts, the transaction has the following effects:

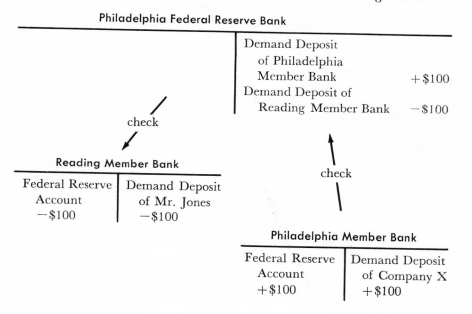

Collection of a Check Between Two Member Banks in Different Federal Reserve Districts

Things become a bit more complicated when two different Federal Reserve districts are involved, for the rather obvious reason that the member banks concerned do not carry Reserve accounts at a common Federal Reserve bank.

Suppose, for example, our Mr. Jones in Reading (Philadelphia Federal Reserve district) makes out a check to pay a bill to Firm Y, located in New York City (New York Federal Reserve district). In this case, when Firm Y deposits the check in its New York member bank, this bank sends it into the New York Federal Reserve, to initiate the collection process. The New York Federal Reserve bank, as before, increases the reserve account of the New York member bank but this time, it cannot collect from the bank on which the check is written. What solution exists for this problem?

For just such cases, the Federal Reserve System maintains an office in Washington with the revealing title of Interdistrict Settlement Fund. Each Federal Reserve bank "deposits" gold certificates at the Interdistrict Settlement Fund. These "gold certificate deposits" are then used to settle interdistrict claims.

Returning to our example, the New York Federal Reserve bank would, after increasing the New York member bank's reserve account, send a wire to the Interdistrict Settlement Fund stating it had received a check for $100 written on a bank in the Philadelphia Federal Reserve district. The Interdistrict Settlement Fund would respond to this by increasing the New York Federal Reserve bank's gold certificate deposit account, while decreasing that of the Philadelphia Federal Reserve bank.

In the meantime, the check would be sent directly from the New York Reserve bank to the Philadelphia Reserve bank where the latter would reduce the Reading bank's reserve account, as well as its own claim on the Interdistrict Settlement Fund, and then send it, at long last, to Reading. In terms of T-accounts all this looks like the following:

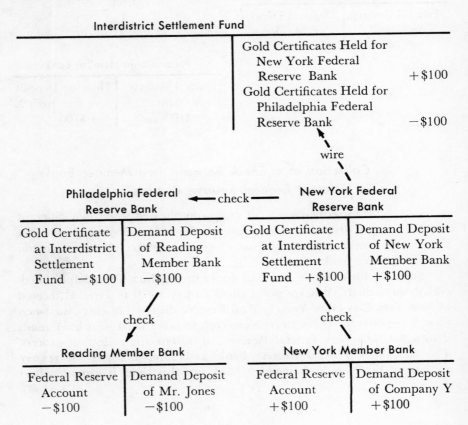

Interdistrict Settlement Fund

| | Gold Certificates Held for New York Federal Reserve Bank   +$100 |
| | Gold Certificates Held for Philadelphia Federal Reserve Bank   −$100 |

wire

Philadelphia Federal Reserve Bank ◄—— check —— New York Federal Reserve Bank

| Gold Certificate at Interdistrict Settlement Fund −$100 | Demand Deposit of Reading Member Bank −$100 | Gold Certificate at Interdistrict Settlement Fund +$100 | Demand Deposit of New York Member Bank +$100 |

check   check

Reading Member Bank   New York Member Bank

| Federal Reserve Account −$100 | Demand Deposit of Mr. Jones −$100 | Federal Reserve Account +$100 | Demand Deposit of Company Y +$100 |

Collection of a Check Deposited in a Nonmember Bank, but Written on a Member Bank

When nonmember banks become involved in the check collection procedure, some complications are added but there is little substantive change. Generally nonmember banks use a large member bank in a nearby city, as a "correspondent" bank, in about the same way member banks use their district Reserve banks.

If, for example, a check written on a Reading member bank gets deposited by Firm Z in a Chester, Pennsylvania, nonmember bank, it would be likely that the Chester bank would have a Philadelphia member bank as a correspondent. If so the Chester bank would keep a checking account at its Philadelphia member bank correspondent, a main purpose of which would be to facilitate the collection of just such a check as the one we are considering.

Here, the Chester nonmember bank would send the check to its Philadelphia member bank correspondent, receiving in return an increase in its checking account there. The Philadelphia member bank would, in its

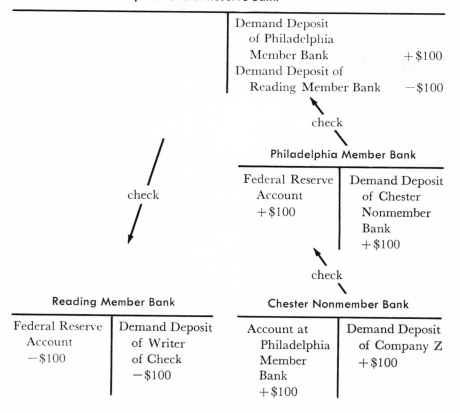

Philadelphia Federal Reserve Bank

	Demand Deposit of Philadelphia Member Bank +$100
	Demand Deposit of Reading Member Bank −$100

check

Philadelphia Member Bank

Federal Reserve Account +$100	Demand Deposit of Chester Nonmember Bank +$100

check

check

Reading Member Bank

Federal Reserve Account −$100	Demand Deposit of Writer of Check −$100

Chester Nonmember Bank

Account at Philadelphia Member Bank +$100	Demand Deposit of Company Z +$100

turn, forward the check to the Philadelphia Federal Reserve bank, which would collect it and then forward it to Reading. The T-account effects for this check would be as shown above.

A More Detailed Discussion of Check Collection— Federal Reserve Float

The preceding examples are perfectly adequate descriptions of the check collection process for most purposes. Indeed, in any future examples we may use in this book, we shall rely on them fully.

However, they are oversimplified, rather than exact descriptions. And the oversimplification involved, while justified as a means of cutting out unnecessary detail, does have the serious deficiency of eliminating explicit recognition of a concept of some significance, called *Federal Reserve Float*. This section attempts to correct that deficiency.

Let us refocus on the case of the check written on Member Bank X but deposited in Member Bank Y in the same Federal Reserve district. In our earlier example of this case, we assumed that the bank sending the check in immediately got an addition to its reserves, while the bank on which it was written lost reserves as soon as the check reached the Federal Reserve bank. Now we must recognize that, strictly speaking, neither of these is correct.

When a member bank in which the check is deposited sends it to the Federal Reserve bank it does *not* immediately increase its Federal Reserve account, but instead marks it up to a *temporary* account called its *Federal Reserve collection account*.

Thus, the initial T-account effect would actually be:

Member Bank X

Federal Reserve Collection Account +$100	Demand Deposit of Check Depositor +$100

The important difference here is the fact that the bank may *not* count its Federal Reserve collection account as a part of its legal reserves. When the check is received by the Philadelphia Federal Reserve bank it, instead of immediately altering the reserve accounts of the two member banks involved, will indicate its receipt of the check by entering that amount in two temporary accounts entitled *uncollected cash items* and *deferred availability cash items*. The T-account effects would be:

Philadelphia Federal Reserve Bank

Uncollected Cash Items +$100	Deferred Availability Cash Items +$100

The *uncollected cash item* entry is a temporary account to allow for the fact that the Federal Reserve bank will shortly (as soon as Bank Y receives the check) have a claim on Bank Y. When the bank on which the check is written receives it, the Federal Reserve bank will remove the *uncollected cash item* entry and, at that time, mark down the reserve account of Bank Y. Then, and only then, does that bank lose reserves from the check.

The *deferred availability cash items,* on the other hand, is a temporary account which recognizes that the Federal Reserve bank owes that amount to Member Bank X but that credit for additional legal reserves is being temporarily withheld—deferred—for a certain period of time.

Now the Federal Reserve bank maintains a time schedule for each member bank in its district. This schedule categorizes each bank according to the *average time it takes for a check to go from the Federal Reserve bank to each particular member bank.* If, for example, the usual amount of time for mail delivery to Bank Y in our example were two days, Bank Y would be in the "two day" category. The significance of this category lies in the fact that any bank sending in a check on Bank Y would know that, *whether the check was actually delivered to Bank Y in the usual time or not,* it could take credit for additional reserves automatically after waiting the prescribed two-day period.

In the usual case, the check *would* be received by Bank Y at the end of two days, at which time the following T-account entries would be appropriate:

Federal Reserve Bank

(5) Uncollected Cash Items −$100	(3) Deferred Availability Cash Items −$100 (4) Demand Deposits of Bank X +$100 (6) Demand Deposits of Bank Y −$100

Bank Y		Bank X	
(7) Federal Reserve Account − $100	(8) Demand Deposit of Check Writer − $100	(1) Federal Reserve Collection Account − $100 (2) Federal Reserve Account + $100	

Entries (1), (2), (3), and (4) are necessary to recognize that the scheduled time having elapsed, Bank X eliminates the temporary *Federal Reserve collection account* and takes credit for a $100 addition to its legal reserves, while the Federal Reserve bank eliminates the temporary *deferred availability item* account because the reserve credit to Bank X is no longer deferred.

Entries (5) and (6) are to take account of the fact that, since Bank Y has now actually received the check, the temporary *uncollected cash item* account can be eliminated and collection actually made by marking down Bank Y's reserve account.

There is, however, another possibility. If, after the scheduled two-day period has elapsed, Bank Y has for some reason *not* yet received the check, Bank X will automatically get its additional reserves (because the scheduled time period is up) but Bank Y will not yet lose any (because it has not yet, in fact, received the check).

In this case the T-account entries at the end of this two-day period would be:

Federal Reserve Bank		Bank X	
	Deferred Avail-ability Cash Item — $100 Demand Deposit of Bank X + $100	Federal Reserve Collection Account — $100 Federal Reserve Account + $100	

For the moment (and until the check *is* actually received by Bank Y) the Federal Reserve's balance sheet still shows a $100 uncollected cash item, but no deferred availability cash item for this check. Also, for the same time period, *both banks are entitled to claim that $100 as a part of their legal reserves.* What has happened is that, because of the methods it uses to collect checks, the Federal Reserve has added to the volume of member-bank legal reserves just as surely as if it had made a loan to a member bank for $100. In this case, *Federal Reserve float* has arisen.

As the above example illustrates, Federal Reserve float increases whenever a bank that has sent in a check for collection receives an addition to its reserves before the check actually reaches the bank on which it was written, so that its reserves are reduced. Such an increase, raising as it does the total legal reserves of the system, is conceptually precisely the same as a very short-term interest free loan of reserves by the Federal Reserve.

For the System as a whole the amount of Federal Reserve float can always be determined from the balance sheets of all Federal Reserve banks, as the excess of uncollected cash items over deferred availability cash items. For example, in May of 1966, uncollected cash items totaled $6.4 billion while deferred availability cash items equaled $4.9 billion. As of that date, therefore, Federal Reserve float totaled about $1.5 billion.

Since they necessarily involve increases in the total of member bank reserves, and therefore in their lending capacity, rises in Federal Reserve float are watched closely by Federal Reserve officials. Anything that slows down the normal delivery of the mails—a rail strike, a crippling storm— can markedly raise bank reserves at least temporarily via this rather involved route and may require offsetting action.

It is important that the student familiarize himself with the nature of Federal Reserve float and with the actual details of check collection. However, since specific detail can sometimes be a burden when considering other matters, we shall, in the remainder of this book, revert to the more simplified versions covered in the preceding sections. Specifically, in any future examples involving check collections, we shall ignore the "temporary" accounts just discussed and assume that reserve changes take place immediately.

RESERVE REQUIREMENTS

Under present law, member banks are required to "back up" their deposit liabilities with a specified amount of *legal* reserves. This requirement is, without question, the cornerstone of the System's power to control deposit expansion.

Within limits specified by Congress, the Board of Governors has complete power to implement this control. Specifically, the Board's area of authority consists of: (1) specifying within limits, which member-bank assets are eligible to be counted as a part of their legal reserves, and (2) setting the required reserve ratio—the minimum percentage of outstanding deposits which must be kept in legal reserve form.

At present the member-bank assets that qualify as legal reserves are vault cash and balances held at Federal Reserve banks. Consequently a member bank's total legal reserves always equal the sum of its Federal Reserve account plus its vault cash.

The Board of Governors' area of discretion in the setting of required reserve ratios is a bit more complicated. To begin with, the member banks are divided into two groups, *reserve city* or *country* banks, according to the size of the city in which they are located. As of the moment, member banks located in approximately the fifty largest cities are classified as reserve city banks, while all the rest have been placed in the country bank category. For all banks with the reserve city classification, required reserve ratios applicable to demand deposits may be varied at the discretion of the Board of Governors, anywhere between 10 percent and 22 percent. For country banks, the minimum ratio that the Board may apply to demand deposits is 7 percent, while the maximum is 14 percent. Required reserve ratios for time deposits, at *all* member banks, may be varied between 3 and 6 percent. Table 4-2 summarizes these limits.

There is, of course, nothing to prevent a member bank from holding *more* legal reserves than its outstanding deposits and required reserve ratios dictate. The bank that does so is said to have *excess reserves*—total legal reserves that exceed the minimum amount necessary to back up present deposits.

TABLE 4-2   Legal Limits to Board of Governors' Authority to Vary Required Reserve Ratios[a]

		Minimum	Maximum
Reserve City Banks	— Demand Deposits	10%	22%
Country Banks	— Demand Deposits	7	14
All Banks	— Time Deposits	3	6

[a] The percentages applicable to demand deposits apply to "net" demand deposits, which are defined as gross demand deposits minus cash items in process of collection and demand deposits due from other domestic banks.

Perhaps a numerical example will help clarify the terminology here. Suppose Bank A, below, is a reserve city bank that is subject, at the moment, to required reserve ratios applicable to demand and time deposits of 20 percent and 5 percent respectively.

Bank A

Cash	$ 50	Demand Deposits	$2,100
Federal Reserve		Time Deposits	2,000
Account	500	Other Liabilities	
Loans and Securities	4,000	and Net Worth	650
Other Assets	200		
	$4,750		$4,750

Its total legal reserves equal $550, the sum of its Cash and Federal Reserve Accounts. Its *required reserves*, the legal reserves now required to back up its deposits, total $520, a figure that results from adding 20 percent of present demand deposits to 5 percent of time deposits. Its excess reserves, therefore, equal $30.

The student should remember the following simple relationship:

Total Legal Reserves
(Cash + Federal Reserve Account) =

Required Reserves
(Required Reserve Ratios × Deposits) + Excess Reserves

Given the necessary data to compute any two of these totals, the student should be able to produce the third with no difficulty.

Reserve requirements do not have to be met on a daily basis. For reserve city banks, if the average amount of legal reserves for each *seven-day period* equals the required percentage of the average amount of deposits outstanding for the same period, the requirement is met. This, of course, means that a bank may fall below the required reserve ratio on any given day as long as it acquires an offsetting excess of reserves on some other day within the same seven-day period. Country banks are treated even more leniently, with a fourteen-day period in which to meet the requirement.

For the bank that fails, within the time period allotted, to meet the reserve requirement, various penalties are assessable. Generally the offending bank is subjected to a fine, the amount of which is directly related to the size of its reserve deficiency. For repeated offenses more serious penalties, such as expulsion from membership in the System and/or revocation of national bank charters, are also possible.

It is perhaps natural to think of required reserves as primarily a source of liquidity for the bank. Indeed, there can be little doubt that earlier reserve requirement legislation *was* aimed largely at providing liquid funds in case of sudden unexpected withdrawals. But those days have long since passed. Such a view constitutes, in fact, a serious misconception regarding the major role of reserve requirements.

Far from providing for bank liquidity needs, they are the fulcrum or cornerstone on the basis of which our monetary authorities limit the supply of money and credit in the economy. And this is a far more important function than partially providing for bank liquidity.

THE CREATION AND DESTRUCTION OF MONEY BY COMMERCIAL BANKS

It is a natural, but serious mistake, to visualize demand deposits as a segment of our money supply that results solely from the deposit of currency into a checking account. Such a view is not only incorrect in fact, but gives rise to serious misconceptions regarding the real significance of demand deposits—the debts of banks—as truly independent mediums of exchange.

The truth is, of course, that the bulk of the demand deposit portion of our money supply originates, not from the deposit of currency, but from commercial bank lending. It can, in fact, be said that *whenever a commercial bank makes a loan or purchases a security* (with the exception of a purchase from a Federal Reserve bank) *it creates new money and thereby expands the money supply*. Similarly, whenever a loan at a commercial bank is paid off, or a security is sold (except to a Federal Reserve

Bank) money is thereby destroyed and the money supply cut. Let us see why this must be the case.

The Creation of Money

Whenever a bank makes a loan, it accepts the borrower's IOU, in return for which it makes available the proceeds of the loan in money form. It would be highly unusual for the proceeds of a loan to be granted in the form of currency, because generally both the bank and the borrower find demand deposits more convenient. In the usual case, the borrower accepts the proceeds in the form of an increase in his checking account, which the bank is able to make available (assuming it has sufficient reserves) simply by writing the account up on its books. In either case, however, the money supply is increased.

In the extremely unlikely case where the proceeds do take the form of currency, the T-account effects of a $10,000 loan would be:

Bank X

Loans (Borrower's IOU)	+$10,000
Cash	−$10,000

Since we have defined the money supply as excluding vault cash, this transaction, by putting the currency into the hands of the public, does indeed raise the money supply.

In the more usual case where the borrower accepts a write-up of his checking account, the T-account effects would be:

Bank X

Loans + $10,000	Demand Deposits + $10,000

The bank here simply exchanges its IOU for that of the depositor but, of course, whereas the borrower's debt is usually quite illiquid, the bank's debt is a spendable medium of exchange. The money supply has once again been increased.[3]

---

[3] If the bank *discounts* a note it, in effect, takes the interest out in advance. If, for example, the above note for $10,000 was discounted at a rate of 6 percent for one year, the borrower would receive only (approximately) $9,400, although he signed a note agreeing to pay back $10,000 one year hence. In this case the T-account effects on Bank X's balance sheet would be:

Bank X

Loans and Discounts + $10,000	Demand Deposits	+ $9,400
	Unearned Discount	+ $ 600

Similarly, whenever a commercial bank purchases a security (except from the Federal Reserve) its payment has the effect of raising the money supply. If the payment should, for some unusual reason, be made in cash, the T-account effects would be:

Bank X

Cash — $10,000	
Securities + $10,000	

If the seller of the security accepts a checking account in payment, the money supply effect, as before, is the same.

Bank X

Securities + $10,000	Demand Deposits + $10,000

The Destruction of Money

When a loan matures, and is paid off by the borrower, the money supply is cut. This is true as an immediate effect whether the repayment is made in cash or by check.[4]

Where cash is the instrument of payment the T-account effects are:

Bank X

Cash + $10,000	
Loans — $10,000	

Where a check on a checking account is used, and assuming that the borrower's checking account is held at the lending bank, the results would be:

Bank X

Loans — $10,000	Demand Deposits — $10,000

[4] The bank's future lending power, however, will certainly be more enhanced if repayment is made in cash.

In either case the money supply is cut in exactly the reverse of the process by which it was created. We need not show the T-accounts involved in the sale of securities to make the same point.[5]

THE LIMITS TO COMMERCIAL BANK MONEY CREATION, ASSUMING NO CASH DRAIN AND NO TIME DEPOSITS

At first glance, the road to profit for the commercial banker appears to afford remarkably easy access. Unlike the manufacturer, who must pay to hire the resources needed to produce his product, the banker can merrily create the "product" that provides his income—money for loan—by the mere stroke of a pen. What a wonderfully simple means of amassing profits! "You give me your IOU for $100,000 and I will reciprocate by giving you mine for the same amount, providing you agree to pay me $6,000 of interest for doing so." What a seemingly effortless way of earning a living!

But alas, as is so often the case, there are a few flies in the ointment. It is true that the banker has every reason for desiring to expand his loans, thereby expanding the money supply by an equivalent amount. For when he can do this, he does indeed raise his income. But his ability to do so is limited on a number of fronts and for a variety of reasons. We turn now to a consideration of the limits to the lending (and money creating) capacity of commercial banks. We shall approach this topic in three sections. First, our focus will be restricted to the individual commercial bank and the limitations on its ability to create more money. Then, we shall switch to a consideration of the banking system as a whole under the highly oversimplified assumptions of no cash and no time deposits.

---

[5] Of course the above examples ignore any interest payment involved. If, for example, 6 percent interest had been charged for a one-year $10,000 loan, the T-account effects on repayment would actually be:

Bank X

Loans — $10,000	Demand Deposits — $10,600
Accrued Interest — $ 600	

assuming that the interest had been accrued on the bank's books during the year as it had been earned.

In the case of a discounted note, the repayment would affect the balance sheet of Bank X in the following manner:

Bank X

Loans and Discounts — $10,000	Demand Deposits — $10,000
	Unearned Discount — $ 600
	Undistributed Profits + $ 600

Finally, in the next chapter, we shall attempt a closer approach to reality by relaxing our assumptions and admitting cash drain and time deposits into the picture.

The Single Commercial Bank

The individual commercial bank, as a profit-seeking institution, has a natural desire to maximize its ownership of earning assets—loans and securities. Since, as we have just seen, such assets can be readily acquired by the simple act of creating more demand deposits, an obvious question arises. What keeps commercial banks from expanding the money supply to infinite proportions in their quest for added profits? What limits the individual bank's money creation?

To begin with, any issuer of demand deposits must be prepared to pay *cash on demand* to any depositor who requests it. Consequently, *even if there was no required reserve ratio at all*, commercial banks could not freely expand loans (and demand deposits) without limit. As long as people desire to hold their money partly in the form of demand deposits and partly in the form of cash, any expansion in the former will likely induce an increase in the latter. If, for example, a bank possesses $1 million in cash and has, at the moment $40 million of demand deposits outstanding, the $1 million may be just adequate to meet usual demands for cash on the part of the holders of the $40 million. Any increase in loans (and therefore in demand deposits) in this case would, consequently, raise the demand deposit total, and the attendant risk of cash withdrawal, to a level at which $1 million in cash would be insufficient. Such a bank, then, would be unable to grant more loans.

The risk of cash withdrawal, however, is not the most important limitation on the single bank's loan expansion potential. Far more confining is the restriction that is imposed by the combination of the *required reserve ratio* coupled with the *likelihood that borrowers of newly created deposits will write checks on them which will be deposited in other banks*.

Let us revert, once again, to an example. Suppose Member Bank X, subject to a required reserve ratio of 20 percent, has the following assets and liabilities:

Bank X

Cash	$ 10,000	Demand Deposits	$600,000
Federal Reserve Account	125,000	Other Liabilities and Net Worth	100,000
Loans and Securities	560,000		
Other Assets	5,000		

Assuming no time deposits, Bank X has excess reserves totaling $15,000 ($135,000 minus 20 percent of $600,000). The very existence of excess reserves indicates unused lending power available to the bank. As a profit-maximizing institution we can assume that Bank X will be desirous of exploiting its full loaning (and interest earning) capacity. Just how far can it go?

If the required reserve ratio were the only limitation it seems clear that, at least initially, it could *legally* lend an additional $75,000. For if a 20 percent required reserve ratio means anything, it signifies that each dollar of reserves can, at maximum, back-up $5.00 of demand deposits. Therefore $15,000 of excess reserves can be used legally to back up $75,000 of additional demand deposits.

No banker, however, can afford to be satisfied with considering only what is legal today, without some concern with what is likely tomorrow. And the truth is that if Bank X *should* lend out an additional $75,000 on the basis of its present $15,000 of excess reserves, it will certainly be in trouble tomorrow.

Let us take a long look at the consequences of a single bank lending out, as in this case, an amount equal to five times its excess reserves. Immediately after the loan is granted, Bank X's balance sheet would be altered to look like this:

Bank X

Cash	$ 10,000	Demand Deposits	$675,000
Federal Reserve		Other Liabilities	
Account	125,000	and Net Worth	100,000
Loans and			
Securities	635,000		
Other Assets	5,000		

Bank X is, for the moment at least, within the limits of the law, since its $135,000 of total legal reserves are exactly 20 percent of its outstanding demand deposits. But it had better beware the future.

The borrower of the $75,000 can certainly be expected to begin writing checks on his newly created account almost immediately. After all, who borrows money at interest without the intent of spending the money? Bank X must count on $75,000 worth of checks being written in short order.

Now the important question is—where will those checks end up? If they are redeposited by the check recipient into accounts at Bank X, it will lose no reserves and be in no difficulty. If, however, they are deposited in a *different* member bank, then Bank X can expect to lose $75,000 of reserves as a result of their collection through the Federal Reserve.

Which eventuality is most likely? The answer is obvious. Since Bank X is only one out of 13,800 commercial banks in this country—any of which might receive the check—the odds on its returning to Bank X would appear prohibitively small. And if the likely thing happens and $75,000 of checks are written, deposited in a different bank, and collected via the Federal Reserve, Bank X will find itself in the following position:

Bank X

Cash	$ 10,000	Demand Deposits	$600,000
Federal Reserve		Other Liabilities	
Account	50,000	and Net Worth	100,000
Loans and			
Securities	635,000		
Other Assets	5,000		

Its legal reserves are reduced to $60,000, while its required reserves are $120,000. It has a $60,000 deficiency, which, if not made up shortly, will lay it open to fines or other penalties. Clearly no single bank would knowingly place itself in this situation.

In fact, for the reasons just discussed, commercial banks making loans must *expect* to lose reserves shortly by the amount loaned. Consequently the prudent banker must limit his lending (and money creating) activities to a scale that will not subject him to the embarrassment and expense of a reserve deficiency. The only completely safe practice is to limit his new loans to the *amount of his excess reserves* rather than a multiple of them. This is, in fact, the usual custom of commercial bankers.

If Bank X should follow the "working rule" of lending just the amount of its excess reserves, $15,000, the expected loss of reserves which follows the granting of the loan will not leave it with a reserve deficiency. Immediately after making the loan, its balance sheet would be:

Bank X

Cash	$ 10,000	Demand Deposits	$615,000
Federal Reserve		Other Liabilities	
Account	125,000	and Net Worth	100,000
Loans and			
Securities	575,000		
Other Assets	5,000		

Then, after the borrower writes checks, the recipient deposits them in a different bank, and they are collected via the Federal Reserve, it would be left with:

Bank X

Cash	$ 10,000	Demand Deposits	$600,000
Federal Reserve		Other Liabilities	
Account	110,000	and Net Worth	100,000
Loans and			
Securities	575,000		
Other Assets	5,000		

Its remaining reserves of $120,000 are just sufficient to meet the requirements of the law and it can go on about its business. Its prudence, in limiting its loans to the amount of its excess reserves, has paid off.

Summing up, the individual commercial bank is limited in its lending and money-creating activities by (1) the likelihood of cash withdrawal and (2) the legal reserve requirement, coupled with the likelihood that it will quickly lose reserves (to other commercial banks) in the full amount of any loan it makes. To protect himself against either or both of these threats, the single commercial banker can safely lend out only *the amount of his excess reserves*.

The Commercial Banking System, Assuming No Cash Withdrawal or Time Deposits

No one bank can safely expand the money supply by more than the amount of its excess reserves. But if we widen our horizon to encompass all 13,800 commercial banks, or the banking system as a whole, we find, not surprisingly, that potential expansion is considerably enhanced. With each single bank along the way expanding to its safe maximum, the sum created by all is bound to be greater.

In this section, for simplicity, we shall assume that there is no cash withdrawal and no conversion of demand deposits to time deposits. Thus we are considering a banking system in which all demand deposits created as a result of bank loans are kept in that form. Anyone who subsequently acquires them prefers to hold them as demand deposits rather than convert them to cash or transfer them to savings accounts.

With these simplifications, which will be dropped in the next chapter, the results are apparent. Unlike the single bank case, when loans are made and checks written on the newly created deposits, there is no loss of reserves for the system. For the loss of reserves by the bank that made the loan is exactly offset, from the vantage point of the system as a whole, by the gain of reserves on the part of the bank in which the checks are deposited.

If, in this case, the banking system starts out with excess reserves of $15,000, and none of these reserves can be lost to the *system* through cash withdrawal, conversion to time deposits, *or through transfer to another bank*, then the maximum possible expansion of deposits and loans is only reached when every dollar of excess reserves is used to support its maximum permissible amount of demand deposits.

If, for example, the required reserve ratio is 20 percent (⅕), this means that at maximum each $1.00 of reserves may support *$5.00* of deposits. Consequently, $15,000 of excess reserves could, at the extreme, back up five times that amount, or $75,000 of new demand deposits. If the required reserve ratio were 10 percent (⅒), each dollar of reserves could back up $10 of deposits, and $15,000 of excess reserves would not be "used up" until $150,000 of demand deposits had been created. Finally, a 25 percent (¼) required reserve ratio would imply that each dollar of reserves can support $4.00 of deposits so that $15,000 of excess reserves would be sufficient to "back up" $60,000 of additional deposits.

It is not coincidental that in each of the preceding examples, the maximum possible expansion of demand deposits by the banking system as a whole equals the *reciprocal of the required reserve ratio times its excess reserves.* Under the assumptions we have made, that is the formula for computing maximum potential deposit (and loan) expansion for the banking system as a whole.

To compute maximum potential deposit and loan expansion by the entire commercial banking system (no cash withdrawal and no conversion to time deposits):

$$\frac{1}{\text{Required Reserve Ratio}} \times \begin{array}{c}\text{Excess Reserves} \\ \text{of System}\end{array} = \begin{array}{l}\text{Maximum Possible} \\ \text{Expansion of Demand} \\ \text{Deposits and Loans}\end{array}$$

Some memorization of pat formulas is useful for handling economic issues; but memorization alone is sterile without a thorough understanding of the *reasons* that lie behind the formulas. Let us take a brief look beyond the mere mathematics of the final outcome, to the *process* whereby this result may be achieved.

Suppose, for example that we have a banking system in which no bank has excess (or a deficiency of) reserves except Bank A, which, at the moment, is in the following condition:

Bank A

Cash	$ 50,000	Demand Deposits	$2,000,000
Federal Reserve		Other Liabilities	
Account	380,000	and Net Worth	300,000
Loans and			
Securities	1,800,000		
Other Assets	70,000		

If the required reserve ratio for all banks is 20 percent, Bank A (and the banking system as a whole) has $30,000 of excess reserves. Of course, we know immediately that, given these facts, the banking system as a whole can increase loans and demand deposits by $150,000 before the expansion limit is reached. Then, and only then, will every dollar of reserves be backing up its legal limit of $5.00 of deposits. Then, and only then will every dollar of excess reserves have been "used up" in the sense that it will have become part of the required reserves.

But our interest here is in the process by which this limit is approached. It all starts, of course, in Bank A, the only bank with the present capacity to grant additional loans. As a single bank, Bank A, for reasons discussed earlier, will find its ideal combination of profitability and safety, by following the working rule of lending out an amount just equal to its excess reserves. The T-account effects of its doing so will be:

Bank A

Loans + $30,000	Demand Deposits + $30,000

It is to be expected that the borrower will then write checks on his newly acquired account and that the recipient of those checks will deposit them in another bank. If the other bank is Bank B (and, to simplify, a member bank) it will immediately send the checks in via the Federal Reserve for collection. The effects of this step are:

Bank A		Bank B	
Federal Reserve	Demand Deposits	Federal Reserve	Demand Deposits
Account	− $30,000	Account	+ $30,000
− $30,000		+ $30,000	

Now, of course, the wisdom of Bank A's forebearance in lending only the amount of its excess reserves becomes evident. The expected has happened and it has lost reserves equal to the loan granted. But, since it retains $400,000 of legal reserves, it is still able to support the remaining $2 million of demand deposits. It has done all the money creating it could and is now safely out of the picture.

But whereas Bank A has lost all its excess reserves, the banking *system* has not. The $30,000 of reserves, lost by Bank A, have been gained by Bank B. And now Bank B is in a position to grant a loan.

Bank B, which, it will be remembered, started with no excess reserves, now has received a $30,000 boost in its total reserves and an equivalent increase in its demand deposit liabilities. Remembering that $6,000 of the added reserves are required to back up the added deposits, we see that Bank B has excess reserves of $24,000. It can, therefore, loan that amount.

Bank B

Loans + $24,000	Demand Deposits + $24,000

At this point, $54,000 of newly created money exists. The $30,000 created by Bank A is still held as a deposit in Bank B and an additional $24,000 has just been created by Bank B. As before, the borrower can be expected to write checks on the full $24,000 and the checks will in all likelihood be deposited in a different bank (Bank C), which will, in turn, send them through the Federal Reserve collection machinery.

Bank B		Bank C	
Federal Reserve Account — $24,000	Demand Deposits — $24,000	Federal Reserve Account + $24,000	Demand Deposits + $24,000

Bank B loses $24,000 of the $30,000 of reserves it originally acquired but the $6,000 it retains is sufficient to back up the $30,000 demand deposit that is still there. As before, however, another bank has gained the reserves that Bank B has lost. And, since the $24,000 of added total reserves provides Bank C with $19,200 of *excess* reserves (added total reserves, $24,000, minus 20 percent of added demand deposits, $4,800), it can now add further to the credit and money supply, as shown below.

Bank C

Loans + $19,200	Demand Deposits + $19,200

At this point, $73,200 of new money exists, $30,000 created by Bank A and still in Bank B, $24,000 created by Bank B and now in Bank C, and $19,200, just created by Bank C. It is hardly necessary to continue with this description, the future course of which must be obvious by now. Bank C will shortly lose $19,200 of reserves and deposits while Bank D will gain them. Bank D will then have excess reserves of $15,360 and will lend that much. It, in turn will lose that amount to Bank E, which will then be in a position to create an additional $12,288, and so on.

Note that at each step along the way, individual commercial banks add to the money supply, 80 percent of the amount added by the preceding bank. What we have, then, is a process in which, if the original excess

TABLE 4-3 Summary of Process of Demand Deposit Expansion by Entire Banking System, No Cash or Time Deposits

Banks	New Money Created by:	New Loans Made by:	Newly Created Demand Deposits Retained by:	Original Excess Reserves Retained as Required Reserves by:
A	$30,000	$30,000	—	—
B	24,000	24,000	$30,000	$6,000
C	19,200	19,200	24,000	4,800
D	15,360	15,360	19,200	3,840
E	12,288	12,288	15,360	3,072
F	9,830	9,830	12,288	2,458
G	7,864	7,864	9,830	1,966
H	6,291	6,291	7,864	1,573
I	5,033	5,033	6,291	1,258
J	4,026	4,026	5,033	1,007
K	3,221	3,221	4,026	805
L	2,577	2,577	3,221	644
M	2,062	2,062	2,577	515
N	1,650	1,650	2,062	412
O	1,320	1,320	1,650	330
P	1,056	1,056	1,320	264
Q	845	845	1,056	211
All Other	3,377	3,377	4,222	845
Total by Banking System as a Whole	$150,000	$150,000	$150,000	$30,000

reserves can be taken to be x, money is created in the following amounts.

	Bank A		Bank B		Bank C		Bank D	
Amount of New Money Created	x	+	.8x	+	.8(.8x)	+	.8[.8(.8x)]	+

This series of money supply additions clearly make up an infinite declining geometrical series, the formula for the addition of which is:

$$\frac{1}{(1 - \text{the common multiple})} \text{ x or, in this case, } \frac{1}{(1 - .8)} \text{ x} = \frac{1}{.2}\text{x} = 5x$$

Since, in the case we are describing, (1 − the common multiple) must always equal the required reserve ratio, the rationale for our earlier

$$\frac{1}{\text{Required Reserve Ratio}} \times \text{Excess Reserves}$$

formula becomes clearer. The process of expansion just described is depicted in tabular form in Table 4-3.

So much for the expansion potential of the banking system under the highly oversimplified conditions herein assumed. We must proceed now to approximate more closely the conditions of the so-called "real world." This is the task set up for the next chapter.

5

Commercial Bank Expansion and Contraction

A solid basis for understanding complex institutions sometimes necessitates suppression of the detail of the "real world" situation in order to isolate and magnify main underlying causal mechanisms. So it is with commercial banking.

For purposes of throwing into bold relief the central fact that multiple credit creation results from fractional reserve banking, the oversimplified version presented at the end of the preceding chapter probably does a better job than a more detailed, "realistic" discussion. But if the ultimate objective is to consider practical policy measures in a going economy, some of the more important complicating factors must be reinjected into the picture.

The Federal Reserve's Board of Governors, for example, can hardly carry out its real world obligations by blandly assuming without further concern for what, in fact, *will* happen—that with a 20 percent required reserve ratio, $1 billion of excess reserves will produce a $5 billion rise in the money supply. This result will be realized, in fact, only if the public withdraws no cash, converts no demand deposits to time deposits, and if the banks are unwilling to carry any excess reserves. If the public or the commercial banks should happen to be so uncooperative as to violate these assumptions, then the $5 billion money supply increase simply will not come about. The Board of Governors must be concerned not with what "would be if the world fit the assumptions," but with what, in fact, *will* happen in the world that exists.

The fact is that people *do* desire to hold more currency when their money supply as a whole increases. They *do* tend to convert some added demand deposits to time deposits as their wealth grows. Banks *do*, depending on conditions, sometimes hold excess reserves, rather than lending up "to the hilt." Our problem, in the first section of this chapter, is to develop a framework that will permit us to determine how much the money supply will increase, under more realistic given conditions. Then, in the second section, we shall consider the reverse situation—how do banks respond to a *deficiency* of reserves and what is the process whereby the money supply is decreased?

COMMERCIAL BANK CREDIT EXPANSION UNDER MORE REALISTIC CONDITIONS

The Public's Preferred Asset Ratio

In the act of granting loans or purchasing securities, commercial banks provide the public with the most convenient medium of exchange, demand deposits. Once the loans are made, however, and the deposits are in the hands of the public, it is the public, and not the banks, who will determine, according to its preferences, whether those funds will remain in demand deposit form, be converted to currency, or transferred into some near money form such as a time deposit.

For example, from December, 1960, to December, 1963, commercial banks acquired approximately $54 billion of additional loans and securities. Almost certainly, in the process of acquiring them, the banks created a similar amount of demand deposits. Yet, during the same period, Federal Reserve statistics show an increase of demand deposits at commercial banks totaling only about $10 billion! How can this wide discrepancy between loans, securities, and demand deposits be explained?

A full and completely accurate explanation would involve a number of highly technical transactions, which need not concern us here. However, the main answer is tied up in the fact that the public was simply not willing to keep its added $54 billion entirely in demand deposit form. As it acquired, through bank purchase of loans and securities, more demand deposits, it exercised its prerogative to exchange some of them for currency and some for increased time deposits. This is illustrated by the fact that, during the same 1960 to 1963 time span, currency in circulation rose by about $4 billion and commercial bank time deposits shot upward by almost $40 billion.

The public, it would seem, has a mind of its own. Commercial banks may create nothing but demand deposits but the public can freely transform these into desired proportions of other assets. Indeed, it is not unreasonable in this connection to refer to the public's relative desire for the three assets—demand deposits, time deposits and cash—as its *preferred asset ratio.*[1]

If data from the 1960-1963 period is used, it would appear that the public's preferred asset ratio was $10 in demand deposits to $40 in time deposits to $4.00 in cash. (Or, since it is the ratio and not the absolute figures which matter here—1 to 4 to .4) If so, this means that, from every $54 in demand deposits which the banks create in the process of loaning that amount, the public withdraws $4.00 in cash and transfers $40 to savings accounts.

The Process of Expansion, Allowing for Cash Withdrawal and Time Deposits

What significance has all this for our consideration of maximum potential money supply increases? Simply this—if the system starts with $10,000 of excess reserves and a 20 percent required reserve ratio, demand deposits can, at maximum, be raised by $50,000, providing all of the $10,000 of excess reserves can be used to back up demand deposits. If, however, some of these reserves are drawn out of the banks in cash form and others are used up to "back" increases in time deposits, the maximum increase in demand deposits is going to be substantially less than $50,000.

Suppose, for example, that the banking system has excess reserves of $10,000 (all in Bank A); that the required reserve ratios for demand and time deposits are 20 percent and 5 percent, respectively, and that the public's preferred asset ratio is $2.00 in demand deposits for every $2.00 in time deposits for every $1.00 in currency.

Bank A, as before, can be expected to make a $10,000 loan creating, at the same time, $10,000 of new demand deposits.

Bank A

Loans + $10,000	Demand Deposits + $10,000

Once again, the borrower will write $10,000 of checks almost immediately and all will likely end up in another bank, which will collect them via the Federal Reserve.

Bank A		Bank B	
Federal Reserve Account — $10,000	Demand Deposits — $10,000	Federal Reserve Account + $10,000	Demand Deposits + $10,000

[1] It should be pointed out that this phrase is used in a broader sense in other connections in economics. Despite the risk of confusion, we shall use it here with this more limited meaning simply because it seems to be the most apt title for the concept we are considering.

At this point, however, the new element enters the picture. If we can assume that the depositor at Bank B is an "average" member of the public, he does not *want* to increase his holdings of demand deposits by $10,000 while holding no more time deposits or currency. He wants these three assets to rise at a 2 to 2 to 1 ratio. What can he do?

Well of course he can *put* his $10,000 into those proportions by writing a $2,000 check for cash and transferring $4,000 from his checking to his savings account. This will leave him with $4,000 of demand deposits, $4,000 of time deposits, and $2,000 of currency—exactly what he wants.

Bank B

Cash — $2,000	Demand Deposits — $6,000
	Time Deposits + $4,000

But note the effect of this on Bank B's excess reserve position. Instead of the $8,000 of exces reserves, which B would have had as a base for further monetary expansion had the depositor not exercised his privilege of trading some of his demand deposits for cash and time deposits, Bank B now has only $7,000. The $10,000 of total reserves received was reduced by $2,000 by the cash withdrawal and $800 is required to support the remaining $4,000 of demand deposits, while $200 is tied up as required reserves behind the $4,000 of time deposits. Consequently, Bank B can safely add only $7,000 to the money supply.

The same thing, of course, is true all along the line. After Bank B makes its $7,000 loan, the newly created deposit and $7,000 of reserves will end up in Bank C. Once again, if the Bank C depositor is representative, he will withdraw cash (in the amount of $1,400) and transfer half the remaining amount into his savings account ($2,800) leaving him with $2,800 of demand deposits. Bank C is thus left with excess reserves of only $4,900 to continue the system's expansion.

Computing the Maximum Potential Expansion of Demand Deposits in the System as a Whole

The process just described will, of course, reach its limit only when all of the original $10,000 of excess reserves are "used up," in the sense that they are either withdrawn from the banks in the form of cash or become required reserves needed to back expanding demand and time deposits.

To determine the maximum possible expansion in demand deposits,[2]

---

[2] Note that in this case the expansion of demand deposits will not be the same as the expansion in money supply or in loans. The growth in the money supply includes both the increase in demand deposits and currency in the public's hands, while the growth in loans will be even larger.

we must first compute the *coefficient of demand deposit expansion*. This can be defined as a "number that can be multiplied times the initial excess reserves of the system to determine the maximum possible permanent increase in demand deposits." We have already discussed such a coefficient, without naming it, in the previous chapter. Thus, we have determined that the coefficient of demand deposit expansion for a single bank in a many-bank system is *one*. And, under the restricted assumptions of no cash withdrawal or time deposits, we found the banking system's coefficient to be the *reciprocal of the required reserve ratio applying to demand deposits*.

Under the more realistic, but decidedly more complex conditions assumed in this chapter, the coefficient of demand deposit expansion can be determined by use of the following expression:

$$\frac{1}{R_d + C + (R_t \times T)}, \text{ wherein:}$$

R_d = the required reserve ratio applying to demand deposits.
C = the amount of currency desired by the public *per dollar of demand deposits.*
R_t = the required reserve ratio applying to time deposits.
T = the amount of time deposits desired by the public *per dollar of demand deposits.*

In the example used thus far, where the required reserve ratios for demand and time deposits are 20 percent and 5 percent and the public's preferred asset ratio is $2.00 in demand deposits for every $2.00 in time deposits and $1.00 in currency, the coefficient of demand deposit expansion would be:[3]

$$\frac{1}{.20 + .50 + (.05 \times 1.0)} = \frac{1}{.75} = 1\frac{1}{3}$$

[3] An alternative method of obtaining the same result would be to set the three desired assets up in tabular form as below, recording the given preferred asset ratio in the second column, and then, for each of the three assets, compute the excess reserves "used up" either as required reserves or reserves withdrawn from the bank in the third column. The third column is then added and this sum is divided into the amount of demand deposits listed in the preferred asset ratio column.

	Preferred Asset Ratio	Excess Reserves "Used Up" as Required Reserves or Withdrawn from Bank	
Demand Deposits	$2.00	(20% x $2.00)	$ .40
Time Deposits	$2.00	(5% x $2.00)	.10
Cash	$1.00		1.00
			$1.50

$$\frac{2.00}{1.50} = 1\frac{1}{3}$$

Note that there is no difference between the two procedures if the preferred asset ratio is reduced to the point where the demand deposit figure is one.

Computing the Maximum Possible Expansion in Currency, Money Supply, and Loans

As already indicated, the coefficient of demand deposit expansion must be multiplied times the system's excess reserves to compute the maximum expansion of demand deposits. For the current example, the coefficient of expansion, $1\frac{1}{3}$, times the original excess reserves, $10,000 gives a maximum increase in demand deposits of $13,333.[4]

Once the demand deposit figure has been determined, one need only refer to the preferred asset ratio to obtain that for cash and for time deposits. If, as the ratio indicates, the public insists on just as many time deposits as demand deposits, the maximum increase in time deposits must also be $13,333. And, since the ratio indicates that an attempt will be made to keep currency at a level half as large as demand deposits, the increase in cash in circulation must be one-half of $13,333, or $6,667.

The increase in the money supply, consisting of a $13,333 rise in demand deposits and a $6,667 rise in currency, totals $20,000.[5] The loan expansion that is the basis for all these changes is equal to $33,333, the sum of the expansion in demand deposits, time deposits, and cash in circulation.

We might express the results of the entire procedure in a consolidated T-account for the entire system as follows:

Bank System

Cash	— $ 6,667	Demand Deposits	+ $13,333
Loans	+ 33,333	Time Deposits	+ 13,333

Implications for Monetary Control

Before we turn to the possible reaction of banks to reserve deficiencies, it will be useful to point out the implications of some of the preceding material for monetary control. Since, at any point in time, the

[4] This, of course, is the maximum demand deposits *after* the public has put its assets in the desired proportion. A good many more demand deposits are actually created when loans are made but many of them are given up in favor of cash or time deposits.

[5] The money supply expansion potential could also be computed directly by using:

$$\frac{1 + C}{Rd + C + (Rt \times T)}$$

which is a coefficient of money supply expansion.

potential increase in the money supply is a direct function of the expression

$$\frac{1}{Rd + C + (Rt \times T)} \times \text{Excess Reserves}$$

it is apparent that changes in the *actual* money (and credit) supply can be brought about by changes in any of the following:

1. The volume of excess reserves
2. The required reserve ratio, applying to demand deposits (Rd)
3. The required reserve ratio applying to time deposits (Rt)
4. The public's *preferred asset ratio* (determining C and T in the equation)
5. The degree to which commercial banks are willing and able to use the excess reserves they have

Through their so-called monetary policy weapons, the Federal Reserve System can directly control items 1, 2, and 3, although other agencies such as the Treasury Department also affect the volume of excess reserves. Items 4 and 5, on the other hand, are largely outside of the System's direct sphere of control. In fact it is often necessary for the Federal Reserve System to employ its credit control tools so as to affect 1, 2, or 3, in a direction needed to counteract *unfavorable* changes in the money supply and credit conditions, triggered by changes in 4 or 5. It will be helpful to keep these factors in mind in the next chapter when the tools of monetary policy are considered in some detail.

COMMERCIAL BANK REACTION TO RESERVE DEFICIENCIES

When excess reserves are present, there is every reason, except in unusually uncertain times, for commercial banks to expand their loans and the money supply. But what can they do in the reverse situation where reserves are insufficient to satisfy the required reserve ratios? Suppose, for example, Bank A is in the position depicted below:

Bank A

Cash	$ 50,000	Demand Deposits	$2,000,000
Federal Reserve		Time Deposits	1,500,000
Account	400,000	Other Liabilities	
Loans and		and Net Worth	500,000
Securities	3,200,000		
Other Assets	350,000		

If the required reserve ratios are 20 percent for demand deposits and 5 percent for time deposits, Bank A clearly has a reserve deficiency totaling $25,000. Such a situation cannot be permitted to continue indefinitely. If it should threaten to do so, Bank A will be forced to take action.

Basically, the bank has only two choices. It must either find a source from which it may obtain added reserves of $25,000 or, failing this, act to reduce its outstanding demand deposits by $125,000. The first alternative, much the preferred method from the bank's viewpoint, would provide it with enough reserves to support its present deposits. The second would reduce its deposit liabilities to a level at which their present reserves would be adequate.

Means of Acquiring More Reserves

There are a variety of ways in which a bank may obtain additional reserves. Perhaps the most likely is via the sale of some of its secondary reserves—its short-term U.S. securities. If our Bank A can find a buyer for $25,000 worth of U.S. securities, its reserves deficiency will probably be erased.

If another member bank should purchase them, the normal means of payment between member banks will provide Bank A with additional reserves at the expense of the purchasing bank.

Bank A	Member Bank Purchasing Securities

U.S. Securities
  — $25,000
Federal Reserve
  Account
  + $25,000
	U.S. Securities
	  + $25,000
	Federal Reserve
	  Account
	  — $25,000

If the purchaser is a nonbank financial institution, like an insurance company, or any member of the nonbank public, payment would nomally be made by a check written on an account at another member bank, the collection of which would, once again, raise Bank A's reserve account by the requisite amount, while lowering that of the other bank.

Bank A	Member Bank on Which Check is Written to Purchase Securities	

U.S. Securities
  — $25,000
Federal Reserve
  Account
  + $25,000
	Federal Reserve
	Account
	  — $25,000
		Demand Deposits
		  — $25,000

If the purchaser should be a Federal Reserve bank, implying, of course, a Federal Reserve open-market purchase, the effects would be:

Federal Reserve Bank		Bank A	
U.S. Securities + $25,000	Demand Deposit of Member Banks + $25,000	U.S. Securities − $25,000 Federal Reserve Account + $25,000	

An attractive alternative to the sale of U.S. securities would be borrowing the needed reserves on the *Federal Funds* market. Federal Funds are excess reserves lent for a 24-hour period by one member bank to another. Generally, the lending bank makes the needed amount of reserves available immediately, in return for a cashier's check (a check that the bank with the deficiency writes on its own reserve account, payable to the lending institution) in the amount of the borrowed funds plus a small interest charge, which is collectable one day later. The effects of borrowing Federal Funds, for Bank A, ignoring the interest charge, would be:

Bank A		Member Bank That Lends Excess Reserves	
Federal Reserve Account + $25,000	Cashier's Checks Outstanding + $25,000	Federal Reserve Account − $25,000 Loans and Discounts + $25,000	

If for some reason, it is difficult for Bank A to acquire the reserves it needs by a sale of securities or borrowing Federal Funds, it can usually borrow them through the "discount window" of the Federal Reserve System. While this approach to the solution of its difficulties may appear to be the most direct and obvious, it is very likely to have the lowest priority among the methods thus far discussed. Member banks have shown themselves to be quite reluctant to avail themselves of the Federal Reserve's discount facilities. We shall touch upon this reluctance further in the next chapter. For the moment it is sufficient to point out that borrowing from the Federal Reserve is, to most member banks, an unattractive solution to a reserve deficiency.

Now one very important fact regarding all the above methods of acquiring additional reserves deserves stress. If the Federal Reserve System is enforcing a so-called *tight money* policy, making it hard to obtain additional reserves, Bank A's position is complicated greatly.

To begin with, a sale of securities to the Federal Reserve System would not be possible. If the Open Market Committee is following a tight money line, it will be selling, not buying. In addition, if the restrictive monetary policy has been in effect for some time, the amount of excess reserves available at other member banks is likely to be minimal. This would seem to rule out selling securities to other member banks or borrowing Federal Funds. Unless the other member banks possess excess reserves, these solutions are unavailable.

It would still be possible to sell securities to some member of the nonbank public, of course, but while this may ease Bank A's reserve problem, it will simply transfer it to another member bank. The reason is that the purchaser of the securities pays for them by a check on his member bank so that the $25,000 addition to reserves that A acquires comes at the expense of the bank on which the check was written. If, as is likely during a period of restrictive monetary policy, this other bank had no excess reserves to begin with, it now is in the same difficult position in which Bank A found itself. And somewhere, sometime, this sort of "passing the buck" must end.

In such a situation, Bank A, reluctant or not, may therefore be forced to resort to borrowing from the Federal Reserve. And such an out would be even more unpalatable than usual during a tight money period, since it is at just such a time that the Federal Reserve discount rate would be pushed to higher levels.

Contraction of Loans and Deposits

In the long run a squeeze on the member banks such as that described above would, if the pressure is maintained, probably force the system into the other alternative, a reduction in deposits outstanding. As we saw earlier, deposits are reduced when bank loans are paid off. If forced to this extreme in dealing with a reserve deficiency, the banks can do two things. To the extent they have made loans that are subject to *call* (broker's loans are often call loans, which must be paid back at the discretion of the bank), they can call for their payment. In the case that these are repaid by checks written on accounts at Bank A, the effect, of course, is:

Bank A

Loans — $125,000	Demand Deposits — $125,000

In the event that the quantity of call loans outstanding is insufficient to do the job, Bank A can obtain the same sort of result by simply refusing to renew other loans that reach their maturity date and must be paid off. One of the techniques of bank portfolio management is to arrange for a maturity structure of earning assets such that some are coming due, if not every day, at least on some regular basis. Consequently, although under happier circumstances the loans that are coming due would be immediately reissued, under the assumed stress of a persistent reserve deficiency, they must be permitted to disappear.

Theoretically, if the acquisition of new reserves is impossible, this process of reducing demand deposits via a reduction in loans outstanding must continue until deposits are reduced by five times the reserve deficiency (assuming, as we have, a 20 percent required reserve ratio). In fact, this is the necessary result only if all loans are paid off by drawing down demand deposits. If we should reintroduce the concept of a public's preferred asset ratio at this point, it would become necessary to take account of the fact that, as the public's demand deposits were falling, they would desire a reduction in cash and time deposits also. Consequently, with the release of required reserves from some time deposits plus the inflow of cash reserves from the public, the required reduction in demand deposits would be something less than five times the original deficiency. We shall not bother to attempt to illustrate this point numerically, but the student should be aware of it and its significance.

SUMMARY—DEPOSIT EXPANSION AND CONTRACTION

It may be helpful, at this point, to draw together the various possibilities for expansion and contraction of deposits discussed in this and the preceding chapter. This is done below in outline form.

A. Potential Expansion of Demand Deposits When Excess Reserves Exist[6]

1. Single Member Bank $1 \times \text{Excess Reserves} = \dfrac{\text{Increase in}}{\text{Demand Deposits}}$

2. Entire Commercial Banking System, Assuming No Cash Drain and No Time Deposits

$$\frac{1}{R_d} \times \frac{\text{Excess}}{\text{Reserves}} = \frac{\text{Increase in}}{\text{Demand Deposits}}$$

---

[6] It should be noted that these formulas provide the maximum possible expansion in demand deposits, assuming all excess reserves are used. If the banks retain some excess reserves by their own choice, the *actual* expansion of demand deposits will be less than the maximum.

3. Entire Commercial Banking System, Assuming Conversion of Some New Demand Deposits into Cash and Time Deposits

$$\frac{1}{R_d + C + (R_t \times T)} \times \frac{\text{Excess}}{\text{Reserves}} = \frac{\text{Increase in Demand}}{\text{Deposits}}$$

B. Potential Destruction of Demand Deposits Resulting from a Reserve Deficiency

1. Assuming that as Loans Are Repaid, Demand Deposits Are Decreased but There Is No Reduction in Cash in Circulation or in Time Deposits

$$\frac{1}{R_d} \times \text{Reserve Deficiency} = \frac{\text{Decrease in}}{\text{Demand Deposits}}$$

2. Assuming that as Loans Are Repaid, the Decrease in Demand Deposits is Accompanied by a Decrease in Time Deposits and in Cash in Circulation

$$\frac{1}{R_d + C + (R_t \times T)} \times \frac{\text{Reserve}}{\text{Deficiency}} = \frac{\text{Decrease in}}{\text{Demand Deposits}}$$

6

The Nature and Effectiveness of Monetary Policy Tools

It was pointed out in Chapter 3 that the Federal Reserve's main function is to "control the supply of money and credit, and thereby regulate the cost of credit (the interest rate) in a manner that will affect aggregate demand in a direction that will contribute to the achievement of full employment, stable prices, and rapid economic growth." This is the goal of monetary policy.

In this chapter we shall be primarily concerned with a description and evaluation of the means to that end. What are the characteristics of the weapons available to Federal Reserve authorities, with which the evils of excessive unemployment, inflation, and sluggish economic growth may be combatted?

GENERAL VS. SELECTIVE CONTROLS

It has become customary to separate the various monetary policy tools into two categories, general and selective. General credit controls are those, the implementation of which, alter the total supply of credit available to borrowers in general without singling out for discriminatory treatment, intentionally at least, any particular group of borrowers that desires credit for a specific purpose. The total supply of credit may be cut, for example, but it is the "credit market" rather than the monetary authorities which determines which particular potential borrowers are rationed out. Selective credit controls, on the other hand, are specifically aimed at altering the quantity of credit available for specified groups of borrowers that are borrowing to finance the purchase of a particular item, or selected group of items.

Included in the Federal Reserve's arsenal of general credit controls is the power to alter reserve requirements and discount rates, as well as open-market operations. As of the present, the only selective credit control available is the power to set margin requirements on the purchase of securities; in the past, however, credit buying of real estate and of certain consumer durable goods have also been selectively controlled.

GENERAL CREDIT CONTROLS

The Power to Alter Required Reserve Ratios

The original Federal Reserve Act allowed the Board of Governors no discretion in the area of reserve requirements. It set up fixed required reserve ratios for the member banks in each group and specified the member bank assets that could be counted as *legal* reserves.[1]

It was in 1933 that the Congress first gave the Board of Governors temporary authority to alter required reserve ratios, and in 1935 this temporary power was granted on a permanent basis. Then, in 1959, the Board received additional discretion in a law authorizing it to permit vault cash, as well as accounts at the Federal Reserve banks, to count as legal reserves. Consequently, as noted in Chapter 4, the Board may now set required reserve ratios behind demand deposits anywhere between 10 percent and 22 percent for *reserve city* banks and between 7 percent and 14 percent for *country* banks. Similarly, it may alter the required reserve ratio for time deposits at all member banks anywhere between the limits of 3 percent and 6 percent.

The Effects of Altering Reserve Ratios

A simple example may help bring out the potency of this credit control tool. Suppose that member banks have a consolidated balance sheet as depicted below:

All Member Banks (billions of dollars)

Cash and Federal Reserve Account	12	Demand Deposits	100
Loans and Securities	90	All Other Liabilities and Net Worth	5
All Other Assets	3		

[1] From 1914 to 1917, both vault cash and deposits at Federal Reserve banks could be counted as "legal" reserves. From 1917 to 1959, however, vault cash was not counted. Since 1959, the Board has received authority to permit member banks to, once again, include cash, as well as their Federal Reserve accounts, as "legal" reserves.

Now, if the present required reserve ratio is 10 percent for demand deposits, the member banks possess $2 billion of excess reserves, which[2] can be used to back up a $20 billion increase in demand deposits and loans.

Whether such a monetary expansion should be permitted to take place would depend, of course, on a careful assessment of economic conditions. If, for example, full employment has been reached and there are indications that inflationary pressures exist, a strong case for credit restraint could be made. It seems clear that, in the absence of restraint, spenders who need borrowed funds to carry out their spending plans, will find a commercial banking system willing and able to meet their needs.

If the Board of Governors does decide that its own and the nation's goals would be impeded by a $20 billion money supply increase, it can forestall that undesirable development by simply raising the required reserve ratio behind demand deposits from 10 percent to 12 percent.

Notice that such action has a double effect. Not only does it wipe out the System's excess reserves by transferring the former $2 billion of excess reserves into the required reserve category, but it also reduces the coefficient of demand deposit expansion from ten to 8.33 (reciprocal of 12%). And, of course, this sharp reduction in the supply of loanable funds available will be likely, as is the case with anything in relatively shorter supply, to raise the price that borrowers must pay to obtain them. That is, the rate of interest will be increased. Thus, excess spending is combatted from two directions. First, lenders have fewer funds to lend and must now turn down some requests of potential spenders, which they would previously have granted. Second, the price charged for the loan of funds which *are* still available will be higher, further discouraging spenders who would add to the inflationary pressures.

Of course, deficiencies in spending, along with threatening recession, would be combatted by a lowering of required reserve ratios. Referring back to the balance sheet for all member banks, suppose the required reserve ratio is already 12 percent (implying no excess reserves) and that recession is threatening. In this case, a reduction of the ratio to 10 percent would (1) transfer $2 billion of the system's reserves from the required to excess reserve category; (2) increase the coefficient of demand deposit expansion from 8.33 to 10, and (3) lead to a lowering of interest rates because of the increased potential supply of loanable funds. All three of these developments would be in the direction of facilitating more borrowing and, hopefully, more spending with borrowed funds.

A Weapon Infrequently Used

Without taking a stand, as yet, on the larger question of the effectiveness of monetary policy as a whole, one can unequivocally

2 Ignoring the possibility of conversion into cash or time deposits.

state that, relative to other credit controls, the power to alter required reserve ratios is extremely potent. And yet despite its potency, or perhaps, to some degree, *because* of it, there appears clear-cut evidence that the Board of Governors has come close to abandoning it as a business cycle control device in the past fifteen years.

Whereas, from 1935 to the Korean War, required reserve ratios were raised nine times and lowered ten, in the period from 1951 to the present there have been nine successive reductions without an increase.[3] If this record can be taken as any guide, it appears that the Board has decided to take advantage of recession periods to get reserve ratios lowered but to rely on other credit control weapons when credit-tightening is called for.

There are a number of possible explanations for this behavior. In the first place, commercial bankers have long objected to variable reserve requirements as an altogether too blunt weapon, affecting all banks in a given category equally whatever the differences in their circumstances. Secondly, there is the understandable distaste that member banks feel for being made subject to higher reserve requirements than their nonmember competitors, a complaint that may well carry weight with Federal Reserve officials who are sensitive to the fact that many present member banks have voluntarily joined and are free to leave whenever they choose. Finally, it may well be that the Board, granting the legitimacy of some of the objections to raising reserve requirements, has decided that so long as it can control the credit supply adequately through its other weapons, such as open-market operations, it need not employ this powerful tool as a contracyclical device. If a real emergency comes along requiring a severe restraint on credit, the authority to raise reserve ratios is always there, but for the ordinary business cycle, other means of credit restriction may be more palatable. This, at least, would appear to be a plausible explanation for the pattern of use of this weapon in the past fifteen years.

The Discount Mechanism and the Power to Alter the Discount Rate

One of the privileges of membership in the Federal Reserve System is having the opportunity of borrowing added reserves from a Federal Reserve bank. This privilege—and it is a privilege rather than a right—is granted to all member banks who need to borrow reserves temporarily because of such emergencies as sudden withdrawals, regional economic difficulties, or temporary shortages arising from the tightening of general credit controls. Normally the Federal Reserve banks grant all

---

[3] In November of 1960, the required reserve ratio on demand deposits for country banks was raised from 11 percent to 12 percent, but this coincided with permission to count all vault cash as legal reserves so that the overall effect was a decrease in requirements rather than an increase.

loans requested but they do have the power to refuse where the member bank is considered to be abusing the privilege or using it for other than a stopgap solution to a temporary problem.

Substantial changes have been made over the years in the procedures for granting these loans. In the original Federal Reserve Act, borrowing member banks were required to turn over *eligible* paper to the Federal Reserve bank, to qualify for a loan. This eligible paper was defined, in accordance with the Commercial Loan Theory which pervaded the original Act, as short-term notes (90-day, except for agricultural notes) which the member bank had acquired from businessmen borrowing for working capital purposes.

In 1916, however, the Act was amended to permit member banks to borrow by means of an *advance* rather than the formal *discount* required previously. This meant that the borrowing member bank could borrow by submitting its own IOU to the Reserve bank, rather than having IOU's of its customers discounted there. And even more important, the collateral required to secure these IOU's could be either eligible paper *or* U.S. securities. This amendment not only signified a sharp turn away from the Commercial Loan Theory, but also greatly broadened the scope of the discount mechanism, while markedly simplifying the borrowing procedure for member banks.

Finally, in 1932, a further amendment was passed permitting advances secured by *any sound asset.* The apparent liberality of this change, however, is compromised by the requirement that the interest rate charged on Federal Reserve advances secured by assets other than eligible paper and U.S. securities must be $\frac{1}{2}$ percent higher than the others.

Now, of course, the power to make loans of reserves to member banks is not, in and of itself, a discretionary credit control weapon.[4] The monetary policy tool involved here is the authority to alter the interest rate (or more popularly, the discount rate) charged for these loans. This power, while nominally possessed by the Federal Reserve banks themselves, rests in reality with the Board of Governors through its authority to *review and determine* rates set by the individual banks.

How Discount Rate Changes "Work"

In a period of overbuoyant demand, an increase in the discount rate might be expected to contribute to economic stability in a number of ways. First, since this source of reserves now costs more, some banks that might otherwise have exploited it may shy away. This effect, however, is almost certainly of very slight significance. There is good

---

[4] One might argue, however, that power to grant or not grant loans provides a degree of discretion.

evidence to show that, in the main, member banks borrow from their Reserve banks with great reluctance and only when other, more desired sources are relatively inaccessible. If such borrowing is done only in cases of real need and only when alternatives are not available, it is not likely that a rise in the discount rate will do much to forestall it.

More important among the ways in which discount rate alterations are expected to "work" (that is, restrict credit and ultimately, spending) is their effect on short-term market interest rates. If this source of added reserves now costs more, the increase in the discount rate will almost certainly be reflected shortly in a rise in the short-term interest rates that the member banks charge the businessmen who borrow from them. And if this happens there is at least the possibility that borrowers who would otherwise have borrowed new money and spent it, will not do so.[5]

Of course the effect of a rise in the discount rate depends, to some extent, on its relation to the yield on highly liquid, short-term assets such as Treasury bills. If the discount rate is above the Treasury bill rate two factors work against member bank borrowing. Not only is it cheaper to sell Treasury bills to acquire needed reserves but the member banks' well-known "reluctance" to be in debt to the central bank provides an additional barrier. However, if the Treasury bill yield should be above the Federal Reserve discount rate, cost considerations favor borrowing from the "Fed," higher discount rate or no.

Announcement Effects

Most authorities are agreed that the increases in short-term market rates produced by discount rate rises, while working in the proper *direction* to restrain excessive spending, are probably of little significant aid in combatting inflationary pressures. Somewhat more emphasis has been placed recently upon the psychological "announcement" effects of a change in the discount rate.

The argument runs something like this. Unlike open market operations, which are being carried on continuously, discount rate changes are only made periodically. When such changes are made, especially when they involve a change of *direction,* they are widely interpreted as a signal or indication of the Board of Governors' thinking and of the future course of monetary policy. A rise in the discount rate after a series of reductions, for example, may well indicate that the Board foresees some inflationary pressure and can be expected to use its general credit controls to make credit (and bank reserves) harder to get in the near future.

The effect of such a "signal" of the Federal Reserve's future inten-

[5] The degree to which this will happen depends, of course, on the elasticity of the demand for investment funds, a topic to be discussed later.

tions will depend upon a number of factors. Those who would rely on it as a helpful development, see bankers reacting to the likelihood of a shortage of reserves in the future by slowing down on current loans in order to conserve some "elbow room" for making loans to important customers later on when additional reserves will be difficult to obtain and when the interest return will be more favorable than it is today. If this is the reaction of lenders, the announcement effect of the rise in the discount rate does promote the objectives of the Federal Reserve. Credit extension is slowed down, as is desired.

Critics, however, see some potential problems with this mechanism.[6] If bankers interpret the increase in the discount rate as a "one shot" affair, to be followed in the future by lower rates, it will be in their interest to lend more now, taking advantage of the temporarily higher return available. And if they do so, the expectational effects of the discount rate rise are perverse, encouraging rather than restricting current inflationary pressure.

Nor is that the end of it. There is no reason to assume that reaction to the announcement of a discount rate increase will be restricted to lenders. After all, borrowers and spenders, also armed with expectations about the future, read the newspapers too. And if borrowers and spenders interpret a rise in the discount rate as a heralding of future inflationary pressure, they may well borrow and spend more now because of it in order to beat the rise in borrowing costs and prices which is coming in the future.[7] To the degree this is the case, the discount rate signal has even more seriously perverse effects.

Reflecting all these claims and counterclaims, there is much disagreement regarding the effectiveness of the discount rate as a credit control weapon to combat undesirable business cycle changes. Some are so disenchanted with it that they advocate eliminating the entire discount mechanism. Others, though willing to keep the facility itself, would neutralize it as a discretionary credit control device by requiring that the discount rate be kept at the same level as the yield on Treasury bills. Even among its supporters there are few who feel that the power to alter the discount rate is a very potent business cycle control weapon.

The Role of the Discount Facility Itself

Whatever its weaknesses as a tool for maintaining domestic economic stability, the discount facility itself, as distinct from changes in the rate, does appear to serve several useful purposes. In the first place it

---

[6] See, for example, Warren L. Smith, "The Instruments of General Monetary Control," *The National Banking Review*, Vol. I, No. 1 (September, 1963) pp. 59-64.

[7] At least this would be rational behavior to the degree that they doubt the Federal Reserve's ability to combat the inflation.

is a very important guarantor of the banking system's liquidity, especially in case of a major bank panic. Secondly, some have argued, the fact that individual banks have a temporary source of borrowed reserves permits the Federal Reserve to make freer use of more powerful tools of credit restraint, such as open-market operations than might be the case if the discount "window," serving as a sort of "safety valve," did not exist. Finally, alterations in the discount rate are sometimes useful to deal with Balance of Payments problems. That is, a rise in the discount rate may be used, not just to reduce domestic demand but also to raise short-term interest rates generally as a means of attracting short-term foreign capital to this country (or keeping that which is already here from leaving).

Open-market Operations

There can be no question but that open-market operations are, by a substantial margin, the most important of the kit of monetary policy weapons. Open-market operations, for our purposes, can be defined as *the purchase or sale of U.S. securities by the Federal Reserve System for the purpose of altering the amount of member-bank reserves.*[8]

Policy in this area is determined by the Open Market Committee, which regularly meets, at three week intervals, in Washington. The Committee transmits its orders to an official with the title of System Account Manager, who operates out of the New York Federal Reserve bank.

The basic responsibility of the System Account Manager is to carry out the dictates of the Open Market Committee—to do the buying when purchases are decreed and to do the selling when the reverse is called for. Put this way, the Account Manager may appear to have a purely perfunctory task, that of buying or selling when he is told to do so. Actually this is far from the truth; his is an exacting position requiring an inordinate amount of skill and knowledge of the securities market, in addition to considerable discretion and judgment.[9]

If the Open Market Committee has given orders that imply the purchase of securities, their intent is to increase the quantity of member-bank reserves. The Account Manager, who operates in New York for obvious reason that it is the location of the market for U.S. securities, carries out his orders through the less than two dozen government security dealers in the city.

[8] This definition, it should be noted, excludes from the open-market operation category, purchases of bankers acceptances by the Federal Reserve, a currently unimportant activity that generally *is* considered a type of open-market operation.

[9] The fact is, the System Account Manager is seldom given a specific order to buy or sell a specified quantity of securities. Rather he is given general guidelines about the degree of restriction or ease desired by the Open Market Committee and expected to use his judgment in the specifics of buying or selling required to implement that policy.

The government security dealers are middlemen who bring together buyers and sellers of U.S. securities. They offer a ready market for government obligations by regularly quoting "bid" and "ask" prices on federal government obligations. As middlemen, they purchase securities with the intent of reselling them to institutions and individuals who desire them as a part of their regular portfolios although, when necessary, they sometimes hold some for their own accounts; when they sell, they acquire most of the securities ultimately from the same types of institutions and individuals. Their income is earned primarily for their services of bringing buyer and seller together.

When the Federal Reserve's System Account Manager is given orders to purchase securities, he contacts, generally via telephone, all the major government securities dealers and obtains comparative bids. The dealer who offers the lowest price then generally is awarded the business.

Mechanics of an Open-market Purchase

The actual mechanics of the purchase go something like this. The dealer purchases the U.S. securities from the ultimate seller by means of a check written on his account at a member bank. The Federal Reserve, in turn, pays the dealer for the securities via an officer's check which it makes up on itself and which the dealer can be expected to deposit in his checking account at a member bank. The result is that the Federal Reserve has the securities, the ultimate seller of the securities has an increase in his checking account, and the member banks have more reserves.

The immediate result of an open-market purchase differs somewhat, depending on whether the ultimate seller of the securities is a member bank or not. If we ignore the intermediate role played by the dealer, the T-account effects of a purchase from a member bank would be as follows:

Federal Reserve		Member Bank	

U.S. Securities
  + $100
	Demand Deposits
	  of Member
	  Banks + $100
		U.S. Securities
		  − $100
		Federal Reserve
		  Account + $100	

In this case total member-bank reserves have gone up by the amount of the purchase (making possible, of course, a future expansion in demand deposits by some multiple of this amount), member-bank excess reserves have risen by the amount of the purchase, and there has been, as yet, no increase in the money supply.

If, on the other hand, the ultimate seller turns out to be someone other than a member bank, the T-account effects, again ignoring the transactions of the dealer middleman, would be:

Federal Reserve		Member Bank	
U.S. Securities +$100	Demand Deposits of Member Banks + $100	Federal Reserve Account + $100	Demand Deposit of Seller + $100

Notice that, in this case, while total member-bank reserves still go up in the amount of the purchase, the immediate effect on excess reserves and the money supply is different from the effect when member banks are the sellers. For here, the money supply has already gone up by $100 (in the form of the new demand deposit acquired by the seller of the securities) and excess reserves are increased by less than the amount of the purchase. If, for example, the required reserve ratio applying to demand deposits is 20 percent, the $100 increase in total reserves is composed of a $20 rise in *required* reserves, to back the new demand deposit, and an $80 expansion of excess reserves.

Mechanics of an Open-market Sale

If the Open Market Committee sees a need for credit restraint and calls, accordingly, for a policy involving open-market sales, the reverse of the above is in order. The System Account Manager would contact all government security dealers asking for the prices they would offer to take the quantity of securities for sale. The dealers, in turn, would quote prices that would seem to them low enough to enable them to resell the securities to ultimate holders and still earn a return for their intermediary service. When the sale is made, the dealers would pay the Federal Reserve with checks on their accounts at member banks but would then be repaid by checks written by the ultimate purchasers on their own checking accounts.

If the T-account effects involving the security dealers' role are once again ignored, the effect of a Federal Reserve sale to a member bank would be:

Federal Reserve		Member Bank	
U.S. Securities — $100	Demand Deposits of Member Banks — $100	U.S. Securities + $100 Federal Reserve Account — $100	

Total reserves as well as excess reserves are reduced by the full amount of the sale while, for the moment at least, there is no effect on the money supply.

If the ultimate purchasers are not member banks, the T-account effects would be:

Federal Reserve		Member Banks	
U.S. Securities — $100	Demand Deposits of Member Banks — $100	Federal Reserve Account — $100	Demand Deposit of Purchasers — $100

Total reserves are cut by the amount of the open-market sale but here the money supply is immediately cut by $100 and excess reserves go down by only $80 (assuming a 20 percent required reserve ratio).

Individual Federal Reserve banks have no discretion regarding their own participation in open-market operations. When the System Account Manager buys securities he is, in effect, doing so on behalf of all twelve Federal Reserve banks and the total increase in the System's portfolio of securities is apportioned among all the Reserve banks. Similarly, if the Account Manager, in pursuance of orders from the Open Market Committee, sells securities, the individual Federal Reserve banks' portfolios of U.S. securities will each be proportionately reduced, regardless of their own desires in the matter.[10]

Most open-market operations are carried out in shorter term U.S. securities, usually 90-day Treasury bills. For example, in 1964, $9.4 billion of the $10.5 billion of gross outright open-market security purchases were in Treasury bills while all $5.4 billion of gross outright sales were carried out in bills.

The "Bills Only" Controversy

Indeed, from 1953 until 1961 the System followed a policy, popularly known as the "bills only" policy, of restricting its open-market operations almost entirely to Treasury bills. This procedure reflected, in part, a reaction to the wartime bond support program of the Federal Reserve under which the System's commitment to using open-market

10 Of course, individual Federal Reserve bank presidents, when they are members of the Open Market Committee, do have a voice in determining the overall policy. But even this is making a System-wide decision, not one applying just to their particular bank.

operations to maintain all U.S. securities at par effectively "froze" the interest rate yields on these obligations.

Widespread opposition to this policy whereby the Federal Reserve used its main credit control weapon to fix bond prices and the interest rate structure led System officials to adopt, in 1953, the so-called bills only policy. It was felt that by concentrating the Federal Reserve System's open-market operations only on short-term securities, the Federal Reserve would be doing the most it could to permit government bond prices and the interest rate schedule to seek their own levels in the market, while at the same time employing open-market operations to appropriately alter the volume of bank reserves.

It is true that purchases and sales of short-term securities do have less effect on security prices and yields than similar operations in long-term obligations. However, there was far from unanimous agreement to the wisdom of the bills only approach. Critics felt, among other things, that there were some positive virtues to directly affecting long-term interest rates by buying and selling longer-term securities also. It was their position that restricting open-market transactions to short-term obligations only was an unnecessary relinquishment of the power to directly affect any desired interest rate with this instrument.

The controversy over the merits of "bills only" raged until early 1961 when a change in the economic environment, led the System to abandon it. The circumstances that precipitated this change were discomfortingly high levels of unemployment coupled with a discouragingly high deficit in the balance of payments. It was felt that the domestic unemployment problems could be eased by somewhat lower long-term interest rates, while a reduction in the balance of payments deficit required higher short-term rates to cut down on the outflow of short-term capital.

In response, the System switched from the bills only policy to what has come to be called *operation twist*. The new policy has consisted of keeping enough restraint on short-term credit to push up short-term interest rates while, at the same time, easing up sufficiently on long-term credit to permit long-term interest rates to fall. The latter goal, implying as it did purchases of long-term U.S. securities, required an abandonment of the bills only policy. As a result, over one-half billion of securities with maturity dates five years or more into the future were purchased during 1964.

The Advanatges of Open-market Operations

Open-market operations clearly bear the bulk of the burden of monetary policy. The main reasons for their primacy are clear. To begin with, the initiative for their implementation is entirely in Federal

Reserve hands and not, as with the discount mechanism, partly with the member banks. Secondly, with a portfolio of over $40 billion and the ability to purchase many more if conditions warrant, the System has sufficient power to alter bank reserves within very wide limits via the weapon.[11] Thirdly, the open-market device is a model of flexibility. Because it is used continuously it does not carry with it the psychological "announcement effects" that accompany alterations in the discount rate or required reserve ratios. Consequently, it is entirely feasible to "operate by feel," buying today and then reversing to a sale tomorrow if conditions warrant. Open-market operations can be made as powerful as a sledge hammer or as discriminating as a surgeon's scalpel. In an area replete with controversy there is remarkable unanimity with respect to the preeminence of open-market operations among monetary policy weapons.

SELECTIVE CREDIT CONTROLS

If the government should take some action to reduce sharply the supply of eggs produced in the United States, their price would have to rise, assuming a free, competitive market. Since fewer eggs would be available some people who would have eaten eggs under the old conditions would now be unable to do so. But the mechanism for determining which particular consumers get "cut out" of the egg market would be the impersonal one of the price system. Those who are unwilling (or unable) to pay the higher price, we say, are "rationed out" by the increase in price.

Contrast this situation with one wherein the government simply decreed that all consumers living in New York City would have to go without eggs next year. Here, as before, government action has had the effect of cutting out certain people from egg consumption; but whereas in the former case, the government does not specify the particular individuals who will do without (leaving it to the forces of the market to determine that), in the latter case it does.

This comes pretty close to illustrating the difference between general credit controls and selective ones. Under general credit controls, government action may be taken to reduce the total supply of credit available, but the credit "market" determines which particular credit users will have to do without. Under selective credit controls government takes action to alter the amount (or terms) of credit available for specific groups of people that desire to use it for a particular purpose.

In past years the Congress has given the Board of Governors authority

11 The power to expand reserves via purchases was becoming rather narrow until the Congress acted to eliminate the gold certificate requirement behind member-bank deposits. Now, however, that limitation has been greatly relieved.

to impose selective credit controls on three different groups of credit users —those who purchase securities on credit, those who purchase consumer durables on credit, and those who buy real estate with borrowed funds. As of today, the authority with respect to real estate and consumer durables has lapsed, leaving margin controls on the purchase of stock as the only selective control now available to the Board.

The Power to Set Margin Requirements on the Purchase of Stock

In 1934, the Securities Exchange Act gave the Federal Reserve's Board of Governors the authority to set margin requirements on the purchase of stocks. Acting on this basic legislative authority the Board of Governors subsequently issued Regulations T and U, specifying the details of the control. Briefly, the Board is empowered to specify what proportion of the purchase price of stocks may *not* be borrowed from brokers or commercial banks.[12] If, for example, the margin requirement is at 70 percent (as it was in mid-1966), banks and brokers that loan money for the purpose of financing stock purchases may only lend 30 percent of the purchase price. Alternatively, a 70 percent margin requirement indicates that the buyer of stock must put up 70 percent of the purchase price in cash.

Experience in the 1920's and early 1930's, of course, provided the background and impetus to the initial margin requirement legislation. The stock market boom of the 1920's was generously fed by bank credit. Purchases of stock on very thin margins (with the bulk of the purchase price borrowed) were common. Inevitably this meant that the safety of a significant proportion of bank loans depended on fluctuations in stock prices. When the stock market crash came in 1929, the rapid decline in market prices quickly wiped out the equity of many owners, leaving the banks (and many brokers who had in turn borrowed from banks) with collateral that was decreasing in value at an alarming rate. Chaos followed. Banks were forced to sell the securities, to attempt to meet their commitments to depositors, with the effect of depressing the stock market still further while pouring more fuel on the fires of the bank panic that ensued. It was indeed a time for action and among the many laws passed in response to the crisis was the authority for the setting of margin requirements any place between zero (no cash required to purchase stock) and 100 percent (banks and brokers may not loan anything to finance stock purchases).

[12] More specifically, Regulation T controls loans for stock purchase from security dealers to purchasers, while Regulation U has to do with loans from *any* commercial bank (member or nonmember) to either brokers or purchasers of stock.

Entirely aside from the general philosophical issues regarding selective controls, a number of problems have emerged concerning the implementation of margin requirements. In theory, at least, control is effected through the lender who is expected to determine the intended use of the funds that he is lending. Generally this problem is simplified by the fact that, when stocks are to be purchased, the stock itself composes the collateral for the loan.

Weaknesses of Margin Requirements

However, a number of leakages in the network of control have appeared over the years. To begin with, a borrower may deny any intention of purchasing stocks with his borrowed funds, pledge other assets as collateral for the loan, but then go ahead and buy stocks anyway. Or he may purchase stocks with cash he would normally use to purchase materials and supplies and then borrow money to finance the material and supplies purchase, pledging the stocks he already has as collateral for the loan. In addition lenders other than commercial banks and brokers, who are not subject to margin requirements, may increase their security loans when brokers and commercial banks are being held down by high margin requirements. And, indeed, some of these nonregulated lenders may be getting the funds they lend to finance security purchases from commercial banks themselves.

Despite these weaknesses in practice, most authorities feel that margin requirements serve a useful purpose. That purpose, however, is not quite the same as for general credit controls. While a tightening of general credit controls may combat rises in the *general* price level, there is considerable doubt that increases in margin requirements accomplish the same results. For they are aimed, as their name indicates, *selectively* at one segment of the economy. If they are successful they damp down on excessive speculation in the stock market and stock price increases but there are grounds for doubting their effectiveness as a means of combatting general inflation of the prices of goods and services. After all, holding down on the use of credit to purchase stocks does not in any way cut the quantity of credit available to buy other things. And it is entirely possible that the credit that would, in the absence of margin requirements, have been used to purchase stocks, may now be used to purchase something else.

The Power to Limit the Use of Credit by Buyers of Real Estate and Consumer Durable Goods

During World War II, the Board of Governors was given the power to limit the credit that could be granted on the purchase of a number of major consumer durable goods. Although this authority ended in 1947, it was granted again during the Korean War, starting in 1950. In addition, 1950 saw the first grant of authority to the Board of Governors to control credit used to finance the purchase of real estate.[13] Authority for both controls lapsed in mid-1952, and the Board now has no power in either area.

Consumer credit controls were enforced on a specific list of major consumer durable goods. They took the form of minimum down payment requirements coupled with maximum repayment periods for the amount borrowed. Controls over the use of credit in the purchase of real estate limited the size of the mortgage that could be granted to a specified percentage of the market value of the home and also set up maximum terms for the length of the mortgage.

Although both these efforts at selective controls now fall in the category of history, debate over the wisdom of their possible use in peacetime continues. This is especially true with respect to controls over consumer credit which many feel should be given to the Federal Reserve on a standby basis, to be used when conditions warrant. Those favorable to a law granting such authority cite the destabilizing role that they believe consumer credit has played in the business cycle in recent years. Opponents counter with the argument that an extension of selective controls in peacetime is inimical to the philosophy of a free enterprise, consumer-directed economy.

The argument here is a basic one on which we shall postpone full consideration to a later chapter. But the issues involved can be noted here briefly:

1. How effective are selective controls as an addition to our ability to deal with economic instability?
2. How serious are the inroads on economic freedom which selective controls imply?
3. How effective a job does the credit market do, if it (rather than the government via selective controls) is relied upon to allocate credit in a manner that will maximize consumer desires?

These issues will be dealt with at some length in Chapter 19.

MORAL SUASION

In addition to the general and selective credit control devices, some notice should be taken of the rather vague, ill-defined area usually referred to as *moral suasion*. Properly speaking moral suasion is

[13] Actually the control over real estate credit was shared by the Board of Governors and the Housing and Home Finance Administration.

not really a *control* device at all, since it involves voluntary cooperation by, rather than coercion of, the member banks. It might best be described as an attempt, on the part of Federal Reserve authorities, to persuade banks to voluntarily tailor their lending policies to the desires of the System, thereby reducing the need for more overt credit control measures.

This attempt to persuade comes through many channels. During the periodic examinations made of state member banks, discussions with bank officers often turn to the System's overall aims in its credit policy. At periodic banquets and meetings held for bankers in their district, representatives of the Reserve bank hammer away at the reasons for and wisdom of, recent policy actions. In their frequent publications, the Board of Governors and the twelve Federal Reserve banks carry the message very much further. Much of this, it is true, might well be put under the heading of mere public relations but to the most sanguine supporters of moral suasion it accomplishes much more. If bankers do respond to these many appeals to "do right" creditwise, the burden that must be borne by the other tools of monetary policy is proportionately reduced.

For all the natural appeal of the voluntary way of doing things, it seems fair to observe that, barring some unusual and compelling incentive to cooperate, the moral suasion approach probably, in and of itself, accomplishes little. However our experience with it during the Korean War provides some basis for optimism in times of national emergency.

At that time, at the urging of the Federal Reserve, the credit industry, including nonbank lenders as well as commercial banks, set up the National Voluntary Credit Restraint Committee. The purpose of the committee was to draw up a set of standards, specifying those uses of credit which were in the national interest and those that were not. The entire approach was voluntary but there is considerable evidence to the effect that the Committee elicited widespread cooperation among lenders and that the Federal Reserve's task of controlling credit expansion was thereby measurably relieved.

However this experience cannot be taken as evidence of the peacetime effectiveness of moral suasion. The Korean War provided a sufficient sense of national emergency and patriotic fervor to partially overcome the normally powerful drive to maximize profits. It is impossible to say what the future will hold but there can be little question that the voluntary approach will be less effective without the special incentives involved in a national emergency.

7

Effects on Money Supply and Bank Reserves Resulting From Actions of the Public and the Treasury

INTRODUCTION: DYNAMIC VS. DEFENSIVE MONETARY POLICY

Control of the money and credit supply through affecting the quantity of member-bank reserves is the major responsibility of the Federal Reserve System. But while the "Fed" is the only institution for which alterations in bank reserves and the money supply are the deliberate essence of policy, it is by no means the only one whose activities actually do affect reserves and the money supply. For there are at least two other important forces in the economy whose activities, though primarily motivated by other considerations, do, in fact, alter the money and reserve supplies.

The nonbank public, to name one, may markedly affect the quantity of money and bank reserves, as a result of a decision to switch from currency to demand deposits, or vice versa. And the Treasury Department, whose prime responsibilities are quite far removed from determining or altering the money supply, may nevertheless affect it mightily, in any one of a number of ways.

The result is that the Federal Reserve System, to whom the money supply *is* a matter of prime importance, must employ its monetary policy weapons to *offset* or *prevent undesirable* changes in bank reserves and the money supply which may be caused by these other groups, as well as to *actively* promote *desirable* changes in them. Monetary policy, to employ a pair of terms that have come to be generally accepted, has its *defensive* and its *dynamic* aspects.[1]

Defensive policy is underway when the System employs, for example, open-market operations to combat an unfavorable change in bank reserves which has come about as a side effect of actions by the public or the Treasury. Dynamic policy, on the other hand, involves the use of monetary policy weapons, not just to prevent unfavorable changes, but to promote favorable conditions. The line between the two is perhaps tenuous, but it contains enough meaning to provide a useful distinction.

Indeed, at least one competent authority argues that the very fact that open-market operations are sometimes used for defensive purposes and sometimes for dynamic purposes, so that the direction of policy is never quite clear on a day-to-day basis, is one of their important virtues as a policy weapon.[2] This attribute frees them from the psychological "announcement effects" that are so characteristic of discount rate and reserve ratio changes.

In any event, the purpose of this chapter is to explore the many ways in which public and Treasury actions can alter bank reserves and the money supply, thereby possibly creating the need for Federal Reserve defensive operations.

EFFECTS OF CHANGES IN THE PUBLIC'S PREFERRED ASSET RATIO

It was pointed out in Chapter 5 that a change in the public's preferred asset ratio can produce changes in the potential money supply. Our purpose here is to review this point and place it into context as one of the ways in which bank reserves and the money supply can be altered by a non-Federal Reserve action.

Suppose, for example, that the public's preferred ratio as between demand deposits, time deposits, and currency has been $5.00 to $5.00 to $1.00, and that the required reserve ratios applying to demand and time deposits are 20 percent and 5 percent respectively. Finally, let us assume that the public has succeeded in putting its assets into the desired pro-

---

[1] Robert V. Roosa coined these appropriate terms in his excellent booklet entitled *Federal Reserve Operations in the Money and Government Securities Markets,* published by the New York Federal Reserve bank in 1956. In fact, however, the terms are used somewhat differently here from the way in which Roosa uses them.

[2] See W. L. Smith, "The Instruments of General Monetary Control," *The National Banking Review,* Vol. I, No. 1 (September, 1963).

portions and that the consolidated balance sheet for all commercial banks is as follows:

Commercial Banking System

Cash and Federal		Demand Deposits	$100
Reserve Account	$ 35	Time Deposits	100
Loans and Securities	170	Other Liabilities and	
Other Assets	20	Net Worth	25

Under the assumed conditions, the banking system has total reserves of $35 and excess reserves of $10 while the money supply totals $120 ($100 of demand deposits and $20 of currency outside the banks).

Assume now that the public's preferred asset ratio changes so that $3.50 demand deposits for every $5.50 in time deposits for every $2.00 in currency is desired. To accomplish this $20 would have to be withdrawn in cash, and demand and time deposits would have to be reshuffled until the former was $70 and the latter was $110. This would give the public $70 in demand deposits, $110 in time deposits, and $40 in currency, or just the desired proportion. The effect of all this switching around on the banking system's balance sheet would be:

Commercial Banking System

Cash and Federal		Demand Deposits	$ 70
Reserve Account	$ 15	Time Deposits	110
Loans and Securities	170	Other Liabilities and	
Other Assets	20	Net Worth	25

But now all sorts of things have changed. The money supply has declined from $120 to $110. Total bank reserves have been pulled down from $35 to $15. And most significant of all, the banks have been catapulted from a position of $10 excess reserves (which, under the old conditions, could have supported a loan increase of almost $50) to a reserve deficiency of $4.50.

If, when all this was happening, unemployment was excessive, one would certainly expect to see the Federal Reserve pitch in and use its monetary policy tools defensively in order to feed the system more reserves and help prevent a potentially disastrous deflationary squeeze. The example is no doubt extreme but it does illustrate how changes in public preferences may sharply alter bank reserves and the money supply.

EFFECTS OF TREASURY ACTIVITIES

The U.S. Treasury, of course, is primarily charged with meeting the nation's fiscal needs. At the risk of oversimplifying what is, in fact, a monumental task, this responsibility might be said to boil down to seeing to it that the federal government always has on hand the funds that are necessary to carry out the spending programs set up by the Congress.

This alone involves a number of fundamental duties including the collection of taxes, borrowing by sale of government securities when required spending exceeds tax revenue, handling the cash balances of the federal government including those arising from a tax surplus, and refunding when necessary, the outstanding federal debt. Each of these duties provides the Treasury with major areas of discretion, such that the impact on the economy of handling the job one way or the other must be given careful consideration.

For example, if a deficit must be financed, it makes a difference what type of securities are sold. If a tax surplus is in the offing, different ways of handling it will have substantially different impacts on the economy. If a sizable portion of the national debt is approaching maturity and there is no tax surplus available to meet the bill, the choice of the type of obligation to sell to borrow the needed funds can be of crucial importance. And even the apparently simple decision of determining the location of the Treasury's cash balances involves matters that are by no means inconsequential.

In this section we shall attempt to deal with the consequences for bank reserves and the money supply, of several of the more important Treasury activities. Specifically, we shall take a look at the effects of gold inflows and outflows, the effects of changing the location of Treasury cash balances, the effects of financing deficits and disposing of surpluses in various ways, and the effects of refunding the existing national debt.

Treasury Purchase or Sale of Gold

Since 1934, the U.S. Treasury has committed itself to buying all gold offered to it at a fixed price of $35 per ounce. Similarly, it has agreed to sell gold for dollars at that price to all licensed users of gold.[3]

---

3 Licensed users of gold have included Americans who have a legitimate use for gold, such as dentists or jewelry makers, and all foreign monetary authorities. Actually, the "commitment" to buy or sell gold at a fixed price can be withdrawn at any time at the Treasury's discretion.

Purchase of Gold. When gold is purchased, the Treasury makes payment with a check written on its account at the Federal Reserve. If the seller of the gold deposits his check in a checking account in one of our commercial banks, both the money supply and total member bank reserves are increased by that amount.

Federal Reserve		Member Banks	
	Demand Deposit of Member Banks + $100	Federal Reserve Account + $100	Demand Deposit of Seller of Gold + $100
	Demand Deposit of U.S. Treasury − $100		

Issuance of Gold Certificates. Now the Treasury possesses more gold and it is authorized, as noted earlier, to issue gold certificates, dollar for dollar, on the basis of that gold. If, as is usual, it does so, it will deposit the gold certificates in the Federal Reserve bank, receiving in return an increase in its checking account there.

Federal Reserve Banks	
Gold Certificates + $100	Demand Deposit of U.S. Treasury + $100

Note that it is the purchase of gold and not the issuance of gold certificates which directly leads to the increase in member-bank reserves and the money supply. Under present law the only effect of the issuance of gold certificates (beyond the fact that the Treasury's checking account is restored to its former level) is the fact that, since these are legal reserves required behind Federal Reserve Notes outstanding, they give the Federal Reserve System the authority to issue more Federal Reserve Notes.

A sale of gold by the Treasury, of course, has the opposite effects. The sale itself reduces member bank reserves and the money supply while the required withdrawal of gold certificates from the Federal Reserve reduces, in its turn, their ability to support Federal Reserve Notes. We need not tarry with all this because it has been discussed earlier. It is repeated here because it is one of the areas within which Treasury operations do affect the prime concerns of the Federal Reserve—the money supply and bank reserves.

The Location of Treasury Cash Balances—Tax and Loan Accounts

Another very important task of the Treasury, the handling of which can markedly affect commercial bank reserves, is the management of its cash balances. These balances consist, beyond a small amount held in the form of currency and coins, of checking accounts at the twelve Federal Reserve banks and at over 11,000 specified commercial banks.

The latter, Treasury checking accounts at commercial banks, are called *Tax and Loan Accounts*. As their name implies these accounts are used to receive funds being paid in to the federal government by taxpayers as well as by those who, through the purchase of U.S. securities, are loaning money to the government. A commercial bank can qualify to receive and hold such deposits by meeting certain specified requirements and as the 11,000 plus figure indicates, most of our banks have done so.[4]

Why, the reader may ask, does the Treasury keep checking accounts at commercial banks *and* at Federal Reserve banks? Why not simplify matters by keeping all their demand deposits at the Federal Reserve? A moment or two of reflection will clear up this matter.

When taxes are paid in by the public or when loan funds are made available to the government, the taxpayer (or security purchaser) generally writes a check on his account at a commercial bank to make payment. If these funds were deposited directly into the Treasury's accounts at the Federal Reserve, the immediate effect would be to reduce bank reserves and the money supply by that amount, as the T-accounts below indicate.

Federal Reserve Banks		Member Banks	
Demand Deposits of Member Banks — $100 Demand Deposit of U.S. Treasury + $100	Federal Reserve Account — $100	Demand Deposit of Taxpayer — $100	

When the Treasury spends out of its accounts at Federal Reserve banks, the effects on the money supply and bank reserves are, of course, the other way around. The Treasury makes out a check payable to some member of the public; he deposits it in his account at his commercial bank and the collection process raises bank reserves.

[4] A commercial bank can qualify as a "special depository," thereby becoming eligible to hold tax and loan accounts by pledging certain specified securities as collateral and by being recommended by the Federal Reserve bank in its district.

Federal Reserve Banks		Member Banks	
	Demand Deposits of Member Banks + $100 Demand Deposit of U.S. Treasury − $100	Federal Reserve Account + $100	Demand Deposit of Person Paid by Treasury + $100

If the money collection and money disbursement sides of Treasury operations were always perfectly coordinated their opposing effects on reserves and the money supply would neatly offset one another so that no major disturbance would be forthcoming. But, unfortunately, no such neat offset occurs. Treasury receipts, both from taxes and security sales, arrive in an uneven pattern throughout the year, bulking particularly large on April 15 when settlement for the personal income tax is due and at the end of each quarter when corporate payments come in. It would require a prohibitively strange spending pattern for the two to mesh perfectly. And, if for example, spending should be spread out evenly throughout the year while receipts arrive in the "bunches" that our tax laws dictate, the banking system would be subject to the most disturbing kind of an influence—substantial net losses of reserves around the end of each quarter, offset only over time by government spending.

It is for the purpose of minimizing the disturbing effects of Treasury operations on the banking system that the tax and loan accounts at commercial banks have been established. Under this arrangement, most taxes (and loan funds) are paid in initially to a tax and loan account at a commercial bank. Since this simply represents a change in the ownership of demand deposits still in commercial banks, no loss in bank reserves results.

The Treasury, however, does not choose to subject itself to the administrative chaos that might be involved in making its disbursements directly out of the tax and loan accounts located at over 11,000 different commercial banks. Its expenditures, with rare exceptions, are made through checks written on its accounts at Federal Reserve banks, a source that is regularly replenished, as expenditures are planned, from the tax and loan accounts.

The Mechanics of Tax and Loan Accounts

The entire mechanism works as follows. Tax and loan proceeds are paid directly into the tax and loan accounts. Consequently, the irregularity of receipts does not affect the quantity of bank reserves. As these funds are needed for expenditures they are transferred from the tax and loan accounts at commercial banks into the Treasury's accounts at Federal Reserve banks.

These transfers are accomplished via *calls* on the commercial bank depositories, which are generally issued from four days to one week before the funds are actually transferred.[5] The funds are generally transferred just prior to the need for spending them so that, although the transfer does reduce commercial bank reserves temporarily, their almost immediate disbursement pumps the funds back into the system. In this way the disturbing influences of Treasury operations on bank reserves can be minimized.

If, for example, $10 billion should be collected in federal taxes on April 15, and the funds should be spent at a rate of $500 million per day thereafter, the T-account effects would be as follows. On April 15, taxes are collected:

Commercial Banks

	Demand Deposits of Taxpayers — $10 billion Demand Deposits of U.S. Treasury + $10 billion

On April 16 and each day thereafter for 20 days, funds are transferred to Federal Reserve Banks:

Federal Reserve

	Demand Deposits of Member Banks — $500 million Demand Deposits of U.S. Treasury + $500 million

Commercial Banks

Federal Reserve Account — $500 million	Demand Deposits of U.S. Treasury — $500 million

and the Treasury spends the funds:

[5] Actually, most commercial banks with tax and loan accounts—those with average daily Treasury balances of under $200,000—get one week's notice before transfers are made. Those with average Treasury balances between $200,000 and $500 million generally get about four days notice before withdrawals, while the sixty-odd banks with tax and loan accounts over $500 million, although normally also receiving four days notice, may expect changes in the amount withdrawn at the Treasury's discretion without prior notice.

Federal Reserve		Commercial Banks	
Demand Deposits of U.S. Treasury − $500 million Demand Deposits of Member Banks + $500 million	Federal Reserve Account + $500 million	Demand Deposit of Those Paid by the Treasury + $500 million	

The Monetary Aspects of Fiscal Policy: Effects on Bank Reserves and the Money Supply of Alternative Means of Financing Deficits and Disposing of Tax Surpluses[6]

A common practice in introductory economics courses is to distinguish sharply between monetary and fiscal policy. The former is generally defined as action by the Federal Reserve System to alter the quantity of bank reserves and the potential money and credit supply so as to ultimately affect the level of aggregate demand in the necessary direction for stability and growth. Fiscal policy, on the other hand, is usually described as alterations in tax and/or expenditure programs, also aimed at promoting stability and growth via effects on aggregate demand.

The two sets of policy tools thus are seen to be distinctly different means for achieving the same final objectives. Fiscal policy "works" (affects aggregate demand) largely through altering the income available to spending groups. Monetary policy, on the other hand, works primarily through a change in the degree of liquidity of the wealth held by the community.

Such distinctions are useful for throwing into broad relief the central difference between two techniques. But, valuable though it may be to emphasize the conceptual differences between them, it is important to recognize that many times a single policy action involves them both.

This is particularly true of fiscal policy, the execution of which is the particular responsibility of the Treasury department. If, for example, the Congress cuts taxes to raise demand, the *fiscal* policy effects of the action have to do with increased consumption and investment spending by those groups whose disposable incomes have been increased by the tax cut.

But that is not all there is to it. If the tax cut has reduced governmental revenue below its expenditures, it is the task of the Treasury to

6 In this section we shall oversimplify by ignoring the tax and loan accounts, assuming for the moment that both tax and loan funds are deposited directly in the Treasury's Federal Reserve Account. The complexity that this simplification overcomes is considerable and the final effects on bank reserves and the money supply of each operation are unchanged in any case.

raise the funds needed to fill the deficit. The particular means it chooses to carry out this responsibility, whether it prints new money or borrows, and if so, from whom it borrows, are matters which can profoundly affect the money supply and bank reserves. And the overall effect of the deficit on aggregate demand will depend, to some extent, on these matters.

The Financing of a Budget Deficit

The Treasury can finance a current deficit in a number of ways. It might, under certain conditions, simply permit the extra spending to draw down its cash balances. It may, again within specified limits, choose to provide the money in the form of newly printed currency. Or, what is most likely with deficits of any significance, it may find it necessary to issue new securities to borrow the needed funds.

The scope of the first two of these alternatives is severely limited. The Treasury can print some new currency for deficit spending but its authority to do so is quite restricted. If, for example, it possesses some silver (or gold) which is not now backing silver certificates (or gold certificates), it can if it chooses, have these certificates printed and deposited in its Federal Reserve account for spending. But this source, as of now, is of only token significance.

Similarly, the expedient of drawing cash balances down below their normal levels can only be relied upon temporarily, and for very small deficits. To the degree these balances are needed for operating purposes, they must be rebuilt quickly so that little long-run advantage is gained from using them to finance deficits.

In any case, the effects on money supply and bank reserves are the same whether new currency is printed or cash balances are drawn down. In neither case does the raising of the funds to meet the deficit affect bank reserves or the money supply.[7] In both cases, the spending of the funds raises both the money supply and bank reserves. As we shall see shortly, the monetary effects of these methods are the same as could be expected from a sale of securities to the Federal Reserve.

The funds to finance most budget deficits, however, must come from borrowing—the issuance of new U.S. securities by the Treasury. And the effects on the money supply and bank reserves will differ markedly depending upon who the buyer is.

Borrowing from the Nonbank Public. If, for example, the securities

---

[7] This is true if the cash balances drawn down are those kept in accounts at Federal Reserve banks. If funds are transferred from tax and loan accounts at commercial banks and then spent, the transfer, of course, does reduce both the reserves and the money supply.

are sold to members of the nonbank public, the T-account effects of the sale are:

Federal Reserve		Member Banks	
	Demand Deposits of Member Banks — $100 Demand Deposit of Treasury + $100	Federal Reserve Account — $100	Demand Deposits of Security Purchasers — $100

When the funds thus raised are spent, the effects of this step are:

Federal Reserve		Member Banks	
	Demand Deposits of Treasury — $100 Demand Deposits of Member Banks + $100	Federal Reserve Account + $100	Demand Deposits of Those Paid by Treasury + $100

As the T-accounts demonstrate, a Treasury deficit financed by sale of securities to the nonbank public has no net effect on either the money supply or bank reserves. The money supply is cut by $100 when the security purchasers make their payment but it is immediately increased again by an equal amount when the government makes its expenditure. Similarly, member-bank reserves go down by $100 when the security purchasers' checks are cleared but come back up again when the money is spent.

A word of caution is in order here. The statement that a budget deficit financed by sale of securities to the nonbank public has no net effect on bank reserves or the money supply must not be taken to mean that it has no effects on the economy *at all*. For we have here an example of fiscal policy wherein, despite the absence of a change in the money supply, aggregate demand will almost certainly be altered.[8] The student must be careful not to jump to conclusions that do not follow.

Borrowing from Commercial Banks. The effects are different if the

---

[8] However, as we shall see in the next section, the magnitude of the impact on aggregate demand *is* affected by the fact that no more money is available.

securities are sold to commercial banks. In this case, the T-account effects would be as follows for (1) sale of securities:

Federal Reserve Banks		Member Banks	
	Demand Deposits of Member Banks — $100 Demand Deposit of Treasury + $100	U.S. Securities + $100 Federal Reserve Account — $100	

and (2) expenditure by Treasury:

Federal Reserve Banks		Member Banks	
	Demand Deposits of Member Banks + $100 Demand Deposit of Treasury — $100	Federal Reserve Account + $100	Demand Deposits of Those Paid by Treasury + $100

Here, the member banks pay for the securities by, in effect, writing a check on their accounts at Federal Reserve banks. This lowers bank reserves but does not alter the money supply. When the Treasury spends the funds, member-bank reserves are raised once again to their old level and, because those who are paid by the Treasury have increased checking accounts, the money supply is increased. What has happened is that the member banks have provided the Treasury with newly created funds to spend rather than, as in the previous case, the public lending the government part of the money supply that already exists.

The careful student, however, will note that the effect of this entire operation is to *reduce* member-bank excess reserves. This, of course, follows from the fact that total reserves are unchanged while demand deposits have increased.

Borrowing from the Federal Reserve. The sole remaining mechanism for financing a budget deficit is by sale of securities to the Federal Reserve banks. If this is done the monetary effects are considerably more potent —(1) sale of securities:

Federal Reserve		Member Banks
U.S. Securities + $100	Demand Deposit of Treasury + $100	No Effect

(2) expenditure by Treasury:

Federal Reserve		Member Banks	
Demand Deposits of Member Banks + $100 Demand Deposit of Treasury − $100	Federal Reserve Account + $100	Demand Deposits of Those Paid by Treasury + $100	

Since the Federal Reserve creates the funds lent to the Treasury and since their expenditure increases both the money supply *and* bank reserves by the full amount, we have here a situation in which the banks obtain a substantial amount of excess reserves with which they may increase the money supply even further. Clearly, if the intent of the deficit is to raise aggregate demand, this course will accomplish more than the other two.

In fact, as noted earlier, there is no real difference, so far as the economic effects are concerned, between financing a Treasury deficit by sale of securities to the Federal Reserve and running the printing presses. And this should hardly be surprising. In either case the Treasury is simply obtaining its spending money from another government agency. Why should it make a difference whether the money creator is the Federal Reserve or the Bureau of Engraving?

In recognition of the fact that direct borrowing from the Federal Reserve by the Treasury has identical effects to running the printing presses, the Congress has seen fit to place a rigid limit on the practice. The Federal Reserve may hold, at any one time, no more than $5 billion of U.S. securities purchased directly from the Treasury. In actual practice, at least in peacetime, it very seldom purchases any such new issues.

The World War II Bond Support Program. But, as our past experience vividly demonstrates, the pressure of necessity sometimes leads to a violation of the spirit, even though not the letter of the law. A case in point was the so-called *bond support* program of the Federal Reserve System during World War II. Under this arrangement the Federal Reserve, for reasons we shall not go into now, stood ready to purchase, at par, all (already outstanding) U.S. securities offered to them.

Now, of course, this amounted to an open-ended commitment to make open market purchases without limit, thereby providing the banks with additional reserves. Suppose now, that the U.S. Treasury was prepared to sell a new $20 billion issue of securities to finance a deficit. The law forbade the Federal Reserve to purchase all of *them*, but it *could* buy other securities already in the hands of the banks or the public. The effects were as follows—(1) Federal Reserve purchases of old securities from member banks:

Federal Reserve		Member Banks	
U.S. Securities + $20	Demand Deposits of Member Banks + $20	Federal Reserve Account + $20 U.S. Securities − $20	

(2) treasury sale of new securities to member banks:

Federal Reserve		Member Banks	
	Demand Deposits of Member Banks − $20 Demand Deposit of Treasury + $20	U.S. Securities + $20 Federal Reserve Account − $20	

(3) expenditure by Treasury:

Federal Reserve		Member Banks	
	Demand Deposits of Member Banks + $20 Demand Deposits of Treasury − $20	Federal Reserve Account + $20	Demand Deposits of Those Paid by Treasury + $20

A careful inspection of these transactions will reveal that the effects of all this on money supply and bank reserves are precisely the same as if the new securities issued by the Treasury had been purchased directly by the Federal Reserve. Yet this simpler procedure, because its effects, in turn, are essentially the same as running the printing presses, is forbidden by law! It would seem that there is, indeed, more than one way to skin a cat.

The Handling of a Tax Surplus

When tax revenues are in excess of government expenditures, the Treasury's area of discretion has to do with the handling of the surplus. Two major possibilities present themselves. The Treasury might simply hoard the surplus, either in its commercial bank tax and loan accounts or in its checking account at the Federal Reserve. Or, it may use it to retire a portion of its outstanding debt. If it chooses this alternative, the effects on the money supply and bank reserves will differ depending on whose securities are retired.

If a tax surplus is held in the tax and loan accounts at commercial banks, its collection will reduce the public's money supply but leave bank reserves as well as excess reserves unaffected.[9] If, however, the surplus is transferred to the Treasury's Federal Reserve account, and hoarded there, its effect will be to lower the money supply and bank reserves by the amount of the surplus and excess reserves by a lesser amount, the magnitude of which depends on the required reserve ratio. Clearly the second alternative is more contractionary than the first.

The hoarding of tax surpluses is reasonable economically, depending on the state of the economy, but is often hazardous politically. When a large national debt on which interest is accruing exists, it is extremely difficult to justify holding a tax surplus when it might be used to reduce the level of debt. Consequently, the usual practice of the Treasury is to employ surpluses to retire outstanding securities.

Retiring Securities Held by Nonbank Public. If the securities retired are those held by the nonbank public, neither the money supply nor bank reserves are altered in the final analysis. As the T-accounts below indicate, the reduction in bank reserves and the money supply which result from collection of the tax surplus and its deposit in the Federal Reserve are exactly offset by the expansion that the retirement of the securities causes —(1) collection of tax surplus and deposit in Federal Reserve:

Federal Reserve		Member Banks	
	Demand Deposit of Member Banks — $100	Federal Reserve Account — $100	Demand Deposit of Taxpayer — $100
	Demand Deposit of Treasury + $100		

[9] Since the money supply, by our definition, excludes Treasury deposits, it is reduced by the collection of the surplus. However, the amount of demand deposits behind which commercial banks are required to maintain reserves is unchanged, so that, despite the drop in the money supply, as defined, required reserves are unchanged.

(2) use of surplus to retire securities held by nonbank public:

Federal Reserve		Member Banks	
	Demand Deposit of Treasury − $100 Demand Deposit of Member Banks + $100	Federal Reserve Account + $100	Demand Deposits of Security Holders + $100

Retiring Securities Held by Commercial Banks. A tax surplus used to retire securities held by the member banks would reduce the money supply but leave total member-bank reserves unchanged, thereby raising excess reserves. This is the case because, while the reduction in bank reserves caused by the collection of the surplus is replaced when the securities are retired, no increase in demand deposits occurs to replace the money given up by the taxpaying public. Thus, the collection of tax surplus and deposit in Federal Reserve:

Federal Reserve		Member Banks	
	Demand Deposit of Member Banks − $100 Demand Deposit of Treasury + $100	Federal Reserve Account − $100	Demand Deposits of Taxpayers − $100

and the use of surplus to retire securities held by member banks:

Federal Reserve		Member Banks	
	Demand Deposit of Treasury − $100 Demand Deposit of Member Banks + $100	U.S. Securities − $100 Federal Reserve Account + $100	

Retiring Securities Held by Federal Reserve. Finally a tax surplus could be used to retire U.S. obligations held by the Federal Reserve banks themselves. This approach, as the T-accounts below demonstrate, will result in a reduction of both the money supply *and* member bank reserves by the amount of the surplus, thereby, assuming the banking system had some to begin with, reducing excess reserves in addition. It does so because this use of the surplus funds restores neither the public's demand deposits nor the member banks' reserves that were drained away in tax collection. The student should note that these monetary effects are identical to those that would result from hoarding the surplus in the Treasury's Federal Reserve account—(1) collection of tax surplus and deposit in Federal Reserve:

Federal Reserve		Member Banks	
	Demand Deposit of Member Banks — $100 Demand Deposit of Treasury + $100	Federal Reserve Account — $100	Demand Deposit of Taxpayers — $100

(2) use of surplus to retire securities held by Federal Reserve banks:

Federal Reserve	
U.S. Securities — $100	Demand Deposit of Treasury — $100

Treasury Debt Refunding

One of the Treasury Department's weightier responsibilities is the refunding of debt which matures each year when no tax surplus is available to retire it. This, of course, requires the sale of new securities to raise the funds with which to retire those coming due and the Treasury, as the issuer, is free to tailor the type and maturity of the new issue to its desires. Certain types of securities especially appeal to particular groups of lenders so that the Treasury, in designing the nature and special characteristics of the new issue can reasonably effectively determine its purchaser.

This, too, provides a means of altering bank reserves and the money supply, and the possibilities are many. By way of example, assume that $100 million of securities held by the Federal Reserve are approaching maturity and that the Treasury chooses to raise the funds to pay them off by selling an equivalent amount of new securities to the nonbank public. The effects of these transactions are shown below in T-account form—

(1) sale of new securities to nonbank public and deposit of funds in Federal Reserve account:

Federal Reserve		Member Banks	
Demand Deposits of Member Banks — $100 Demand Deposit of Treasury + $100		Federal Reserve Account — $100	Demand Deposits of Purchasers of Securities — $100

and (2) use of new funds borrowed to retire maturing securities held by Federal Reserve banks:

Federal Reserve	
U.S. Securities — $100	Demand Deposits of Treasury — $100

The result of this particular refunding operation is to reduce both the money supply and member bank reserves by the full amount of the refunding operation, a monetary effect that is sharply contractionary.

We shall not take the time here to go through the monetary effects of all the possible refunding combinations. This is an exercise the student might prefer to work out on his own. It is clear, however, that substantial increases or decreases in the economy's liquidity are possible via the debt-refunding mechanism.

SUMMARY—THE MAJOR DETERMINANTS OF BANK RESERVES AND THE MONEY SUPPLY

It should be clear from the past several chapters that our money supply is subject to a variety of influences. It may be helpful to attempt to draw these various determinants together, at this point, by way of summary.

It will be recalled from Chapter 5 that, given a certain amount of excess reserves, the maximum possible *increase* in demand deposits can be computed from the expression:

$$\frac{1}{R_d + C + (R_t \times T)} \times \text{Excess Reserves.}$$

The maximum possible increase in the _money supply_, including both the demand deposit and currency elements, then, was computed by adding to the above, an amount equal to:

$$C \left[\frac{1}{R_d + C + (R_t \times T)} \right] \times \text{Excess Reserves}$$

to account for the expansion in currency.

It should be clear that it is also true that the maximum possible _money supply_ at any time equals:

Demand Deposit Component

$$\frac{1}{R_d + C + (R_t \times T)} \times \text{Total Reserves} +$$

Currency Component

$$C \left[\frac{1}{R_d + C + (R_t \times T)} \times \frac{\text{Total}}{\text{Reserves}} \right]$$

or, what comes to the same thing,

$$\frac{1 + C}{R_d + C + (R_t \times T)} \times \text{Total Reserves}$$

To put this rather imposing equation into so many words, it implies that the maximum supply of money at any time depends on:

1. The required reserve ratios (R_d and R_t)
2. The public's relative preferences for demand deposits, time deposits and currency (C and T)
3. The quantity of bank reserves.

Before venturing further let us be sure that the role that each of these major factors plays in determining the potential money supply is understood fully.

Required Reserve Ratios

It is clear that, other things being equal, the higher the required reserve ratios the smaller the potential money supply and vice versa. This, of course, is precisely why the Federal Reserve was given this power. Further belaboring of the point hardly seems necessary.

Public Preference Ratio for Demand Deposits, Time Deposits, and Currency

Also, it should be clear that changes in the public's relative preferences for demand deposits, time deposits, and currency will alter the potential money supply. Other things being equal, the money supply will be larger the stronger the public's preference for demand deposits relative to the other two. An increase in the relative desire for time deposits on the other hand, since this asset is only a near money, will tie up more of the existing reserves behind it and reduce the maximum that the money supply can attain. More complicated changes in the preferred asset ratio with less clear-cut effects on the money supply abound, but the two noted above are sufficient to illustrate the point.[10]

The Quantity of Member-bank Reserves

As we have seen, far and away the most important sources of changes in the money supply are changes in the quantity of legal reserves possessed by the banks. This strategic item is subject to alteration by actions of the Federal Reserve, the Treasury, or the public.

Table 7-1 represents an attempt to bring together all the many influences on the size of member-bank reserves which we have discussed in the past several chapters. The table lists the major items, changes in which will alter the quantity of member-bank reserves plus, in each case, an example of a specific activity that could cause such a change. The student would be well advised to study Table 7-1 with care.

Although a few of the more minor influences on member-bank reserves have been omitted from Table 7-1, it includes all the important ones, and the student who has mastered it and the logic lying beneath it has a reasonably complete understanding of the determinants of the supply of money. Our next, and even more important task, is to begin the construction of a theoretical framework within which we can see something about the significance, in terms of the goals of our economy, of changes in the money supply.

We possess a pretty sterile bundle of technical information if all we know are the determinants of the size of the money supply. We must turn now to consideration of the more fundamental question, "What difference does it make if the money supply *does* change?"

---

[10] An interconnection between this factor and the next should be noted at this point. A decline in the public's desire for cash along with an increase in its preference for demand deposits has the effect of increasing the quantity of member-bank reserves. This effect is listed in Table 7-1, as in item 6.

TABLE 7-1   Major Determinants of Member-bank Reserves[a]

Factors That Can Increase (Decrease) Member-bank Reserves	*Specific Actions That Would Cause Changes in These Factors*
1. Increase (Decrease) in Federal Reserve Ownership of U.S. Securities	1. The Federal Reserve System open market operations in outstanding securities, or sale of new securities directly to the Federal Reserve System by Treasury to finance deficit spending, or refunding operation involving sale of new securities to the Federal Reserve System
2. Increase (Decrease) in Federal Reserve Discounts and Advances	2. The Federal Reserve System makes loans of reserves to member banks via discount mechanism
3. Increase (Decrease) in Federal Reserve Float	3. Uncollected Cash Items differs from Deferred Availability Cash Items in the Federal Reserve System balance sheet as a result of the check collection mechanism
4. Increase (Decrease) in Gold Stock	4. Treasury buys or sells gold
5. Increase (Decrease) in Treasury Currency in Hands of Member Banks, Public or Federal Reserve Banks	5. Treasury issues more currency, e.g., silver certificates, by depositing it in the Treasury's account at the Federal Reserve
6. Decrease (Increase) in currency and coins in hands of public	6. Public withdraws currency and coins from commercial banks by writing checks on accounts held there
7. Decrease (Increase) in Treasury Deposits at FRS	7. Treasury (a) changes location of its cash balances to commercial bank tax and loan accounts, (b) draws down its Federal Reserve Account to finance deficit spending, and (c) deposits and keeps new Treasury currency in its Federal Reserve Account

[a]This table is a simplification of the usual "Sources and Uses of Member Bank Reserves" table regularly reported in the *Federal Reserve Bulletin*. For a more complete explanation, see the Appendix to this chapter.

APPENDIX

DERIVATION OF "SOURCES AND USES OF MEMBER BANK RESERVES" STATEMENT

Table 7-1 contains a simplified and somewhat truncated version of the more formal "Sources and Uses of Member Bank Reserves" statement. This data, published monthly in the *Federal Reserve Bulletin* is a complete summary of all the factors that can affect bank reserves. Increases in *source* items will, other things being equal, raise member-bank reserves while increases in *use* items will, *ceteris paribus*, reduce member-bank reserves. The source-use table for January 31, 1965, was as follows:

"Sources"—Factors Supplying Reserve Funds (millions of dollars)		*"Uses"—Factors Absorbing Reserve Funds (millions of dollars)*	
U.S. Securities owned by Federal Reserve System	$36,856[a]	Currency in Circulation	$38,540
Federal Reserve System Discounts and Advances	304	Treasury Deposits at Federal Reserve	929
		Other (Nonmember Bank) Deposits at Federal Reserve	361
Federal Reserve Float	1,577	Treasury Cash	653
Gold Stock	15,185	Other Federal Reserve Accounts	1,039
Treasury Currency Outstanding	5,400		

[a] Includes minor amounts of acceptance and industrial loans held.

This statement is derived from a consolidated balance sheet for all Federal Reserve banks, as of that date, plus a partial Treasury balance sheet containing the Treasury's monetary accounts. In order to throw somewhat more light on the logic behind the source-use statement depicted here, let us run through its derivation.

The consolidated Federal Reserve balance sheet for January 31, 1965, was as follows:

Federal Reserve Balance Sheet (millions of dollars)

Assets		Liabilities and Capital Accounts	
(1) Gold Certificates	14,906	(8) Federal Reserve Notes	33,706
(2) Cash	193	(9) Demand Deposits of Member Banks	17,801
(3) Discounts and Advances	304	(10) Demand Deposits of U.S. Treasury	929
(4) U.S. Securities	36,856[a]	(11) Demand Deposits of others	361
(5) Uncollected Cash Items	5,330	(12) Deferred Availability Cash Items	3,753
(6) Bank Premises	102	(13) Other Liabilities	638
(7) Other Assets	654	(14) Capital Accounts	1,157
	58,345		58,345

[a] Includes minor amount of acceptances held.

The Treasury monetary accounts, as of January 31, 1965, consisted of:

Treasury Monetary Accounts (millions of dollars)

Assets		Liabilities and Capital Accounts	
(15) Gold Stock	15,185	(18) Gold Certificates	14,906
(16) Treasury Currency Outstanding	5,400	(19) Treasury Currency Outside Treasury	5,148
(17) Federal Reserve Notes Held in Treasury	121	(20) Treasury Cash	653
	20,706		20,707

Before we attempt to illustrate how these two statements may be combined and consolidated to produce the source-use statement on the preceding page, definitions of some of the entries in the Treasury Monetary Account may well be in order.

Treasury Currency Outstanding (16) includes all the Treasury Currency (including silver dollars, silver bullion, silver certificates, coins, U.S. Notes, and

minor amounts of other currency in process of retirement), which is held by anyone in the economy including the public, the member banks, the Federal Reserve
Banks, *and the Treasury itself.* Of the $5,400 of Treasury Currency Outstanding,
for example, $252 million is held by the Treasury itself [item (16) minus item
(19)], $193 million is held by the Federal Reserve Banks (item 2) and the remain-
ing $4,955 million is held by the member banks and the public.

    Treasury Currency Outside Treasury (19) includes, as the title indicates all
Treasury Currency Outstanding that is not held by the Treasury. It includes the
$4,955 million held by the member banks and the public plus the $193 million
held by the Federal Reserve banks.

    Treasury Cash (20) is really a balancing item composed of three sepa-
rate items:

1. The value of gold held by the Treasury which is not now supporting gold
certificates [(15) minus (1)].
2. The value of silver held by the Treasury which is not now supporting
silver certificates or Treasury Notes of 1890.
3. All Federal Reserve Notes plus all Treasury Currency held in the Treasury's vaults. [The last two combined equal the sum of items (16) and
(17) minus item (19).]

Conceptually, then, the Treasury Cash entry measures the funds that the Treasury has at its disposal without writing checks on its Federal Reserve or tax
and loan accounts.

    Deriving the source-use table requires that we combine the statements of the
Federal Reserve and of the Treasury. This, of course, can be done by listing all
the assets from both statements on one side and all the liabilities and capital
accounts from both on the other. That is:

    A. $(1) + (2) + (3) + (4) + (5) + (6) + (7) + (15) + (16) + (17) = (8) + (9)$
$+ (10) + (11) + (12) + (13) + (14) + (18) + (19) + (20)$

Since we are interested in spotlighting the determinants of member-bank
reserves, it will be useful to rearrange the above equality to read:

    B. $(9) = [(1) + (2) + (3) + (4) + (5) + (6) + (7) + (15) + (16) + (17)] -$
$[(8) + (10) + (11) + (12) + (13) + (14) + (18) + (19) + (20)]$

From here on the procedure is simply to consolidate the items in the awk-
ward expression above so as to reduce it to the minimum number of basic determinants. This involves four operations.

1. Consolidating items (5) and (12), replacing them with the source item,
"Federal Reserve Float"
2. Consolidating items (6), (7), (13), and (14) and replacing them with the
use item, "Other Federal Reserve Accounts"
3. Consolidating items (2), (8), (17), and (19) and replacing them with the
use item, "Currency in Circulation"
4. Eliminating gold certificates from each side (1) and (18).

Let us run through these four computations, one by one. Since Federal
Reserve Float is the difference between Uncollected Cash Items and Deferred
Availability Cash Items we can easily amend expression B. by subtracting (12)
from (5) and, entering the positive result as Federal Reserve Float. This gives us:

C. $(9) = [(1) + (2) + (3) + (4) + (6) + (7) + (15) + (16) + (17) +$ Federal Reserve Float$] - [(8) + (10) + (11) + (13) + (14) + (18) + (19) + (20)]$

If we now add items (6) and (7) and subtract the sum of items (13) and (14), and, since the result is negative, enter it as "Other Federal Reserve Accounts" on the minus side, we have:

D. $(9) = [(1) + (2) + (3) + (4) + (15) + (16) + (17) +$ Federal Reserve Float$] - [(8) + (10) + (11) + (18) + (19) + (20) +$ Other Federal Reserve Accounts$]$

Next, we can consolidate four more of our original items into a single entry entitled "Currency in Circulation" if we sum items (8) and (19) and subtract from this, the total of items (2) and (17). What this step gives us is the amount of currency currently held outside the Treasury and the Federal Reserve banks. That is, it includes the currency in the hands of the nonbank public and the member banks. This computation produces:

E. $(9) = [(1) + (3) + (4) + (15) + (16) +$ Federal Reserve Float$] - [(10) + (11) + (18) + (20) +$ Other Federal Reserve Accounts $+$ Currency in Circulation$]$

Finally since items (1) and (18) both report the amount of gold certificates, with opposite signs, they can be eliminated giving us:

F. $(9) = [(3) + (4) + (15) + (16) +$ Federal Reserve Float$] - [(10) + (11) + (20) +$ Other Federal Reserve Accounts $+$ Currency in Circulation$]$

We have now arrived at the irreducible list of sources and uses with which we started. When the positive factors on the right of the equality sign in expression F. are listed on the reserve-supplying side and the negative factors on the reserve-absorbing side, we have:

"Sources"—Factors Supplying Reserve Funds (millions of dollars)		"Uses"—Factors Absorbing Reserve Funds (millions of dollars)	
(4) U.S. Securities owned by Federal Reserve System	36,856	Currency in Circulation	38,540
(3) Federal Reserve System Discounts and Advances	304	(10) Treasury Deposits at Federal Reserve	929
(15) Gold Stock	15,185	(11) Other Nonmember Bank Deposits at Federal Reserve	361
(16) Treasury Currency Outstanding	5,400	(20) Treasury Cash	653
Federal Reserve Float	1,577	Other Federal Reserve Accounts	1,039

The table above provides us with a convenient means of isolating the causes of changes in member-bank Federal Reserve accounts over time. Any increase in a source item (or decrease in a use item), in and of itself, tends to increase member-bank Federal Reserve accounts. Conversely, any increase in a use item (or decrease in a source item) will lower the quantity of reserves member banks keep at the Federal Reserve.

For example, it might be noted that from the end of 1960 to the end of 1964, member-bank Federal Reserve accounts rose by almost $1.3 billion. This rise took place despite the fact that the nation's gold stock fell by over $2.5 billion during the period while currency in circulation rose by over $6.5 billion. The major offsetting source of reserves was a nearly $10 billion increase in Federal Reserve ownership of U.S. securities. The conclusion? In the 1960-1964 period, open market operations more than offset the drain on reserves created by our gold loss and expansion in currency circulation. The details of the source-use changes for this 1960-1964 period were as follows:

Factors Expanding Member-bank Federal Reserve Accounts
(millions of dollars)

U.S. Securities Owned by Federal Reserve System	+	9,878
Discounts and Advances	+	172
Federal Reserve Float	+	758
Treasury Currency Outstanding	+	5
Other Deposits at Federal Reserve System	−	378
Total Sources		11,191

Factors Reducing Member-bank Federal Reserve Accounts
(millions of dollars)

Gold Stock	−	2,566
Currency in Circulation	+	6,679
Treasury Cash	+	187
Treasury Deposits at Federal Reserve System	+	422
Other Federal Reserve Accounts	+	64
Total Uses		9,918

The result of all this was a net four-year rise of $1,273 million in member-bank reserves at Federal Reserve banks.

One word of caution is in order. While prior to 1959, it was correct to refer to our list of source-use items as the Sources and Uses of member-bank reserves, this is no longer quite accurate. Prior to 1959, no member-bank vault cash could be counted as legal reserves to fulfill the reserve requirements. Consequently, the factors that determined the size of member-bank deposits at the Federal Reserve determined, at the same time, total member-bank reserves.

Now, however, vault cash held by member banks is counted as a part of legal reserves. Consequently, the $1,273 million rise in member-bank deposits at the Federal Reserve between 1960 and 1964 is only a part of the total increase in legal reserves. For during this period $1,050 of the increase in Currency in Circulation noted took the form of an increase in member-bank vault cash. The result is that total member-bank reserves rose by the sum of $1,273 and $1,050, $2,323 from December, 1960, to December, 1964.

II

MONETARY AND INCOME THEORY

8
Introduction to Theory

This is perhaps an appropriate time for a look at what the military calls the "big picture." The maze of T-accounts and transactions that we have just completed in the preceding section is, unfortunately, almost ideally suited to losing sight of the proverbial forest because of the trees. Let us step back and take a broad view of our progress.

WHERE WE HAVE BEEN AND WHERE WE ARE GOING

In a sense we have, in the previous section, approached our subject backwards. For, as the reader will recall, we started out with a consideration of how much credit (and money supply) could be created by the banking system if we had *given* to us, the system's excess reserves, the appropriate required reserve ratios, and the public's preferences for holding demand deposits, time deposits, and cash. Then in succeeding chapters, we went about discussing the factors that can alter these given conditions, namely, Federal Reserve actions, public changes in preferences, and U.S. Treasury action. The purpose of all this, of course, was to arm ourselves with a basic knowledge of all the major factors that play a role in determining the money supply in the United States. Unfortunately, however, even complete information about what determines or can change the money and credit supply is, though interesting, a pretty sterile bundle of information if left to stand on its own feet. The student is perfectly entitled to a skeptical "so what?" at this point.

We turn now to deal with that "so what?" Armed with our technical knowledge of what *makes* the money and credit supply change, we must come to grips with the far more significant question of what *difference* it makes if the money and credit supply *does* change. To be more specific,

155

to what degree and in what circumstances do changes in the money and credit supply affect, for good or ill, our major economic goals of maximum production, full employment, stable prices, and rapid economic growth?

The answer to this question lies squarely within the bailiwick of economic theory, the subject of this section. In order to deal adequately with the effect of changes in the money supply on our ecomonic goals we will, in the following chapters, be concerned with building up, via income determination, monetary, and interest rate theories, a "model" of the economy through which we can trace the effect of changes in monetary and other variables.

Before proceeding, let us delve briefly into the "whys" of economic theory.

Why, the reader may ask, must we resort to abstract, sometimes difficult, theory, to discuss our problems? Why must we rely on oversimplified, artificial "models" of the economy, sometimes even going so far as to present them in purely mathematical terms? Why not stick to the much advertised "real world" in which we all live?

The answer to these queries, of course, is that there is no other way. With an economy and a set of economic problems as complex as those with which we are faced, it is only a "pipedream" to talk about sticking strictly to a description of the so-called real world. It is much too complicated. In order to bring order out of chaos, we *must* abstract from the highly complex reality in which we live. There is no alternative to theory if we would discuss the likely effects of an alteration in the money supply on the economy.

But the conclusions drawn from an oversimplified, abstract theory of the economy are most certainly *not* in conflict with the real world. Not, at any rate, if the theory is sound. Indeed, the old saw that, "that's all right in theory but it will never work out in practice" is a nonsense statement. If a theory does not work out in practice (or in the real world) in the vast majority of cases, it is simply *not* all right in theory either.

It may help the student who reacts negatively to the use of "theory" and "economic models" to switch terms. What we are about to begin is the building up of a *framework* of our economy, using, as pieces of the superstructure, certain economic variables that appear, as a result of statistical investigation or sheer, deductive reasoning, to be causally related. This framework (or model) can be kept simple, and hence, pretty far removed from complicated reality, or refined, by dropping more and more simplifying assumptions, to the point at which it closely approaches both the reality and the complexity of the real world.

We shall try, in the upcoming chapters, to steer a middle course. On the one hand, our framework of the economy must be complicated enough to be a *reasonably* close approximation to reality. On the other hand, however, we shall attempt to retain enough simplifying assumptions to avoid "muddying up" the picture with detail, so that major, important relationships can be clearly visualized. This, after all, is the purpose of theory.

9 | Theories Aimed at Explaining the Value of Money: the Commodity Theory and the Quantity Theories—Old and New

Ever since certain items became generally acceptable as mediums of exchange, man has been curious about the determinants of their acceptability and purchasing power. Two separate but related issues have commanded most attention.

The first of these has to do with the acceptance of "token," inherently valueless, paper money in exchange for valuable goods and services. Why, it has been asked, have men been so willing to give up goods and services in return for mere slips of paper? The ancient commodity theory of money, covered briefly in the next section, represented an attempt to come to grips with this issue.

Secondly, there is the more complex question of the determinants of the purchasing power of money or, what is the same thing, the price level. In this chapter we shall concentrate on the attempts to deal with this issue via the time-honored quantity theory of money.

COMMODITY THEORY OF MONEY

Given the fact that our first moneys *were* commodities with substantial value in their nonmoney uses, it should not be a surprise to learn that the earlier ideas regarding the source of money's acceptability

158

and value centered on the commodity value of the money substance. Hence, according to the commodity theorists, money was freely accepted as a medium of exchange because the commodity of which it was made (or into which paper money was convertible) had significant value in some nonmoney use. In addition it was argued that the value of money (its purchasing power) varied directly with the quantity of the commodity of which it was made (or "backed").

Now to the modern reader, long since accustomed to nonconvertible paper money, such a theory may sound incredibly naïve. And though it would, indeed be naïve to apply it in this form to today's world, some defense of the earlier commodity theorists seems in order.

It will be remembered that the first moneys *were* commodities—commodities that evolved naturally to their money use. There can be little doubt that these commodity moneys *were* acceptable in exchange largely because of the nonmoney value of the commodity itself. And, it seems reasonable to assume that their purchasing power—the amount of goods and services obtainable for each money unit—would tend to vary directly with the quantity of the commodity. Consequently, *many years ago* the commodity theory undoubtedly was a fairly reasonable and at least partly valid hypothesis.

But time and changing customs have a sneaky way of playing tricks on long-established "truths." A combination of government issue, the legal tender power, and most important of all, a growing willingness among the public to accept certain tokens at an exchange value far exceeding their commodity value, have long since cut the ground out from under the commodity theory. It is certainly no longer true, and has not been so for many years, that the acceptability or the value of money is determined by the commodity of which it is made (or backed).

But the idea died hard and, indeed, in the general public's mind is probably not completely dead yet. How many times does one hear, even today, statements which imply that the value of the American dollar is somehow directly and fundamentally derived from the gold held in Fort Knox? Sadly, all too often.

Nor have members of the general public been the only victims of the trap of commodity theory reasoning in modern times. Not so many years ago some prominent economists and public officials relied upon the commodity theory as the major rationale for a devaluation of the U.S. dollar.

In that ill-starred venture of 1934, it was thought, strange though it may sound today, that the alarming spread of unemployment might be reduced if the sharp decline in the price level and its attendant squeeze on profit margins could be reversed. The argument used was almost unbelievably naïve.

It was thought by the scheme's backers that raising the dollar price of gold from \$20.67 per ounce to \$35 per ounce would, because it reduced the amount of gold backing the dollar by about 40 percent, reduce the value (purchasing power) of the dollar by 40 percent. A reduction in the purchasing power of the dollar by 40 percent would, of course, be reflected in a 70 percent rise in the price level.

But what happened when the devaluation was carried out? The price level was affected very little and what little rise *did* take place would be very difficult to attribute to the devaluation. This experiment, or rather its failure as a means of cutting the value of the dollar, should have laid to rest for all time the idea that the commodity backing the dollar determines its value. The value of the American dollar rests on a far more substantial foundation than the value of the yellow metal contained in Fort Knox.

THE QUANTITY THEORIES

Of much greater significance for the theory of money are the so-called *quantity theory* approaches. These too, represent attempts to explain the relation between money and the price level and, like the commodity theory, trace their origins back very many years. Unlike the commodity theory, however, the quantity theory has been able to adapt itself, over the years. As earlier, cruder versions have been challenged and discredited, newer, more sophisticated hypotheses have been developed to replace the old. If long survival under constant attack can be taken as a measure of the strength of an idea, the quantity theory must be awarded an honored position in economic thought. For, albeit in a form much altered from that of its origin, the quantity theory continues today to be a lively source of debate among monetary theorists.

As its name implies, the quantity theory, in all its versions, looks to the quantity of money as the main causal determinant of changes in the price level. If the theory is valid its implications for monetary policy are indeed enormous. For, as we have seen, the quantity of money is subject, given sufficient skill by the monetary authorities, to reasonably precise control. If the price level should be responsive to the supply of money, however indirectly and tardily, knowledge of the relationship would obviously be invaluable to policy makers.

Of course, none of the so-called quantity theories has been so naïve as to simply posit the proposition that, without some logical behavioral process, prices automatically follow the money supply, willy-nilly. Developed by brilliant thinkers, all quantity theories worthy of the name have attempted to explain the process—the causal sequence—whereby a larger money supply leads to higher prices and vice versa.

But theorizing about relationships in a complex economy requires order and simplification in order to avoid a hodge-podge of confusing detail. It requires, among other things, a simplified framework of the economy within which the important variables stand out as clearly as do super highways on a large-scale road map. In a phrase, what is needed is a "way of looking" at the economy which will screen out the unnecessary detail while retaining the crucial variables, and provide the foundation for the construction of a cause-and-effect theory.

Each version of the quantity theory has relied upon a variant of what has come to be called the *equation of exchange* as its way of looking at some of the important variables in the economy. Since these equations are the framework upon which the quantity theories are built, we shall consider them in the next section before going on to discuss the theories themselves.

The Equation of Exchange

Transactions Version

The *transactions version* of the equation of exchange is largely the product of the brilliant mind of Irving Fisher, one of the finest American economists of the early twentieth century. Fisher, as we shall see shortly, was a quantity theorist, but our interest in this section is only with the equation of exchange around which he organized his theory, not the theory itself.

Fisher's (transactions) equation of exchange was simply a complicated way of stating an obvious truth. Starting from the unassailable proposition that for every dollar spent by a buyer, a dollar is received by a seller, we can proceed without difficulty to the equally obvious statement that, for any given group (assuming, of course, no transactions outside the group) during any given time period, the dollar value of everything bought equals the dollar value of everything sold.

Though it may appear to be absurd to stress such an obvious truism as "amount bought equals amount sold," that is really all that the equation of exchange says. The equation itself (in the transactions version) is:

$$MV \equiv PT, \text{ wherein:}$$

M = the average supply of money during the period
V = the number of times per period (rate) the average dollar is spent to buy *anything* (for short, transactions velocity)
P = the price, per unit, of everything sold[1]
T = the number of things sold (for short, *transactions*)

---

[1] Of course we could not actually compute such an average price. To use the equation for measurement would require the use of a price index here. However, there is nothing wrong or difficult with the *concept* of an average price per unit and since we are not going to be concerned with measurement, we shall stick to the above, conceptually clearer, definition of P.

Let us look at what this equation says, using some assumed values for the four variables. Suppose M equals $100, V equals 15, P equals $2.00 per unit, and T equals 750.

We have, of course, assumed values that make the equation balance, but the student must understand that we *must* do this because we are dealing with a definitional identity. Consider, for example, the left-hand side of the equation, MV (M times V). If $100 of money exists during the period and each dollar of it is spent 15 times, when the two are multiplied the result, $1,500, is simply *total expenditures* on everything during the period.

The right-hand side of the equation, PT (P times T) reflects 750 items sold at an average price of $2.00 each. What does the multiple of these two items show, other than *total receipts* from selling what was bought? Actually, then, $MV \equiv PT$ simply says that the value of what was bought during the period equals the value of what was sold—a definitional identity. MV does not just equal PT in equilibrium, nor is some economic process required to bring these two totals into equality with one another. They are equal at all times because they are defined that way.

But, the reader may be thinking, of what use is it to dress up an obvious identity into this form when everyone already grants that the amount bought equals the amount sold? The answer to this question is very simple. When we break total expenditures down into the two components M and V, we have spotlighted two variables, the money supply and the rate of spending it, which do fluctuate and which do affect the level of expenditures. And when we divide total dollar receipts down into P and T, we have again separated out two important variables, changes in which have important implications for economic welfare.

But the skeptical reader should not give up so easily. The statement that $MV \equiv PT$ *is,* as such, merely a sterile framework. It is *not* a theory. It does *not* say that MV *causes* PT, nor does it imply the reverse causation. We shall, presently, discuss some examples of cause and effect theories that have been built on the equation of exchange. But the equation of exchange itself (as distinct from cause and effect theories built upon it) should be regarded only as a sterile framework that permits a spotlighting of four important variables in our economy.

Income Version

A second version of the equation of exchange which is often employed is the *income* version:

$$MV_y \equiv P_yO, \text{ wherein:}$$

M = the average supply of money during the period

V_y = the number of times per period (rate) the average dollar is spent to buy *newly produced goods and services* (for short, income velocity)

P_y = the price, per unit, of *newly produced goods and services*

O = the number of physical units of *newly produced goods and services* sold (for short, output)

Once again we are dealing with an identity. The left-hand side of the equation, MV_y, now equals total expenditures on newly produced goods and services whereas the right-hand side, P_yO, equals the dollar value of newly produced goods and services sold. The amount spent on new goods and services equals the amount received from selling them.

But the income version represents a formulation much different from the transactions version. MV (transactions) equals total expenditures on *everything sold*; newly produced goods and services, sales of already existing goods, purely financial expenditures to purchase stocks and bonds, and intrabusiness expenditures such as for raw materials. Similarly PT in the transactions version reflects the value of *everything sold* including not only new goods and services but everything else.

In the income version, MV_y is a much smaller total than MV because it only counts the expenditures for new production. And P_yO is much smaller than PT because it too, only records the sales of newly produced items. A dollar may be spent 15 times per year but it may be spent only 3 of those times on newly produced goods and services. In this case V would be 15, but V_y only 3. The difference represents spending for already existing goods, stocks and bonds, raw materials, etc. The total number of *transactions* may be 750, but newly produced items sold may be only 100. In this case, T would be 750 and O, 100. The difference again reflects the many items sold during the period which are not currently produced.

The Cash Balance Equation

Finally, let us take a brief look at a third version of the equation of exchange, the cash balance version, developed by scholars at England's Cambridge University many years ago (and sometimes referred to as the Cambridge version).

Their equation may be stated as:

$$M \equiv k \, P \, T,[2] \text{ wherein:}$$

[2] There is no reason why this equation could not also be put in income terms. As such, it would read $M = K_y \, P_y \, O$ with k_y, P_y, and O all being defined in terms of currently produced goods and services. To cut down on the detail we shall ignore this in our discussion.

M = the average supply of money during the year
P = the price, per unit, of everything sold
T = the number of things sold
k = the proportion of the total value of transactions (PT) that the public holds in money balances[3]

After some reflection it becomes apparent that this, too, is a definitional identity. Since the money supply that exists *must* be held by *somebody* at any point in time, k, as defined above, turns out to be a fraction that equates the two sides. In fact, as must be obvious $K = 1/V$. If, for example, $M = \$100$, $P = \$2.00$ and $T = 500$ then V would have to equal 10 and k would have to equal $\frac{1}{10}$. Why? Because if the value of total transactions (PT) equals $1,000 and $100 of money *exists*, since someone must, at any point in time, hold all the money that exists, the proportion of total transactions which the public holds in money balances must equal $1/10(\$100/\$1,000)$.

It would appear, then, that the cash balance equation says nothing different from the transactions version of the equation of exchange. Both are, in this form, definitional identities, with the latter using the speed of spending to equate the two sides and the former using its reciprocal. And yet the cash balance approach, despite its formal similarity to the others, paved the way to some novel ideas in monetary theory.

Equilibrium Conditions vs. Definitional Identities

As definitional identities, neither the cash balance nor the equation of exchange approaches add much that is significant to our understanding of the working of the economy. As long as V and k are defined in terms of what people *do* do with money rather than what people *desire* to do with it, the equations are sterile truisms offering, in and of themselves, no insight into the forces that lead to economic change.

It was in this area that the Cambridge cash-balance equation made its unique contribution. While it was rather difficult for scholars to conceive of people being unable to spend money at a desired rate (a "desired" V different from the "actual" V) it was very much easier to imagine peo-

---

[3] It should be noted that this definition does some violence to the actual Cambridge position. In fact, k in the Cambridge equation was a behavioral variable. It represented the proportion of PT which people *desired* to hold, rather than the proportion they *actually* hold. In these terms $M = k P T$ is not a definitional identity, but a condition that only holds in equilibrium, when the amount of money people *actually* hold represents the fraction of PT which they *desire* to hold. To the earlier proponents of this approach, however, the difference was not significant. For it was argued that k (desired) like V, was reasonably constant, that T also was reasonably constant and that therefore, anytime $M \neq k P T$, only M and P could change to restore equilibrium. The result was a Quantity Theory not much different from those built on the $MV = PT$ framework.

ple possessing cash balances that were bigger or smaller than the desired proportion of PT (a desired k different from the actual k).

After all, the supply of money that exists, and which must be held by someone in the community at any point in time, is determined by the monetary authorities. And it may be an amount that is larger or smaller than the public feels is desired in light of the volume of transactions it is needed to finance. For example, if P = $2.00, T = 1,000 and the present money supply (M) equals $500, the actual k must be ¼. The public has no choice but to hold a money supply that is one-fourth the size of its total transactions. If, however, the public does not really *want* to hold that much money when its transactions total $2,000, some changes are going to be forthcoming.

Unless the monetary authority chooses to change the money supply, the public, although unwillingly for the moment, will have to hold all $500. But, if for example, the desired k is ⅕, individual members of the public, having larger money balances than they desire, are going to be attempting to get rid of the excess. They might, for example, use the plethora of cash to raise their consumption spending.[4]

Individuals may succeed in lowering their money balances in this way but, of course, the community as a whole cannot, because money spent by one member of society is received by another (the seller of the consumer good in this case) and the total amount held by all is undiminished. However, the very effort to reduce money balances will eventually lead to an equilibrium situation (where the actual k equals the desired k). For added consumer spending must raise PT, and by the time this total is increased to $2,500, the $500 of money that exists will be just exactly sufficient to meet the desired k of ⅕.

It is important that the student see the difference between the definitional identity, M ≡ kPT, where k is *defined* so as to make the equation balance, and an equilibrium situation, wherein the actual k is the same as the "desired" k. Conceptually, the point is the same as that which is involved in supply and demand analysis where the amount bought always equals the amount sold even though the quantity demanded only equals the quantity supplied at the equilibrium price.

In any case, the cash balance version of the equation, spotlighting as it did the demand for money to hold rather than the velocity of spending, has proved to be the most useful formulation for the simple reason that it led scholars to a more fruitful line of inquiry. Why, the Cambridge scholars asked themselves, do people desire to hold a nonincome earning asset such as money anyway? What rational motivations for demanding money balances are there? Some of the most important theoretical break-

[4] They might also use it to purchase securities, thereby lowering interest rates, but we shall, for the moment, overlook this possibility.

throughs in economics have resulted from efforts to answer these questions and it was the cash balance equation that provided the easier format for dealing with them.[5]

Three Examples of the Quantity Theory

Whatever the relative merits of the different equations, one point should be clearly understood. None of them is a theory. As definitional identities none of them, in and of itself, sheds any light on cause and effect in the economy. They do provide a useful way of organizing some of the economy's key variables but it remains for the theoretician to provide hypotheses regarding the nature of cause and effect relationships between the variables. To say that MV *equals* PT is merely to present an obvious truism. No theory is involved. To say, however, that MV *causes* PT is to promulgate a theoretical hypothesis that argues that MV is an active variable while PT is a passive one; that while a change in MV can cause a change in PT, no change in PT can come about without alterations in MV being the causal force.

The quantity theories have all argued that M, in the equation of exchange, is a key causal variables and that P, (or PT) is a passive one that "results from" the level of M. Over the years, however, the several versions of the quantity theory have differed notably in detail and degree of sophistication.

The Crude Quantity Theory

Although its origins can be traced back over two hundred years, what we shall here refer to as the *crude* quantity theory still appears to be given currency by some modern-day men of affairs. In its simplest form this theory argued that: *"The price level is determined by the money*

---

[5] For future reference, let us establish one more point about the left-hand side of the income version of the equation of exchange, if V_y is defined as *desired* income velocity.

$$MV_y = \frac{\text{Total expenditures on Newly}}{\text{Produced Goods and Services}} = C + I + G$$

Total spending on new goods and services can be broken down in two different ways. In the equation of exchange it is broken down in a way that spotlights the money supply and the rate at which it is spent. Another method of breaking down the same total is by spending groups—consumption spending, investment spending, and government spending on goods and services. While we shall not make much of this relationship now, the student should bear it in mind when we come to the next chapter and the so-called "modern" theory of income determination. As we shall see, the basic difference between those who choose to use the older income version of the equation of exchange and those who adhere to the newer theory to be discussed in Chapters 10-13 is that while the former find it more useful to emphasize the money supply—velocity breakdown of total expenditures—the latter group considers a breakdown by spending groups more fruitful. We shall return to this comparison later. Let it simply be observed at this point that *both* approaches are useful; neither is "wrong."

supply in a manner such that changes in the money supply lead to equal proportionate changes in the price level in the same direction."

Let there be no mistake about one thing. In the extreme form stated above the crude quantity theory is certainly incorrect as a mechanism for explaining changes in the price level. This can easily be proven by a look at the logic that underlies the theory.

The argument of the crude quantity theorists was buttressed by some of the important pillars of classical economic theory.[6] These included the arguments that:

(1) A free enterprise economy contains within it, a mechanism which will reasonably promptly restore those conditions necessary for full employment when any tendency toward a deficiency in aggregate demand appears; hence, a full-employment level of output was looked upon as a "norm."

(2) Income received by rational individuals would be disposed of in only two ways—spending on consumption and lending out the amount not spent at interest; hence, holding idle money balances was considered irrational.

Now let us employ the income version of the equation of exchange to illustrate the impact of these two hypotheses on those who espoused what we have chosen to call the crude quantity theory. This is:

$$MV_y \equiv P_y O$$

If the economy *does* contain a built-in mechanism that will maintain a near full-employment level of output at all times, the main reason for drastic, short-run changes in O is removed. It is still true that over a period of time O will rise as a result of growth in the labor force, capital equipment and changing technology. But these features of economic growth only have effect slowly, at a fairly steady rate (such as 3 percent per year) over long periods of time. The likelihood of a 10 percent to 25 percent cutback in O in a short period of time, such as was typical of our Great Depression, is ruled out by assumption. Hence it could be argued, O, while not absolutely fixed, cannot change much from year to year.

And what about V_y? The second Classical assumption pretty well takes care of it. Except in the rare case of a financial panic, it is irrational to hold idle money balances (that is, it is irrational to hold a portion of the existing money supply to a zero velocity). Hence, the one main possibility for sharp, short-run changes in V_y is also ruled out by assumption. The velocity of spending is affected, it is true, by changes in the industrial and financial structure, a speedup in check collection, changes in the frequency of paydays, and the like. But these, too, are the kinds of changes that only take place slowly over long periods of time. The sharp changes

[6] This should not be taken to imply that all classical economists espoused the crude version of the quantity theory.

in V_y which would be possible if people should suddenly decide to hold half the money supply in idle (zero velocity) balances are ruled out by the dictum that such behavior is irrational.

Now, *if it were true* that both V_y and O change only slightly in the short run and that any changes in either are likely to be, as a result of the long-run forces working on each, in an upward direction, then the "crude" quantity theory follows directly from the definitional nature of the equation of exchange. If V_y and O change only slightly, and in the same direction, it must follow that changes in M would be associated with essentially equal-porportional changes in P_y in the same direction.

Under the assumptions noted, how might the recipient of additional money (as a result of an open market operation for example) make use of it? He must, of course, either spend it on consumer goods or save it. If he spends it on consumer goods, full employment being assumed, it can only raise consumer goods' prices. If he saves it, he must either purchase capital goods directly or "financially" invest by purchasing securities. Hoarding his saved funds is ruled out by assumption as irrational. If he uses his savings to purchase capital goods directly, the full-employment assumption once again requires that prices must rise. If he purchases securities, this must raise their prices (and thereby lower their market yield and the rate of interest in the economy) calling forth additional purchase of capital goods by others which raises prices. There is no way out. Increased M must spill over, one way or another into increased prices.

Of course the underlying assumptions of stable V_y and O are really untenable and therefore the theory based on them is, in fact, equally invalid. The price level can and has been affected many times by sharp changes in V_y and it is equally true that any changes in MV_y (total expenditures on newly produced goods and services) may spend themselves partially or wholly in affecting O, as well as in affecting P_y. The money supply is by no means the sole determinant of the price level, and the student should be alert enough to recognize the fallacies involved when versions of the "crude" quantity theory emerge as the basis for political speeches or newspaper editorials, as they still all too often do.

The Fisher Quantity Theory

It would certainly be misleading to represent all so-called quantity theorists as subscribing to the naïve theory discussed above. The leading exponent of a more refined version of the quantity theory in the United States was Professor Irving Fisher, a scholar who was anything but naïve.[7]

---

[7] See Irving Fisher, *The Purchasing Power of Money* (New York, The Macmillan Company, 1926). Fisher, in fact, discussed this issue by use of the transactions version rather than the income version that we use.

Fisher's variant of the quantity theory was carefully qualified to eliminate the most serious fallacies of the crude version. He granted, for example, that *in the transition periods* (during the ups and downs of the business cycle), the velocity of spending might alter significantly, thereby minimizing (or accentuating) the effects of money supply changes on prices. In addition, Fisher was an accurate enough observer of the world about him to recognize that, at times (again, during the transition periods) the effects of increased M might well be partly absorbed by increases in output (O), with proportionately smaller immediate effects on price.

Nevertheless, Fisher concludes, despite his impressive list of careful qualifications that, "we find nothing to interfere with the truth of the quantity theory that variations in money produce normally proportional changes in price."[8] How, the reader may well ask, does he square this conclusion with his recognition that V_y and O may vary?

In effect Fisher is arguing that while V_y and O may change during transition (business cycle) periods, a longer run comparison between two similar stages in a business cycle would find V_y and O returning to approximately the same levels leaving any change in M in that interim to work itself out on prices. And while Fisher himself grants that "periods of transition are the rule and those of equilibrium the exception,"[9] he feels that if we know that a doubling of the money supply at point X in business cycle 1 will lead to a doubling of prices by the time a similar point in the next cycle is reached, we have a pretty valuable piece of knowledge.

Is the most sophisticated Fisher quantity theory valid? It seems unlikely that many present-day economists would defend it despite Fisher's careful qualifications. And yet it can hardly be said to have been disproved.

Over the long pull there *is* a rather impressive relationship between changes in the money supply and the price level although it is far from a perfect correlation. In addition most of the critics of the quantity theory have concentrated their fire on divergences between the two which might well be considered transitional in nature by Fisher and, therefore, no exception to his argument.

For example, it has been argued quite persuasively that the public and the banks have devised means of making a constant (or decreasing) money supply finance a greater quantity of expenditures in expansion periods, thereby partially frustrating so-called *tight money* policies by raising the velocity of circulation. In such a situation prices rise without a rise in the money supply. If these arguments are valid, and they appear to be quite well documented, they indicate that *during the expansion phase of the cycle,* we may see prices rise even though the money supply does not.

8 *Ibid.*, p. 183.
9 *Ibid.*, p. 71.

The importance of such a pattern can hardly be questioned; yet the carefully qualified Fisher quantity theory could be said to allow for it as a transitional episode.

Similarly, there can be no doubt that, during both phases of the business cycle, changes in the money supply may be largely absorbed through changes in the level of output (O). In the contraction phase, even if the money supply falls we would not expect to see prices falling proportionately. Instead, for some time at least, the level of output would decline as workers were laid off without much, if any, price decline. Similarly, in the initial recovery phase of an expansion, increased money supply may, to the degree it raises expenditures, cause output and employment to expand rapidly with little price increase. But here again we are considering the transitional effects that Fisher carefully allowed for.

The New Friedman Quantity Theory

Whatever the merits of Professor Fisher's views, it seems clear that the Great Depression and the theoretical contributions of Keynes' *General Theory* in the 1930's convinced the preponderant majority of economists that the quantity theory was an inadequate, if not downright erroneous theoretical apparatus. Indeed, serious reservations regarding the validity of *any* version of the quantity theory undoubtedly still dominate the profession.

But the quantity theory, in very much altered form, has staged a sharp comeback in recent years, largely as a result of the exhaustive and penetrating contributions of Professor Milton Friedman of the University of Chicago.[10]

The *new* quantity theory, however, differs significantly from all the older versions in that it no longer represents an attempt to directly relate the price level to the money supply. Instead, in its new *Friedman* form, the money supply is said to be the major determinant of P_yO, or the value of output. To put this statement in a somewhat different form, Friedman argues that, in the $MV_y \equiv P_yO$ formulation: (1) V_y (or inversely, the demand for money) is a fairly stable or at least reasonably predictable magnitude so that, when M changes, the product of P_y and O must change by a similar proportion, and (2) the direction of causation is from M to P_yO and not that other way around. That is, it is M that causes P_yO to be what it is, not P_yO that determines M.

[10] See M. Friedman, ed., *Studies in the Quantity Theory of Money* (Chicago, University of Chicago Press, 1956); M. Friedman and Anna J. Schwartz, "Money and Business Cycles," *Review of Economics and Statistics*, Vol. XLV, Supplement; M. Friedman and David Meiselman, "The Relative Stability of Monetary Velocity and the Investment Multiplier in the United States, 1897-1958," *Stabilization Policies* (Englewood Cliffs, N.J., Prentice-Hall, 1963).

In making his case, Professor Friedman has provided an impressive volume of empirical evidence to show that, in fact, the money supply and the value of current output have moved along together. The longer run relationship revealed by the Friedman data is particularly striking although Professor Friedman believes the relationship, albeit with a long and variable lag, to hold in a shorter-run, business cycle sense also.[11]

In addition to his empirical evidence Friedman relies heavily on a theory of asset choice to explain the close relationship that he sees between money and P_yO. Since the publication of Keynes' *General Theory*, it had become general to argue that money affected the level of income only *indirectly* through changing the rate of interest which, in turn, led to alterations in aggregate demand. In the "Friedman" quantity theory this connection between money and income is significantly supplemented by a *direct* effect of money on income in which a change in the supply of money leads to a series of alterations in asset holders' balance sheets, which ultimately lead to changes in the demand for new goods and services.

We shall not attempt to delve more deeply into the new quantity theory at this point. It is at present in a highly unsettled state and much more time and careful investigation will be required before the extent of its validity is a subject of general agreement.

The policy implications of the theory, however, seem clear. If Friedman's arguments should stand the test of time, they will have (1) placed the supply of money back near the center of the economic stage, rather than in the wings to which it had been pretty much relegated since the 1930's, and (2) given a potent "shot in the arm" to monetary policy as the major stabilization device.[12]

IMPORTANCE OF THE EQUATION-OF-EXCHANGE APPROACH TO THEORY

There can be no doubting the fact that many important contributions to economic understanding have been made through the use of the equation of exchange mechanism. However it is equally undeniable that the majority of economists today find it preferable to use the more

[11] It should be noted that for most of his investigations Friedman defines the money supply to include time deposits as well as currency and demand deposits, a definition which differs from that in most common usage today. However, he also defends his hypothesis when the more conventional definition of money is used.

[12] It should be noted here, however, that Professor Friedman himself finds the lag between money supply and income changes so long and variable that he recommends abandoning discretionary monetary policy altogether in favor of a fixed annual money supply increase.

recently developed theory of income determination to be discussed in the following chapters. The author shares the opinion of this majority.

But the student must not be misled. The widespread preference for the so-called income-expenditure approach to theory is a purely utilitarian choice. Those who today shun the equation of exchange approach to the economy do so, not because there is anything invalid about the statement that $MV_y \equiv P_yO$. Indeed, we have already stressed the point that this is a definitional truth. The switch to the newer approach has arisen simply out of the conviction that a clearer picture of the economic process, its why and wherefores, can be gleaned from breaking down total expenditures on newly produced goods and services into segments according to spending groups rather than into the two components, money supply and velocity. But in the hands of a skilled technician, the same things can be said either way.

As for the specific quantity theories discussed earlier, the crude version is clearly invalid whereas the more refined *Fisher* version is sufficiently qualified to defy clear-cut evaluation. The jury is simply not yet in on the new Friedman version for although it has already picked up impressive support, many economists of equal stature remain dubious.

As for the equations themselves, all three versions are, of course, valid as presented. Any one, then, is appropriate to use as a framework of the economy. Of the three, there seems little doubt that the cash balance version presented the relevant variables in a manner most conducive to later trailblazing developments in monetary theory. It is to the core of these developments that we turn in the next chapter.

10

The Simplified Theory of Income Determination

INTRODUCTION: THE CLASSICAL BACKDROP AND ITS OVERTHROW

Besides the quantity theory, classical economic theory (pre-1935) contained a body of reasoning which led many of its earlier followers to the belief that there existed, within a free enterprise economy, a mechanism that would swiftly, surely, and automatically restore full employment whenever the ugly spector of involuntary unemployment reared its head. Hence, the long cherished philosophy of *laissez faire*—let the economy alone.

The Classical Theory

The main mechanism involved was thought to be the rate of interest. Briefly, and in highly oversimplified form, the classical argument ran this way:

1. The very process of producing any given value of goods leads to an equivalent amount of income being earned by *someone* for producing them. (If $500 billion worth of goods are produced, $500 billion of income is earned for producing them.)

2. Ignoring government and foreign trade, the recipients of this income must dispose of it either by spending it to buy consumer goods or not spending it on consumer goods. If we define saving as income received, not spent on consumer goods, all income is either consumed or saved. (Suppose of the $500 billion income, $400 billion is spent on consumption and $100 billion is saved.)

3. What is needed to keep the following period's production at the same high $500 billion level is for everything produced this period to be sold. Demand, therefore, must total $500 billion.

4. The other element of demand, besides consumer expenditure, needed to be sure all $500 billion of goods are bought is investment spending—spending by business to buy newly produced capital goods. (In our example, if investment spending is $100 billion—equals saving—that, plus the $400 billion of consumer spending, will provide enough demand to buy everything produced. Note here that the condition needed to ensure enough demand to buy everything produced is for investment spending to equal saving.)

5. What is needed then is something that will cause investment spending to be as large as saving. The required mechanism is the rate of interest.

(a) The rate of interest is determined where the quantity of funds supplied by savers equals the quantity of funds demanded by investors.

(b) Since people only save money (refrain from consumption) in order to receive the reward of interest (hoarding is irrational) the quantity saved will be larger, the higher the interest rate. (The savings *schedule* will be positively sloped with respect to the rate of interest.)

(c) Since interest is one of the costs a businessman must incur in order to invest, the quantity invested will be larger, the lower the rate of interest. (The investment schedule will be negatively sloped with respect to the rate of interest.)

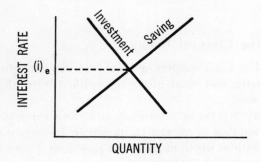

FIGURE 10-1

6. With this set-up (and assuming that the interest rate is a flexible price) a deficiency of demand to buy what has been produced cannot exist for long. For, if saving *should* exceed investment, the rate of interest will

be bid down, and this movement in the interest rate will at one and the same time expand the quantity invested and lower the quantity saved until the two come together.

Consequently, movements in the rate of interest will keep investment equal to saving which, in turn, guarantees that everything produced is bought so that producers need not lay off workers because of unsold inventories from this period's production.[1]

Keynes and His Attack on the Classicals

It was a rosy picture. But it was a bad theory, because it did not really "fit the facts." It did not accord with our experience in the "real world." Through the many years during which this theory dominated thinking there were challengers, some of them very important. But the final overthrow of the heart of the structure, at least in England and the United States, awaited the Great Depression of the 1930's and the publication of J. M. Keynes' General Theory of Employment, Interest and Money in 1936.

It did not take an economist to recognize, in the early 1930's, that something must be wrong with a theory that argues that full employment is the "norm," and unemployment simply a temporary interruption that will soon be automatically eliminated by movements in the interest rate. When upwards of one-fourth of the labor force is pounding the pavements seeking nonexistent jobs, the man on the street, being unencumbered with the niceties of any theory, saw clearly that something pretty fundamental was wrong. So, too, did the already famous British economist, John Maynard Keynes.

After a long struggle to break out of the well-worn track of classical reasoning, Keynes consolidated his new ideas into his now famous General Theory. In it he confessed that his work was the result of ". . . a struggle of escape from habitual thoughts and modes of expression. . . . The difficulty lies, not in the new ideas, but in escaping from the old ones, which ramify, for those brought up as most of us have been, into every corner of our minds."[2]

Keynes leaves no doubt about the purpose of his study. It is, on the one hand, to expose the fallacies of the classical theory and, on the other, to construct a new framework, a new theory, to replace it. No fence

[1] The above description of the classical ideas is admittedly highly oversimplified and should not, by any means, be taken as a complete evaluation. It is included here for pedagogical, rather than analytical reasons and it omits much of the classical argument, not the least of which is the assumption of flexible wages and prices.

[2] J. M. Keynes, General Theory of Employment, Interest and Money (London, Macmillan and Co., Ltd., 1936), p. viii.

straddler, he boldly states in his first chapter that the classical analysis is valid only in very special circumstances: ". . . which happen not to be those of the economic society in which we actually live, with the result that its teaching is misleading and disastrous if we attempt to apply it to the facts of experience."[3]

With this statement as a springboard, Keynes goes on to point out specific fallacies in the classical reasoning and to develop his own framework of analysis. It is essentially this framework that we call here the *modern* theory of income determination and to which we shall shortly turn.

Before doing so, it should be pointed out to the reader that the theory that will be developed in Chapters 10 through 13 should not be taken to be an exact reproduction of Keynes' *General Theory*. His famous volume is now over thirty years old and has had to weather the storm of controversy its author expected. As is true of all new ideas, substantial portions of what Keynes said have been deleted and many things he did not foresee, have been added. What we will be going through, then, is not *Keynes' theory* but what now has come to be accepted as an important, integral part of economic theory. We are concerned, not in evaluating Keynes, but in making use of his major contributions to our discipline.

One final word before proceeding. While the fact that Lord Keynes made the most vital contributions to the "modern" theory of income determination is hardly debatable, it would be less than just to leave the impression that his was the only voice raised in opposition to classical economics. Although many names might be mentioned, it seems clear that that of Knut Wicksell, a giant among the impressive list of outstanding Swedish economists, deserves a special place of honor. Written many years before the *General Theory*, Wicksell's work in many ways anticipates a great deal of the substance of what has since been referred to as the *Keynesian revolution*.

Let us now turn from the background and the developers of the "modern" theory of income determination to the theory itself.

THE GENERAL APPROACH

The *theory of income determination* is just what its name implies—an attempt to say something about how the level of income and production gets determined in a modern capitalistic economy. But its implications run deeper. If we can develop a theory that tells us how the level of production is determined, and what can make it change, we shall

3 *Ibid.*, p. 3.

be in a position to go further and say something about what determines the level of employment, prices, and the like. Our goal, then, is to develop a theoretical framework that will permit us to discuss, in an organized fashion, the factors that affect our ability to achieve the generally accepted economic goals of full production, full employment, and stable prices.

We start off with the rather common sense view that, since in a free enterprise economy, producers can only be expected to produce that which they can sell, the level of expenditures on newly produced goods and services is the main direct determinant of the level of production.[4]

Now as pointed out earlier, there are two alternative ways of looking at total expenditures on newly produced goods and services, or *aggregate demand* as we shall refer to it. One could take the so-called equation of exchange approach and break aggregate demand down into the components of M and V_y. Or, if it appears to provide a better insight into the causation involved, the alternative of subdividing total expenditures by spending group can be adopted. The "modern" theory of income determination is built around the latter alternative.

Simplifying Assumptions

To keep our analysis within manageable proportions, some simplifying assumptions are necessary. For the time being we will be talking about an economy in which the following complications are ruled out by assumption.

1. There are no exports or imports.
2. There is no business saving. (No retained earnings or depreciation allowances.)
3. All taxes are personal taxes and "lump sum." (Not related to the level of income and not withheld at the source.)
4. The government makes no transfer payments. (All its expenditures are for newly produced goods and services.)
5. Neither investment nor government spending is related to the level of income. (The size of each is determined "autonomously" —by something other than the level of income—and changes in the level of income do not affect the amount of either.)

Most of these assumptions will be dropped later, but for the moment, they are useful for simplifying the picture.

---

[4] This is, of course, a relatively short-run viewpoint. In the longer run one would have to consider not only the determinants of the level of aggregate demand but also the quantities and qualities of productive factors available and the state of technology. We are, in what follows, assuming these factors essentially fixed, thereby bypassing discussion of the area that has come to be called economic growth.

What are the effects of our assumptions? What is the nature of the economy with which we are dealing?

1. There are only three elements of aggregate demand—consumption, investment, and government spending. (The potential fourth, spending by foreigners, is ruled out.)
2. All income resulting from production is received by individuals (in the form of wages, rent, interest, or profits).
3. Since there are no taxes other than personal taxes, no government transfers and no corporate retained earnings or depreciation allowances, no distinction need be made between total production and income (GNP), net national product, national income, or personal income.[5]

Definitions and Symbols

In what follows, it is essential that the student be aware of the definitions and symbols of the terms being used. They are presented below.

1. *Consumption Expenditures* (C)—spending by households to buy newly produced consumer goods and services.

2. *Investment Expenditures* (I)—intentional spending, primarily by business, to buy newly produced capital goods and additions to inventory.

Note two things about this definition. In the first place, expenditures to buy already existing capital goods or to buy stocks and bonds (sometimes referred to as *financial investment*) are *not* a part of investment for our purposes. Secondly, increases in inventories which are not *intended* (that is, those that arise because of a disappointing sales experience) are

---

[5] We are also assuming that there is no social security tax. In fact, the relationship between these national aggregates, in a nonsimplified economy is:

$$
\begin{array}{ll}
& \text{Gross National Product} \\
& \quad minus \quad \text{Depreciation Allowances} \\
equals & \text{Net National Product} \\
& \quad minus \quad \text{Indirect Business Taxes} \\
equals & \text{National Income} \\
& minus \left\{ \begin{array}{l} \text{Social Security Taxes} \\ \text{Corporate Profits Taxes} \\ \text{Corporate Retained Earnings} \end{array} \right. \\
& plus \quad \text{Government Transfer Payments} \\
equals & \text{Personal Income}
\end{array}
$$

The reader should recognize that, by assumption, we have eliminated all difference between these four concepts so that any volume of total production (GNP) leads to an equal amount of income received by persons (PI).

Personal income, in our economy, provides the wherewithal to pay personal taxes, leaving income recipients with *disposable income*, which they can consume or save as they choose.

not a part of investment. To employ the terminology often used by economists, we are using investment in the *ex ante* (planned) sense rather than the *ex post* (actual) sense.[6]

3. *Government Expenditures* (G)—spending by government to purchase newly produced goods or services. This would include purchasing government goods from business firms, as well as purchasing the current productive services of government employees.

4. *Taxes* (T)—total collections of taxes by government from individuals.

5. *Saving* (S)—that portion of income received by individuals (Personal Income) which is neither paid in taxes nor spent on consumer goods during the period. (Alternatively, saving could be defined as "that portion of Disposable Income not spent on consumer goods during the period.")

It is extremely important that the reader recognize that we are defining saving negatively. Saving is not something individuals *do* with their income; it is something they *do not do*.

Perhaps the point can best be illustrated with an example. Suppose an individual receives $5,000 of income. Out of this he pays $800 in taxes and of the remaining $4,200, he chooses to spend $3,500 on consumer goods. By definition, his saving is $700. This is the amount of income he does *not* spend on taxes or consumption.

What *does* he do with the $700 we are calling saving? We do not know, but he may do *anything* with it except pay taxes or spend it on consumer goods. He may, for example, put it in his saving account at a bank. He may lend it to somebody in return for his IOU. He may use it to buy stocks and bonds. He may simply hoard it, either in a cookie jar at home or in a checking account at his bank. He may use it (although this is rare and should not lead the reader to any conclusions about the connection between saving and investment) to buy a piece of equipment for his business in which case he is both saving *and* investing. Or, to carry the illustration to absurd lengths, he may even *lose* the money. The point is, so long as he receives income which he *does not* use for taxes or consumption spending, no matter what he *does* do with it, that portion of his income is, *by definition*, saved.

6. *Total production* or *total income* (Y)—the total value of new goods and services produced during the period, or the total income received by individuals for production carried out during the period. (Alternatively this might be called GNP or PI. A third term often used in economics to refer to the production side of it is *aggregate supply*.)

---

[6] See the Appendix at the end of this chapter for a more extensive discussion of the *ex ante-ex post* relationships. We have previously used the term *investment* in Chapter 1, when we were referring to financial investment by financial intermediaries. From this point on, however, *investment* will be used only in the sense defined above.

7. *Disposable Income* (DI)—total income after taxes. It is all used for consumption spending or saving, by virtue of our definition of saving.

The Problem of Time

One of the thorniest conceptual problems in economics is the question of time periods. In fact, of course, production and the receipt of income from it are continuous processes not really divisible into finite time periods. It is convenient, nevertheless, to draw an arbitrary line to divide time into segments for purposes of our analysis.

The productive process into the "real world" rolls along something like this:

$$\text{production} \rightarrow \text{income} \rightarrow \text{spending} \rightarrow \text{production} \rightarrow$$
$$\text{income} \rightarrow \text{spending} \rightarrow \text{production, etc.}$$

In order to be able to talk in terms of finite time periods and avoid the use of the calculus, we shall arbitrarily break up this sequence in the following way:[7]

Period 1

$$\overbrace{\text{Production}_1 \rightarrow \text{Income}_1 \rightarrow \text{Spending}_1}$$

Period 2

$$\overbrace{\text{Production}_2 \rightarrow \text{Income}_2 \rightarrow \text{Spending}_2}$$

To identify the time period involved, we shall add subscripts to the symbols introduced above; C_1 means consumption spending in period 1, S_2 means saving in period 2, and so forth.

---

[7] Technically speaking we are relying on a "production lag" to separate our time periods. We shall be assuming that the production that takes place in period 2 is determined on the basis of sellers' experience during period 1. An alternative method would involve reliance on an "expenditure lag" wherein, as is indicated below.

Period 1

$$\overbrace{\text{Expend}_1 \rightarrow \text{Production}_1 \rightarrow \text{Income}_2}$$

Period 2

$$\overbrace{\text{Expend}_2 \rightarrow \text{Production}_2 \rightarrow \text{Income}_1}$$

income earners are assumed to be paid for work done in period 1 in that same period, but cannot use their income until the following period.

A More Detailed Conceptual Picture of the Production Process Over Time

Figure 10-2 below illustrates, in some detail, the conceptual framework of the productive process that we will be envisaging in the upcoming analysis.

Production in period 1 equals the income earned from production in period 1. That is simply to say that $500 billion worth of goods must lead to an equivalent amount of income having been earned by *someone* (including the owners of the business) for producing them. This income is then paid in taxes to the government, spent to buy consumer goods, or, by virtue of our definition of saving, saved.

$$Y_1 \equiv C_1 + S_1 + T_1$$

Now, still within period 1, the goods that have been produced are put up for sale. In our economy, the only spending to buy them must come from consumers, investors, or government.

$$\text{Aggregate Demand}_1 \equiv C_1 + I_1 + G_1$$

There is, of course, no reason why the level of spending in period 1 should be just sufficient to buy what has been produced during the period. That is, $C_1 + I_1 + G_1$ does *not* necessarily have to equal Y_1.

However, the experience of sellers in disposing of what they produced in period 1 will, of necessity, affect their decisions when determining the level of production of period 2.

THE CONDITIONS FOR STABLE, RISING, AND FALLING PRODUCTION

We are now in a position to state the conditions that will:
1. Cause production and income to rise from period 1 to period 2.
2. Cause production and income to fall from period 1 to period 2.
3. Cause production and income to stay the same in period 2 as they were in period 1.

The latter situation is a special one in economics, generally referred to as the *equilibrium* level of production and income. The meaning here is not really different from a whole host of equilibrium concepts used in the field: the equilibrium price, the equilibrium size of industry, equilib-

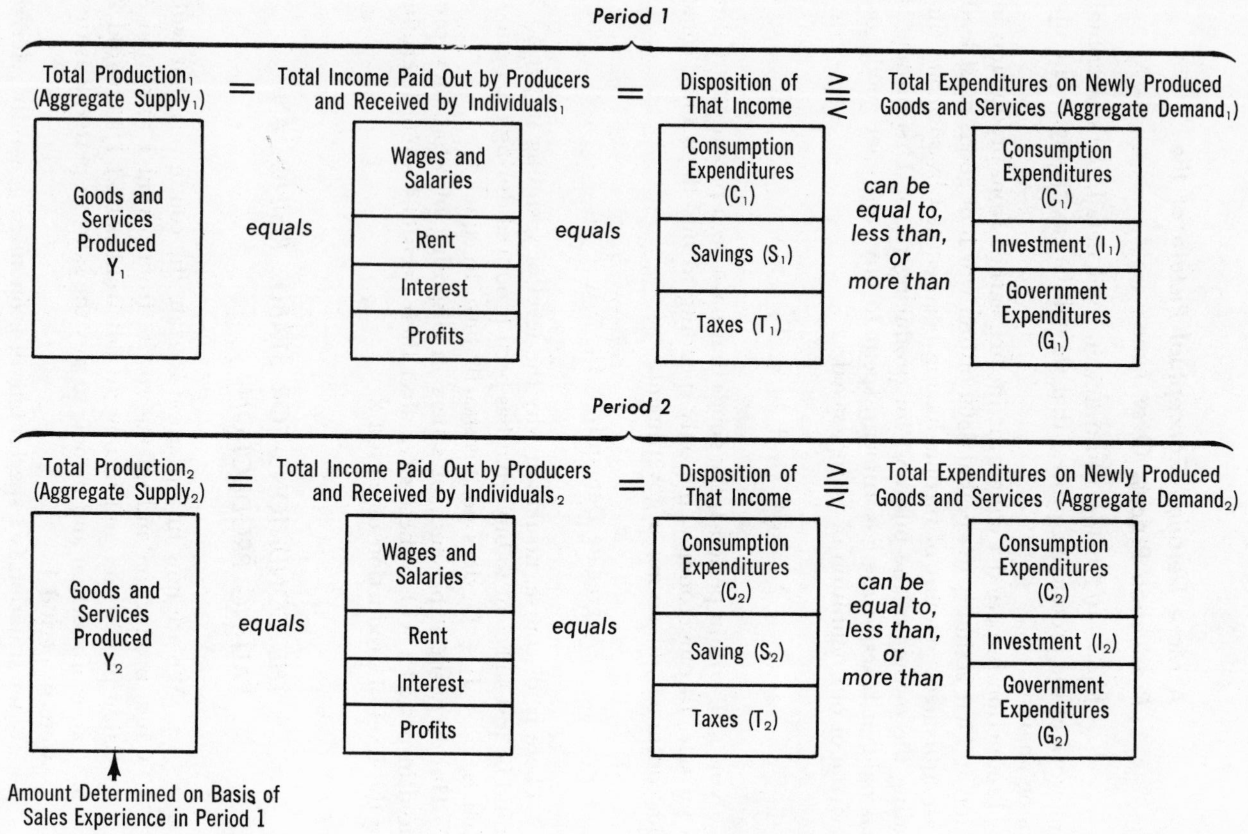

FIGURE 10-2 Conceptual Picture of Production Process

Period 1

Total Production₁ (Aggregate Supply₁) = Total Income Paid Out by Producers and Received by Individuals₁ = Disposition of That Income ≷ Total Expenditures on Newly Produced Goods and Services (Aggregate Demand₁)

Goods and Services Produced Y₁

equals

| Wages and Salaries |
| Rent |
| Interest |
| Profits |

equals

| Consumption Expenditures (C₁) |
| Savings (S₁) |
| Taxes (T₁) |

can be equal to, less than, or more than

| Consumption Expenditures (C₁) |
| Investment (I₁) |
| Government Expenditures (G₁) |

Period 2

Total Production₂ (Aggregate Supply₂) = Total Income Paid Out by Producers and Received by Individuals₂ = Disposition of That Income ≷ Total Expenditures on Newly Produced Goods and Services (Aggregate Demand₂)

Goods and Services Produced Y₂

Amount Determined on Basis of Sales Experience in Period 1

equals

| Wages and Salaries |
| Rent |
| Interest |
| Profits |

equals

| Consumption Expenditures (C₂) |
| Saving (S₂) |
| Taxes (T₂) |

can be equal to, less than, or more than

| Consumption Expenditures (C₂) |
| Investment (I₂) |
| Government Expenditures (G₂) |

rium in the Balance of Payments, to note a few. Equilibrium is a state of balance. It is a position *towards which* forces are pushing.[8] It is, finally, a position that once achieved, will tend to be maintained.

The Three Fundamental Conditions—Aggregate Demand and Aggregate Supply

What level of production, achieved in period 1, will tend to be maintained in the following period? The answer results from simple logic. It makes sense to argue that if the goods and services produced in period 1 are all sold to buyers (consumers, investors, and the government) during the period, producers have reason to be satisfied with period 1's production level and to continue it in the following period. If, in other words, aggregate demand in period 1 ($C_1 + I_1 + G_1$) just equals aggregate supply (the level of production), everything produced is bought. Producers' inventories neither rise because of a disappointing sales experience nor fall because of an unexpectedly heavy demand. There is, therefore, no reason to alter production schedules for the next period. The *equilibrium* level of production has been achieved.

But what if sales experience in period 1 is disappointing? What if aggregate demand during the period is *less* than enough to buy everything produced? If, for example, producers set their production schedules at a $500 billion level, but find that the three spending groups purchase only $450 billion of them, what then? If this is the case, producers find themselves with an unintended rise in their inventories amounting to $50 billion worth of unsold goods. It is certainly not difficult to predict the result. Production in period 2 will undoubtedly be scaled down to permit a "working off" of these excessive inventories. To employ the usual economic terms, if aggregate demand is *less* than aggregate supply during period 1, period 2's production can be expected to be cut below that of period 1.

Finally, what is to be expected if demand exceeds producers' expectations? What if $500 billion of goods and services are produced in period 1, but buyers purchase $550 billion? Such an experience is a happy one for sellers, who find they have sold, not only everything produced during the period but $50 billion more out of their inventories on hand. The only logical response to this "seller's market" situation is to raise production schedules in the following period to meet the higher demand and, perhaps, to build inventories back up to the desired size.

[8] This, at least, is true of a stable equilibrium position, which is the only case we shall consider.

We have, then, three conditions:

1. Condition for stable production as between periods 1 and 2 (the equilibrium condition)—when aggregate demand₁ *equals* aggregate supply₁
2. Condition for rising production as between periods 1 and 2—when aggregate demand₁ *exceeds* aggregate supply₁
3. Condition for falling production as between periods 1 and 2—when aggregate demand₁ *is less than* aggregate supply₁

The Three Fundamental Conditions—$S + T$ and $I + G$

Now it is sometimes useful to state these three conditions in a different way. The student should learn both, but it is of great importance that he remember that they are simply alternative ways of saying the same thing. The logic—the "why"—of the three conditions, however they are stated, remains the same as that discussed above.

Let us use a numerical example to illustrate the alternative approach to our basic conditions. Suppose production in period 1 (aggregate supply) is $500 billion. It is then definitionally true that total income earned is $500 billion. It is also definitionally true that the sum of $C_1 + S_1 + T_1$ is $500 billion, because of our concept of saving. Finally, let us suppose that taxes equal $70 billion, and consumption spending $380 billion so that saving, by definition, is $50 billion. We have, then, a situation such as is depicted below:

Production (Aggregate Supply₁) $500 billion	≡	Income Earned₁ $500 billion	≡	C_1 $+$ S_1 $+$ T_1	$380 billion 50 billion 70 billion
					$500 billion

Since $C_1 + S_1 + T_1$ is, by definition, always equal to aggregate supply in period 1, there is no reason why we cannot use the former total, rather than the latter, in our fundamental conditions. And, since aggregate demand in period 1 is nothing but the sum of expenditures by the three spending groups, it is optional whether we use the total figure and call it aggregate demand or the sum of its components, $C_1 + I_1 + G_1$.

We can, then restate our fundamental conditions in the following way:

1. Condition for stable production as between periods 1 and 2—when $C_1 + I_1 + G_1 = C_1 + S_1 + T_1$
2. Condition for rising production as between periods 1 and 2—when $C_1 + I_1 + G_1 > C_1 + S_1 + T_1$

3. Condition for falling production as between periods 1 and 2—
when $C_1 + I_1 + G_1 < C_1 + S_1 + T_1$

Indeed, we can go one step further. Recognizing that the same quantity on each side of an equality or inequality sign can be dropped without altering the sense of our statements, we can eliminate consumption spending from the above and end up with:

1. Equilibrium condition $\rightarrow I_1 + G_1 = S_1 + T_1$
2. Condition for rising production $\rightarrow I_1 + G_1 > S_1 + T_1$
3. Condition for falling production $\rightarrow I_1 + G_1 < S_1 + T_1$

One fact here can hardly be overemphasized. The student who commits these three conditions to memory without taking the slight time and trouble required to understand their common-sense logic is doing himself a great disservice. If he does not "see" that the condition $I_1 + G_1 > S_1 + T_1$ is simply another way of expressing the condition aggregate demand exceeds aggregate supply, which, in turn, is simply the economist's way of saying more was bought than was produced, he is missing, at the outset, the fundamental common sense logic of the entire theory of income determination. If he simply memorizes, he ends up with a strictly mechanistic picture of our theory which bars him from a true appreciation of its value. He is likely to be the student who, because of his lack of comprehension of the basic cornerstone of the entire theoretical apparatus, refers scornfully to this portion of the theory as being too mechanical and inapplicable to the so-called "real world." He who does has very likely missed the point at the very beginning.

At the risk of belaboring the obvious, let us resort to a numerical example to illustrate, once again, the logic involved. Suppose, as before, total production in period 1 equals $500 billion and that taxes are $70 billion and consumption spending $380 billion. Then, as before:

Total Production₁ (Aggregate Supply₁)		Total Income Earned₁		Disposition of Income Earned	= > <	Total Expenditures (Aggregate Demand₁)
$500 billion	=	$500 billion	=	C₁ $380 billion		C₁ $380 billion
				+		+
				S₁ $ 50		I₁ ?
				+		+
				T₁ $ 70		G₁ ?
				$500 billion		

Now aggregate demand during period 1 is composed of $380 billion of consumer spending plus investment and government spending. Suppose I_1 equals \$45 billion and G_1 equals \$75 billion. Then $I_1 + G_1 = S_1 + T_1$ *and* aggregate demand is just enough to equal aggregate supply. Everything produced is bought, no more and no less.[9]

If, however, I_1 should be \$50 billion and G_1, \$75 billion, $I_1 + G_1$ exceeds $S_1 + T_1$ by \$5 billion, and aggregate demand exceeds aggregate supply by the same \$5 billion. Producer's inventories are drawn down by \$5 billion providing the impetus for an increase in production next period.

Finally, what if I_1 equals \$45 billion and G_1, \$70 billion? Then $I_1 + G_1$ is \$5 billion *less* than $S_1 + T_1$ and aggregate demand is \$5 billion less than aggregate supply. Consequently, \$5 billion of goods produced in period 1 go unsold and it is this unwelcomed increase in producers' inventories which motivates a cutback in the new period's production.

THE DETERMINANTS OF CONSUMPTION SPENDING AND THE CONSUMPTION SCHEDULE

It is one thing to know that when $I + G > S + T$, production should logically rise. It is quite another, and more difficult question, to ask *how much* production will rise. In order to deal with this question we must look behind the figure we have thus far simply assumed for consumption spending, to its determinants.

The Determinants of Consumption Spending

It is not difficult to amass a rather imposing list of factors which help to determine the level of consumer spending. Among the most important are the following:

1. *Level of Disposable Income.* Clearly, the most important of all is the amount of income earned and available *to* spend. Both as a matter of common sense, and as a result of extensive statistical investigation, there can be no doubt that this is a major, indeed *the* major, determinant. But it is not the only one.

2. *Consumer expectations regarding future prices, incomes, and availability of goods.* A rational man who confidently expects future prices to be higher, will have a strong incentive to spend a larger percentage of his income on consumer goods now, while prices are still relatively low, than he would in the absence of such an expectation.

Similarly, a man who expects his income to be higher in future years,

---

[9] The student should note that equilibrium does *not* require that $I_1 = S_1$ or that $G_1 = T_1$. The only requirement is that the *sum* of I and G equal the *sum* of S and T.

would be quite within the bounds of logic to spend a larger percentage of his income on consumption now, than he would if he did *not* expect higher future incomes.

And finally, if people expect, as appears to have been the case at the start of the Korean War, that, because of wartime priorities, such things as automobile tires and consumer durables may not be freely available for some years, they are motivated by their personal self-interest (if not by patriotic fervor) to "stock up" now on those consumer goods they expect to need.

3. *Real value of consumers' liquid wealth.* Other things equal the man (or society) who possesses a large amount of liquid wealth will be free to spend a larger percentage of his income on consumption than would be the case if he needed to build up, via saving, a contingency reserve fund.

4. *Community's present stock of consumer durables.* Presumably the greater the stock of consumer durables now held by the public, and the newer they are, the less need for consumers to buy more. This, then, would be a negative variable, causing consumption spending to vary inversely to it, other things being equal.

5. *Social customs and attitudes toward saving.* Other things being equal, the attitude of the public toward the virtues of saving will certainly matter. One would expect, for example, a community whose social mores classify savings as a highly ranked virtue, to spend less on consumption than another community similar in all respects except this sociopsychological bent toward saving.

The Consumption Schedule Defined

Like almost all economic variables, consumption spending is affected by many factors. Yet if we are to deal with consumption analytically, we must devise a method of expressing these many interrelationships in a simplified manner. The method used is that of the consumption schedule (or function).

A community's consumption schedule presents *the amounts that will be spent on consumption at all possible levels of income, other factors being considered given.*

Let us once again resort to an example. Suppose we have taken a survey of the American people asking each citizen the following question: "Assuming that your expectations, wealth, ownership of consumer durables, and attitudes toward saving stay as they are today, how much will you spend to buy consumer goods if your income is 0, $100, $200, $300, $400, $500, or $600?" If we total up the responses received, we could easily draw up a table such as is depicted below.

Possible Levels of Disposable Income	Consumption Expenditures
$ 0	$ 50
100	100
200	150
300	200
400	250
500	300
600	350

Such a table, assuming that our survey elicited valid responses of what people *would* spend on consumption at various income levels *is* a consumption schedule (or consumption *function*).

If it seems strange to single out one determinant of consumption, income, and hold all the others "fixed," the student is asked to recall the concept of the market demand for a good. Whereas the quantity of a good consumers are willing and able to take depends not only upon its price but also upon consumer tastes, incomes, the prices of related goods, and the like, the demand curve we use generally assumes all the determinants except price fixed and then shows the relation between price and the quantity demanded. A change in any of the determinants other than price, we say, will shift the demand curve itself.

This concept, first introduced in the case of market demand, is precisely paralleled by the consumption schedule. Here, too, we select the one determinant that seems most important and assume the others fixed. Here, too, a change in the main variable (income) will lead to a different amount consumed but will not change the consumption schedule itself. This is perfectly analogous to a change in price changing the quantity demanded but not shifting the demand curve itself. It will be well worth the reader's time to think through the similarities in these two important economic tools before proceeding.

Methods of Expressing a Nation's Consumption Schedule

Assuming that we have made our survey and have figures on the responses received, there are three basic methods for expressing them as a consumption schedule. We can, as we have already done, report them in tabular form; we can show the same figures geometrically in a line; or we can express the relationship algebraically in an equation.

A Table to Express the Consumption Schedule—The APC, APS, MPC, and MPS

Let us once again assume that we have made the necessary survey and have totaled up the responses given. The result, as before, is:

1 Possible Levels of Disposable Income	2 Consumption Expenditures	3 Savings
$ 0	$ 50	$ —50
100	100	0
200	150	+50
300	200	100
400	250	150
500	300	200
600	350	250

As indicated before, columns 1 and 2 constitute the community's consumption schedule. Similarly, columns 1 and 3, reflecting as they do, the amount that will be saved at all possible levels of income, make up a *savings schedule*.

If one already has all the figures that make up the consumption and savings schedule, he needs nothing else for a full picture. However, there are several expressions that partially reflect the *nature* of the relation between income and consumption and saving which may be used to describe that relationship. These are the average propensity to consume, the average propensity to save, the marginal propensity to consume and the marginal propensity to save.

1. *Average Propensity to Consume.* This may be defined as "consumption expressed as a fraction of income." In the above example, the figures are such that the APC is different at each level of income. For instance, when income is $200, the APC is $150/$200 = ¾; when income is $400, the APC is $250/$400 = ⅝; when income is $600, the APC is $350/$600 = ⁷⁄₁₂.

2. *Average Propensity to Save.* The APS is "saving expressed as a fraction of income." It too, changes as income changes, becoming larger the higher the income level. It is ⅓ when income is $300; ⅜ when income is $400; ⅖ when income is $500; and ⁵⁄₁₂ when income is $600.

Note that, since by virtue of our definition of saving, all disposable income must either be spent on consumption or saved:

$$APC + APS = 1$$

3. *Marginal Propensity to Consume.* The MPC is a more important concept for our analysis than the APC. It is defined as "the *change in* consumption expressed as a fraction of any *change* in income."

We have chosen figures for our numerical example which, unlike the APC, result in the same MPC at all income levels. Although it is probable that, in fact, there is a slight decline in the economy's MPC as income rises, the above assumption is close enough to reality for our purposes and it possesses the virtue of greatly simplifying the analysis. We shall therefore maintain this assumption of a constant MPC in all future examples.

For the consumption schedule given, the MPC at all levels of income is ½, since every $100 *change* in income leads to a $50 *change* in consumption spending in the same direction. The student should check the figures to verify this for himself.

4. *Marginal Propensity to Save.* The MPS is definable as "the *change in* saving expressed as a fraction of any *change in* income." This too, in our example, is ½ at all income levels—each $100 increase (or decrease) in income calling forth a $50 increase (decrease) in saving.

The relation between the MPC and the MPS, as that between the APC and the APS, is such that their sum equals unity:

$$MPC + MPS = 1$$

This, of course, is because any *addition to* income must, by virtue of the saving definition, lead either to *added* consumption or *added* saving.

Graphical Representation of Consumption and Saving Schedules

The data provided above can also be represented graphically. The consumption schedule (or function) can be plotted in a two-dimensional diagram, as in Figure 10-3.

With expenditures on the vertical axis and income on the horizontal, each dot in Figure 10-3 represents the amount of consumption spending at a particular level of income. When the dots are joined by the line we have labeled C, we have a graphical representation of the community's consumption schedule.

For those who are geometrically minded it may be helpful to point out that the slope of C function *is* the MPC; therefore, the steeper the C

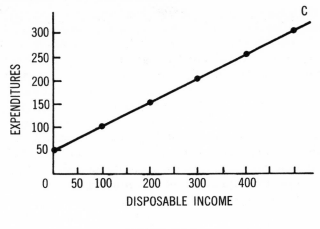

FIGURE 10-3

function the larger the community's MPC (and conversely the smaller its MPS).

The same thing may be done for the savings schedule, except that here the vertical axis represents saving rather than consumption spending.

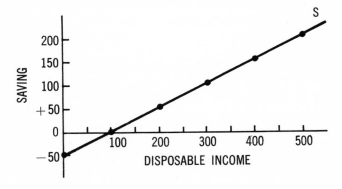

FIGURE 10-4

Here again, the slope of the Savings function represents the MPS. The line starts below the horizontal axis because, as the figures presented earlier indicate, saving is negative when income is zero. For the same reason the C function starts at the positive amount of $50, when income is zero.

Algebraic Representation of Consumption and Saving Schedules

Finally, the relationship between consumption and income can be stated algebraically. The straight line in Figure 10-3 and the figures in tabular form can equally well be expressed by the equation:

$$C_1 = .5DI + 50$$

Such an equation is merely a third way of representing the facts contained in the consumption schedule we are discussing. The student should verify for himself the fact that when any of the income levels given earlier are plugged into this equation, the resulting figure for consumption is the same as that from the table. In such an equation, the constant term (50, in our example) is always the amount of consumption spending when disposable income is zero and the coefficient of the disposable income variable (.5, in our example) is always the marginal propensity to consume.

CHANGES IN THE EQUILIBRIUM LEVEL OF PRODUCTION: THE MULTIPLIER CONCEPT

A Numerical Example

Earlier, we showed that when $I + G > S + T$ (that is, aggregate demand exceeds aggregate supply) production and income must rise. We are now prepared to tackle that more difficult question of *how much* production and income will rise before equilibrium ($I + G = S + T$) is restored.

The answer is inherently tied in with the consumption function concept just discussed. That is, *because* consumption spending gets bigger when income rises, and *because* consumption spending is a part of aggregate demand requiring further rises in production and income, any initial rise in spending, such as investment or government spending, will set off a whole chain of events in the economy which will raise production and income by some *multiple* of the original increase.

Perhaps a numerical example with two economies is the best way to make the point. Suppose we look, simultaneously, at two different economies, A and B, in Tables 10-1 and 10-2.

It may help, at this point, to recall the simplifying assumptions under which we are working. Total production (aggregate supply) churns out an equal amount of income. This income is partly dispersed in the payment of taxes (which are assumed to be a fixed amount, not varying with

TABLE 10-1   Economy A (MPC = ½)

1 Possible Levels of Production (Aggregate Supply) (GNP)	2 "Lump Sum" Taxes Collected	3 Possible Levels of Disposable Income (1-2)	4 Consump- tion Ex- penditures	5 Saving (3-4)	6 Investment Spending	7 Govern- ment Spending
100	50	50	100	−50	45	55
200	50	150	150	0	45	55
300	50	250	200	50	45	55
400	50	350	250	100	45	55
500	50	450	300	150	45	55
600	50	550	350	200	45	55

income). The amount left after taxes is disposable income, which house-holds either consume or save. The amount they choose to spend on consumption, together with investment and government spending, makes up aggregate demand. Consequently, for Economics A and B above, column 1 is aggregate supply and the sum of columns 4, 6, and 7 is aggregate demand.

To determine the equilibrium level of production in Economy A we can either find the place where aggregate demand just equals aggregate supply or employ the equivalent alternative of locating the point where I + G = S + T. The student should verify for himself the fact that

TABLE 10-2   Economy B (MPC = ¾)

1 Possible Levels of Production (Aggregate Supply) (GNP)	2 "Lump Sum" Taxes Collected	3 Possible Levels of Disposable Income (1-2)	4 Consump- tion Ex- penditures	5 Saving (3-4)	6 Investment Spending	7 Govern- ment Spending
100	50	50	75	−25	45	55
200	50	150	150	0	45	55
300	50	250	225	25	45	55
400	50	350	300	50	45	55
500	50	450	375	75	45	55
600	50	550	450	100	45	55

Economy A's equilibrium level is $300. Note also that at any level of production less than $300, more will be bought than is produced, while at any production level above $300, there will not be enough spending to purchase everything turned out.

In Economy B, for precisely the same reasons, the equilibrium level of production is $400. In this case also, any level of output less than $400 will be faced with a demand that absorbs more than the amount produced, whereas a production level of over $400 will be so high that the spending propensities in the economy will not be enough to buy it all.

Finally, it should be noted that the two economies are exactly alike in all but one respect—their consumption functions. The citizens of Economy B are clearly the "bigger spenders" with a marginal propensity to consume of ¾, rather than the ½ that is the case for Economy A. The explanation for this difference is to be found in the other, *nonincome* determinants of consumption discussed in the previous section.

Graphical Presentation of the Same Data

While we are about it, let us see how the above data for Economies A and B might be depicted graphically. Figure 10-5 refers to Economy A, while Figure 10-6 is for Economy B.

In both diagrams, the elements of Aggregate Demand (C, I, and G) are measured off vertically, and the level of income earned appears on the

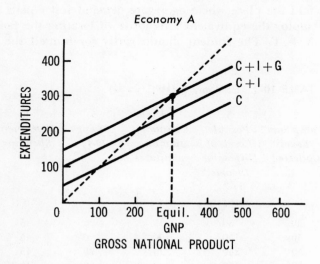

FIGURE 10-5

horizontal axis. The line labeled C in each is the consumption function that corresponds to the data from columns 1 and 4 in Tables 10-2 and 10-3. It should be noted that what is plotted here is the relation between consumption spending and GNP, not that between consumption and disposable income. The line labeled C + I results from adding the amount of investment spending (here, $45 at all levels of income)[10] to the amount of consumer spending at each income level. The C + I + G, or aggregate

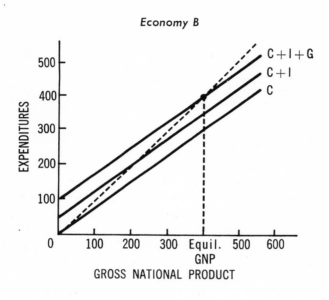

Economy B

FIGURE 10-6

demand line, is computed by adding the $55 of government spending to the C + I total at each level of income. The dashed 45° line is the locus of all points equidistant from the two axes. Since one axis measures aggregate supply and the other aggregate demand, it should be clear the 45° line contains all points of equilibrium.

There is, in each graph, only one level of production which satisfies the conditions for equilibrium. That is where the C + I + G (aggregate demand) line crosses (equals) the 45° line. Here, and only here, the amount being produced is all bought by spenders. Here, and only here, aggregate demand equals aggregate supply.

[10] Our assumption that investment spending is the same at all possible levels of income is equivalent to denying the existence of an "accelerator" in these economies.

The Multiplier, Initiated by a Rise in Investment

Now suppose each of our two economies has reached the equilibrium level of production—A at $300 and B at $400. What effect will a $50 rise (to $95) in the level of investment spending have?[11]

The initial impact is obvious. In each economy, aggregate demand will, in the first instance, exceed aggregate supply by $50. That is, Economy A will find that its $300 aggregate supply encounters a $350 aggregate demand, while in Economy B the $400 of goods turned out will be met by $450 worth of spending. In both cases, inventories will be drawn down and therefore production in the following period can be expected to rise.

The question we are concerned with here is—"by *how much* must the level of production rise before it reaches a new equilibrium level?"

The Multiplier Process

It is not difficult, with the aid of Tables 10-2 and 10-3 to determine the new equilibrium levels for Economies A and B. If, in Economy A, investment rises to $95 and government spending remains at $55, their total is $150 and equilibrium requires that saving plus taxes (remember, equilibrium is where $I + G = S + T$) also equals $150. Such a position is only reached when production has risen by $100, to $400. Similarly, in Economy B, when the sum of investment and government spending rises to $150, what is needed to restore equilibrium is a rise in $S + T$ to the same point. This would require a rise there by $200, to a new equilibrium production level of $600.

Because a $50 rise in investment forces production up by $100 in Economy A, we say the "multiplier" for that country is *two*. Because a $50 rise in investment spending leads to a $200 rise in Economy B's equilibrium level of output, we say that the multiplier for that nation is *four*.

But this is all too automatic. Simply reading results from tables does nothing to make clear the logical causation involved in the *process* by which production is forced up. We need to take the time to ferret out the economic logic involved before turning the whole thing into what too many look upon as sterile arithmetic. We need, in other words, to deal with the "whys" of the multiplier process. *Why* does production in Country A rise by double the initial rise in investment? *Why* does production

[11] The reader should note that we are referring to a permanent rise in the level of investment, not a one period rise. The assumption is that investment rises to $95 and stays there rather than falling back to $45 in the following period. Also, we are assuming all other things remain unchanged.

Agg Sys (GNP) = C + I + G

in Country B rise by twice as much as that in Country A? Why and what is the process that we refer to as the multiplier?

Let us concentrate first on Country A. If the only change in spending propensities which takes place is a $50 rise in investment, why is a $50 rise in production not sufficient to restore equilibrium?

TABLE 10-3   The Movement Toward Equilibrium of Economy A (MPC = ½)

	Time Period						New Equilibrium
	1	2	3	4	5		
Production and Income	$300	$300	$350	$375	$387.50	→	$400
C	200	200	225	237.50	243.75	→	250
I	45	95	95	95	95	→	95
G	55	55	55	55	55	→	55
T	50	50	50	50	50	→	50
S	50	50	75	87.50	93.75	→	100

Table 10-3 provides us with a period-by-period picture of the multiplier process. Within each time period it is assumed that the total income earned from production is all disposed of by paying taxes, spending on consumption, and saving. Secondly, it is assumed that the level of aggregate demand (sum of C, I, and G in any period) determines the level of production in the following period. That is, we are assuming that producers always adjust their production levels to the level of the *previous* period's demand.[12]

In period one the production of $300 is met by an equivalent aggregate demand so that there is no apparent reason for changing production levels in period 2. As between periods 1 and 2, Economy A is at equilibrium. In period 2, the $300 of earned income is again split between taxes ($50), consumption ($200), and saving ($50). But in this period, investors suddenly decide they want to increase their purchases of capital goods from the old level of $45 to the higher level of $95. Thus, aggregate demand in period two turns out to be $350, while production was only $300 (I + G > S + T by $50). Consequently, inventories of sellers in period 2 are drawn down and we expect them to raise production in the follow-

[12] This is not the only possible assumption or even necessarily the most likely one, but *some* assumption must be made. The fact is, that whether or not producers anticipate by raising production to a *higher* level than the previous period's demand, the final equilibrium level is unchanged. We adopt this assumption simply as the most convenient available one for purposes of exposition.

ing period. By assumption, we take the amount of this production rise to be $50 so that production (and income earned from production) in period 3 is $350.

Up to this point, the multiplier process has not entered the picture. But it begins to show up in period 3. Here, $50 of added income is earned and, since we assume taxes do not rise, it is all available to recipients as disposable income to spend on consumption or save. How do they split this new income? The *marginal* propensity to consume of $\frac{1}{2}$ tells us that half of it will be spent on consumption and half will be saved. Consequently, consumption spending in period 3 rises by $25 to $325 and saving goes up to $75. The result (of the additional consumption spending) is that once again aggregate demand ($375) exceeds aggregate supply ($350). The $50 rise in production which took place in period three was not enough to restore equilibrium because demand, in the form of added consumer spending, rose still higher. This is the heart of the multiplier idea.

Assuming, once again, that producers react to the disequilibrium of period 3 by raising period 4's production by the amount of the excess demand experienced in period 3, production will go up to $375. Once again, however, the $25 of added income earned as a result of this production boost leads to a $12.50 rise in consumption and an equal rise in saving. Aggregate demand in period four is thus $387.50 while aggregate supply was only $375.

There is no need to carry the discussion further. The point is that, via some such process, *production must keep on rising until it is so high that the sum of taxes and saving is high enough to equal the higher level of I + G.*

The multiplier effects show up in periods 4, 5, 6, 7, etc., where production is pushed up beyond the $350 level, because the added income earned from additional production leads to additional consumption spending. The multiplier then results entirely from the fact that a rise in production leads to a rise in income which, leads to a rise in consumer spending which, in turn, causes production to be raised further in the following period, etc.

Table 10-4 provides the same period-by-period picture of the rise to the new equilibrium in Economy B. Why is the multiplier larger in this case? Why does production rise further before reaching the new equilibrium? Because here, consumers who get added income spend a larger portion of it, thus adding more to aggregate demand in each period and consequently, more to production. Or, to approach it from the other direction, saving rises less rapidly here as income rises (the MPS is smaller). Since equilibrium requires that saving rise by enough to offset (equal) the higher level of investment that started it all, the lower the propensity

$C = 0.75$
$mpc = 0.75$
$mps = 0.25$

TABLE 10-4   The Movement Toward Equilibrium of Economy B (MPC = ¾)

	Time Period						New Equilibrium
	1	2	3	4	5		
Production and Income	$400	$400	$450	$487.50	$515.60	→	$600
C	300	300	337.50	365.60	386.70	→	450
I	45	95	95	95	95	→	95
G	55	55	55	55	55	→	55
T	50	50	50	50	50	→	50
S	50	50	62.50	71.90	78.90	→	100

to save the greater the rise in income required to "call forth" the necessary amount of saving.

The multiplier, and its workings can also be visualized in graphical terms as Figures 10-7 and 10-8 indicate. In each of these graphs the rise in investment spending is indicated by the vertical distance between the $C + I_1 + G$ line (where $I_1 = \$45$) and the $C + I_2 + G$ line (where $I_2 = \$95$). The change in the equilibrium level of production and income is the horizontal distance between GNP_1 and GNP_2 which, in turn, are located by the point where $C + I_1 + G$ and $C + I_2 + G$ cross the 45°

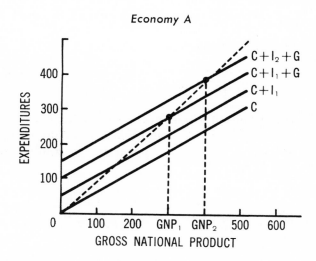

FIGURE 10-7

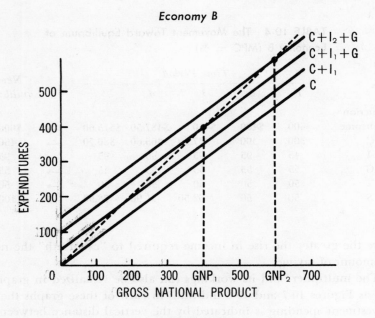

FIGURE 10-8

line. The multiplier is the horizontal distance between GNP_1 and GNP_2 in each case, divided by the vertical distance between $C + I_1 + G$ and $C + I_2 + G$.

Multiplier Definitions

It is one thing to understand and be able to describe the multiplier *process*. It is quite another to define and compute the multiplier itself.

An adequate definition of the multiplier would appear to be: "The multiplier is a number that, when multiplied times any original change in aggregate demand, gives you the change in the equilibrium level of income and production."

That is:

$$\text{Multiplier} \times \begin{array}{l} \text{Any Original} \\ \text{Change in Aggregate} \\ \text{Demand} \end{array} = \begin{array}{l} \text{Change in} \\ \text{Equilibrium Level} \\ \text{of Production} \end{array}$$

Or

$$\text{Multiplier} = \frac{\text{Change in Equilibrium Level of Production}}{\text{Any original change in Aggregate Demand}}$$

It should be noted that the multiplier is reversible. Any *decline* in aggregate demand can set off a multiplied *decline* in output for the reverse reasons.

Computing the Multiplier

The examples of the workings of the multiplier process in Economies A and B should have made it clear that the *size* of the multiplier in any economy is inherently tied up with the marginal propensity to consume and save in the economy.

To be more specific the size of the multiplier may always be determined by use of the formula:

$$\frac{1}{1 - \text{MPC}}$$

In an economy such as the one we are dealing with here, where taxes are not related to income, we can also compute the multiplier from the expression:

$$\frac{1}{\text{MPS}}$$

Either expression is simply the mathematical formula for adding up an infinite series where each addition to the series (of added production) is a fixed percentage (the MPC) of the previous addition.[13]

These formulas cannot be applied indiscriminately. In the simplified cases we are working with up to now, the assumption that taxes do not vary as income varies is crucial. It has the effect of avoiding any variance between the MPC out of disposable income and the MPC out of GNP, thereby leaving saving as the only "leakage" to be considered when

---

[13] The general expression, if b is used to represent the MPC, is: (1) Change in Production = Original Change in Spending $(1 + b + b^2 + b^3 \ldots + b^n)$; multiplying both sides by b, we have (2) b change in production = Original Change in Spending $(b + b^2 + b^3 + b^4 \ldots + b^n + b^{n+1})$; subtracting 2 from 1, we have (3) $(1 - b)$ Change in Production = Original Change in Spending $(1 - b^{n+1})$; if b is less than 1, b^{n+1} becomes infinitely small in infinity and we are left with (4) $(1 - b)$ Change in Production = Original Change in Spending, or

$$\frac{\text{Change in Production}}{\text{Original Change in Spending}} = \frac{1}{1 - b}$$

See Barger, *Money, Banking and Public Policy*, Rand McNally & Company (1962), p. 346. This, incidentally, is precisely the same formula used for determining the maximum possible increase in demand deposits for the system as a whole when there is no cash on time deposits.

GNP rises. If we were dealing with the more realistic case where taxes are based on income and rise as it does, the expression for the multiplier would be:

$$\frac{1}{1 - \text{MPC out of GNP}}$$

The reciprocal of the marginal propensity to save would *not* provide the actual multiplier because, in such a situation, not only saving, but also taxes act as a drag on the expansion of production.[14]

The Multiplier, Initiated by a Rise in Government Spending

Perhaps it is unnecessary to make the point specifically, but the student should keep in mind that the multiplier is a *general* concept. The multiplier process can just as readily be set off by a rise in government spending as by a rise in investment and a cut in government spending may initiate the same sort of downward multiplied spiral as a cut in investment.

Referring once again to the numerical examples of Economies A and B, a $50 rise in government spending, rather than in investment, would, other things being equal, lead to the same final results. The only difference for Economy A would be that $50 of the $100 rise would be accounted for by government, rather than investment spending. The same may be said of the $200 rise in Country B. A student can hardly understand the theory underlying fiscal policy until he recognizes the part the multiplier process plays in it

The Multiplier, Initiated by an Upward Shift in the Consumption Function

It was pointed out earlier that there are a number of determinants of consumption, including not only income but wealth, stock of consumer durables, consumer expectations, and the like. The latter are assumed constant when any consumption function is drawn and a change in any of them shifts the level of the consumption function.

Clearly, consumption spending can rise, either because income has risen permitting increased consumption or because one of the other determinants has changed leading to greater consumption spending out of the

[14] The expression $1/(1 - \text{MPC out of GNP})$ is equivalent to $1/[1 - \text{MPC out of DI}$ (Tax rate as percentage of GNP)] or $1/(\text{MPS out of GNP} + \text{Tax rate as percentage of GNP})$.

same income. It would be convenient to be able to distinguish verbally between these two possibilities.

Such a distinction is possible with the aid of the familiar economic terms, *autonomous* and *induced*. An induced change in consumption spending may be defined as *a change in consumption spending which is caused by a rise in income*. The multiplier effect is solely a result of induced consumption spending.

On the other hand, an increase in consumption spending which occurs because of an upward shift of the consumption function itself (which has, in turn, been caused by changes in consumer expectations, wealth, and so forth) may be referred to as an autonomous rise in consumption.

Perhaps, once again, the distinction can be made clear with an example. Suppose we are dealing with a country in which, at the moment, the consumption function is:

Income	Consumption
$ 0	$ 50
100	100
200	150
300	200
400	250
500	300
600	350

If, because of a rise in investment or government spending, income should be increased, consumption spending would also rise. Such an increase would be an induced rise in consumption caused by a movement along a given consumption function.

On the other hand, if consumer expectations should change so that the entire consumption function is raised, as below, the $50 rise in consumption spending is autonomous.

Income	Consumption (Before Change in Expectations)	Consumption (After Change in Expectations)
$ 0	$ 50	$100
100	100	150
200	150	200
300	200	250
400	250	300
500	300	350
600	350	400

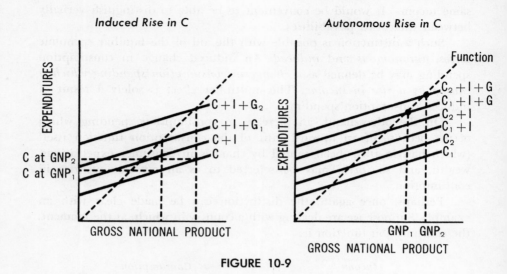

FIGURE 10-9

Now while induced changes in consumption *are* the heart of the multiplier process, autonomous changes in consumption can, exactly like investment and government spending, *set off* the multiplier. Suppose we illustrate, by assuming an economy whose equilibrium is upset by an upward shift of the consumption function itself from $C = \frac{1}{2}GNP + \$50$ in period 1 to $C = \frac{1}{2}GNP + \$100$ in period 2.

Table 10-5 and Figure 10-10 show the result. In period 1, equilibrium has been achieved. In period 2, however, there is an autonomous rise in consumption by \$50 which is the result of an upward shift of the consumption function itself.

TABLE 10-5 Movement Toward Equilibrium After Rise in Level of Consumption Function

	Time Period						New
	1	*2*	*3*	*4*	*5*		*Equilibrium*
Production and (GNP) Income	\$300	\$300	\$350	\$375	\$387.50	→	\$400
C	200	250	275	287.50	293.75	→	300
I	45	45	45	45	45	→	45
G	55	55	55	55	55	→	55
T	50	50	50	50	50	→	50
S	50	0	25	37.50	43.75	→	50

This autonomous rise in consumer spending then, leads into the same multiplied expansion as before. The rise in consumption spending in period 2 is autonomous; the *further* rise in consumer spending in succeeding periods is *induced*.

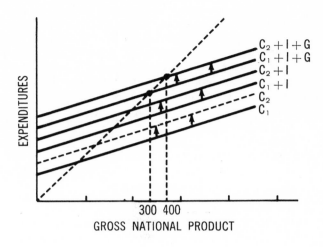

$C_2 + I + G$
$C_1 + I + G$
$C_2 + I$
$C_1 + I$
C_2
C_1

EXPENDITURES

300 400
GROSS NATIONAL PRODUCT

FIGURE 10-10

APPENDIX

EX POST VS. *EX ANTE* SAVING AND INVESTMENT

For a good many years the difference between *ex post* and *ex ante* variables in economics has been a source of difficulty and confusion. For that reason we have, up to now, skirted the issue by defining all our terms in the *ex ante* sense. It is not only possible, but it seems to the writer, preferable, to keep *ex post* terminology out of the regular analysis altogether.

However, for those who will be doing more advanced work in economics, the distinction should be made.

Basically, the difference between *ex ante* and *ex post* variables is simple. *Ex ante* refers to the amount savers and investors *plan* or *intend* to save and invest while *ex post* refers to the *actual* (or *realized*) saving and investing carried out, including both intended and unintended increments.

How is it possible for investment plans and results to diverge? Very easily. In any period in which the inventories of businessmen rise sharply because of an unexpectedly poor demand, they find that they have *actually* invested more than they had intended. They have bought the plant and equipment that they planned but they end up the period with additional investment in inventories, which was quite unintended.

And in a period of unexpectedly heavy demand, the reverse will be true. They may have bought all the plant and equipment they intended but at the end of the period their *actual* investment will be less than that by the amount of their *unintended* disinvestment in inventories.

Now how about saving? Is it possible for savers to save more or less than they had planned? Of course, but it requires a change in our method of dividing time into periods to demonstrate the possibility. Suppose, instead of looking at the time sequence of the production process as:

Period 1

Production		*Income*		*Use of Income*[15] $C + S$		*Aggregate Demand*[15] $C + I$
(1)	=	(2)	=	(3)	$\substack{> \\ = \\ <}$	(4)

we draw our time period, dividing-line, at a different point as below:

Period 1

Use of Income From Previous Period $C + S$		*Aggregate Demand* $C + I$		*Production*		*Income*
(1)	$\substack{> \\ = \\ <}$	(2)	=	(3)	=	(4)

In the latter case, we are assuming that people are paid at the *end* of the period, for production done, but that they are not free to dispose of this income until the following period. If it helps to make sense of this, it is as if workers are paid at 5 P.M. on the last day of the month but, since the stores are closed then, they cannot spend their income until the next day, the first of the following month, which is a new time period.

In this circumstance, suppose the APC is $\frac{3}{4}$. If the income available from

[15] For purposes of simplicity, we shall deal with a no government economy, wherein there are no taxes so that all income is consumed or saved and there is no government spending so that aggregate demand is composed of only consumption and investment.

the previous period's production is $400, they will spend $300 on consumption and save $100. But if investors spend $140 to buy capital goods, aggregate demand will be $440, production will rise to $440, and income earners will find themselves with $440 of income at the end of the period. Therefore, if we consider saving during the period *relative to the income earned during the same period, actual* saving (*ex post*) turns out to be $140 (income earned during the period minus consumption spending during the period), whereas consumers' original intentions (*ex ante*) were to save $100.[16]

Which is the "correct" way of defining saving and investment? There is no problem with answering this one. Both *ex ante* and *ex post* definitions of saving and investment are "correct." The possibility of error arises in misuse or confusion of the two.

When defined *ex post*, saving and investment are always, and definitionally equal. This can best be shown by numerical example. If we return to our production-lag concept of time periods, suppose production and income are $500, consumption spending is $400, and investment spending during the period is $150. Here, *ex ante* (as well as *ex post*) saving is $100 (Inc. $500—Cons. $400) and *ex ante* investment, $150. *Ex post,* or realized investment, however, turns out to be only $100 because the intentional $150 spending on capital goods is partially offset by $50 of unintended inventory decreases.

Use of the expenditure lag time period concept produces the same *ex post* equality. If $500 of income is available at the beginning of the period, and consumers spend $400 on consumption, *ex ante* (planned) saving is $100. But if, during the period investment spending (both intended and actual) turns out to be $150, pushing production and income earned during the period up to $550, *ex post* saving (income earned during the period minus consumption spending during the period) will turn out to be $150, or the same as investment.

How can we summarize these relationships? Saving and investment, *ex post*, are always, and definitionally equal. Saving and investment, *ex ante*, are equal *only when production has reached its equilibrium level.* At the equilibrium level of production and income, *ex ante* saving = *ex ante* investment = *ex post* saving = *ex post* investment. At any level of production *above* equilibrium, while *ex post* saving still equals *ex post* investment, *ex ante* saving exceeds *ex ante* investment. At any income level *below* equilibrium, *ex ante* investment exceeds *ex ante* saving.

---

[16] The thoughtful reader may note another quantity that can equally well, or perhaps even more legitimately, be considered intended saving during the period. An APC of ¾ is a psychological phenomenon that does describe consumers' intentions. Consequently, with income of $440 earned during the period it would be perfectly valid to argue that intended saving (if consumers had time to do what they would really *like* to do) is $110 (¼ of $440).

11

Investment Spending

INTRODUCTION

Mastering economic theory is not unlike erecting a building. Even the finest of superstructures will produce a faulty finished product if the foundation is weak. We should, therefore, make sure that the essence of Chapter 10 is clearly in mind before plunging more deeply into the analysis.

We have seen that the modern theory of income determination rests upon the basic assumption that it is the level of expenditures to purchase newly produced goods and services which determines how much will be produced. More specifically we have argued that production will tend toward the level where aggregate demand just equals aggregate supply—the equilibrium level.

Of the three elements of aggregate demand, consumption, investment, and government spending, only consumption has thus far been carefully considered. We have seen that, whereas many factors affect the level of consumer spending, income is far and away the most important; so important, in fact, that we refer to the relation between income and consumption as a functional relationship, the consumption function.

The existence of the so-called "multiplier" in the economy is, indeed, due solely to the fact that consumption spending is so heavily dependent on income. Any autonomous rise in consumption, investment, or government spending, we have argued, will not only cause production to rise, but, by causing rises in income will *induce* further rises in consumption spending so that before a new equilibrium position is reached, production will have risen by a multiple of the original increase.

Multiple changes in the level of production and income (and, indirectly, in employment and/or prices), then, can emanate from autonomous changes in any of the three elements of aggregate demand. What we need to know more about are the possible causes of the autonomous changes which initiate these cumulative income changes.

We already know something about the causes of autonomous changes in consumption spending. Consumer expectations, consumer wealth, the existing stock of consumer durables, etc., all can, by changing, cause autonomous consumption changes. But the truth is that while these factors *can* be important in initiating income changes, they generally do so only in the short run. Consumption spending, in the long run at least, is a relatively stable, passive portion of aggregate demand, changing in significant amount only when income does.

Not so for the other two elements. Both investment spending and government spending can be highly volatile, setting off repeated cumulative changes in the nation's income in one direction or another. We must, if we are to be able to say much about the economy, know more about them and the causes of their erratic behavior.

Unfortunately, not much can be said, from the economic point of view, about the determinants of government spending. At least not in the context in which we are considering it. The level of such spending is so heavily dependent on essentially noneconomic factors, such as international affairs, that a discussion of economic determinants hardly seems warranted. We will, therefore, reluctantly pass it by, with the important reminder that, as one of the major tools of fiscal policy, government spending can and does have significant effects on the level of income.

This leaves investment, perhaps the most volatile of the elements of aggregate demand. We turn, in the remainder of the chapter, to a consideration of the determinants of the level of investment spending, the causes of its volatility, and the effects of its erratic behavior on the level of income in the economy.

The Determinants of the Level of Investment Spending

Investment, the reader will remember, has been defined as "intentional spending to buy newly produced capital goods and additions to inventory." The question before us is what causes such spending to be large or small?

If one were to start out and, reasoning from sheer common sense, list the factors that would appear to affect the level of investment spending, the list would be imposing. Among others, the following would certainly be included.

1. Expected future levels of demand (to buy products produced on machines bought today)

2. Expected future wage and material costs (to purchase the labor and materials needed to operate the machine, or to use *instead* of the machine)
3. Expected future taxes
4. The current price of the machines to be bought
5. The interest cost of borrowing the money to buy the machine (or to forego the potential interest return on one's own money in order to buy the machine)
6. Future consumer tastes. (Will they shift away from products that can be produced on the machines available to be purchased?)
7. Pace of technological change. (Will a better machine soon make those available now obsolete?)
8. The "gambling spirit" of entrepreneurs
9. The existing stock of capital goods

There can be no doubt that each of the factors on this partial list plays a role in the determination of the level of investment spending in any period. The problem that confronts us is how can all these factors be organized to develop a reasonably accurate, yet not too unwieldy theory?

Essentially what economists have done is to cover almost all these individual determinants under the somewhat vague phrase "businessmen's expectations of future profits." We say that the level of investment spending today depends upon "businessmen's expectations of future profits" which, in turn, depends on almost all the factors in the foregoing list. But such sweeping generalities, while formally correct, are not very helpful for purposes of analysis. We need to see how all these variables are handled.

The Marginal Efficiency of Investment—Its Computation From the Point of View of a Single Firm

It should help clarify matters if we attempt to follow through the logical thought process of an individual businessman considering the purchase of a particular machine.

Suppose Mr. Jones is trying to decide whether or not to buy a certain machine, the price of which is $100,000, for his business. If he is a profit-maximizer what does he consider in arriving at his decision?

He knows that if he buys the machine and uses it in production, his total revenue will increase. The machine will add to his ability to produce and, assuming he can sell this added ouput, its use adds to his firm's gross income. That's the good side of it. On the negative side, he realizes that certain added costs will accrue from buying and using it. His costs will be increased not only by the initial price of the machine, but also by the interest cost he incurs to finance the purchase and by the added labor and material costs that will necessarily be encountered in order to operate it. Presumably, his decision about whether to purchase it or not will rest on the balance of good versus bad. If it is expected to add more to his revenue than to his costs he can increase his profits by buying it. On the other hand, if expected costs from buying and using it exceed expected added revenue from selling the goods produced on it, he will forego the opportunity.

It is apparent that the investment decision is full of "ifs." Our businessman must first estimate the expected added revenue as a result of purchasing the machine. What does such an estimate entail? It requires that he "guess" at:

1. The physical productivity of the machine per year
2. The economic life of the machine (which involves a guess at how soon his competitors may come up with a better machine, which will make this one obsolete)
3. Consumer demand for the product produced on the machine (which involves not only a forecast of consumer tastes but also an estimate of the course of the business cycle)

Fraught with difficulty though it may be, no investment will be made by a profit maximizer without, explicitly or implicitly, considering all these imponderables. Let us assume that our Mr. Jones has done so and has come up with a "best guess" that the annual added total revenue he will derive from selling products produced on the machine is $80,000. Furthermore, he expects this added revenue to continue for five years, the expected useful life of the machine.

Now let us consider the negative side. Mr. Jones knows that buying the machine will add to his yearly costs by the following:

1. The initial cost of the machine, $100,000, spread over 5 years, or $20,000 per year
2. The interest cost involved in financing the purchase (assuming it is 5 percent on $100,000 or $5,000)[1]

He must also guess once again the added costs he will incur yearly from operating the machine. Here he must estimate:

1. Added labor cost (to operate the machine)
2. Added material cost (to feed into the machine)
3. Added taxes that he will incur as a result of selling more and earning more income

---

[1] In fact, of course, since $20,000 of the original cost is being recovered each year, the interest cost would be substantially less than $5,000, if the interest rate is 5 percent, because the full $100,000 is only borrowed in the first year. We are ignoring this complication here to simplify the arithmetic involved.

Let us assume that once again he has gazed into his crystal ball and has come up with the following "best guesses":

1. Added yearly labor cost—$25,000
2. Added yearly material cost—$15,000
3. Added yearly taxes—$7,500

Now, if we put all his estimates together this would appear to be the picture:

Expected added annual revenue		$80,000
minus: Expected added annual costs		72,500
Original cost of machine	$20,000	
Interest cost	5,000	
Labor and material cost	40,000	
Taxes	7,500	
Expected added annual profits		7,500

In this case, the purchase of the machine would appear to be advisable, yielding an addition to profits of $7,500 for each of the next five years. It would seem that, in order to maximize his profits, Mr. Jones must make the investment.

But hold on. We have omitted something that is absolutely crucial in the investment decision. The $7,500 expected annual profit figure we have come up with may be Mr. Jones' "best guess," but it is, at best, a guess. Mr. Jones thinks this $7,500 is the greatest likelihood but, as any businessman must, he knows that there is some (lesser) chance that he will reap a greater profit and also some (lesser) chance that if he buys the machine he will *lose* money. Can we ignore the risk involved altogether by assuming that Mr. Jones will always act on his best guess despite the fact that he is aware things *might* turn out differently?

That depends on how much of a gambler Mr. Jones is. Let us suppose, for purposes of argument, that whereas a $7,500 annual profit is *most* likely (there being 50 chances out of 100 that this will be the result) there are also 5 chances out of 100 that he will lose $5,000 per year, 20 chances out of 100 that he will just break even, 20 chances out of 100 that he will make an annual profit of $15,000 and 5 chances out of 100 that he will make $20,000 profit per year.

If that's the case, his outlook on the likely profitability of the investment would look something like Figure 11-1. This, of course, is a probability distribution that, in this case, turns out to be a symmetrical curve.

The problem facing Mr. Jones has now been complicated. Would he be as willing to accept this set of probable results as a *certain* $7,500 profit

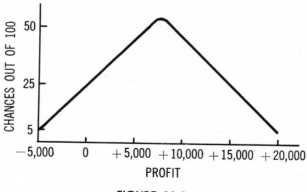

FIGURE 11-1

per year? It all depends on his own makeup. If he's a relatively conservative man, he would prefer a certain $7,500 to this range of possibilities even though the chances of loss may appear to be offset by equal chances of larger gain. In such a case the risk involved is a positive detriment that would lessen the chance that he would buy the machine. If, on the other hand, he is a gambler by nature, he might positively prefer this set of probabilities to a certain $7,500, putting more store in the possibilities of greater profit than in the equal likelihood of loss.

There is no safe way of characterizing all businessmen with respect to their attitude toward the risk involved. However, it would seem that most would be on the conservative side, preferring a certain $7,500 to the range of probabilities listed in Figure 11-1. If that *is* the case for Mr. Jones we had better take account of his aversion to risk in his investment decision.

Suppose that to cover his risk, Mr. Jones insists that his best guess on the profitability of a $100,000 investment be at least $5,000. If this is the case, that $5,000 *risk-allowance* will have the same effect in deterring his purchase of the machine as would be an additional out-of-pocket cost of $5,000. There is no reason why we cannot consider it explicitly, as another cost, like wages, interest, etc., that must be covered.

Now that we have covered everything we can state definitely that if Mr. Jones is a profit maximizer he will buy the machine because he expects, after all costs including enough to cover his risk, a profit of $2,500 per year on the machine. In fact, under these conditions, he would buy the machine if he expected a profit of $1.00 per year from it.

We must now put all of Mr. Jones' figures into the form in which economists generally use them. The reader should be aware that there is no change in substance in what follows, from what we have already covered. The change is only one of form and we go through it because it is the form that economists generally use.

The economist uses the term *marginal efficiency of investment* to refer to "the expected annual rate of return on an investment."[2]

It would be computed, in the case of Mr. Jones, in the following manner: the expected annual addition to total revenue ($80,000 here) would be reduced by the expected annual addition to cost, *except for interest cost*.

In this case, it would be:

Expected annual revenue		$80,000
minus: Expected annual costs		72,500
Return of original investment	$20,000	
Labor and materials	40,000	
Risk allowance	5,000	
Taxes	7,500	
Expected annual profits		7,500

Oversimplifying considerably[3] we can say that the *marginal efficiency of investment*—the expected annual *rate* of return on the investment—is $7,500/$100,000 or 7.5 percent. Theoretically, the machine will be purchased as long as the MEI is higher than the only cost not yet considered, the rate of interest. In Mr. Jones' case the MEI on the machine is 7.5 percent and the rate of interest is 5 percent, so the investment should be made. If the interest rate had been 8 percent however, the MEI would not be high enough to cover it and the machine would *not* have been purchased.

---

[2] The more formally correct definition is "that rate of discount which will equate the expected annual dollar profits to the original cost of the machine." The discussion in this section oversimplifies the concept, but the gain from simplicity more than overcomes the loss in rigor.

[3] To be more exact, the MEI here is that rate of discount needed to equate the expected stream of revenue (before allowance is made for *either* the interest cost *or* the $100,000 original cost of the machine) to the cost of the machine. This can be computed by use of the formula:

$$C = \frac{R}{(1 + r)} + \frac{R}{(1 + r)^2} + \frac{R}{(1 + r)^3} + \frac{R}{(1 + r)^4} + \frac{R}{(1 + r)^5} \text{ wherein:}$$

C = the original cost of the machine ($100,000)
R = the expected annual revenue before allowance for depreciation or interest ($27,500)
r = the required rate of discount—the MEI

Our 7.5 percent figure ignores the fact that part of the original investment is being paid off each year.

In general we can say that (if investors are profit maximizers) investment will always be carried out if the MEI (adjusted for risk allowance) exceeds the rate of interest. If the interest rate exceeds the MEI, the investment would not be profitable and will not be made.

The Marginal Efficiency of Investment Schedule for the Economy as a Whole

At any point in time many potential investments are under consideration by many different firms in many different industries. If we "add up" all these for the economy as a whole, we may end up with a result something like the following. *M.E.I. = MARGINAL EFFICIENCY OF INVESTMENT*

dollars of expenditure to be spent during the next year Dollars Worth of Investment Projects (billions of dollars)	With an MEI (Expected Rate of Return) of at Least:
10	20%
15	18
20	15
25	13
30	10
34	8
38	5
40	3
42	1

Such a result could equally well be expressed graphically, as in Figure 11-2.

Why do we end up here with a downsloping curve? Why do we imply with our example that the marginal rate of return to be expected from $40 billion worth of investment is less than that to be expected from $20 billion worth? Because each investment figure includes all the projects with a higher rate of return plus the *additional* projects that are expected to realize the lower rate. For example, when investment is pushed from $30 billion to $34 billion, the marginal expected rate of return falls from 10 percent to 8 percent. The investment projects that can be expected to yield *at least* 10 percent total up to $30 billion, but the total for which a return of *at least* 8 percent is expected is $4 billion higher because it includes both the $30 billion for which a 10 percent return is expected *plus the additional* $4 billion worth of projects for which returns of 9.5 percent, 9 percent, 8.5 percent, and 8 percent are expected.

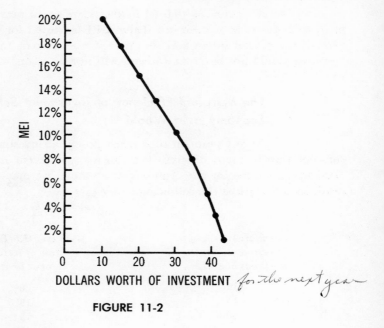

FIGURE 11-2

The curve we have in Figure 11-2, however, is not yet an investment demand schedule, which is what we are seeking. For the direction of causation is the reverse of what is needed. Figure 11-2 tells us *the effect upon the expected rate of return which results from varying the volume of investment*. What we need is a curve that tells us *the volume of investment that will result from varying one of the factors which is a determinant of investment*.

Assuming, however, that the data for Figure 11-2 have been arrived at after adjustment for risk allowances, as well as all other costs except the interest cost involved, and that the goal of the businessmen involved is to maximize profits, we can easily turn it into an investment demand schedule. What we have in Figure 11-2 is a picture of the expected rates of return of various amounts of investment before the interest cost has been met. If we now measure off the interest rate (i), as well as the MEI, on the vertical axis we shall have what we are looking for.

We can now say that if the interest rate (the determination of which we shall soon discuss) is 10 percent, then, in order to maximize profits, businessmen will invest $30 billion. At a 10 percent rate of interest, if they invested less than $30 billion they would be leaving unexploited some investment opportunities with an expected rate of return of *more* than 10 percent, or with a rate of return high enough to cover the interest

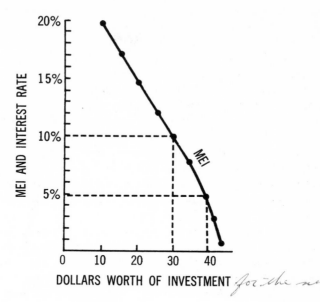

FIGURE 11-3

cost *plus* add something to profits. They would not, on the other hand, invest more than $30 billion because all projects beyond the $30 billion level have an expected rate of return which is *less* than the 10 percent needed to just cover the interest rate.

Similarly, if for some reason the rate of interest should fall to 5 percent, investment spending would rise to $38 billion because $8 billion worth of investment projects, which did not promise enough return to fully cover a 10 percent interest charge, *are* expected to be profitable enough to more than cover a 5 percent rate. In summary, *the MEI curve tells us the amount that profit-maximizing businessmen will spend on investment, at each possible rate of interest.*

DETERMINANTS OF THE LEVEL OF THE MEI CURVE OF THE ECONOMY

For the student who followed through on the logical thought process of our mythical Mr. Jones is arriving at the MEI for *his* particular $100,000 investment, most of the factors that determine the level of, or cause shifts in, the economy's MEI curve will be apparent. Nevertheless, since we are now talking about the determinants of the level of the *entire*

MEI curve for the *economy as a whole* rather than the consideration behind *one* prospective investment for *one* businessman, we had better list some of the more important determinants.

1. *Technology.* There can be no doubt that technological progress, whether in the form of the development of new methods of production or new products, has profound effects on the level of the MEI curve. Although there are exceptions, we can assume that improvements in the state of technical knowledge *usually* tends to raise the MEI curve.

2. *Stock of Capital Goods on Hand.* To the degree that the stock of capital goods in the economy increases more rapidly than the other factors of production, we will, other things being equal, encounter diminishing marginal productivity of capital. Consequently, the larger the stock of capital goods already on hand, relative to the other productive factors, the lower the level of the MEI curve.

3. *Tax Policy.* Just as our Mr. Jones' decision was affected by the level of taxes he expected to have to pay, so must the outlook of all prospective investors be influenced by tax policy. This applies not only to corporate profits tax rates but also such less obvious factors as changes in the rate at which depreciation is permitted for tax purposes. Clearly any tax change that has the effect of reducing taxes on the income earned from successful investment would, other things being equal, tend to raise the community's MEI curve.

4. *Businessmen's Psychology.* Since investment spending is entirely an activity that "pays off" only in the future, its volume is inevitably influenced by the psychology of investors. Even the hard economic facts that underlie the estimate of the rate of return from an investment are colored by the psychological makeup of those who make the investment decisions, because "future expectations" involve a degree of crystal ball gazing that, by its very nature, cannot be based entirely on economic fact. If the investor group is composed primarily of "gamblers," the risk allowance will be smaller and the resulting investment, larger than if investors were extremely cautious by nature.

5. *Social and Political Atmosphere.* Just as the interpretation of economic facts is influenced by psychology, so must it be affected by apparent changes in the social or political structure within which the economy functions. Rationally or irrationally, the illness of a president, the election of a seemingly hostile Congress, the intensification of social problems will affect businessmen's expectations. In large part, of course, the effectiveness of such developments as determinants of investment depends upon the effect they appear likely to have on such fundamental economic facts as tax policy, and the like. Nevertheless, they would seem to be sufficiently different in origin to justify a separate listing.

This is hardly an exhaustive list, but it does include some of the most important determinants of the MEI curve's level. A change in any one will alter the expectation of return from investment all along the line thereby raising or lowering the MEI curve itself.

The Significance of the Slope (or Elasticity) of the MEI Curve

While there can be no doubt that the MEI falls to the right, there is considerable doubt and disagreement as to *how rapidly* it falls. In this section, we shall say what we can about the actual slope (or elasticity[4]) of the MEI curve and then explore its implications.

Is the usual MEI curve for the American economy relatively steep or relatively flat? The truth is, we do not really know. Extensive efforts have been made to find out, but as yet there appears to be no conclusive proof one way or the other. Some scholars have attempted to get at the issue via the survey technique in which businessmen are asked the relative importance of various factors as determinants of investment. Although the survey results almost unanimously reveal the interest rate as a factor of generally minor importance, this approach falls short of conclusively demonstrating that the MEI curve is inelastic.[5] Other investigators have employed econometric techniques with indifferent success. Others, with and without resort to empirical evidence, have theorized that such things as risk allowances, corporate profits taxes, and short *payoff* periods make for an inelastic investment demand curve.

Perhaps continued effort along these lines will pay off with more definitive results in the future. Until that point is reached, however, an agnostic view appears most appropriate. We just do not know how elastic or inelastic the MEI curve is.

But the question is a vitally important one, especially in its implications for the effectiveness of monetary policy. If it could be shown that the MEI curve was highly elastic (relatively flat) over most of its range, this would be equivalent to saying that slightly lowering the rate of interest (with a given MEI curve) will make profitable and call forth substantial amounts of additional investment spending. And a highly inelastic MEI curve carries exactly the opposite implications. Let us look at Figure 11-4 to examine this point.

[4] Although the slope and elasticity of a demand curve are not identical with the exceptions of the limiting cases of perfectly elastic and perfectly inelastic curves, we shall oversimplify here by ignoring the difference. Specifically, we shall refer to a relatively steep MEI curve (or a steep portion of an MEI curve) as inelastic and to a relatively flat curve (or portion thereof) as elastic.

[5] See below for a further discussion of this point.

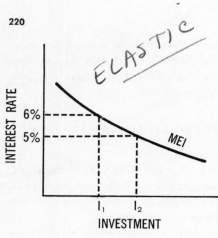
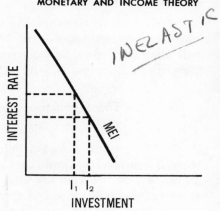

FIGURE 11-4

In the graph on the left, we have drawn a relatively flat MEI curve to represent a high degree of elasticity. On the right, the fairly steep curve is intended to depict a case of low elasticity. It can be seen that a reduction in the interest rate from 6 percent to 5 percent permits a relatively large increase in the volume of investment in the elastic case, but only a small increase where the MEI is decidedly inelastic. An *easy money* policy designed to raise aggregate demand via a lowering of interest rates would clearly be more successful, the more elastic the MEI. The reverse reasoning applies, of course, to the effectiveness of interest rate increases induced by a *tight money* policy.

Before leaving this area, it seems in order to point out that the statement that investment is highly elastic with respect to the rate of interest is not necessarily the same thing as arguing that the interest rate is *important* as a determinant of the level of investment. Perhaps another example will help make the point.

In Figure 11-5, we have drawn a pair of MEI curves that are highly elastic over most of their ranges. Suppose that initially, the MEI curve applicable for our economy is MEI_1, and the rate of interest is 6 percent. This would mean that the volume of investment spending would be I_1. Now, suppose Federal Reserve policy lowers the interest rate to 4 percent in order to combat a developing recession. *If the MEI curve does not shift,* the reduction in interest rates will permit a substantial increase in investment spending up to I_2. But, in fact, there is good reason to expect a shift in the curve itself as businessmen's expectations are adversely affected by the developing recession. If the MEI curve shifts to the left to MEI_2 at the same time as the interest rate is reduced, the new volume of investment will be I_3, a very slight increase. Thus we have a situation

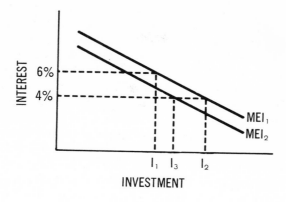

FIGURE 11-5

wherein, even though investment is highly elastic with respect to the rate of interest, changes in the other factors (businessmen's expectations) affecting investment work in the opposite direction, and keep investment from rising much.

The reverse, of course, is also possible. If the MEI curve is highly elastic and monetary policy raises interest rates to combat a developing inflation (the purpose being to cut investment spending), the elasticity of the investment demand curve does not guarantee that investment spending will be diminished. For the optimism generated among businessmen by the boom conditions may be reflected in an upward shift of the MEI curve itself, producing a smaller decrease in investment than a stable, elastic curve would lead one to expect. Indeed, there may even be an increase.

If, in fact, shifts in the MEI curve itself are so frequent and significant as to "swamp" the effects on investment of interest rate changes, then one must conclude that even if the MEI is *elastic,* interest is not an *important* factor in determining investment. It is partly this possibility that led us to state earlier that replies to surveys by businessmen to the effect that interest was not an important factor do not necessarily prove that the MEI curve is inelastic.

The Accelerator Effect

There is one determinant of investment which we have thus far ignored. Since it does not fit in easily with the discussion just completed, we have chosen to cover it separately.

Businessmen, it would seem, must adjust their buying of capital goods not only to fit their expectations of the future, but also to fit the facts of the present. One of the most important of these facts is the current level of demand for finished consumer (and capital) goods.

If the current demand for finished consumer (and capital) goods is high, meeting this demand requires a high level of production. A high level of production in turn, requires more (or better) factors of production; more labor as well as more capital goods. Consequently, it would appear that the higher the level of demand for finished products, the higher must be the rate of purchasing capital goods to produce them.

In general terms what we are talking about here is the *acceleration principle*. This time-honored economic phenomenon argues that the demand for capital goods (investment spending) is *derived* from the demand for the finished goods, which they are designed to produce.[6] No one wants machines for their own sake, but only to use in producing more final goods. The number of machines needed must then depend in some way on the demand for the things they can turn out.

All this is rather elementary and obvious. The real question is "in what *way* does the demand for capital goods depend on the demand for the goods they produce?"

Perhaps a numerical example will help. Table 11-1 contains data for an industry in which the assumptions are made that (1) each machine can produce 10 units of final product per period and (2) 10 percent of the machines on hand during any period wear out via depreciation during the period.

As Table 11-1 shows, slight fluctuations in the demand for the finished good lead often to greatly magnified changes in the demand for capital goods. For instance, in period two, a 20 percent increase in consumer demand causes, under our assumptions, a 200 percent increase in the purchase of machines. Similarly, the approximately 13 percent rise in consumer demand in period 10 (over the previous period) leads to an increase in investment of over 130 percent.

The reader may note from the example that the real determinant of acceleration investment is not the *level* of consumer demand (or income) but the *rate of change in* consumer demand (or income). To emphasize this point let us state more formally that according to the acceleration principle, *the volume of investment spending depends upon the rate of change in income (or demand).*

We have already seen that, sometimes, a small increase in demand leads to a much larger relative rise in investment. Thus, to the extent that the principle is operative, it should be clear that it tends to reinforce any change in the level of business activity. An on-going expansion in

[6] This is so in much the same way that the demand for any productive resource is said to be derived from the demand for the product it is intended to produce.

TABLE 11-1 Accelerator Example

Time Period	Number of Units of Final Product Demanded	Number of Machines on Hand at Beginning of Period (10 Percent of Machines on Hand Wear Out Each Period)	Number of Machines Needed to Meet Demand for Final Product (Each Machine Produces 10 Units of Produce)	New Machines Purchased to Meet Demand (Gross Investment)
1	1,000	90	100	10
2	1,200	90	120	30
3	1,600	108	160	52
4	1,800	146	180	34
5	1,800	162	180	18
6	1,700	162	170	8
7	1,600	153	160	7
8	1,500	144	150	6
9	1,500	135	150	15
10	1,700	135	170	35

production and income may well, via the accelerator mechanism, be reinforced.

But that is not the most interesting facet of the accelerator idea. Look back to Table 11-1 in period four. Here, although consumer demand has continued to rise (from 1,600 to 1,800 units), investment demand has actually fallen! The same sort of thing, to a different degree, is shown in period nine where, despite the fact that consumer demand has not risen, investment expenditures exhibit a rise.

How can we generalize about this behavior and its implications? In addition to sometimes moving more rapidly in the same direction as consumer demand, acceleration investment seems, sometimes, to move in the *opposite* direction. Let us put it this way. *Acceleration investment depends upon the rate of change in consumer demand* (or income). *When consumer demand is rising* (falling) *at an increasing rate, acceleration investment increases* (decreases).[7] *When, however, the rate of increase* (decrease) *of consumer demand slows down, the acceleration principle may cause an absolute drop* (rise) *in investment spending.*

Put this way, the acceleration principle provides a most important additional tool for understanding the business cycle. In the first place it interacts with the multiplier to help explain why upward (downward) movements in production and income tend to become cumulative leading to the familiar upward (downward) spiral of the business cycle. If, for example, a rise in investment spending sets off an upward movement, the economy is propelled further by the additional induced consumption that makes up the multiplier. This consumption rise, in turn, activates the accelerator causing more investment, and the cycle continues. Roughly, this multiplier-accelerator interaction works as below:

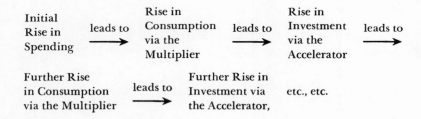

Secondly, our accelerator provides some explanation for the turning points of the business cycle. As long as consumption is increasing ever more rapidly, the accelerator reinforces the upswing. As soon, however, as the *rate of increase* in consumption slows, the accelerator principle

[7] As we have seen, generally this happens at an even faster rate.

permits an absolute drop in investment which can start the whole economy downward towards recession.

The accelerator principle as discussed, however, is not without its weaknesses. The numerical relationships we derived in Table 11-1 depend upon an assumption of fixity in the relation between output and number of machines which is seldom found. In the first place, when demand rises producers will often wait for a time to determine how permanent the rise is before buying new machines. In the meantime, they may meet the increased demand by working their present capacity overtime. Secondly, a rise in demand, especially when it takes place near the end of a recession, may often be met by calling into use machines already on hand which, because of the previous low demand, had been lying idle.

For these and other reasons,[8] the *formal* structure of theory which follows in Chapters 12 and 13 will omit consideration of the acceleration principle. That is, we shall go on in the next two chapters to complete formulation of a model of the economy which assumes that investment depends solely on the relation between the marginal efficiency of investment and the interest rate, leaving out altogether any reference to the rate of change in demand as an additional determinant.

We do this primarily for the advantage of simplicity. Despite its weaknesses and the complications it introduces, the accelerator idea is a perfectly viable one.

SUMMARY

We have now what amounts to half a theory. We have seen that, given the rate of interest, the marginal efficiency of the investment schedule will tell us the volume of investment at which producers will maximize expected profits. This volume of investment spending, along with the level of government spending and the consumption function, will permit us to determine the equilibrium level of production and income.

All this can be expressed graphically, as in Figure 11-6.

If the rate of interest is given to us as i_o, the volume of investment spending will be I_o. When this volume of investment is added (vertically) to the consumption and government spending curves, we find that the equilibrium level of income and production is Y_o.

Of course different assumptions for the curves involved would give us different answers. If businessmen's expectations became worse, the MEI curve itself would shift to the left, in which case an interest rate of i_o

---

[8] We wish to keep the model as simplified as possible.

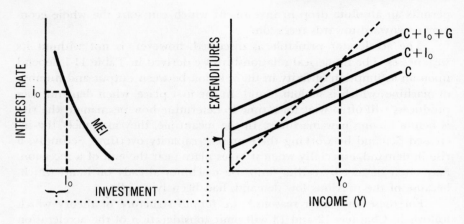

FIGURE 11-6

would produce a smaller volume of investment and, consequently, a lower equilibrium level of income. If one of the determinants of the consumption schedule, such as income taxes or consumer expectations, should change from what is depicted to produce a higher or steeper consumption function, the equilibrium level of income would be higher even with the same level of investment.

A good deal can be said about the economy with the aid of this "half model" alone. But we must go further. In order to complete the picture we need to know how the rate of interest is determined. This is the subject of Chapter 12. Once it is completed, we will have covered all the pieces of our simplified model of the economy, and be in a position to go ahead in Chapter 13 and use it in its entirety.

12

The Rate of Interest

What determines *the* rate of interest is an age-old question. Economists have battled for years over the proper explanation of its determination and, if the truth be told, the battle is not over yet. Fortunately for us, however, enough solid ground of agreement has been established to permit a fairly confident discussion of where we now stand and how we got there.

This chapter is divided into three main sections. After some introductory comments limiting the area of discussion, we shall take a brief look at a somewhat oversimplified version of the classical economists' theory of interest. Although this, like some other elements of classical theory, has since been replaced, discussion of it will help us understand more thoroughly the current theories.

Following the classical theory, we shall turn to the loanable funds theory of interest, one of the two currently accepted theories. Finally, in the last and most lengthy section, we shall consider the newest theory of all, the liquidity preference theory. This theory will be considered at somewhat more length than the others for it is the one which we choose to incorporate into our model of the economy.

LIMITATIONS OF THE AREA OF DISCUSSION

It is a gross oversimplification to discuss "the" rate of interest. The fact is, of course, that there are many different rates of interest ruling in any economy at any given time. What do we mean by *the* rate of interest?

The rate of interest should be taken to mean the rate of return which is paid to a lender who has lent his money for a long period of time by a borrower for whom the chances of default are extremely remote. In other words, the return on a long-term, virtually riskless security would provide a good measure of what we mean by *the* rate of interest. There is no better example than the interest paid on a long-term U.S. government security.

But what about all the other rates being paid? At any one time, even if we had already determined "the" rate of interest to be 4 percent, one could find examples of a whole structure of rates ranging from perhaps 1 percent to as high as 30 percent or more. What explains the divergences from our "pure" 4 percent rate?

To answer fully such questions we would have to become deeply involved in a complicated discussion of the *structure* of interest rates. This, we shall not do.

Suffice it to say that interest rates above and below the "pure" rate are largely explainable by differences in the term of the loan, the costs of collection and the risk involved. We shall, in the discussion that follows, ignore such differences in order to permit concentration on the forces that determine the "pure" long-term "riskless" rate of interest.

The Classical Theory of Interest

The earlier classical economists looked upon money as merely a "veil" that partially concealed, but did not really alter any of the basic "real" forces in the economy. This was as true of their interest theory as of other elements of their elegant structure.

To the classical mind, the rate of interest was a "real" phenomenon, depending on the marginal physical productivity of capital and the disutility associated with saving (postponing consumption).

Their reasoning ran something like this:

Interest, of course, is what must be paid for the right to borrow money. But this amount is a price which, like all other prices, is determined by demand and supply. The demand for borrowed money comes, almost entirely from businessmen, who desire to use the funds to purchase capital goods. The supply, on the other hand, comes from individuals who, having decided not to spend all their income on consumption, have some left over in the form of saving, available to lend out.

But we must look behind these surface phenomena for a fuller understanding. The amount of borrowed money demanded by businessmen depends, at bottom, on the marginal productivity of capital goods. If the productivity of any added machine is expected to be high enough to more than cover the interest cost of financing its purchase, it must be bought to maximize profits. However, additional capital goods, when combined with the other factors of production will produce diminishing marginal productivity. Therefore, more such goods will be bought only at lower rates of interest because their lower productivity will not cover higher rates. That is to say the demand for borrowed funds (reflecting as it does the diminishing productivity of capital) will look like this:

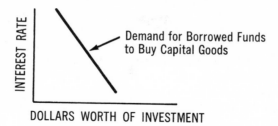

FIGURE 12-1

On the other side of the market, the supply of funds made available by savers is motivated by the opportunity of receiving interest on funds not spent for consumption. Actually it is irrational for people to refrain from spending their income on consumption (and suffer the disutility that is associated with such abstinence) and then hoard their saved money. For any rational man would prefer some interest return on his savings to none. Therefore, since it is the reward of interest which motivates saving, we can expect a greater quantity saved, the higher the rate of interest. The supply of savings, then, would look like this:

FIGURE 12-2

The equilibrium rate of interest will, of course, be determined at the point where demand and supply intersect.

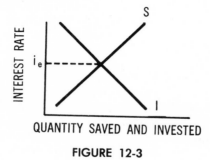

FIGURE 12-3

According to this reasoning this equilibrium rate of interest reflects both the real marginal productivity of capital goods and the real disutility suffered by savers as a result of their abstinence.

Though it was the dominant theory for a good many years, the classical theory, as stated above at any rate, simply does not hold water. Over the years, the following deficiencies of it, as an explanation of the interest rate, were pointed out:

not true

1. Bank creation of new money (or destruction of existing money) also affects the interest rate.
2. As economies developed more fully, consumers and government came to be important users of borrowed funds, in addition to businessmen buying capital goods.
3. The following basic classical assumptions were called into question:

   true

   (a) It is irrational to hold idle money
   (b) More would be saved, the higher the interest rate

FLOWS OF FUNDS

not needed

THE LOANABLE FUNDS THEORY OF INTEREST

These criticisms of the early classical theory led to corrections that have produced a sharply amended version, which we call the *loanable funds* theory. It is a perfectly correct way of looking at the determination of the interest rate, the choice between it and the *liquidity preference* theory being largely a matter of convenience.

The loanable funds theory takes the straightforward common sense position that the rate of interest is the "price that must be paid for the right to use loanable funds." It, like the classical theory that preceded it, goes on to argue that the way to get at the determinants of this price is to look into the components of the demand for, and the supply of, loanable funds. Unlike the earlier classical theory, however, it includes far more than saving and investment among these components.

The Components of the *Supply* of Loanable Funds include:

1. Saving out of current income

   plus

2. New money created by banks (or *minus* money destroyed)

   minus

3. Funds saved or newly created which are *hoarded*, that is, not lent out (or plus any dishoarding of funds, saved and hoarded in previous years)

For example, suppose that in a given year $500 of income is received of which $400 is spent on consumption. Saving out of current income is then $100. If, during the year, the banks create an additional $50 as a result of making loans to business, this must be added to the $100 to get at the total supply of loanable funds made available. But, suppose the savers choose to *lend out* only $70 of the $100 they have saved, and hold the other $30 in idle balances (hoard it). In this case the amount of loanable funds which is actually supplied (and which therefore enters into determination of the interest rate) is $120 ($100, saving, + $50, new money, − $30, hoarded).

If, on the other hand, saving was $100 and new money creation, $50, suppose that customers decided to lend out not only the full $100 they had saved out of this year's income but also another $20, which they had hoarded in idle balances last year. In this case the supply of loanable funds would be $170 ($100, saving, + $50, new money, + $20, dishoarded).

On the other side of the market are all those who desire to borrow these loanable funds. The largest demander (in peacetime) is business, which borrows for the purpose of financing its investment expenditures. Secondly, the government, when it must borrow funds to finance deficit spending, certainly affects the interest rate. Finally, consumers who buy on credit use up a far from insignificant portion of the available loan funds.

The Components of the Demand for Loanable Funds, therefore, include:

1. Business demand to finance the purchase of capital goods (investment)

    plus

2. Government demand to finance deficit spending (or minus government surplus)

    plus

3. Consumer demand to finance consumer credit

If we look at supply and demand together, with each expressed as a curve, we get something that looks very much like the simplified version of the classical theory sketched earlier but which is, in fact, a far more complete picture.

It provides us with a perfectly correct way of looking at interest rate determination which is widely accepted and used by economists today. There exists, however, an alternative theory of somewhat later vintage which is equally correct. We shall use it more extensively because it fits in more easily with the rest of our theoretical model. We turn now to consider this alternative—the liquidity preference theory.

LOANABLE FUNDS THEORY OF INTEREST

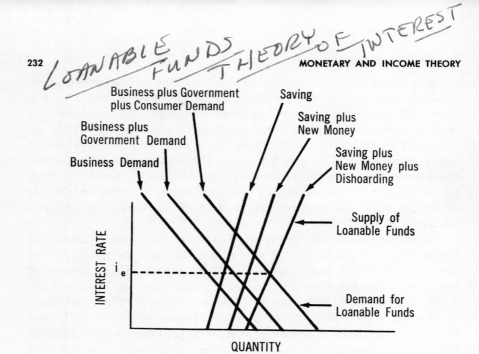

FIGURE 12-4

STOCKS OF MONEY

THE LIQUIDITY PREFERENCE THEORY OF INTEREST

J. M. Keynes, when he wrote his epic *General Theory*, concocted an interest theory with an entirely different approach. After a man decides how much of his income to save, said Keynes, he then must make a second decision regarding the use of his new savings. Basically, two alternatives are open to him. He can lend out what he has saved and receive the reward of interest for doing so, or he can hold on to his saved money in the form of (perhaps, temporarily) idle balances, receiving, instead of interest, the advantage of increased liquidity during the period.[1] If one looks at it in this way, interest appears to be *the price that must be paid to get people to give up the advantage of liquidity*.

It would seem to follow from this that, the lower the rate of interest, the greater the quantity of money demanded for cash balances and the smaller the supply of funds to lend. Conversely, the higher the rate of interest, the smaller the quantity of money demanded to hold and the larger the supply of loan funds.

But here we encounter a logical problem. The amount of money

[1] We assume, here, that he does not use his savings for purposes of direct investment.

which exists at any point in time is under the control of the monetary
authorities—the Federal Reserve System and the Treasury in the United
States. And the fact is, whatever the supply of money *is*, it *must* be held
by *somebody*.[2]

If, for example, the supply of money is $100, and the interest rate
is at such a high level that, people in the aggregate only *want* to hold
$50, whether they like it or not they must hold $100 because there is
$100 to be held. Any individual, of course, can react to this unsatisfactory
situation by spending his excess money on goods or perhaps securities. But
this will not directly solve the problem for the community as a whole since
when Mr. A spends his excess money, it merely ends up in the hands of
the Mr. B from whom he bought something. And, of course, if Mr. B then
succeeds in getting rid of his excess money, it will transfer the problem to
Mr. C, and so forth.

We have arrived, once again, at a supply and demand situation. On
one side of this market there is a supply of money (which is a certain
number of dollars at any point in time), the size of which is determined by
the monetary authorities. On the other side, there is a demand for money
to hold by the community as a whole with the quantity demanded being
larger, the lower the rate of interest. If today's rate of interest is at such
a level that people do not *willingly* hold the supply of money which exists
(that is, if the quantity supplied exceeds the quantity demanded) their
efforts to get rid of the excess will (in a manner we shall soon discuss)
lower the rate of interest until it reaches the level at which people do willingly hold in cash balances the supply of money which exists. To the
liquidity preference theorist, then, the equilibrium rate of interest is *that
rate of interest which equates the demand for money to the supply of
money*. Note that we have returned to a demand for money concept
entirely consistent with the "kP_yO" of the cash balance equation discussed
earlier in Chapter 9.

Before plunging more deeply into the intricacies of the liquidity
preference theory, the reader should make certain that he sees the essential difference between this approach and the loanable funds version. To
the loanable funds theorist, interest is the price that equates demand for,
and supply of, *loanable funds*. According to the liquidity preference doctrine, interest is the price that equate the demand for, and supply
of, *money*.[3]

[2] We exclude, of course, money that is in the mail.
[3] According to the loanable funds theory, the determinants of interest are *flows*
(measurable only as a rate of flow within a finite time period), whereas the liquidity
preference theorists' supply of and demand for money are *stocks* (measurable as of a
point in time).

The Demand for Money

Almost the whole of Part I was devoted to discussing the determinants of the supply of money. We need not repeat that material here. But our coverage of the demand for money thus far has been, to say the least, highly superficial. We have, as yet, done no more than allude to the fact that there is some sort of inverse relation between the level of the interest rate and the quantity of money demanded. We must do better than that. We must know more about this demand for money.

When Keynes introduced his liquidity preference theory, he argued that there were three rational motives for holding (demanding) money. He entitled these the transactions, precautionary, and speculative motives. In our discussion we shall ignore the precautionary motive[4] and deal separately with the transactions and speculative demands.

The Transactions Demand for Money

All of us have some need to hold money balances for some period to cover our requirement for cash between paydays. We shall define transactions balances in just this way—*money, held in cash form temporarily, for the purpose of financing needed expenditures for goods and services between paydays.*

If the transactions demand is defined as above, the only way a person could avoid having *some* transactions demand for money would be by spending, instantaneously, his entire paycheck, and then passing all the time until his next pay period without any spending money whatsoever. While many of us may feel we act almost like this, the fact is that none of us can operate without *some,* however small, transactions balance. Any man who has change in his pocket or a positive balance in his checking account has a transactions demand, if these are funds he intends to spend to buy goods and services before his next paycheck arrives.

Probably the best way to look at the transactions demand for money is via the simple diagram in Figure 12-5.[5] We depict there, the transactions balances held by a man who is paid $600 per month, on the first

---

[4] The precautionary motive would consist of money balances held, over and above those needed to finance transactions or take advantage of speculation on movements in the interest rate, to cover contingencies such as accident, sudden illness and the like. We do not treat it separately because:

1. Its determinants would be quite similar to the transactions demand.

2. Widespread availability of highly liquid, yet interest-earning instruments such as savings accounts and U.S. Savings Bonds would appear to have sopped up a large majority of funds held for precautionary purposes.

[5] This device is used by G. Ackley in his excellent text, *Macroeconomic Theory* (New York, The Macmillan Company, 1961), pp. 113-117.

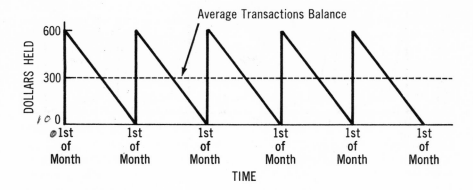

FIGURE 12-5

of each month and who spends this money at a constant rate throughout
the month, ending up with a zero balance at the end of the month. Such
a person has, on the average, $300 of transactions balances—$600 on the
first of the month, $580 on the second, $560 on the third, and so forth,
until, on the thirtieth, he spends his last $20.

If so prudent a spending pattern seems hardly applicable to anyone
we know, we can just as easily depict the more familiar case (to most of
us) of the man who spends most of his income shortly after payday by
the same device.. Suppose our subject receives $600 on the first of each
month, but spends $500 of it in the first day, spreading the other $100 out
equally over the remaining twenty-nine days of the month.

Such a man's transactions balances are depicted in Figure 12-6. He,
of course, has a much smaller average demand for transactions money
than his more "prudent" counterpart. On the average he holds somewhat
more than $50 for transactions purposes—$600 for one day, $100 on the
second, about $96.55 on the third, and so forth, spending his last $3.45
(approximately) on the thirtieth day.

It should be clear by now that all of us have some (however small)
transactions demand for money. And, although it is equally obvious that
we differ widely among one another in the size of our individual transactions demands, it is not individual differences that most concern us in
the task at hand. What is more important for our purposes here are the
determinants of the size of the transactions demand for the community as
a whole. What kinds of changes in the economy could significantly increase or decrease the entire community's transactions demand?

The most obvious determinants are four—the community's payment
habits, the degree of vertical integration of production, the development

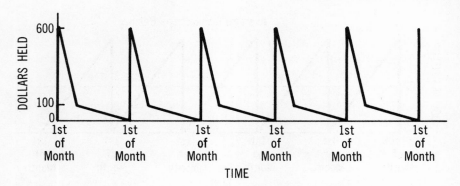

FIGURE 12-6

of the economy's financial system and the level of income. Let us discuss these in order.

Suppose our prudent individual who, it will be remembered, received $600 each month and spent it all with the perfect regularity of $20 per day until his balance was exhausted on the thirtieth day, is notified by his company, that, henceforth, he will be paid twice monthly, on the 1st and 15th. What effect, if any, will such a "speeding up" of his paydays have on his transactions demand, other things being equal?

Figure 12-7 depicts the situation. His previous payment and spending pattern is shown by the solid line and the new, "two paydays per month" arrangement, by the broken line. Assuming that he remains "prudent" and continues to spend just $20 per day, it can easily be seen that his average transactions demand for money has been cut in half. Whereas before he held, on the average, $300 in transactions balances, now he finds he can get along just as well with a mean balance of $150.

If such a speedup in payment habits occurs throughout the economy, the result is clear. A smaller stock of money will suffice to do the same work as one twice as large. In terms of the equation of exchange, since money sits idle for a shorter period of time, on the average, the velocity of spending is raised. The same level of spending (MV_y) is thereby obtainable with a smaller supply of money. We can say then that *a speedup in payment habits tends to reduce the transactions demand for money,* whereas a slowdown in frequency of payment would raise the transactions demand.

The second determinant is the degree of vertical integration of production. If there is little vertical integration of production, each step in the productive process being carried out by separate firms, each firm must carry some transactions cash balance. If, on the other hand, production is carried on from raw material to finished product within the same, highly integrated firm, there exists at least the possibility that a smaller total transactions balance will be needed to finance the entire process.

Thirdly, the development of the country's financial system will certainly be a determining factor. A highly developed financial system, wherein borrowing to finance needed purchases is easily and economically available, will permit an individual to get along on a substantially smaller cash balance than would be the case where it is very difficult to obtain credit. Consequently we can say that the more highly developed the financial system, other things being equal, the lower the transactions demand for money.

Finally, the level of income itself appears to be a quite important determinant. This is simply to say that the higher a person's income, the greater his transactions and therefore the greater his need for transactions cash balances. The point can perhaps be best illustrated as shown in Figure 12-8.

Here the solid lines, as before, indicate the fluctuation in cash balances under the assumptions that our subject's monthly pay is $600 and he spends it evenly over the month. If his monthly income should now be raised to $800 and he should still choose to spend it all at a steady rate before his next payday, his transactions balance would behave in a manner depicted by the broken lines. Clearly the rise in income raises his transactions demand for money. With a $600 monthly check his average transactions balance is $300 while, with $800, the average for the month rises to $400.

While all four of these factors clearly affect the size of the transactions demand, the first three would appear to change only slowly over the long run. That is, while a change in payment habits, degree of vertical

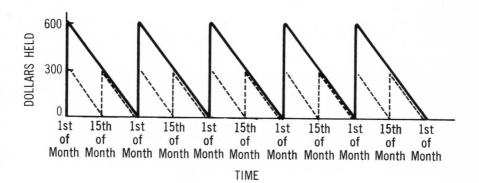

FIGURE 12-7

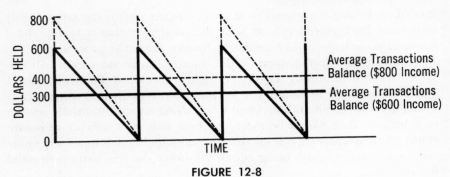

FIGURE 12-8

integration, or the "maturity" of the financial structure will certainly affect the transactions demand *when they change*, all three change only slowly over a long period of time. Hence, within any short-run context, these three are not likely, *in fact*, to cause significant changes in the size of the transactions demand. The level of income, on the other hand, is subject to significant short-run as well as long-run changes. The result is that, in practice, the transactions demand for money changes, in the short run, largely in response to changes in the level of income.

To take account of these considerations, we will depict the transactions demand for money graphically in Figure 12-9.

Here the level of income is measured off on the vertical axis and quantity (of transactions funds demanded) on the horizontal axis. The transactions demand curve itself is upsloping indicating that the quantity of transactions balances demanded rises as income rises. The *slope* of this curve, on the other hand, depends on the other three determinants. For example, the effect of a speedup of payment habits, further vertical integration, or a significant advance in the nation's credit facilities, would be to steepen the curve itself. Opposite changes in any of these three would have a tendency to move the curve to a flatter position.

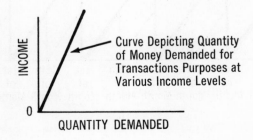

FIGURE 12-9

We have then, in Figure 12-9, a curve that tells us that with a given set of payment habits, vertical integration and financial system, we can determine the quantity of money demanded for transactions purposes directly from the level of income.

The Keynesian Speculative Demand for Money

One area of the classical theory that Keynes questioned was whether it was rational for people to hold (to hoard) money balances of an amount greater than that necessary to fulfill transactions (and precautionary) needs. He argued that, in the case where an individual expects the rate of interest to rise in the near future, holding additional idle money balances was eminently rational. Such a motive for demanding idle money has come to be known as the speculative demand for money, although the Keynesian reasoning has since been supplemented by the contributions of others, as we shall see shortly.

Relation Between Bond Prices and Interest Rates

To understand fully the speculative demand for money à la Keynes, we must do some preliminary spadework on the relation between bond prices and interest rates.

In order to keep the discussion as simple as possible without losing anything fundamental, we shall work with an example in which the bonds involved are perpetuities. That is to say, we shall be discussing bonds that have no maturity date. The borrower (issuer of the bonds) agrees to pay interest to the holder forever, but the principal is never to be paid back. In such a case, the only way a bondholder can get his principal back (he hopes) is by selling the bond to someone else.

Suppose we take, for our example, a bond that is originally issued by the lender at a par value and purchase price of $1,000. The bond carries a coupon rate of 4 percent, which is to say the issuer agrees to pay, in perpetuity, 4 percent of the par value of the bond ($40) annually to the holder. Finally, let us assume that the market rate of interest, which we shall define as the *rate of interest being paid elsewhere in the economy on securities of a risk similar to this one*, was also 4 percent when the bond was originally issued.[6] These figures are listed below in the first line of Table 12-1.

[6] This is simply a common sense assumption. If the market rate of interest had been 5 percent when the bond was originally issued, no rational lender would have bought it because, by definition, similar investments were available which paid more. On the other hand, if the market rate of interest had been 3 percent, the issuer of this bond would be foolish to attach a coupon rate of 4 percent to his obligation. Presumably, he could, in such a case, attract borrowers by paying less. Simple logic leads us to expect the coupon rate of a newly issued bond to approximate the market rate of interest then existing.

TABLE 12-1   An Example—The Relation Between Interest Rates and Bond Prices

Date	Par Value	Coupon Rate	Coupon Payment	Market Rate of Interest	Market Value of Bond
When Issued	$1,000	4%	$40	4%	$1,000
Five Years Later	$1,000	4%	$40	5%	$ 800
Ten Years Later	$1,000	4%	$40	2%	$2,000

Now the par value, coupon rate, and coupon payment are printed on the face of the security and, as such, cannot change while the bond is outstanding. The issuer is committed to paying $40 per year to the holder, regardless of any other changes in the economy.

The market rate of interest and the market value of the bond, however, are something else again. The former, as we know, can easily change as a result of changes in money supply, saving, investment, hoarding, dishoarding, and the like. Our task here is to understand how such changes in interest rates cause changes in bond prices.

Suppose, in our example in Table 12-1, that five years after the bond is issued the market rate of interest rises from 4 percent to 5 percent. At what price can the holder of the bond sell it? Clearly, he will find no rational man willing to pay $1,000 for it since this would be tantamount to accepting a $40 per year income when otherwise similar alternatives are available paying $50 per year. If an actual return of 5 percent on an investment is available elsewhere, the maximum price for which our bond can be sold to rational men is $800 (.05 X = $40). That is, since $40 is all that this bond pays, the rational investor will be willing to pay an amount that "$40 is 5 percent of," and no more.

The holder of the bond when the market rate of interest rises, then, will suffer a $200 capital loss if he sells it. A rise in the rate of interest has thus had the effect of lowering bond prices.

If we look further into the future, say ten years from the date of issue, and assume that by that time the market rate of interest has fallen to 2 percent, we get the reverse result. Now the holder of this bond paying $40 per year can expect to find a buyer who will pay substantially *more* than the $1,000 par value. For if 2 percent is a prospective buyer's best alternative, he should be willing to pay up to $2,000 to acquire our bond (.02X = $40). In this case, the seller of the bond realizes a handsome capital gain.

While the case of a bond with a fixed maturity date requires more complicated arithmetic, it is no different in principle.[7] By way of summary we can say that *whenever interest rates fall, bond prices rise, and vice versa.*

This relationship is purely arithmetical and should be interpreted as definitional rather than as a cause and effect proposition. To say that interest rates rise is just another way of saying that bond prices fall. To say that bond prices rise is just another way of saying that interest rates have fallen. We shall therefore proceed to use them interchangeably.

An Example of the Advantage of Holding Speculative Balances

Let us get back to the speculative demand for money. If a person confidently expects the rate (all rates) of interest to rise in the near future, he is, according to Keynes, perfectly justified in holding idle (speculative) money balances over and above his needs for transactions and precautionary purposes for that period. Indeed, he would be irrational if he did not do so.

It is a simple matter to demonstrate the point. Suppose Mr. Jones expects the interest rate to rise from the present 4 percent level to 5 per-

---

[7] In the case of a bond with five years till maturity, for example, the present value can be computed from the formula

$$V = \frac{R}{1+i} + \frac{R}{(1+i)^2} + \frac{R}{(1+i)^3} + \frac{R}{(1+i)^4} + \frac{R}{(1+i)^5} + \frac{P}{(1+i)^5,} \quad \text{wherein:}$$

V = annual coupon payment
R = present market value of the bond
i = market rate of interest
P = par value of the bond, to be repaid at maturity

The expression above can be reduced to:

$$V = R \frac{1 - \frac{1}{(1+i)^5}}{i} + \frac{P}{(1+i)^5}$$

Our example of a prepetuity, in which the interest is paid forever [so that $k/(1+i)^5$ becomes infinitely small and the last term $P/(1+i)^5$, is zero] reduces the formula to $V = R/i$. As the limiting case, the change in present value resulting from any given change in the rate of interest will always be larger for a perpetuity than for the more realistic case of a bond with a fixed maturity date. Also, the closer the bond is to the maturity date, the less the change in its market price which will result from an interest rate change.

cent within six months. If we return to the example from Table 12-1, he would have to pay $1,000 for the bond if he should buy it today while the market rate is still at 4 percent, but if his expectation turns out to be correct, he can buy it six months from now for $800. Of course by holding idle money for the six month period, he would be foregoing, an interest return of $20 (half a year's interest). But there is certainly nothing irrational about giving up $20 interest return in order to be able to save $200 on the purchase price of the bond!

It is true that our example needs qualification. The reduction in bond prices to be expected from a 1 percent rise in interest rates is always larger for a perpetuity than for the more realistic (but more difficult) case of a bond with a fixed maturity date. Secondly, we would have to assume that our "speculator" does not know exactly when, within the six-month period, the interest rate change will take place. If he were sure that it would take place exactly at the end of six months, he would be better off to put his cash in a savings account, and collect the interest for most of the period, drawing it out and buying the bond just before the expected drop in bond prices occurs. If he is uncertain, however, he will be better off to hold the cash.[8] Finally, we must assume that he is confident enough of his expectation to be willing to gamble on it.

None of these qualifications appear serious enough to undercut the main point, however. Holding idle speculative balances when expecting a rise in interest rates is a perfectly reasonable course.

The Community's Speculative Demand for Money

Granting that holding idle money for speculative purposes makes sense, what determines the size of this demand on the part of the community as a whole? Obviously, the more people who expect interest rates to rise, the greater the speculative demand. But this does not advance us very far, since it leaves unanswered the fundamental question—what leads people to expect changes in interest rates?

One way to handle this more fundamental question is to consider people's ideas regarding the *normal range* of interest rates. Our ideas of *high* or *low* interest rates are usually formulated in light of our recent experience. If we have become "used to" interest rates that have varied from 2 percent to 6 percent, we tend to think of 6 percent as pretty high and 2 percent as quite low. If, on the other hand, we have become accus-

---

[8] If he is not sure when his expectation will be fulfilled, and he has to give notice (perhaps wait for 30 days) to draw his money out of a savings account, he will be better off holding the cash because bond prices may change again in an upward direction before he can make his purchase.

tomed to rates varying from 4 percent to 10 percent, 7 or 8 percent does not seem unusually high while anything below 5 percent appears to us as low.

People's conceptions as to what *is* the normal range of interest rate fluctuation must certainly form part of the basis for their expectations regarding *changes* in rates. For example, if a person, because of his recent observations, forms the judgment that, normally, interest rates fluctuate within a 2 percent to 6 percent range, the existence, now, of an 8 percent rate will lead him to expect, almost compellingly, a drop in rates. An 8 percent interest rate appears abnormally high to him and he expects a fall. Similarly, an actual 1.5 percent rate appears abnormally low, leading him to expect an increase.

The same thing applies to the whole community. If the entire community feels that 2 percent is as low as interest rates are going to get and 6 percent is as high as they are likely to go, when interest rates actually reach (or perhaps even surpass) 6 percent everyone will expect them to fall. If, on the other hand interest rates actually get down to (or below) 2 percent everyone will expect them to rise.

Under such circumstances, we should expect rational people to hold *no* speculative money balances when the interest rate is 6 percent because at such a level, they unanimously expect bond prices to *rise* and they will go out and buy them now, rather than wait. Conversely, when the rate of interest is down at 2 percent we can expect people to hold very large speculative money balances because all look for interest rates to rise (bond prices to fall) and it will be in their interest to hold their saving in money form until they do.

Following this logic it would appear that the community's speculative demand for money will vary inversely with the rate of interest. At low rates the quantity demanded for speculative purposes will be large whereas at high rates, speculative balances will be small.

Of course our discussion thus far oversimplifies greatly. No individual is quite sure just where the upper and lower interest rate limits are. Although he may feel that the normal range is 2 percent to 6 percent, he is not quite certain, for example that rates will not start rising again after dipping to 3 percent. Therefore, instead of holding no speculative balances until a 2 percent interest rate is reached, he may hold *some* at 3 percent but even more at 2 percent, where the likelihood of a rise is even greater. If the rate of interest should actually reach 1 percent, and this is so low that he is positively convinced it *must* rise, then he will rationally hold *all* his saving in idle speculative balances, betting on a drop in bond prices, which appears all but certain.

What kind of speculative demand for the community as a whole would result if all individuals behaved as above? Clearly, the quantity of money demanded for speculative reasons would vary inversely with the rate of interest. The demand for speculative balances would look something like Figure 12-10.

Here we depict a situation in which no speculative funds are held when the interest rate reaches 15 percent presumably indicating that, when interest rates are that high *no one* expects a further increase and, therefore, no one holds any speculative money balances. At a rate of 12 percent, however, some few people expect a rise in interest rates, so there is a small positive quantity demanded. The lower the interest rate, the more people come to expect a rise, consequently, the greater the quantity of speculative funds demanded. By the time the rate of interest gets down to as low as 1 percent, according to Figure 12-10, everyone is convinced that interest rates must rise, so that the speculative demand becomes infinite. This area (the flat portion) of the speculative demand-for-money curve has been given the name, *liquidity trap*, and has a significance to which we shall return shortly.

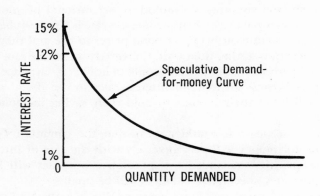

FIGURE 12-10

Post-Keynesian Amendments and Additions to the Concept of a Speculative Demand for Money

The significance of a speculative demand for money was truly enormous. If, as Keynes argued, it is perfectly rational for a man to hold onto money as an asset—to demand money balances in excess of the amount needed to finance transactions—then a number of long-since accepted "truths" had to be reevaluated.

For one thing, if the demand for money (k in the cash balance equation, or $1/V_y$) is subject to so unstable a determinant as peoples' expectations, then we must be much less sanguine about the effects of changes in the money supply on expenditures than were the early quantity theorists. If a sudden change in the demand for money (or in the velocity of spending) occurs, expenditures may be altered without any money supply change or, alternatively, changes in the money supply may be partly or wholly offset by opposing changes in the demand for money (velocity of spending). The money supply becomes a less all-important variable and monetary policy, a substantially less sure policy tool. Certainly the liquidity preference theory of interest, with the speculative demand for money playing the star role, was a major Keynesian contribution.

But the *General Theory* was a pioneering work of the 1930's and Keynes' successors have had some thirty years to comprehend, ponder, debate, and improve upon his theoretical framework. A significant portion of all this later work has gone into amending, although not replacing, his insights into the demand for money as an asset.

According to Keynes:

1. People hold speculative money balances because of expectations of interest rate increases (and accompanying capital losses on bonds).

2. The quantity of speculative money balances demanded is larger, the lower the interest rate (that is, the speculative demand curve has a negative slope) because, the lower the rate, the more intense the expectation of a rise become.

3. The *level* of the speculative demand curve for money depended on the range over which people considered interest fluctuations to be *normal*. If, for example, the normal range in the public's mind was from 2 percent to 6 percent, the curve would become flat at 2 percent and cut the vertical axis at 6 percent. If, on the other hand, the public's ideas of normality should change to the point where they considered 4 percent an unusually low rate and 10 percent a high one, the speculative demand curve would shift to the higher limits set by the 4 percent and 10 percent figures.

Some post-Keynesians, while accepting the validity of the concept of an asset demand for money (a demand for money in excess of that needed to finance transactions) have expressed reservations with regard to Keynes' heavy dependence on speculation as its raison d'être.

It has been pointed out, for example that one can explain the negative slope of the asset (speculative) demand-for-money curve without any reliance at all upon the concept of a normal range of interest rates. Even if the public has no prior conceptions regarding the likely direction of movement of interest rates, the mere knowledge that they are likely to change in either direction may give rise to a down-sloping asset demand-for-money curve. For the mere risk that interest rates may rise (even though there appears an equal chance that they could fall) would cause "risk averters" to hold some cash rather than committing themselves entirely to bonds now.

Nor, in the opinions of many, is the *level* of the asset demand for money curve adequately explained by the range of the public's interest rate expectations. For one thing, we could expect the quantity of money held as an asset to be smaller, at any given rate of interest, the greater the variety and safety of near moneys available. Surely, it has been argued, a community whose claims to wealth consist of nothing but money and highly illiquid bonds, will find a need to hold a larger percentage of its wealth in the form of money than another community in which many diverse near moneys, issued by a variety of financial institutions, are available to compete with money as a means of satisfying this desire for liquidity.

And, again, the volume of the community's wealth itself must certainly be a factor. A wealthier community, in order to maintain a portfolio of assets which, in some sense, satisfies its relative desires for liquid and illiquid assets can be expected to demand more money to hold for asset purposes than a similar but poorer community.

In summary, our speculative demand-for-money curve (or what has now become an *asset* demand for money, recognizing that money is demanded as an asset not only for speculative but also for other reasons) will have a higher level:

1. The greater the community's wealth
2. The less the variety of other liquid assets available (which, in turn, would be likely to be a function of the stage of development of the nation's financial system)
3. The higher the range of interest rates which the community looks upon as normal.

The curve will be steeper:

1. The wider the range over which the average person believes interest rate fluctuation is normal
2. The greater the disparity of opinion among the public as to the normal range of interest rates. For example, if half the population considers 1 percent a normal low and 6 percent a normal high, while the other half considers 5 percent the likely low and 10 percent the high, the total community's asset demand for money will be steeper (stretching from 1 percent to 10 percent) than if everyone agreed on a range from 1 percent to 6 percent.

THE TOTAL DEMAND FOR MONEY

Now we must bring our two pieces together. The total demand for money is the sum of the transactions demand and the asset (speculative) demand and our main task here is to combine the two, both conceptually and graphically.

We concluded earlier that the quantity of money demanded for transactions purposes changes primarily as a result of changes in the level of income. The quantity demanded for asset purposes, on the other hand, varies with the rate of interest. How can we depict these two in the same graph?

Figure 12-11 deals with this problem. In part (a) the transactions demand is drawn while in part (b) the asset demand is reproduced. In part (c), the two are combined to form the total demand for money.

Since there is no way to show variations in three variables (interest rate, income level, and quantity of money demanded) in a two-dimensional diagram, explicit reference to one must be eliminated. Our choice, as indicated by Figure 12-11c is to eliminate income and plot the total demand-for-money curve with the vertical axis measuring off changes in interest rates and the horizontal axis, quantity demanded.

How then do we take account of the unquestioned fact that changes in the level of income, by changing the quantity of money demanded for transactions purposes, will change the total demand for money? Very simply.

As Figure 12-11 shows, we must draw a new total demand-for-money curve for each level of income. For example in part a, when the level of income is Y_1, the quantity demanded for transactions purposes is D_{T1}. For this particular income level, a fixed number of dollars is demanded for transactions purposes. We take account of that amount in part c by the dashed vertical line labeled D_{T1}. Then, to form the total demand for money, we simply "add on," horizontally, the additional quantities demanded at various rates of interest for asset purposes. The result is the *total demand for money when the level of income is at Y_1.*

If the level of income should rise to Y_2, a whole new demand-for-money curve is required. Such a change in income would raise the amount demanded for transactions purposes to D_{T2} in part a, which, in part c is reflected by the dashed vertical line labeled D_{T2}. When the (assumed unchanged) asset demand is added to this larger transactions demand, the result is a higher total demand for money, labeled Total Demand for Money$_2$.

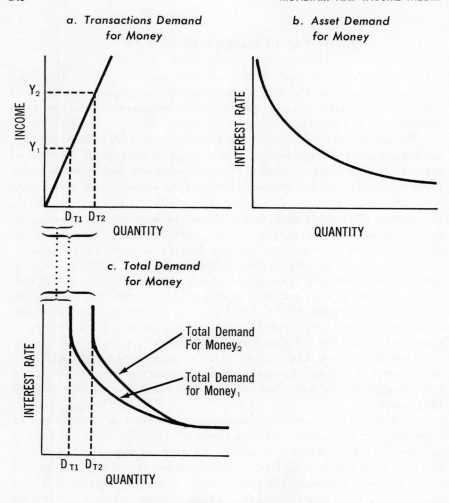

FIGURE 12-11

We arrive then, at a diagram in which changes in the level of income shift the whole demand-for-money curve, while changes in the rate of interest (by altering the quantity demanded for asset purposes) change the quantity demanded via movements along a given demand curve.[9]

9 We have chosen for purposes of simplicity to ignore, at this point, the possibility pointed out by several authorities that the transaction demand for money may become responsive to the rate of interest when the latter reaches some relatively high level. Such a possibility could result from the fact that, when the rate of interest gets very high, the cost, in terms of income foregone, of maintaining normal sized transactions balances

THE DEMAND FOR MONEY, THE SUPPLY OF MONEY, AND THE EQUILIBRIUM RATE OF INTEREST

Now that we have made our way through the reasoning that underlies the concept of demand for money, we are prepared to put it together with the supply and discuss the determination of the equilibrium rate of interest.

Supply and demand are shown together in Figure 12-12. The supply of money, being a certain number of dollars at any point in time, is shown as a vertical line. In the diagram, the equilibrium rate of interest is i_e.

Why must the rate of interest tend toward the point where the demand for money equals its supply? Suppose that, for the moment, the actual rate were i_1. At this rate, the quantity of money people *desire* to hold for transactions and asset purposes is less than the supply that exists (which they *must* hold). Consequently some people hold some money *unwillingly*.

Now no person needs to hold on to money that he does not want to hold. But, short of giving or throwing it away, what can a man *do* with

---

may become so high that it will force some holders of money to "economize" on their transactions balances. The major impediment to lending out transaction balances on a highly temporary basis in order to earn some return on them is the cost of switching back and forth between money and interest earning liquid assets. This impediment may well be overcome by a sufficiently high interest rate (especially for business firms and governments) so that it becomes worthwhile to struggle along with smaller transactions balances. If our graphs accounted for this possibility, assuming i_1 to be the rate of interest above which the transaction demand becomes responsive to the interest rate, they would become:

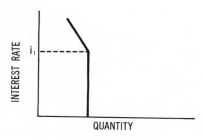

Transactions Demand Curve
with Respect to Interest Rate

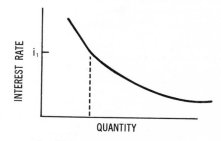

Total Demand-for-money Curve

It is important to recognize the fact that, should such a relationship exist, it has important implications for the effectiveness of a so-called *tight money* policy. If action to raise the rate of interest entices the community to "economize" on its transactions balances, the task of the monetary authorities may be made that much more difficult.

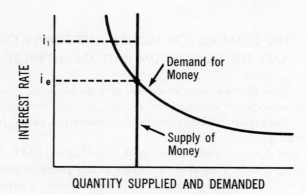

QUANTITY SUPPLIED AND DEMANDED

FIGURE 12-12

money he does not want to hold? One answer, of course, is that he can spend it to buy bonds.[10]

What will be the effects of unwanted cash being spent to buy bonds? Assuming that the supply of bonds available is unchanged, the immediate result can only be a rise in their prices. But, as we have seen, higher bond prices are equivalent to lower interest rates. The market rate of interest will thus be forced down by their action. For how long must this process of buying more bonds with unwanted cash, raising bond prices, and lowering interest rates, continue? Clearly, until there is no more unwanted cash to keep it going. A look back at Figure 12-12 will show that this point will only be reached when the market rate of interest has fallen from i_1 to

[10] We are ignoring the complications that the issuance of equities and the presence of a variety of financial institutions introduce.

We are also omitting the possibility that the person with excess money may choose to spend it to buy consumer goods. If he does we reach an equilibrium rate of interest by a different process. The increased consumption raises income and that, in turn, raises the transactions demand for money. This rise in the transactions demand will shift the total demand-for-money curve up to the right, and the process must continue until the force behind it is eliminated. That is, the demand-for-money curve must continue to rise until it equals the supply that exists at the ruling interest rate.

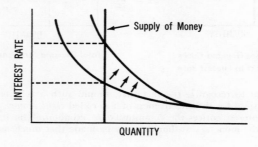

QUANTITY

i_e. Here, equilibrium is restored in the sense that people willingly hold, in their transactions and asset balances, all the money that exists.

Perhaps one more example will help to clarify this point. Suppose, as in Figure 12-13, the rate of interest is originally at the equilibrium level of i_1 and that the Federal Reserve, in pursuance of a tight money policy, upsets this equilibrium by reducing the supply of money from S of M_1 to S of M_2.

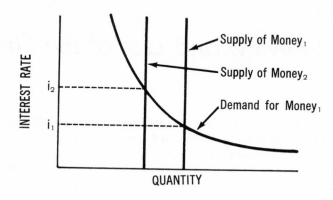

FIGURE 12-13

Immediately after the cut in money supply, individuals find themselves (at the relatively low i_1 interest rate) desiring to hold more money in their transactions and asset balances than there is money to be held. What can they do about this kind of frustration? Individuals can *attempt* to accumulate larger cash balances by not only cutting back on their purchases of bonds but by offering for sale, some of the bonds they already own. Such a cut in demand and increase in supply must reduce bond prices and raise the market rate of interest, with a new equilibrium being established only when interest i_2 has been reached.

13 | *Review and Use of the Theory*

The three previous chapters have been intended to serve as building blocks. Each has concentrated on developing one part of the theory of income determination. The task which remains is to assemble the pieces in order to construct a single, usable, theoretical framework.

Our approach will be two-pronged. First we shall review and summarize the important ideas developed in Chapters 10, 11, and 12, winding up with a graphical[1] model of the economy that encompasses them all. Then we shall go to some lengths to demonstrate how such a model can be used as a framework for analyzing the effects of various changes in the economy, on its performance.

SUMMARY OF THE PARTS AND DEVELOPMENT OF THE WHOLE

A Review

It will be recalled that we started off in Chapter 10 with a discussion of the immediate determinants of the level of production and income. We observed first that production tends to rise whenever aggregate demand exceeds aggregate supply; that production will fall whenever aggregate demand falls short of aggregate supply; and that a change in either direction will stop only when income and production reach the equilibrium level where aggregate demand just equals aggregate supply.

When we looked at this mechanism in more detail we saw that the all important aggregate demand level was composed of consumption

---

[1] This assembly could just as well be done via numerical example, but since it entails many complications, we find that the graphical approach is easier to follow.

spending, investment spending, and government spending. Assuming, as a first approximation, that investment and government spending were autonomously determined by outside forces, we concentrated on the determinants of consumption. Here we concluded that, given consumer expectations, wealth and the like, consumption spending varies with the level of income. These considerations provided us with the basis for producing Figure 13-1 to depict the determination of the equilibrium level of production.

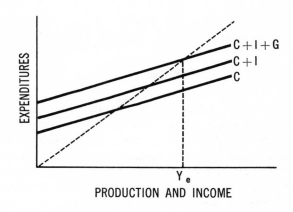

PRODUCTION AND INCOME

FIGURE 13-1

What this diagram told us was that if we were given the amount spent by government and investors and if we had surveyed the public so that we knew how much they would spend on consumption at various levels of income, we could, from these three pieces of information, figure out the equilibrium level of production and income.

But, of course, the amount spent on investment is not a given datum. Consequently, we went on in Chapter 11 to investigate the investment decision somewhat more thoroughly. Here we developed an investment demand schedule, entitled the marginal efficiency of investment schedule, the level of which depended mainly on businessmen's expectations of the future profits to be had by investing. This MEI curve, we said, tells us how much investment spending there will be, at various rates of interest. The two diagrams together, then, provided us with a more complete picture than Figure 13-1 alone does.

Here, as in Figure 11-6, we were able to say *given* the rate of interest, investment spending will be so and so much and that it, along with government spending and the consumption function, will determine the equilibrium income level.

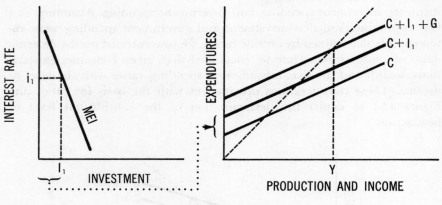

FIGURE 13-2

This, of course, led us finally to investigate what determines the rate of interest. To fit in more easily with our analysis, we chose to emphasize the liquidity preference theory of interest, wherein interest rates depend on the demand for and supply of money. Here we saw that the demand for money is composed of two parts, the transactions and asset demands. The size of the transactions demand depends, most importantly, on the level of income, whereas the quantity demanded for asset purposes varies inversely with the rate of interest. The two together make up the total demand for money, which, along with the supply of money, determines the rate of interest.

Thus, we have made a complete circle. In Figure 13-2, built up on the basis of Chapters 10 and 11, we said that *"given the rate of interest, the MEI schedule plus the consumption schedule and government spending will tell us the level of income."* In Figure 13-3, based on Chapter

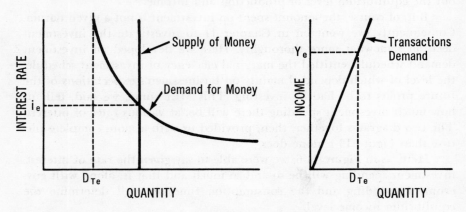

FIGURE 13-3

12, we say that *"given the level of income,* we can compute the quantity of money demanded for transactions purposes, which, along with the asset demand and the supply of money, *will tell us the interest rate."* Clearly these two parts of the analysis are interdependent and need to be combined for a complete theory. That is precisely what we plan to do next.

The Four-diagram Model

Figure 13-4 presents the full theory in diagramatic form. It includes nothing we have not discussed before, the only new feature being the fact that we have combined it all into one four-diagram model.[2]

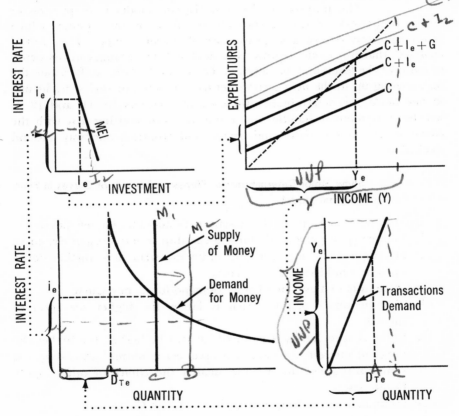

FIGURE 13-4   An Economy in Equilibrium

[2] An alternative method of presenting the same material in two curves is presented in the Appendix to this chapter. The preference for the four-diagram model is based on the feeling that the cost incurred in added clumsiness is more than overcome by the advantage of being able to see, in more detail, "what goes on" when a change takes place.

It is drawn to show an economy at complete equilibrium. That is to say, the *equilibrium* level of income determined in the upper right-hand drawing calls forth (in the lower right-hand drawing) a transactions demand for money which, along with the asset demand and money supply (lower left-hand drawing) determines a rate of interest which permits (upper left-hand) a volume of investment spending which is consistent with the level of income with which we started. This is a long and per-haps, tortuous statement but it will bear study.

The Determinants of the Slopes and Levels of the Curves

The purpose of the four-diagram model is to provide us with a framework for tracing through the effects on the economy which result from any one of a large number of initial changes. The "initial changes" that this model equips us to deal with are changes in the deter-minants of the levels and/or slopes of the curves. In order to facilitate the task coming up in the next section, let us complete our review by listing, in one place, the determinants discussed in Chapters 10, 11, and 12. It will be convenient to handle this in outline form, starting first with the curve in the lower right-hand sector and working our way around clockwise.

Some Major Determinants of Slopes and Levels of Curves in Four-diagram Model

A. Determinants of Slope of Transactions Demand-for-money Curve
   1. Frequency of payment habits—a speedup would steepen the curve
   2. Development of financial and industrial structure—further devel-opment would steepen the curve
B. Determinants of Level of (Total) Demand-for-money Curve
   1. Transactions demand, which is larger the higher the level of income
   2. Level of speculative demand which will be higher, the higher the range of interest rates which people feel is *normal,* the larger the community's wealth, and the smaller the choice of other highly liquid assets
C. Determinants of Position of Supply-for-money Curve
   1. Federal Reserve policy
   2. Treasury policy
   3. Public's *preferred asset ratio*
   4. Commercial bank policy (regarding the extent of use of their reserves)

D. Determinants of Level of MEI Curve
   1. State of technical knowledge—curve usually raised by technological innovations
   2. Stock of existing capital goods—curve is usually lower the more capital goods there are because of diminishing marginal productivity
   3. Level of business taxes—curve is generally higher, the lower the business taxes
   4. Degree of "optimism" or "pessimism" of businessmen regarding future profit prospects—the more optimistic the higher the curve
E. Determinants of Level of Aggregate Demand (C + I + G) Curve
   1. Level of investment which depends on the MEI and interest rate
   2. Level of government spending on goods and services which is considered *autonomous*—that is, determined by noneconomic factors
   3. Level of Consumption Function which depends, in turn, on:
      a. Consumer expectations
      b. Consumer wealth
      c. Consumer tastes (attitudes toward virtues of saving)
      d. Level of personal taxes

EXAMPLES OF USE OF THE COMPLETE THEORY

We are now prepared to make use of our model. Before tracing through a number of specific examples, however, it might be helpful to provide some "ground rules" to facilitate the use of the four-diagram framework.

In the first place, we shall always start off with an economy in equilibrium in the sense in which this condition is pictured in Figure 13-4. That is, we shall assume that prior to a change in one of the curves, the equilibrium rate of interest determined in the lower left-hand graph is consistent with the equilibrium level of income determined in the upper right-hand graph, and vice versa.

Then, we shall assume a change in conditions, which changes one of the curves, and attempt to trace through the effects of that change on the economy, until a new equilibrium position (where once again the rate of interest is consistent with the level of income and vice versa) is reached.

The first task will be to locate the curve (or curves) affected by the assumed change in conditions. Once the nature of this original shift is determined, its effects should be traced through the four diagrams *in a clockwise direction*. That is to say, if the initial change affects the rate of interest determined in the lower left-hand graph, the effect of this on the volume of investment in the upper left-hand graph should be read off

next, followed by a determination of the effect of this change in investment on the equilibrium level of income in the upper right-hand graph,
and so on.

As we shall soon see, it will be necessary to "go around" our four-
diagram model more than once before a new, internally consistent equilibrium is reached. To facilitate discussion we shall refer to these circuits
of our model as "rounds." The end of a round will be assumed to have
been reached each time we determine a new level of income in the upper
right-hand graph.

For example, if our initial change *was* in the lower left-hand graph,
the rate of interest would be affected first. This would, in turn, affect the
level of investment, which would then alter the level of income in the
upper right-hand graph. At this point we have completed round one of
the change toward a new equilibrium. The effect of this change in income
on the transactions demand for money, its effect on the total demand for
money and the interest rate, this secondary effect on investment, and
finally on the level of income, will be referred to as the second round of
the complete change.

The Effects of an Increase in the Supply of Money

Suppose the initial equilibrium of the economy is disturbed
by a Federal Reserve open market purchase from the nonbank public.
This, of course, has the immediate effect of raising the money supply,
which is depicted graphically by moving the supply-of-money curve, in
the lower left-hand graph, out to the right (to S of M_1, in Figure 13-5).

Such a change, other things being equal, will tend to lower the rate
of interest from i_0 to i_1. At this lower rate of interest, the upper left-hand
graph tells us, the amount spent on investment will rise from I_0 to I_1.
Going on over to the upper right-hand graph we then see that, given the
MPC (slope of consumption function), such a rise in investment will raise
the level of income from Y_0 to Y_1. This is the end of the first round and,
as can easily be seen, the open-market operations have had the initial
effect of raising the level of income.

But that is not all there is to it. Such a higher level of income is, in
turn, going to raise the quantity of money demanded for transactions purposes from D_{T_0} to D_{T1}. And this, in turn, will push the total demand-for-
money curve (lower left-hand graph) out to the right from D for M_0 to D
for M_1. Such a shift will *raise* the rate of interest somewhat, from i_1 to i_2
(but i_2 will almost certainly still be lower than i_0). The higher rate of
interest will cut back investment from I_1 to I_2, which, in turn, will reduce
the level of income from Y_1 to Y_2 (Y_2 will still be higher than the original
equilibrium of Y_0).

We have now completed the second round and it can be seen that

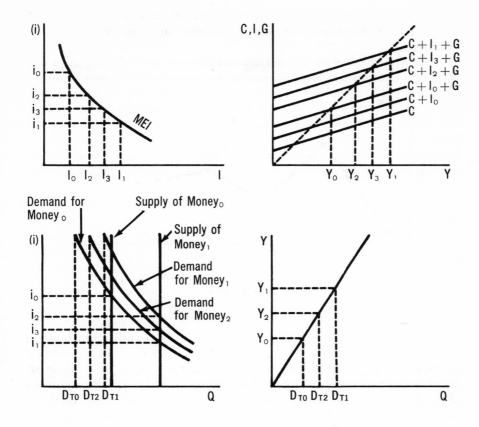

FIGURE 13-5 Effect of Rise in Supply of Money

its effects are to *partially* offset the effects of the first round. The first round, considering the direct effects of the increased money supply raised the income level to Y_1, but the second round, which takes account of the increased transactions demand called forth by that rise in income, operates, in lesser degree, in the opposite direction.

And even yet we are not through. For there is a third round to be considered. The reduction in income (from Y_1 to Y_2) will lower the transactions demand once again (from D_{T1} to D_{T2}) which will lower the total demand for money (from D for M_1 to D for M_2) and lower the rate of interest (from i_2 to i_3). This will permit a rise in investment from (I_2 to I_3), which will raise the level of income again, this time to Y_3.

We need go no further with the detailed description of this adjustment process although it will be apparent to the alert reader that further rounds will be necessary before a new equilibrium is reached in which the rate of interest and the level of income are consistent with one another.

Clearly what we have come up with here is an oscillating approach to a new equilibrium level of income, the nature of which is indicated in Figure 13-6.

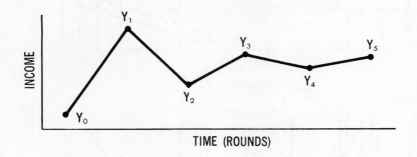

FIGURE 13-6

In Figure 13-6, Y_0 is taken to be the initial equilibrium level of income. Y_1 depicts the rise we get in round one as a result of the increase in money supply. The second round brings us back down to Y_2, while the third round raises income again to Y_3. This oscillating process continues through successive rounds at lesser and lesser amplitude until, finally, a new equilibrium level of income is approached which is consistent with the interest rate.

Now tracing through round after round of the adjustment process that follows any change in conditions is cumbersome, at best. And, fortunately, it is not necessary. We can conveniently generalize regarding the effects of all rounds after the second, in the following manner.

If the given change in conditions is such as to raise (lower) the level of income in round one, unless very peculiar circumstances exist the effects of round two will be to lower (raise) income to a point below (above) that reached in round one but still above (below) the original level. Future rounds will cause further fluctuations *within the limits reached* in rounds one and two. The new, final equilibrium, then, would normally be:

1. Higher (lower) than the original equilibrium
2. Lower (higher) than the income after round one
3. Higher (lower) than the income after round two[3]

[3] The same sort of approach can be used for determining the rate of interest when the change has finally worked itself out. If the change raises (lowers) the rate of interest in round one, it will be lowered (raised) as a result of round two, but not back to the

The student, however, should be aware that an actual adjustment to a new equilibrium need not, in fact, follow the chronological path we have sketched. Our rounds one, two, three, etc., as well as the picture presented in Figure 13-6 are merely expository devices intended to aid the reader in understanding what goes on and why, as a new equilibrium position is approached. They should in no sense be considered descriptions of the "real world" process as it happens but rather, analytical apparatuses to help organize our understanding of the "whys."

Determinants of the Effectiveness of Changes in Money Supply in Affecting the Level of Income

As we observed earlier, one of the main functions of the Federal Reserve System is to control the supply of money in order to contribute to price stability and full employment. In other words the System is to use its controls over the money supply to hold down on inflationary rises in income in boom periods and to contribute to increases in income (in the form of increased production and employment) during recessions.

Having just discussed the *process* through which changes in the money supply affect the level of income, it would appear to be in order to go on to say something about the *magnitude* of the effect of money supply changes on income levels.

As a policy weapon, money supply changes are intended to "work" via their effect on aggregate demand. A cut in the money supply as an anticyclical tool, is "successful" to the degree it cuts or holds down on aggregate demand. Conversely, an increase in the money supply, in the same context, is successful to the degree it raises or holds up aggregate demand. Our question here is: "Under what conditions will changes in the money supply be most effective in achieving their goal of affecting aggregate demand?"

Possible Effects on Interest Rates

Let us look at it first from the point of view of anti-recession monetary policy—a rise in the supply of money. If such a policy is to affect aggregate demand and income levels, it must first lower the interest rate.[4]

---

original position. Further rounds will cause a continued oscillation with the final interest rate being:

1. Higher (lower) than the original
2. Lower (higher) than the interest rate reached after round one
3. Higher (lower) than the interest rate reached after round two

[4] It should be observed that according to the new Friedman version of the quantity theory, money supply increases may raise aggregate demand directly as asset holders seek to trade off the new, unwanted money for other assets, as well as indirectly via an initial lowering of the interest rate. The causal mechanism here, whereby money supply increases transmit themselves into aggregate demand increases, has not, however, been very clearly spelled out.

If the increased supply of money is to lower the interest rate, two conditions must be fulfilled. In the first place, the demand-for-money curve must not rise at the same time, negating the effect of the shift in the supply curve. Secondly, the demand-for-money curve must be downward sloping in the area of the supply change. If, for example, the interest rate is already so low that everyone expects a rise, the relevant portion of the demand-for-money curve will be absolutely horizontal (we will be in the *liquidity trap*) and the increase in supply will not lower the rate of interest. These two possibilities are depicted in Figure 13-7.[5]

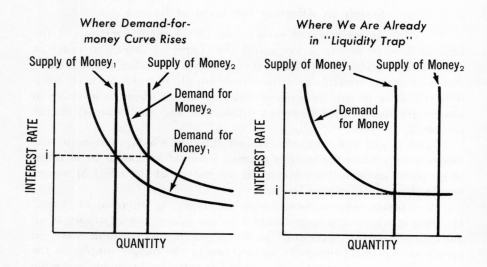

FIGURE 13-7   Situations in Which an Increase in Money Supply Will Not Lower Interest Rates

There are then, two conditions under which an increased money supply will not even affect the interest rate. Monetary policy will, in such circumstances, fail. How about the reverse? Under what conditions will it have the *most* pronounced effect on interest rates? Clearly *the steeper the demand-for-money curve*, in the area affected, *the greater the reduction in interest rates* that will result from a given rise in the money supply. If the type of demand-for-money curve we have been assuming is at all

[5] There are some who feel that, while the demand-for-money curve becomes flatter at lower interest rates, it is going too far to argue that it becomes perfectly horizontal at some low rates. These critics, then, question whether a liquidity trap really does exist. This, unfortunately, is an issue to which our present knowledge provides no definitive answer.

close to reality, this implies that the higher interest rates *are* when we increase the money supply, the bigger the drop in interest rates we can expect. For it is at high interest rates that the demand-for-money curve is steepest.

Possible Effects on Investment

But even if the interest rate *is* reduced, success is not guaranteed. The drop in interest rates is not the end, but merely a means to the end. The goal here is to raise aggregate demand and the hope is that the reduction in interest rates will permit such a rise. Now it is true that, to some extent, lower interest rates will encourage more spending by anyone who spends with borrowed funds. Not only business investors but also government and consumers make use of borrowed funds to finance their spending. But the latter two groups seem to be notoriously insensitive to the interest rate as a cost factor, and we shall oversimplify here by assuming that they do not react at all. This leaves us with only business investors to consider.

How much more investment spending can be expected consequent to a given drop in interest rates? Again, it depends. If the MEI schedule should shift to the left at the same time as interest rates fall, we may get *no* more (or perhaps even less) investment. And, even without a shift in the investment demand schedule, we can expect no more investment if the MEI curve is perfectly vertical in the affected area. These possibilities are depicted in Figure 13-8.

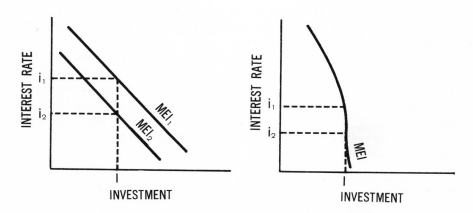

FIGURE 13-8 Situations in Which a Drop in the Interest Rate Will Not Raise Investment

Conversely, the flatter the MEI curve, the more effective is antireces- sion monetary policy. For a flat (elastic) MEI curve will permit a relatively sizable rise in investment spending, as a result of any given drop in interest.

Other Determinants of Effect on Income Levels

If, up to this point conditions are favorable, a rise in aggre- gate demand and the level of income is likely. If so, the policy has been successful. However, the rise in income does not follow automatically even if interest rates are cut and investment spending is increased. If, while all this is going on, either consumption or government spending propensities should fall, the rise in investment may simply keep aggregate demand where it was, and provide no increase in income.[6]

Barring this possibility, the level of aggregate demand must increase and, it will be remembered, increase by a multiplied amount of the rise in investment. This brings us to a third determinant of the effectiveness of monetary changes. If interest rates *are* cut, and investment *is* increased, the favorable effect on aggregate demand and the level of income will be greater, the larger the multiplier (the steeper the consumption function).

Finally, we must consider the *second round* effect. Even if the level of income is raised substantially on the first round, it cannot stay that high so long as a higher income level leads to a larger quantity of money demanded for transactions purposes. The second round effect, in other words, will reduce it. The magnitude of this effect depends clearly upon the slope of the transactions demand-for-money curve. The flatter it is, the more it will cut down on the income rise, and vice versa.

Table 13-1 attempts to summarize the points raised in this section regarding the conditions necessary for money supply changes to be effec- tive in influencing income levels, as well as the situations and develop- ments that can render them ineffective.

It is in recognition of all these potential slips "between the cup and the lips" that many economists point out the indirectness of monetary policy as a means of affecting income. Fiscal policy is more direct in the sense that its effect on aggregate demand, once action has been taken, is more immediate. It does not have to run the gamut of first affecting inter- est rates, then affecting investment, and finally aggregate demand to do its work.

---

[6] It might be noted that, if "success" means restoring full employment, yet another obstacle could appear. Even if the interest rate *is* lowered and even if this does result in an increase in investment, it is a moot question whether *enough* can be done this way to restore full employment. If, for example, a $100 billion rise in income is required to restore full employment, and if the multiplier is 2, a $50 billion rise in investment will be needed to achieve "success." If the MEI curve is very inelastic, it is just possible that increasing the money supply enough to *reduce the interest rate to an irreducible zero level* will not be sufficient. If such a reduction in interest rates raises investment by only $25 billion, full employment is unattainable via this approach.

TABLE 13-1   Determinants of the Effectiveness and/or Ineffectiveness of Money Supply Changes

Changes in Money Supply Will Have Greater Effects on Income if	*Changes in the Money Supply Will be Relatively Ineffective in Changing Income if*
1. The demand-for-money curve is *steep* in the affected area.	1. The demand-for-money curve is *flat* in the affected area.
2. The MEI curve is *flat* in the affected area.	2. The demand-for-money curve shifts to offset the supply change.
3. The consumption function is *steep*.	3. The MEI curve is *steep* in the affected area.
4. The transactions demand-for-money curve is *steep*.	4. The MEI curve shifts to offset the effect of the interest rate change.
	5. The consumption function is flat.
	6. The consumption function or government spending shifts down to offset the rise in investment.
	7. The transactions demand-for-money curve is very flat, causing a large offsetting second round effect.

This too, provides part of the basis for the current widespread opposition to the equation-of-exchange approach to analyzing the economy. It is true that MV_y and $C + I + G$ are simply alternative ways of breaking down aggregate demand, one spotlighting the money supply and the rate of spending and the other focusing on different spending groups. But, say the critics of the MV_y approach, the velocity variable covers up too much. As we have just seen, an increase in the supply of money has a tortuous road to travel before affecting aggregate demand. There are, as we saw in Table 13-1, seven distinct ways in which the effect of a money supply increase on aggregate demand may be altered. If we are viewing the economy in terms of the equation-of-exchange (MV_y) approach, all six of these possibilities must be referred to as changes in the velocity of spending. This, many believe, gives too much significance to the one general term, velocity, for convenient analysis.

The Effects of an Improvement in Businessmen's Expectations of the Future

Suppose, because of important technological improvements, for example, that businessmen's expected returns from investment are sharply increased. Other things being equal, what changes could this be expected to bring about in the economy?

Clearly, the most likely initial major impact would consist of a shift upward and to the right of the MEI curve. As Figure 13-9 shows, this would permit an initial rise in investment spending from I_0 to I_1. This, in turn, would raise aggregate demand (from $C+I_0+G$ to $C+I_1+G$) and raise the level of income from Y_0 to Y_1. And that is the end of "round one."

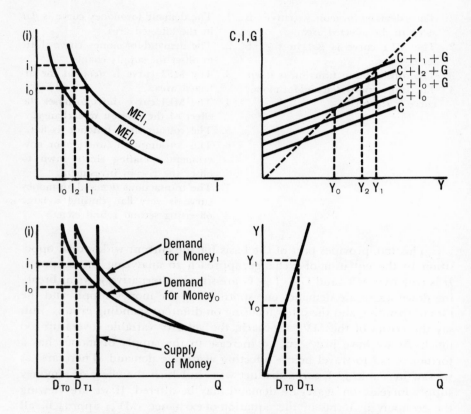

FIGURE 13-9   Effect of Improvement in Technology

The higher income level would raise the quantity of money demanded for transactions purposes to D_{T1} from D_{T0}. This would raise the total demand for money (from D for M_0 to D for M_1) and raise the rate of interest to i_1. A higher interest rate would cause some cutback in investment spending (from I_1 to I_2) which would, in turn, lower aggregate demand and the level of income from Y_1 to Y_2. This marks the end of "round two."

If we should follow this process on to its conclusion at a new stable equilibrium, we would find that the level of income would be somewhere between Y_1 and Y_2. In any event it would be higher than Y_0. The rate of interest would end up finally, higher than i_0, but somewhat lower than i_1.

The Effects of a Speedup in Paydays

Although it is hardly a very likely change, in the short run, it will nevertheless be instructive to trace through the effects of a change in payment habits. Suppose, for example, all business firms suddenly started paying weekly rather than monthly salaries.

As seen in the previous chapter, such a change will reduce the need for transactions balances, thereby increasing the slope of the transactions demand-for-money curve in the lower right-hand graph (from Trans. D for M_0 to Trans. D for M_1) in Figure 13-10. This, at income level Y_0, will

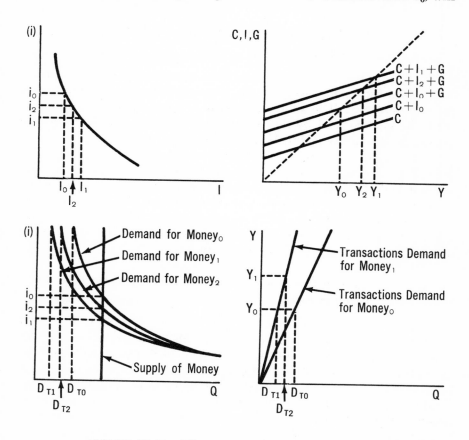

FIGURE 13-10   Effect of Speedup in Payment Habits

lower the quantity of money demanded for transactions purposes from D_{T_0} to D_{T_1}.

The result of the cut in the transactions demand will be a shift in the total demand for money to the left (to D for M_1) and a fall in the rate of interest (from i_0 to i_1). The lower interest rate permits a rise in investment (from I_0 to I_1) which, in turn, raises the level of income from Y_0 to Y_1.

In the second round, the quantity of money demanded for transactions purposes rises from D_{T_1} to D_{T_2}, the total demand for money rises from D for M_1 to D for M_2 and the rate of interest comes back up to i_2. The higher interest cuts back investment to I_2, which lowers the level of income from Y_1 to Y_2. If this were followed through, the final equilibrium level of income would be between Y_1 and Y_2 (and definitely higher than Y_0) whereas the final equilibrium interest rate would be between (i_1) and (i_2), definitely lower than the initial level of (i_0).

The Effect of a Cut in Personal Taxes, Creating a Government Deficit

Our four-diagram model also equips us to trace through the effects of a fiscal policy measure but, as we shall see, the analysis can be more complicated. The additional "wrinkle" introduced here has to do with the method used by the government to finance the deficit that it incurs (or the means of disposing of the surplus).

We already know, from Part I, that if the Treasury raises a deficit by selling bonds to the nonbank public, and then spends the proceeds, there is no net effect on the money supply, whereas borrowing from the banks will increase the stock of money. And we commented then on the fact that the latter course would be the more expansionary of the two. With the aid of our theoretical model, we are now in a position to be more specific about the implications of these two alternatives.

Treasury Deficit Spending Financed by Borrowing From the Nonbank Public

Suppose a government deficit is created by means of a (lump sum) cut in personal taxes (government spending being assumed unchanged), and the amount of the deficit is raised by sale of U.S. securities to members of the nonbank public.

In such a case, while the sale of the bonds cuts the public's money supply, immediate spending by the government will raise it again by an equivalent amount. Hence, on balance, the supply of money is unaffected.

But, of course, aggregate demand *is* affected by the tax cut. By cutting personal taxes the government permits a larger slice of gross income to go to individuals in the form of disposable income. They, in turn, can be counted on to spend a substantial part of it on additional consumption. Graphically, then, the important first effect on our four-diagram model will be to shift the consumption function and the aggregate demand line to the higher level of $C_1 + I_o + G$,[7] as in Figure 13-11. The upward shift will be by somewhat less than the amount of the tax cut, except for the unlikely case wherein the marginal propensity to consume equals one.

The initial rise in consumption permitted by the tax cut, plus the additional "induced" rises in consumption caused by rises in income will

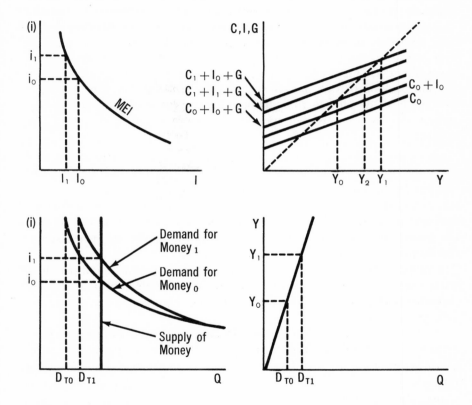

FIGURE 13-11   Effect of Deficit Spending—Deficit Borrowed From Nonbank Public

[7] Since we are not assuming that taxes are related to income, we can show this effect with a parallel upward shift of the consumption schedule. If the cut had been in income taxes, the consumption schedule would become steeper, with a larger multiplier.

drive income up from Y_0 to Y_1. In short order, then, we complete round one. The fiscal policy has had its desired effect by raising aggregate demand and income (and, hopefully, employment along with them).

But, unfortunately, round two will have effects on the rate of interest which will, in some degree, offset part of the rise in income. The increase to Y_1 will raise the quantity of money demanded for transactions purposes from D_{T_0} to D_{T1}; this will raise the total demand-for-money curve to D for M_1 and raise the interest rate from i_0 to i_1. The higher interest rate will cut investment spending back to I_1, which will lower aggregate demand from C_1+I_0+G to C_1+I_1+G and reduce the income level to Y_2. Further revolutions will culminate in a new equilibrium level somewhere between Y_1 and Y_2 and a new equilibrium interest rate between i_0 and i_1.

What are the implications of all this in so many words? Simply this. The reduction in taxes is successful in raising the level of income, but *part* of the good effects on aggregate demand are undercut because the government has financed its deficit in a manner that raised interest rates and cut back on private investment. Since we end up with a higher equilibrium level of income than before the tax cut, the fiscal policy is a success, the rise in consumer spending being greater than the cut in investment.

Treasury Deficit Spending Financed by Borrowing From the Banks

Suppose, in contrast with the case just discussed, the deficit created by the tax cut is financed by sale of U.S. securities to the banks rather than the public. In this case, as pointed out earlier, the money that the government borrows is newly created by the banks and, when spent, the money supply of the public rises.

In terms of our four-diagram model, we again start in the upper right hand graph, showing the upward shift in aggregate demand and the rise in income which is caused by the tax cut. In Figure 13-12, income rises initially from Y_0 to Y_1.

As before, the higher income level will require more money for transactions purposes which, in turn, will raise the demand for money from D for M_0 to D for M_1. But here we encounter something new. By selling bonds to the banks, the government has produced a rise in the *supply* of money also, from S of M_0 to S of M_1. Unlike the situation where the bonds were sold to the public, the effect (if any) on the rate of interest during this second round is indeterminate. In Figure 13-12, we have drawn the relevant schedules so that the changes in the supply of and demand for money exactly offset one another but, of course, this need not always be the case. The interest rate could rise slightly if the increase in demand exceeded that in supply, or fall slightly if the reverse were the case.

So far as general conclusions are concerned, one thing can be said

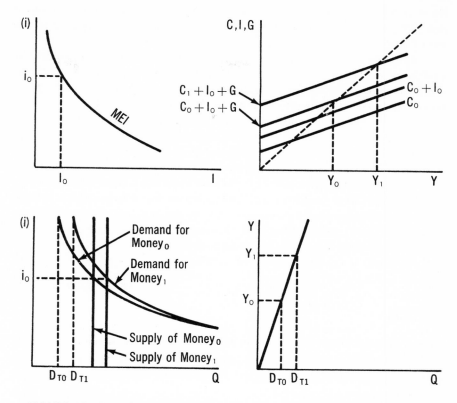

FIGURE 13-12 Effect of Deficit Spending—Deficit Borrowed From Banks

with some assurance. When the deficit is financed via sale of bonds to the banks, the increase in the supply of money which goes along with it will certainly keep the rate of interest from rising as much as it would have had the bonds been sold to the nonbank public with the money supply unchanged. Consequently, private investment spending will be cut back less than in the previous case and the final equilibrium level of income must be higher.

This, then, tells us something more specific about the merits of different methods of handling fiscal policy. If deficit spending is carried out with the express purpose of raising aggregate demand and income, it is better to borrow the deficit from the banks than from the public because the former course will be less likely to raise interest rates and cut back on private investment spending.

These results also permit us to make some generalizations regarding the "best" means of financing deficits when the purpose of the deficit spending is *not* to raise aggregate demand. Take the case of an all-out war effort (such as World War II) where we are already at full employment but the government finds it necessary to operate at a substantial deficit because of very heavy military expenditures.[8]

In such a situation, increases in aggregate demand drive money income up by means of inflationary price rises (in the absence of direct controls over prices). Anything that can be done to hold down on the inflationary rise in aggregate demand will be helpful.

Clearly, the inflationary pressure will be lessened if the deficit is financed by borrowing from the nonbank public, rather than the banks. Why? Because the former course will result in a rise in the rate of interest (demand for money rises but supply does not) which will have the favorable effect of cutting private investment somewhat. If the deficit were financed via sale of bonds to the banks, the increased demand for money, caused by the rise in income, may well be offset by the increase in the supply of money, forestalling any rise in interest rates. Borrowing from the nonbank public is, thus, less inflationary.

The Effect of a Reduction in Government Expenditures, Creating a Tax Surplus

One further example of the operation of our model may be useful. Suppose the government, in order to combat inflationary pressures, cuts government spending without reducing taxes, thereby creating a tax surplus. As in the previous case (where we had to specify how the deficit was financed) we cannot really spell out the effects unless we are told what the government does with its tax surplus. The purpose of the policy is to cut aggregate demand and prevent further price increases but its effectiveness will depend partly on the disposition of the surplus.

Normally, such tax surpluses are used to retire part of the existing national debt. But it makes a difference whether the securities retired are those held by banks or those held by the nonbank public.

Treasury Tax Surplus Used to Retire Securities Held by the Nonbank Public

The reduction in government spending affects the upper right hand graph by reducing aggregate demand and hence, the level of income (from Y_0 to Y_1 in Figure 13-13). This, in turn, reduces the quantity of money needed for transactions purposes and cuts the total demand for money (from D for M_0 to D for M_1).

[8] It may be considered economically necessary to borrow because of fear that the higher taxes that would be necessary to balance the government's budget would seriously impede productive incentives (the worst thing that could happen when the country is at war). On the other hand, political considerations might also lead to deficits at such a time.

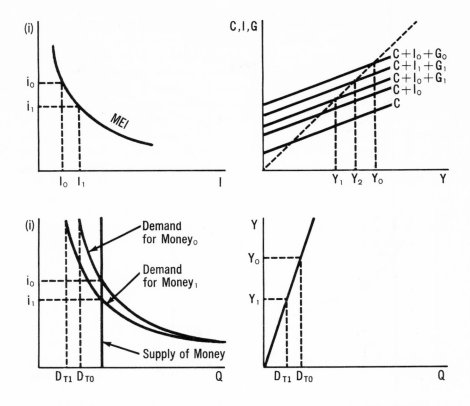

FIGURE 13-13 Effect of Tax Surplus—Surplus Used to Retire Bonds
Held by Nonbank Public

Since the paying off of bonds held by the public places the money collected in taxes back into circulation, the money supply is unaffected and the rate of interest must fall. Such a fall will permit more investment spending (from I_0 to I_1) and this increase will raise aggregate demand back up a bit, offsetting, to some degree, the favorable effects of the surplus.

Treasury Tax Surplus Used to Retire Securities Owned by the Banks

Where the intent of the policy is to cut aggregate demand and combat inflation, more desirable results will be forthcoming from using the tax surplus to retire securities held by the banks. This is because, in this case, the money supply is reduced (see Figure 13-14).

Once again the cut in government spending reduces aggregate demand and the level of income. This will lower the need for transactions

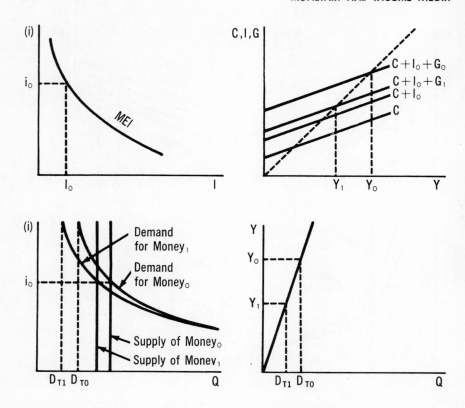

FIGURE 13-14   Effect of Tax Surplus—Surplus Used to Retire Bonds
Held by Banks

balances and lower the demand for money. In contrast with the previous case, however, the lower demand for money need not lead to a reduction in interest rates and an undesirable rise in investment spending. For here the cut in the demand for money may be completely offset by the cut in the supply of money so that interest rates will be unchanged. The result must be a greater total reduction in aggregate demand (and, presumably, inflationary pressure) than is obtainable where the surplus is used to retire public-held securities.

SUMMARY—USE OF THE MODEL

What we have gone through should be sufficient to illustrate the use of our theory. The reader must take over on his own from here. A thorough understanding of the preceding material should be sufficient to permit a "tracing through" of the effects of many changes in economic conditions on the economy (and more specifically on the level of income and the rate of interest).

The four-diagram model, while still far from a "description of the real world," should provide an accurate enough framework to permit thinking about our economy "right side up." Such a result, if achieved, is the important first step in economic understanding.

APPENDIX   *ISLM*
               Hicks — HANSON

AN ALTERNATIVE TO THE FOUR-DIAGRAM MODEL—L-M AND I-S CURVES

The four-diagram model just discussed possesses significant advantages for purposes of tracing through, step-by-step the economy's response to change in any of a number of variables. But is *is* a cumbersome framework.

In an effort to simplify the graphical apparatus required to represent our theory, it has become the most common practice to reduce the four diagrams involved in our more unwieldy model to a single two-line diagram. Students who will be doing more advanced work in economics should familiarize themselves with this graphical device since it is now, by all odds, the dominant representation of the theory employed.

We have seen that a complete equilibrium requires not only that aggregate demand equal aggregate supply (or saving equal investment in a no-government economy) but that the level of income dictated by this equality be such that it produces a demand for money which equals the supply of money at a rate of interest consistent with that level of income. Or, to turn it around, the equilibrium rate of interest which is determined at the point where the demand for, and supply of, money are equal must be at just the level that permits sufficient investment to offset the saving that the public chooses to engage in at that level of income which produces the demand for money with which we started.

For aggregate demand to equal aggregate supply is *not* a sufficient condition in and of itself, to determine the one unique equilibrium level of production in the economy. This is because different rates of interest will produce different equilibrium production levels. If the rate of interest is 6 percent, $75 billion of investment might be forthcoming and the level of income at which saving is just $75 might be $400 billion. A 2 percent rate of interest, on the other hand, may well permit $125 of investment and require income to reach $600 billion before an equivalent amount of saving is called forth.

There are therefore a whole range of income levels at which investment may equal saving, depending on the rate of interest at the moment. We can depict all these possibilities (as well as the upper two diagrams of our four-diagram model) in a single line in the following manner:

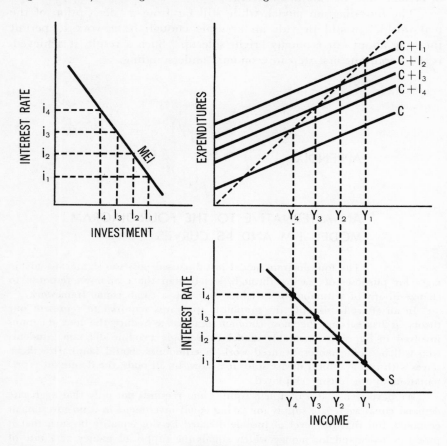

FIGURE 13-15

At each possible rate of interest (i_1, i_2, i_3, i_4) the MEI curve gives us an accompanying level of investment spending (I_1, I_2, I_3, I_4). Along with the given consumption function, each of these investment quantities produces a different level of aggregate demand ($C+I_1$, $C+I_2$, $C+I_3$, and $C+I_4$) and these, in turn, each lead to a different level of income (Y_1, Y_2, Y_3, Y_4). Since the fundamental information that is provided by the upper two diagrams of our four-diagram model is really to indicate the level of income which is sustainable (in the sense that everything produced is bought) for every possible rate of interest, we can construct a new line to present this. In this approach, the rate of interest is measured off vertically, and the level of income, horizontally. For each rate of interest, a dot represents the corresponding level of income. When the dots are joined, we have what has come to be known as an I-S curve.

The I-S curve says no more, and no less than our upper two diagrams. Its level and its shape are determined by all the determinants of the level and shape of the MEI curve and the consumption function. If, for example, an income tax cut should steepen the consumption function, it would at the same time flatten (and raise) the I-S curve. If investors' expectations should improve raising the level of the MEI curve, the I-S curve would shift to the right. If the MEI curve should become steeper, indicating less responsiveness of investors to a change in interest rates, the I-S curve would also become steeper, indicating a smaller change in income associated with each interest rate change, etc., etc.

In an essentially similar manner we can transform the two diagrams on the bottom of our model into a single line, called the L-M line.

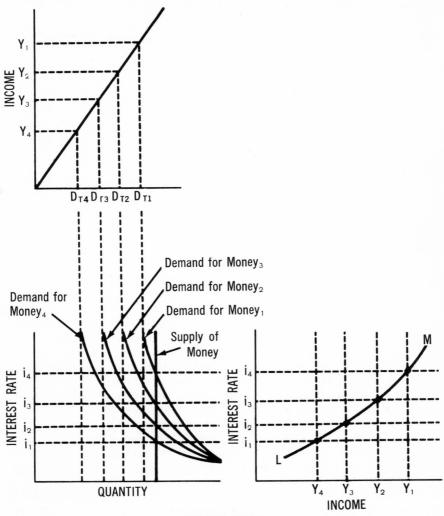

FIGURE 13-16

In this case, each potential level of income, by determining a given trans-actions demand for money, is associated with a certain equilibrium rate of interest. When these two variables, incomes and associated interest rates, are plotted and joined in a line, the result is an L-M curve that provides the same information as the two diagrams at the bottom of the model.

Here, too, the level and slope of the L-M curve is determined by the levels and slopes of the transactions and asset demands for money and the supply of money. A speedup in pay days, for example, will steepen the transaction demand-for-money curve and will lower and flatten the L-M curve. An increase in the community's wealth will shift up the asset (and total) demand-for-money curve and will also shift the L-M curve up and to the left. An increase in the supply of money will shift the L-M curve down and to the right.

If we now put the I-S and L-M curves together in the same surface, we have, in one diagram of two lines only, a simplified representation of everything in our four diagrams.

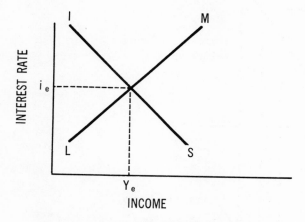

FIGURE 13-17

The point where they cross gives us the one unique pair of values for income and interest rate which are consistent. It is, in short, complete equilibrium.

If, now, an open-market purchase should increase the money supply, the L-M curve will shift to the right and the new equilibrium income level will be higher while the interest rate will be lower. The movement from i_1 to i_2 and Y_1 to Y_2 encompasses all the effects of rounds one, two, three, etc., of our earlier presentation, until a new equilibrium is achieved (Figure 13-18).

It is perfectly obvious that the I-S—L-M curve approach is a simpler, neater mechanism for handling changes diagramatically. For the student who is thoroughly grounded in all the basic determinants of the levels and shapes of these two curves, it is far and away the most efficient means of demonstrating the adjustment to a new equilibrium.

However, it says no more than our more cumbersome four-diagram model. They are simply alternative means of presenting the same relationships, and

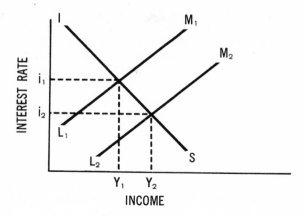

FIGURE 13-18

while the four-diagram approach is the more unwieldy of the two, it has the virtue, especially for the beginning student, of revealing more of the cause and effect process of change.

III

INTERNATIONAL FINANCE

14 | Introduction to International Finance

Simplification is the real goal of economic theory. Consequently it was not only acceptable, but necessary, to proceed within the comfortable confines of an imposing list of simplifying assumptions as we made our way through the income determination model sketched in Part II.

But the luxury of the simplifying assumption carries with it a heavy obligation. The theorist who would say something useful about the world in which we live must be ever mindful of the need to approach reality, even though never really getting there.

A case in point is the assumption, made throughout Part II, of a closed economy—an economy with no foreign trade. As a means of simplifying the analysis there, this assumption was both helpful and usual. But we must realize that to retain it doggedly to the end would result in a distorted theory, quite inappropriate for dealing with some of our most important current problems and issues. We must avoid such a serious omission. That is the purpose of this section.

THE RATIONALE FOR INTERNATIONAL TRADE

The case for international trade is, of course, a simple one. Indeed, it can be justified on substantially the same grounds as money itself. Just as the existence of an efficiently operating money system permits fuller exploitation of the advantages of specialization, so, too, does free, unrestricted international trade.

The reader is no doubt familiar with the time-honored principle of comparative advantage. Given peaceful conditions and abstracting from transportation costs, each nation will be better off (that is, have a higher real level of living) by specializing in the production of those goods in which it has a comparative advantage, while trading for the other things it needs. In its essence the principle of comparative advantage simply states that a nation should obtain its goods and services wherever they cost least in terms of its own resources. If a nation can obtain more units of product X from abroad by producing product Y and trading it to obtain X, than it could by using a similar amount of its resources to produce X at home, it clearly gains by specializing in Y and importing X.

THE IMPORTANCE OF INTERNATIONAL TRANSACTIONS TO THE U.S. ECONOMY

If one were to adopt the parochial viewpoint that the U.S. economy is our only interest, recent data on international trade might seem to imply that U.S. international transactions are relatively unimportant and that devoting several chapters to this topic overstates its importance to us. For example, it could be pointed out that the net contribution to U.S. aggregate demand which results from international trade has recently been in the $5 billion neighborhood, a figure that appears relatively insignificant in the context of a $750 billion economy. Or again, one might point out that even the U.S. *gross* exports of goods and services have, in recent years, totaled only about 5 percent of the U.S. Gross National Product. The fact is, however, that such figures understate the importance of our current topic.

In the first place, the United States is unique in the proportion of its total production going into export business. As Table 14-1 below vividly reveals, most other countries of the world devote a much larger percentage of their total productive effort to turning out goods and services for export.

It should be made clear that the low percentage for the United States does not reflect the fact that it sells little on international markets in absolute terms. Quite the reverse is true, since the United States is the largest single trader in value terms. It is, of course, the very high GNP of the United States that makes its actually sizable export trade look small, when expressed in relative terms.

If one can take the data from Table 14-1 as a rough and ready indicator of the percentage of a nation's employment which depends upon sales to other countries, its relevance is clearer. Whereas one might (quite mistakenly) deprecate the importance of international trade to the U.S.

TABLE 14-1   Percent of Selected Nations' GNP Produced
for Export

Country	Year	Export of Goods and Services, as Percent of GNP
Belgium	1960	34%
Denmark	1961	31
France	1961	15
West Germany	1961	23
Japan	1960	13
Norway	1960	43
Sweden	1961	26
United Kingdom	1961	20
United States	1961	5

SOURCE: *Statistical Yearbook*, 1962, United Nations.

economy, the vital role that it plays in determining the economic welfare of most other nations of the world is clear enough. If from one-fifth to well over one-third of a nation's jobs depend upon production for export, the importance of international transactions can hardly be overstated!

When it is further recognized that, for some countries, a very large percentage of the crucial part of production which must be sold abroad, is intended for U.S. markets the importance of U.S. trade policy is even more apparent. For example, in 1961, 55 percent of Canada's exports were sold in the United States; almost 40 percent of those from Latin America were destined for the United States; and more than 25 percent of Asian exports were shipped there.[1] With some areas depending so heavily on the U.S. markets for sale of their products, it is not difficult to see the point of the old saying: "When Uncle Sam sneezes, some of her trading partners catch pneumonia." Despite their relatively small role in U.S. production, international transactions must command our careful attention.

Nor are these the only reasons why we must devote ourselves to this area. The United States is fortunate in its size, diversity, and rich endowment in natural resources. As such it is far closer to being self-sufficient than are many countries. But it is by no means completely self-sufficient! The relatively small magnitude (about 4 percent of its GNP) of U.S. imports belies their importance to the well-being of the U.S. economy. There are, despite its general affluence, many crucial materials and resources that the United States must import from other countries. Failure to obtain

[1] *Statistical Yearbook*, 1962. United Nations.

them would undoubtedly have the most serious repercussions on the ability of the United States to keep its huge industrial machine operating at full efficiency.

Finally, as the newspapers have made quite clear in recent years, problems in the international sector can have effects that reverberate throughout the entire domestic economy. The recent balance of payments deficits and their attendant gold outflow have created an alarm and spawned a rash of policy proposals that could have serious implications not only for the economy but for the security of the nation itself.

Some critics, for example, have argued that the balance of payments deficits have led the United States to employ monetary policy measures that amount to "letting the tail wag the dog."[2] The implication is that the United States may have taken measures that have been of more harm to its domestic employment situation than of aid to its balance of payments problem. Others have suggested that, because of its deficits, the United States should cut down on its foreign aid or reduce its military commitments abroad despite the political and defense risks involved. We need not take a position now on the merits of these proposals. What is important is clearcut recognition of the fact that their potential effects on U.S. economic welfare are more than sufficient to warrant a careful consideration. Of this there can be little doubt.

METHODS OF MAKING INTERNATIONAL PAYMENTS

For our purposes the really different thing about an international transaction is that two different kinds of money are involved. Whereas a transaction between Americans can be simply settled by the buyer handing dollars over to the seller, a transaction between an American and an Englishman is not quite so simple. For in this case, assuming that the American is the buyer, the English seller wants his own currency, pounds, in payment, while the American buyer normally possesses only dollars.

What solution is available? Stripped to its bare essentials what is required is for the American importer to make two purchases. He must first take the dollars he has and use them to purchase British pounds; then he can go ahead and use the pounds to buy the British goods he desires.

Now the first step in this "double purchase"—the use of dollars to buy pounds—is our chief present concern. Facilitating such exchanges of money is the main function of the *foreign exchange market*.

---

[2] See comments by Senator Douglas and others, in Hearings on the Balance of Payments, Joint Economic Committee, November, 1963.

The foreign exchange market, not unlike most markets, is made up of buyers, sellers, and middlemen. The object of sale, foreign exchange, consists of foreign currency, demand deposits in foreign banks, and other highly liquid short-term claims payable in foreign money. It is, in short, the nation's supply of foreign money, plus very short-term claims to it. The buyers of foreign exchange (from the American viewpoint) are all those Americans who desire to purchase goods or services or perhaps securities from foreigners—essentially, U.S. importers. The sellers of foreign exchanges (still from the U.S. viewpoint) are those Americans who, through the sale of goods or services or securities to foreigners, have acquired foreign money that they would like to convert into dollars—essentially, U.S. exporters.

The middlemen involved in this market are of special concern. It is, of course, their function to bring buyers and sellers together. These middlemen, in the majority of cases, are large commercial banks, located in the nation's financial center (New York, for the United States) acting in the capacity of exchange dealers or brokers.

The commercial banks that perform this vital middleman function in the foreign exchange market arm themselves for their task by establishing a "correspondent" relationship with their counterparts in the financial centers of the other countries of the world. The role of the "correspondent" is an important one. Generally, the American bank will maintain a checking account in its foreign correspondent in the form, of course, of the other country's money. And, in the usual case, the foreign correspondent will reciprocate by maintaining a deposit, in dollars, in the U.S. bank. Besides holding demand deposits for one another, correspondents perform a number of other important services, some of which will be noted below.

So much for the institutional structure of the foreign exchange market. Our major concern is to get some feel for how it works—that is, how international payments are actually made. In what follows we shall make no attempt to describe all the possible means of making such payments. They are many and varied and, indeed, they change as world trade patterns, competitive conditions, and the like, change. What we shall attempt is a description of two of the most prominent mechanisms of payment, leaving greater detail for more specialized treatments. These two will then be relied on, as examples, for our further consideration of international finance.

Let us consider, for our example, a transaction between an American and a British company where the value involved is $280,000 (or, alternatively, if the exchange rate between the dollar and pound is $2.80 per £1, £100,000). In the first case we will consider the mechanism and effects of payment for a U.S. import, in two ways, and then we shall turn it around and look at the mechanism and effects of payment for a U.S. export.

Payment for a U.S. Import

Bank Draft

Far and away the simplest payment instrument in use in international finance is the *bank draft*. A bank draft is simply a special kind of check—an order to pay—which one bank draws on its account at another bank.

Here, the American company would go to one of the large New York banks that deals in foreign exchange[3] and "buy a draft" that the New York bank would draw on its account at its correspondent bank in London. The U.S. importer, for example, would write a check for $280,000 (plus a small service charge) on its own checking account and turn it over to the New York bank in exchange for the draft, which is a check the New York bank makes out for £100,000 on its account at its London correspondent, made payable to the British exporter. The draft is then sent to the exporter, who deposits it in his own account in London.

Let us take a look at the T-account effects of all this. Assuming that the U.S. importer keeps an account at the same New York bank from which the draft is purchased, the effect of its purchase on the New York bank would be as follows:

New York Bank

Due from London Correspondent — $280,000 (£100,000)	Demand Deposit of U.S. Importer — $280,000

When the draft is received and deposited by the British exporter in the London correspondent bank the effects on that bank are:

London Bank

	Demand Deposits of New York Correspondent Bank — £100,000 Demand Deposit of British Export Company + £100,000

And that is all there is to it. The U.S. importer has used his dollars to buy pounds from the middleman, the New York bank, and has trans-

---

[3] It would not really have to go directly to one of these since its own local bank may have a "correspondent" relationship with a New York bank. It is simpler, however, for purposes of exposition to assume that the U.S. importer is located in New York.

ferred these pounds to the British exporter to pay his bill. Sometimes such payments are made immediately on receipt of the goods being shipped but often, especially if the importer is well known, the goods are shipped on a 30-day *open account*. This simply means that payment, by the same means as those described above, does not have to be made until the end of the 30-day period.

Before going on to describe the second mechanism for payment, let us take a look at some of the effects of the transaction above. To begin with, it is clear that payment for this import has reduced the quantity of foreign exchange owned by Americans. *U.S. importers, who provide the demand for foreign exchange owned by U.S. banks,* use up part of it in payment for their imports. In the second place, this transaction has affected the domestic money supply in both countries. The U.S. money supply has been cut ($280,000 of demand deposits owned by the importer having been eliminated) and the British money supply has been increased (£100,000 of demand deposits now being in the possession of the British exporter).[4] *When we pay for imports, our money supply is cut.*

Bill of Exchange

The other mechanism of payment is a bit more complicated. In this case the payment process is initiated, not by the importer but by the exporter. In our example, the British exporter would draw up a *bill of exchange,* a document described by some as a "You owe me." It, in simplest terms, is a paper which states on its face that certain goods are being shipped to a specific U.S. company, for which payment of $280,000 is expected. This bill of exchange can then be taken by the British exporter to his London bank and "sold" to it for pounds at the going exchange rate (less a discount to account for the fact that the London bank will not be immediately repaid). The importer, then, gets his payment in pounds immediately and his London bank has the bill. The London bank will immediately send the bill to its New York correspondent bank, which will, in turn, present it to the U.S. importer for "acceptance."

The U.S. importer "accepts" the obligation stated in the bill by simply signing "accepted" on the face of it. In the usual case, other documents associated with the shipment, most importantly the bill of lading, are attached to the bill of exchange. Upon his acceptance, the bill of lading, which gives the holder the right to go to the docks and claim the goods that have been shipped, is detached by the bank and turned over to the importer.

Sometimes the bill will call for immediate payment by the importer

---

[4] It is to be remembered, of course, that our definition of the money supply excludes demand deposits owned by foreigners.

and sometimes it will call for payment 60 or 90 days hence. In the latter case, the New York bank that now holds it can do one of two things, depending on instructions from its London correspondent. It can hold the bill (an "acceptance" now that it has been signed) until maturity, at which time the U.S. importer must meet his obligation for the face value of the acceptance by writing a check for $280,000 and placing it in the account that the London bank holds at its New York correspondent.[5] In this case the London bank is providing the credit involved.

If, on the other hand, the London bank does not choose to finance the transaction, it will instruct its New York correspondent to rediscount the acceptance in the New York money market. This simply involves finding an American lender who will purchase it at its discounted value and hold it for 60 to 90 days in order to earn the interest involved.

If the U.S. importer is small and not widely known, it may have received advance permission from its own New York bank to have the British exporter draw the bill of exchange on the bank, rather than the importer. Then, when the bank "accepts" it, the acceptance is much more readily salable in the money market, since it is the bank's own promise to pay.

What are the T-account effects with the bill of exchange? When the British exporter sells the document to its London bank, the entries would be:

London Bank

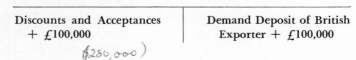

Discounts and Acceptances	Demand Deposit of British
+ £100,000	Exporter + £100,000

If the London bank chooses to remain the owner of the acceptance until its maturity, the effects of final payment by the U.S. importer on the New York bank's balance sheet would be:

New York Bank

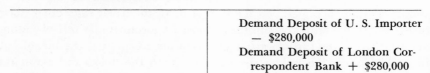

	Demand Deposit of U. S. Importer − $280,000
	Demand Deposit of London Correspondent Bank + $280,000

---

[5] The London bank, which paid the British importer £100,000, less a discount, receives the full $280,000, the difference being the interest it earns for financing the 60 or 90 days of credit. It should be pointed out that the original purchase price agreed upon between the two companies would be such that the discounted amount received by the British exporter would fully compensate it. The American importer, who is really getting the 60 to 90 days credit, bears the interest cost.

These T-accounts ignore the interest involved. In fact the British exporter would receive less than £100,000, by the amount of the discount.

In this case, as in the case of payment by a bank draft, our payment for an import reduces the U.S. domestic money supply and payment for the British export raises the British money supply. There is one difference, however. Instead of U.S. banks using up part of their supply of foreign exchange in payment, British banks have increased their ownership of foreign money. As we will see later, for all practical purposes, the effects of drawing down U.S. claims on foreigners are no different than their increasing their claims on the United States.

Payment for a U.S. Export

Bank Draft

When the United States exports, as might be expected, everything is reversed. If we assume, once again, that a $280,000 sale is involved, the British importer could pay most directly by purchasing a bank draft from his London bank for approximately £100,000 and sending it directly to the U.S. exporter who deposits it in his New York bank. In this case, the T-account entries are:

London Bank		New York Bank	
Due from New York Correspondent Bank — £100,000 ($280,000)	Demand Deposit of British Importer — £100,000		Demand Deposit of U.S. Exporter + $280,000 Demand Deposit of London Correspondent Bank — $280,000

The important effects are:

1. A rise in the U.S. domestic money supply
2. A fall in the British domestic money supply
3. A reduction in the supply of foreign exchange owned by the British.

Bill of Exchange

If, on the other hand, a bill of exchange is used, the U.S. exporter would draw it up and have it discounted at his New York bank. The New York bank would send it to its London correspondent, who would present it to the British importer for acceptance, and, if the New York bank requested, hold it there until maturity. At maturity, the British importer would, of course, pay in pounds, thereby increasing the New York bank's foreign balances. The T-accounts (once again ignoring the interest involved) would look like this—(1) when the bill is orginally discounted at the New York bank:

New York Bank

Discounts and Acceptances + $280,000	Demand Deposit of U.S. Exporter + $280,000

and (2) when the importer pays at maturity:

London Bank

	Demand Deposit of British Importer − £100,000 Demand Deposit of New York Correspondent Bank + £100,000

Once again, payment for a U.S. export raises the U.S. domestic money supply and lowers that of the British, but in this case, instead of the British banks using up their supply of foreign exchange, New York banks increase theirs.

Let us summarize the important results of international transactions which we have thus far uncovered:

1. U.S. Exports
   a. Raise the U.S. Domestic Money Supply
   b. Either Raise the U.S. Supply of Foreign Exchange or Reduce the Supply of Dollars Owned by Foreigners
2. U.S. Imports
   a. Lower the U.S. Domestic Money Supply
   b. Either Lower the U.S. Supply of Foreign Exchange or Raise the Supply of Dollars Owned by Foreigners

THE BALANCE OF PAYMENTS

In any year, of course, there are many transactions between Americans and foreigners such as those just described. It is obviously useful, for policy purposes, to know something about their total and composition for the nation as a whole. This is the purpose of the *balance of payments,* compiled regularly for the United States by the Department of Commerce.

A thorough understanding of the logic, concepts, and organization of the balance of payments is an indispensable first step to any discussion of international trade problems. And yet, such understanding does not always come easily.

Let us begin at the beginning with a working definition. The U.S. balance of payments might reasonably be defined as *"a double-entry listing of all economic transactions between American residents and foreign residents during the year, with those transactions grouped according to the direction of payment required."* One way of presenting a balance of payments statement is shown in Table 14-2.

Before we look, in somewhat more detail, at the various categories of transactions within the balance of payments, one point should be made clear. It is an accounting statement, based upon the fundamental premise of double entry bookkeeping, that there are two sides to every transaction. If the balance of payments is presented as in Table 14-2, *every transaction between Americans and foreigners will affect it in two places,* reflecting the two sides of the transaction.

There are two reasons for stressing the double-entry nature of this statement early in the discussion. In the first place, the student who keeps it in mind will have little difficulty in grasping the point to be explained shortly, that the "balance of payments always balances by definition." Secondly, and of more immediate concern, the logic of the placement (right side or left side) of some of the more difficult-to-handle items will be clearer to the reader who recognizes that while each specific entry in our two-sided statement reveals only half the results of a transaction, its location (right or left side) depends upon it alone. If this statement seems especially difficult to interpret, the reader is asked to be patient. We shall return to this point shortly. Before doing so, however, let us go down the list of the items in Table 14-2.

1. *Exports and Imports of Goods.* There is no problem in understanding and properly locating these. When we export goods we clearly send out something of value for which we expect payment, and when we import goods, the reverse is true.

2. *Exports and Imports of Services.* Only slightly greater difficulty is encountered here. If U.S. ships transport foreign goods or if foreign tourists enjoy U.S. hotels, restaurants, and recreation facilities, U.S. citizens are providing valuable services for foreigners for which the U.S. citizens expect payment. Such items will therefore be left-hand entries, representing exports of services. On the other hand to the extent that foreign ships transport U.S. goods and to the considerable extent that U.S. tourists

TABLE 14-2   U.S. Balance of Payments

Export Items—Transactions Requiring Payment to Americans by Foreigners	*Import Items—Transactions Requiring Payment by Americans to Foreigners*

1. *Exports of Goods*
 2. *Exports of Services*
   Examples:
   a. U.S. ships transport foreign goods
   b. Foreign tourists spend money in the United States
   c. Investment income— amount of interest, dividends, and profits received by Americans on foreign investments
 3. *Long-term Investments* (Export of Long-term IOU's)
   Examples:
   a. Purchase by foreigners of long-term securities issued by U.S. firms and governments
   b. Direct investment by foreigners in U.S. economy
 4. *Short-term Capital Movements—* Net increase in ownership by foreigners of short-term obligations including bank deposits, issued by U.S. firms and governments
 5. *Exports of Gold*
 6. *Unilateral Transfers—*Value of gifts from foreigners to Americans
	1. *Imports of Goods*
	 2. *Imports of Services*
	   Examples:
	   a. Foreign ships transport U.S. goods
	   b. American tourists spend money abroad
	   c. Investment income— amount of interest, dividends, and profits paid by Americans to foreign investors
	 3. *Long-term Investments* (Imports of Long-term IOU's)
	   Examples:
	   a. Purchase by Americans of long-term securities issued by foreign firms and governments
	   b. Direct investment by Americans in foreign economies
	 4. *Short-term Capital Movements—* Net increase in ownership by Americans of short-term obligations, including bank deposits, issued by foreign firms and governments
	 5. *Imports of Gold*
	 6. *Unilateral Transfers—*Value of gifts from Americans to foreigners

spend money traveling abroad, foreigners are providing services for U.S. citizens for which the foreigners must be paid. These, then, are right-hand entries.

Students sometimes have difficulties with another item that we list as a part of exports and imports of services—investment income. This represents interest, dividends, and profits earned during the year on investments owned abroad. The value of the payment of interest, dividends, and profits to Americans, earned on securities and branch plants owned abroad, are considered an export of the services of American capital and, as such, appear on the left-hand side of the balance of payments. The value of interest, dividends, and profits, paid by Americans to foreign owners of U.S. securities or branch plants here, are treated as an import of services, a righthand entry.

How does this treatment fit in with our prior classification of left-hand entries representing things of value done by Americans for foreigners, requiring payment to Americans and right-hand entries representing things of value done by foreigners for Americans, requiring payment by Americans? Very simply. The item that goes on the left-hand (export) side represents the value of the services which U.S. capital invested abroad has performed for foreigners during the year, for which Americans expect payment. This entry is *not* the payment itself (although it is equal to it in amount) but the value of the services rendered for which payment (which will show up elsewhere on the right-hand side) is due. Similarly, the amount of interest, dividends, and profits paid by Americans to foreigners, is taken to represent the value of the services performed by foreign capital invested in the United States—a service for which Americans must pay.

3. *Long-term Investment.* Long-term investment by Americans abroad, a right-hand (import) side entry in our balance of payments consists primarily of purchases by Americans of securities issued by foreign firms and governments with a maturity date at least one year hence, plus direct investment (outright purchase of productive facilities) abroad by American firms. Its counterpart on the left-hand (export) side of the balance of payments includes purchases during the year by foreigners of long-term securities issued by American firms and governments and direct investment by foreigners in the United States.

Since proper handling of these items is sometimes a source of confusion, let us take a closer look. When Americans purchase foreign securities they are, it seems, "exporting" American capital to foreigners. Why then, have we said that such an activity appears on the right-hand (import) side of the U.S. balance of payments?

To answer this question we need, once again, to emphasize the two-sided nature of all transactions. When Americans buy foreign long-term securities what are the two sides? On the one hand, Americans are getting something of value from foreigners—the securities themselves, their IOU's—and, on the other, Americans are exporting their capital to pay for these securities. Looked at in this light it is clear that the entry on the right-hand (import) side is intended to reflect *the value of the securities that Americans* get (import) while the actual "capital export"—actual *pay-*

ment by Americans for the securities—appears somewhere on the other (left-hand, export) side.

Similarly, when foreigners purchase long-term securities issued by American firms and governments, the purchase appears on the left-hand (export) side of the U.S. balance of payments because, in truth, Americans are exporting valuable IOU's to foreigners for which they have a right to expect payment. The actual payment, or the "capital import," if that term is desired, will show up somewhere on the right-hand (import) side.

A word of caution before we go on. The reader should take care to avoid confusing interest and dividends earned with investments. The payments for the former, of course, represent *income* from the services of capital invested in past years. Expenditures on the latter, on the other hand, permit an increase in the *stock of capital* Americans have invested abroad and lay the basis for even greater interest and dividend payments in future years. The two, the volume of U.S. foreign investment and the volume of interest and dividends received are, over the long run, related. It is, however, important to recognize their fundamental differences.

4. *Short-term Capital Movements.* These might equally well be termed "short-term investments" to emphasize their essential similarity to long-term investments. However, the title of "short-term capital movements" is the customary one, so we shall use it.

When Americans increase their ownership of short-term (less than one year until maturity) obligations issued by foreign firms and governments, or, significantly, when Americans increase their ownership of deposits in foreign banks, the transaction appears on the right-hand (import side) of the U.S. balance of payments. This treatment is perfectly parallel with that for long-term investments. Such investments represent an "import of short-term IOU's" for which Americans must pay in some form.

Conversely, an increase in foreign ownership of American-issued short-term obligations, including deposits in U.S. banks, affects the left-hand (export) side of the U.S. balance of payments because it represents an "export of American short-term IOU's" to foreigners, in return for which Americans expect payment of some kind.

Notice that the left-hand entry in this category calls for the net increase in foreign short-term claims on Americans and the right-hand entry calls for the net increase in U.S. short-term claims on foreigners. This is to take account of the fact that particular transactions during the year may either increase or decrease foreign exchange deposits owned and only the net amount on each side is required.

For example, if Americans import $100 worth of goods and pay for them via a draft on balances owned by New York banks, the effect will be to reduce American ownership of foreign exchange. The two offsetting effects on the U.S. balance of payments from such a transaction will be:

Transactions Requiring Payment to Americans	*Transactions Requiring Payment by Americans*
	Imports of Goods + $100 Short-term Capital Movements — $100

Similarly, if foreigners buy goods from Americans and pay via a bank draft that reduces their banks' ownership of dollar deposits at their New York correspondents, the U.S. balance of payments would show exports of goods, offset by an equivalent negative short-term capital movement, both on the left-hand side.

5. *Exports and Imports of Gold.* Transactions in gold affect the balance of payments in the same way as exports and imports of commodities, although, of course, they may have quite different implications. When Americans ship gold to foreigners[6] the foreigners are receiving something of value from Americans for which a payment of some sort must be made. Gold exports, then, are a left-hand (export) side entry. When gold is imported into this country, of course, the reverse is true. Americans are receiving something of value for which they must pay foreigners and the appropriate entry appears on the right-hand (import) side.

There is an area of confusion present in the treatment of both gold movements and short-term capital movements which should, despite the difficulties involved, be met squarely. This has to do with a seeming conflict between the "cause and effect" order of some transactions and the logic we have used to place them on the proper side of the balance of payments.

The point is, perhaps, best made by example. Suppose an American company purchases $10,000 worth of goods from a British manufacturing firm and pays for them via the bill of exchange mechanism whereby British banks end up with larger dollar deposits at their New York correspondents. The two entries in our balance of payments, as a result of this transaction will be:

Transactions Requiring Payment to Americans	*Transactions Requiring Payment by Americans*
Short-term Capital Movements + $10,000	Imports of Goods + $10,000

[6] In fact, of course, usually Americans do not actually ship it to foreigners but, instead, set it aside as the foreigners' property even though it stays in the United States.

Or, alternatively, suppose we export $10,000 worth of goods and are paid directly by a shipment of gold (an unlikely case). Here, the proper entries in our balance of payments would be:

Transactions Requiring Payment to Americans	Transactions Requiring Payment by Americans
Exports of Goods + $10,000	Import of Gold + $10,000

But, one may ask: "If the short-term capital movement in the first example is really a payment for goods imported, how can it logically be listed under the heading 'Transactions Requiring Payment *to* Americans'? And if the gold brought in in the second example is really the payment foreigners make to us for goods we sold to them, why is it listed under 'Transactions Requiring Payment *by* Americans'?"

The question is a natural one and it brings up an important point. While it is true that every single right-hand entry in the balance of payments is balanced *somewhere* by an equivalent left-hand entry (or an equivalent negative right-hand entry), one cannot look at the statement itself and determine cause and effect relationship between particular entries as one *can* in the case of individual transactions, such as the above examples.

The location (right side or left side) of each of the two entries caused by a single transaction is determined independently of any cause and effect relationship involved in the transaction itself. When this point is fully understood, one should have no difficulty recognizing that, looked at on its own merits, when Americans grant foreigners increased deposits in U.S. banks Americans clearly are giving foreigners something of value for which they must be paid. The fact that we happen to know that in this case payment was in the form of imported goods and that the cause and effect sequence is the other way around is beside the point.

Similarly, there can be no doubt that when foreigners send Americans gold the Americans have received something of value for which they must pay. Our incidental knowledge about this transaction, which indicates that Americans did pay by exporting goods and that, in fact, the gold shipment came as a result of the goods shipment, has nothing to do with the proper location of the gold movement in the U.S. balance of payments.

6. *Unilateral Transfers.*   Finally, we must consider the role of *unilateral transfers,* an area of some new difficulty. The problem here arises out of the fact that, by their very nature, these are not two-sided, *quid pro quo*, transactions. They represent gifts between Americans and the

rest of the world and their very name, "unilateral," reflects their one-sidedness.

Because these transactions are one-sided, but the balance of payments is an accounting statement that must balance, a fictitious "other side" of the transactions called unilateral transfers is employed to keep things straight. Once again, an example may he helpful.

If the U.S. government should make a $1 billion gift to foreign governments in the form of a dollar deposit in New York banks, the effect on the U.S. balance of payments would be:

Transactions Requiring Payment to Americans	Transactions Requiring Payment by Americans
Short-term Capital Movements + $1 billion	Unilateral Transfers + $1 billion

It is admittedly, pretty farfetched to think of American gifts to foreigners—the unilateral transfers entry on the right-hand side—as being a transaction requiring payment by Americans. What is the thing of value we are getting in this case which requires us to pay foreigners? One could stretch one's imagination a bit and come up with some sort of answer in defense of this treatment but it is perhaps best to admit that, while the treatment of this entry suggested is perfectly correct, it is pretty difficult to logically fit it in under the tent we have been calling "Transactions Requiring Payment *by* Americans." Let us call it an exception and let it go at that.

A gift from foreigners to Americans of $1 billion in the form of deposits in foreign banks would have opposite effects on U.S. balance of payments. The entries, in this case, would be:

Transactions Requiring Payment to Americans	Transactions Requiring Payment by Americans
Unilateral Transfers + $1 billion	Short-term Capital Movements + $1 billion

Why the Two Sides of the Balance of Payments Must Balance—Some Further Examples

Having stressed the double-entry nature of the balance of payments, it hardly needs to be added that, when all transactions are considered, the two sides must be equal. This, of course, follows from the fact that every single transaction that affects the statement, has offsetting effects. The balance of payments always balances, numerically, by definition. It, like the equation of exchange, is a truism.

The same cannot be said for any part of the balance of payments. If one compares simply a nation's exports and imports of *goods*—the *balance of trade*, to use a common term—there is no necessary reason for equality. A nation can obviously export more goods than it imports or vice versa.

Similarly, there is no particular reason for a nation's exports of goods and services to exactly equal its imports of goods and services. The difference between these two totals, sometimes referred to as a nation's *balance on current account*, can be positive or negative. If it is positive, if exports of goods and services exceed imports of goods and services, the nation is often said to have a *surplus* on current account, while if it is negative, with imports being larger, it is said to be running a current account *deficit*.[7]

We shall conclude this section with a list of examples of the balance of payments effects of particular transactions in the hopes that (1) they will further illustrate the fact that every transaction has offsetting entries, thereby requiring that the balance of payments must balance and (2) they will help clarify some of the areas of difficulty in the preceding material.

1. An American company sells $100,000 worth of goods to a British company, payment being made on a bill of exchange that increases the balances owned by New York banks at their London correspondents:

Transactions Requiring Payment to Americans	Transactions Requiring Payment by Americans
Exports of Goods + $100,000	Short-term Capital Movements + $100,000

2. American owners of securities issued by a British firm receive $50,000 of dividend payments, the mechanism of payment raising the balance owned by New York banks at their London correspondents:

Transactions Requiring Payment to Americans	Transactions Requiring Payment by Americans
Exports of Services + $50,000	Short-term Capital Movements + $50,000

[7] The reader should take care not to confuse the significance of a surplus or deficit on current account with that of a surplus or deficit in the balance of payments as a whole. The latter topic will be discussed below.

3. Americans purchase $250,000 of the common stock of a British company, the payment process raising the dollar balances of London banks owned at their New York correspondents:

Transactions Requiring Payment to Americans	*Transactions Requiring Payment by Americans*
Short-term Capital Movements + $250,000	Long-term Investment + $250,000

4. The U.S. government makes a gift of $500,000 to a foreign government in the form of dollar deposits in New York banks:

Transactions Requiring Payment to Americans	*Transactions Requiring Payment by Americans*
Short-term Capital Movements + $500,000	Unilateral Transfers + $500,000

5. The foreign government spends these dollars to buy goods from U.S. companies, thereby reducing its claims on U.S. banks:

Transactions Requiring Payment to Americans	*Transactions Requiring Payment by Americans*
Exports of Goods + $500,000 Short-term Capital Movements − $500,000	

6. Foreign governments that hold dollar deposits in New York banks spend them to buy $100,000 of gold from the U.S. Treasury:

Transactions Requiring Payment to Americans	*Transactions Requiring Payment by Americans*
Exports of Gold + $100,000 Short-term Capital Movements − $100,000	

EQUILIBRIUM AND DISEQUILIBRIUM IN THE BALANCE OF PAYMENTS

To show that the two sides of a firm's balance sheet are equal reveals nothing whatever about the health or stability of the firm's position. Its balance sheet must always balance, by definition, whatever its economic condition. Similarly, the fact that the amount of a commodity bought is exactly equal to the amount sold, at the present market price, is far from demonstrating that that market price is an equilibrium price which clears the market. The amount bought and the amount sold are definitionally equal and reveal little about the quantity sellers would be willing to sell or the quantity buyers stand ready to buy.

In both cases, a sharp distinction must be drawn between *definitional identities*, things that are defined as equal when the equality itself indicates nothing except the definitions involved, and *equilibrium* situations in which a condition of "balance" or "stability" has been achieved.

So it is with the balance of payments. Equality between the two sides of a nation's balance of payments is a matter of definition. For every nation, at all times, whatever its international trade situation, the two sides of the balance of payments are equal. But such definitional equality says nothing about the stability of its current international trade position. *Equality* in a nation's balance of payments, then, has no significance for its economic welfare.

Equilibrium in a nation's balance of payments is something else again. As in the case of the equilibrium price, equilibrium size of industry, and equilibrium level of income, the term denotes a condition of "balance"—in this case, balance in its international transactions. As in its other uses, the equilibrium position is one of reasonable stability, one from which there are no present forces requiring a change.

Perhaps a fuller understanding of the meaning of equilibrium in the balance of payments can be obtained by first considering some *disequilibrium* situation, in which forces that are causing change *are* present.

The student will recall that in the case of a price above or below equilibrium, the forces that cause a change in price are dissatisfied sellers or dissatisfied buyers, each of whom would like to sell or buy more than he is able to at the ruling price. In the case of an industry of above equilibrium size, the force that causes a contraction in size is the dissatisfaction of those firms that are making below normal profits. And in the case of a level of production above the equilibrium level, the motive force for change comes from sellers who are unable to sell everything they are producing at today's high production schedules.

Examples of Disequilibrium

A nation has a disequilibrium situation in its balance of payments when its two sides are brought into equality by means that cannot be relied upon indefinitely. In such a case the motive force that will sooner or later bring about a change is usually the government of the country involved.[8]

Let us take a look at some examples. Consider a country that has experienced no long- or short-term international investment transactions and no unilateral payments, and has a balance of payments that looks like this:

Transactions Requiring Payment to Americans	*Transactions Requiring Payment by Americans*
Exports of Goods and Services $20 billion Exports of Gold $5 billion	Imports of Goods and Services $25 billion

Clearly, unless it happens to be a gold producing country that can turn out $5 billion of gold annually on a regular basis, its current situation in international trade cannot be indefinitely sustained. It was able, this year, to import $5 billion more goods and services than it exported only because it shipped out gold in payment for the difference. But, since no country has an unlimited supply of gold, sooner or later a change must be forthcoming. This country's balance of payments is therefore in disequilibrium. The development that requires changes is the country's dwindling gold stock. The institution that will sooner or later be forced to act to cause the change will be, in all likelihood, its government.

Gold movements, however, are not the only evidence of balance of payments disequilibrium, nor is an excess of imports of goods and services its only cause. Consider the following case:

Transactions Requiring Payment to Americans	*Transactions Requiring Payment by Americans*
Exports of Goods and Services $30 billion Short-term Capital Movements $4 billion (Buildup of Demand Deposits Owned by Foreigners, in U.S. Banks)	Imports of Goods and Services $28 billion Long-term Investment $6 billion (by U.S. Citizens)

[8] Of course, the need for action will seem more pressing in the case of a deficit than in that of a surplus.

This country, also, has an international transactions situation that is in disequilibrium, despite the absence of gold flows and despite the fact that it is selling more goods and services abroad than it is buying. The reason is that its $2 billion surplus on current account is more than offset by the fact that its citizens are investing heavily at long-term in foreign countries. They are spending $34 billion dollars to buy foreign goods, services, and securities, but are only able to sell $30 billion worth of their own goods and services (and, presumably, no long-term securities). Equality in this country's balance of payments is brought about by the fact that foreigners have been willing to accept a $4 billion addition to their deposits in its banks.

Is this a stable situation? Can it be sustained indefinitely? If this country continues to spend $4 billion more on other countries' goods, services, and securities, can it expect other countries to continue indefinitely accepting increases in their deposits in its banks? Clearly not. As was pointed out earlier, the banks of one country hold deposits in banks of another only as a sort of inventory to meet their needs in financing international transactions.[9] When such deposits rise to the point at which any further additions are superfluous for this purpose, they will be unwilling to finance future transactions in a manner that will build them up to any higher levels. This, in turn, will mean that future excess purchases by citizens of this country can only be financed by using up (via bank drafts) the deposits of foreign money owned by their *own* banks. But, unfortunately, supplies of foreign currency, like supplies of gold, are not unlimited. Sooner or later a change must be made. The country's balance of payments is *not* in equilibrium.

So much for what *is not* equilibrium in the balance of payments. What *is?* Perhaps the best way to explain the equilibrium concept is to begin by dividing the main elements in the balance of payments into *autonomous* and *balancing* entries.

Autonomous and Balancing Entries

An *autonomous* entry in the balance of payments is an international transaction that is not induced by other entries in the statement. That is to say, its *causes,* its basic determinants, are independent economic or political factors, such as different tastes, incomes, relative prices, or national foreign policy. Autonomous transactions unlike balancing transactions, do not occur because of something else in the balance of

9 The exception to this statement which arises when some countries are willing to hold large amounts of a "key" currency as the base of their monetary system will be discussed later.

payments but because the nation's tastes or income or some other such fundamental economic variable dictate them.

Exports and imports of goods and services clearly fall into the autonomous entry category, depending as they do on such things as different tastes, incomes, and relative prices. So, too, does the bulk of long-term investment. The amount of foreign securities which Americans are willing to purchase would appear to be largely a result of their high incomes, which give them the ability to save and invest, and estimates of relative profit prospects here and abroad, which also determine where the investment will take place.

Another type of transaction which belongs largely in the autonomous category is *unilateral transfers*. Let us see why this is the case. Unilateral transfers are of two kinds; from private citizens and from governments. Gifts to foreigners from private U.S. citizens, either as individuals or through private organizations, make up a not insignificant part of total unilateral transfers from the United States. They are fairly sizable because (1) American incomes are high, making such philanthropic acts possible, (2) many Americans are interested in helping the needy abroad, and (3) as a nation of immigrants of more or less recent vintage, many of them have relatives living in other countries about whose welfare they are concerned. With these as determinants, private unilateral transfers would seem to fit solidly in the autonomous category.

Unilateral transfers from the U.S. government result, in large measure, from its so-called "Foreign Aid" program. Here, a distinction must be drawn. If these gifts were considered temporary in nature, with the purpose of providing foreign nations with sufficient dollars to "close a dollar gap" in order to balance their (and the U.S.) balance of payments, they would have to be classified as "balancing" entries. This, indeed, was the situation immediately after World War II. If, however, foreign aid is looked upon as likely to continue into the indefinite future, if its purpose is not to simply erase a dollar shortage but rather to shore up the economies and defenses of selected other countries where the United States feels that such action is in its national interest, then it is not a transaction caused by other factors in the U.S. balance of payments. Under such circumstances, which seem reasonably descriptive of the present program of the United States, foreign aid must be classified as autonomous.

Since we intend using this autonomous-balancing item distinction to define equilibrium, one characteristic common to all autonomous entries should be noted. The basic determinants of each—income levels, different tastes, national security policy, and the like—are variables that are reasonably stable in the short run. Consequently, since their determinants do not change much, the autonomous transactions themselves can be expected to continue at roughly the same levels in the future. It is the likelihood that these transactions will remain fairly stable in the future which makes them ideal for defining the condition for stability—equilibrium.

We have defined *balancing* entries as those that are caused by, or induced by, other items in the balance of payments. Which entries fit this definition? Almost without exception, gold exports and imports take place as a result of developments elsewhere in a country's balance of payments.[10] For example, a nation that imports more goods and services than it exports may be called upon to send gold in payment for the difference. Or, conversely, a country that has a surplus in its current account may find itself receiving gold for that reason. Clearly, such shipments take place because of the current account surplus or deficit, and are balancing items.

The only balance of payments entry not yet considered is *short-term capital movements*. Are they autonomous or balancing items? The truth is, short-term capital movements can be either, but we shall oversimplify and consider them all as balancing items. Most, indeed, are, since usually they take place as a result of an import or export of goods or services or securities. They represent simply the means of paying for these other things.

There is, as noted above, a situation under which short-term capital movements could be autonomous. This would be when owners of foreign exchange choose, because of differences in interest rates or sheer speculation, to move their short-term capital from one country to another. In such a case, it is not other items in the balance of payments which have induced the movement, but quite independent considerations. This would be an autonomous movement.

Having duly noted the possibility of an autonomous short-term capital movement, we shall proceed to ignore it in the rest of this chapter and treat all short-term capital movements as balancing items. Although such a procedure does some violence to reality, the gain from simplifying the definition of equilibrium seems to warrant it. We shall return, in a later chapter, to the reality of autonomous short-term capital movements.

Definition of Equilibrium

Now that we have classified all international transactions as autonomous or balancing, we are prepared to be quite specific about the definition of equilibrium. *A nation has equilibrium in its balance of payments when the autonomous left-hand (export) side transactions*

[10] This of course is not true of a gold producing country that ships out gold as a regular part of its exports of goods.

equal the autonomous right-hand (import) side transactions.[11] That is to say, equilibrium in the U.S. balance of payments would only be achieved when:

<table>
<tr>
<td>
1. Exports of goods
    plus
2. Exports of services
    plus
3. Long-term investment by foreigners in the United States
    plus
4. Unilateral transfers from foreigners to Americans
</td>
<td>=</td>
<td>
1. Imports of goods
    plus
2. Imports of services
    plus
3. Long-term investment by Americans abroad
    plus
4. Unilateral transfers from Americans to foreigners[12]
</td>
</tr>
</table>

Whenever the above condition is not met there is, of course, a disequilibrium condition in the balance of payments. The two main types of disequilibrium situations are popularly called *deficit* and *surplus*.

A nation has a deficit in its balance of payments[13] when the following condition holds:

<table>
<tr>
<td>
1. Exports of goods
    plus
2. Exports of services
    plus
3. Long-term investment by foreigners in the country
    plus
4. Unilateral transfers from foreigners
</td>
<td><</td>
<td>
1. Imports of goods
    plus
2. Imports of services
    plus
3. Long-term investment by its citizens abroad
    plus
4. Unilateral transfers to foreigners
</td>
</tr>
</table>

[11] Some authorities would qualify this definition by holding that it is true only when the nation has full employment. This is to allow for the possibility that a nation might achieve this condition by means of monetary and fiscal policies that have disastrous domestic effects.

[12] Since the full balance of payments must balance, the same condition can be expressed by stating that the sum of the "balancing" items on each side are equal.

[13] The student should be careful not to confuse deficit on current account with deficit in the balance of payments.

Finally, a surplus in a nation's balance of payments can be defined as a situation in which:

1. Exports of goods *plus*		1. Imports of goods *plus*
2. Exports of services *plus*		2. Imports of services *plus*
3. Long-term investment by foreigners in the country *plus*	>	3. Long-term investment by its citizens abroad *plus*
4. Unilateral transfers from foreigners		4. Unilateral transfers to foreigners

Significance of and Adjustments to Balance of Payments Disequilibrium

ATTITUDES TOWARDS BALANCE OF PAYMENTS DISEQUILIBRIUM

To understand the meaning of equilibrium in the level of production is to know that it is not necessarily a "good" situation, merely a sustainable or stable one. It may be "bad" or "good" depending, among other things, on the level of employment.

Does the same thing hold for the equilibrium in a nation's balance of payments? Is it necessarily a good position to be in? The question is a difficult one, not readily subject to a "Yes" or "No" answer. Nor, for practical purposes, does it really need to be answered for equilibrium is, at best, a transitory phase in the so-called "real world," seldom really reached, retained only momentarily. For the great majority of nations, most of the time living reality consists of either a deficit or a surplus. What of these? Is one good and the other bad, or must we resort to our time-honored hedge: "It all depends"?

We have come a long way since the days when the early British economists devoted themselves to battling the then-dominant philosophy of the mercantilists regarding the goal of international trade. To the mercantilists the measure of success of an economy was the size of its stock of precious metals and the prime means of increasing this stock was via the development of a balance of payments surplus. In their view, then, a surplus was good and a deficit, bad.

Imbedded though it was, this mercantilist philosophy could not long hold up, at least in intellectual and official circles, under the determined onslaught of the earlier classical economists. But though the "free trade" disciples won the day in the minds of the intellectuals of their time, the mercantilist idea that accumulation of an ever-increasing gold hoard via balance of payments surpluses was a good thing, died hard in the minds of the general public. Indeed, it is probably fair to say that this ancient disease of the mind is not completely dead yet.

Of course, as the years went by, the arguments in support of the proposition that surpluses were good and deficits bad, took on new sophistication. The emphasis on the accumulation of gold as, in and of itself, a major virtue, soon gave way to stress on objectionable employment, wage rate, or other such effects of deficits. But the implications for policy purposes were not much changed.

There is probably no better evidence of the continuing identification of surplus with good and deficit with bad, than the widespread tendency, until recently, to refer to a surplus as a "favorable" balance of payments and a deficit as an "unfavorable" balance. Indeed, even our present terms of deficit and surplus are not free of misleading connotations since, to many people, the very term "deficit" denotes something bad and "surplus," something good.

It is not really the lingering effects of the intellectual heritage of mercantilist thought which is most responsible for the widespread present-day tendency to look upon surpluses as good and deficits, bad. It is rather the pervasive, yet devastatively misleading habit of identifying the nation and its goals with those of a single business firm. It would, indeed, be difficult to locate a more important single source of economic illiteracy than this one tendency to equate the nation and the firm.

Its simple application to international trade problems is clear and straightforward. "A firm is better off when it sells more (takes in more revenue) than it buys (pays out in costs). Therefore, a nation that is able to sell more to the rest of the world than it buys from it is clearly better off too."

Whatever the appeal of the deceptively simple logic in the above quotation and however much it may seem to be in accord with "common sense," it is neither logical nor sensible. The analogy drawn between the firm and the nation is simply faulty and policy measures based on it are likely to be equally faulty.

Indeed, if we limit our consideration to the exports and imports of goods and services, there is even a case to be made for the reverse conclusion—namely that a nation with a deficit on current account is *better* off, *as long as it can maintain its position*. The point is hardly a difficult one. In terms of economic welfare—in terms of level of living—the deficit nation has the distinct advantage of being able to use all that it can produce with its own limited resources, plus an additional amount of goods and services made available to it by foreigners. If there were only some way of arranging it so that a nation could continue forever, operating with a current account deficit, what a wonderful situation it would have! If such a possibility existed, the proper economic policy for maximizing a country's own economic welfare would clearly be to aim for the perpetual deficit!

But, unfortunately, there is a catch here too. It only works if the nation's trading partners can be hoodwinked into accepting a perpetual surplus so that the day never comes when our deficit nation is required to "pay the piper." And, unfortunately, such an idyllic arrangement is not a very likely possibility.

So we are forced to the conclusion that it is not really possible to classify surplus and deficit under a "good" or "bad" tag. On the one hand, there is nothing especially "good," from a nationalistic economic point of view, about a nation aiming at the perpetual support of other nations (which a permanent surplus on current account would imply). On the other hand, however, a nation cannot expect to reap the short-run benefits of a deficit without, sooner or later, having to settle up accounts. Every nation, over a period of time, must experience both surpluses and deficits and a conscious public policy that aims at the perpetuation of either one, must certainly be mistaken.

And yet, entirely aside from erroneous viewpoints based on mistaken analogies or mercantilist reasoning, it seems quite clear that in most countries there is more worry, more immediate pressure to "do something about it," in the case of a deficit. Indeed, the main focus of this chapter will be on what can be done to eliminate a balance of payments deficit.

Such an attitude is perfectly natural. A nation with a surplus is either receiving gold, increases in its supplies of foreign exchange (or reductions in foreign countries' accumulations of its money), or both. As long as it is willing to accept these in exchange for the extra goods, services, and securities it is shipping out, it does not have to worry about corrective steps. If, on the other hand, a country has a deficit, it must *use up* its present supply of gold and foreign exchange to settle accounts. And *this* is an activity that simply cannot go on any longer than its gold and foreign exchange resources permit.[1]

Consequently, when balance of payments deficits of a persistent character show up, the nation involved is usually quite interested in returning at least to the "middle ground" of equilibrium. We shall be exploring

---

[1] To be accurate about it, a surplus cannot continue indefinitely either. As long as other countries possess means of payment for their deficits, they can continue. But when they run out, neither their deficits *nor* our surpluses can be continued.

later on in this chapter the potential policy measures available to combat deficits, but before launching into the corrective mechanisms it may be in order to comment briefly on the types and causes of the deficits themselves.

TYPES AND CAUSES OF BALANCE OF PAYMENTS DEFICITS

A convenient way of classifying balance of payments deficits is according to cause and duration. We shall refer to temporary, cyclical, and chronic deficits.

Temporary Deficit

A deficit caused by random factors, seasonal changes, and the like is called a *temporary* deficit. Such a deficit is of quite short duration and can be expected to correct itself when the transitory factor that caused it disappears. No nation can avoid short-run deficits of this sort and it is partly in recognition of this fact that all countries keep a supply of foreign exchange on hand—to tide them over—until things swing the other way. For a truly temporary deficit, no corrective action other than time is needed.

Cyclical Deficit

A *cyclical* deficit is a balance of payment deficit caused, as the name implies, by changes in the business cycle, either at home or abroad. This is apt to be of somewhat longer duration than a temporary deficit but, once again, can be expected to correct itself when a different phase of the business cycle is reached.

The effect of the business cycle on a nation's balance of payments can be somewhat complicated and we shall go into it at greater length shortly. However, the broad outlines can be brought out very simply.

The amount spent on imports of goods and services is, at least to the extent the items imported are consumer goods, quite closely related to the nation's income. This means that, in the boom phase of the cycle, when incomes are generally high, imports tend to rise. And, conversely, in the recession phase, the reduction in incomes dictates a reduction in imports. It is through this effect of the business cycle on imports that the nation's balance of payments is affected.

Business-cycle swings can push a nation toward a balance of payments deficit in two ways: through a boom originating at home or a recession originating abroad. In the first case, the movement into the boom, or inflation phase of the cycle, will both cut the nation's exports of goods and services and raise its imports. This will take place because rising domestic prices make the nation's exports more expensive to foreigners and because its rising incomes provide it with the wherewithal to buy more imports. In the second case, that of a recession originating abroad, the nation's exports will fall off because the recession abroad lowers foreign incomes and, hence, the foreigners' ability to buy its products.[2]

Chronic Deficit

A *chronic* balance of payments deficit can be a more serious matter. This is a persistent deficit, caused by some fundamental change in competitive conditions, which the mere passage of time will not correct. Whereas a "normal" supply of foreign exchange will usually suffice to tide a nation over a temporary or cyclical deficit, the case of a chronic deficit requires some type of positive action by the deficit country to forestall the possibility of losing all its foreign exchange reserves (unless, of course, its trading partners take some action that will solve the problem).

Specifically what types of developments can create a chronic deficit? We have had many examples in recent years. The destruction of productive capacity and loss of export markets which seriously hampered Western European countries after World War II is one good example. A shift in consumer tastes away from the product of an essentially "one-crop" economy would be another. Technological improvement in competing industries abroad, enabling them to undersell domestic products, would be a third. And a foreign policy requiring large military expenditures abroad, coupled with substantial unilateral transfers, could contribute to the same thing.

The essence of a chronic deficit is that it will not cure itself. If, of course, the basic conditions that led to it should change, it may disappear without positive action by the nation involved. Barring this happy possibility, however, the country must take some sort of remedial steps or run the risk of losing all its foreign exchange reserves.

How serious a risk is this? What are the more fundamental consequences associated with allowing a deficit to go so far that it will drain the nation's reserve of foreign exchange? On the surface such a development might not appear too serious. What is really so bad about it?

---

[2] On the other hand, the reverse business cycle swings can move a nation toward a balance of payments surplus. A recession originating in that nation will, by lowering its incomes, lower its ability to import. An inflation starting abroad, on the other hand, will raise the purchases of other countries from it (its exports) because of the rise in their incomes, and lower the nation's imports from them because of the rise in their prices.

The point is this. A nation that has had a chronic deficit has, by definition, been importing more goods, services, and long-term securities and making more unilateral transfers than it has been able to "pay for." It has, therefore, been relying on its supply of foreign exchange to make payment. Now, when this means of financing its deficit is exhausted it has no choice but to cut down on its imports and gifts. Whether being forced into such a position has serious consequences for its people depends upon the nature and purpose of its imports and gifts. If it has got into this position because of excessive imports of frivolous luxury goods, it will simply have to "tighten its belt" and do without these things. It has been living beyond its means and must come back to reality. Such an adjustment may be painful, but can hardly be considered of crucial importance to the existence or security of the nation itself.

If, on the other hand, the "excessive" imports include many of the basic necessities of life or if materials absolutely essential to the operation of the nation's economy are included among them, the situation may be more serious. Similarly, if a main "cause" of the deficit is military expenditures and unilateral transfers which the nation's best-informed authorities feel are vital to the defense and security of the nation itself, then the deficit jeopardizes something pretty fundamental.

So a chronic deficit *can* be quite a threat. And, in the light of this, it is not at all surprising that high-level policy makers, confronted with such a situation, should bend every effort to bring it under control, if not reverse it.

INTERNATIONAL MONETARY INSTITUTIONAL ARRANGEMENTS

We have almost reached the point where we can proceed to discuss the policy measures available for dealing with a balance of payments deficit. But we must first learn something about the various possible types of institutional structures available for financing international transactions.

There are, basically, five such structures, with which we shall be concerned. They are:

1. A system permitting freely fluctuating exchange rates
2. The full international gold-coin standard
3. A system in which exchange rates are kept stable by Exchange Stabilization Funds
4. "Floating" exchange rates, with adjustable pegs
5. Exchange controls

Freely Fluctuating Exchange Rates

The first of these, a system of *freely fluctuating exchange rates,* involves the most direct extension of the institutions of the free market to the settling of international transactions. Under such a system, exchange rates are free to fluctuate according to supply and demand, and the government takes no steps to influence them. As we shall see below, in all the other four institutional structures, the government "intervenes" in the foreign exchange market, contributing, through statute or discretionary action, to the determination of exchange rates.

An exchange rate, from the American viewpoint, is simply *the price of a unit of foreign money, in dollars.* The foreign currency is looked upon in the same manner as an ordinary commodity, as something that is bought and sold for dollars, at a price that depends upon the demand for it and the supply of it. To say that the exchange rate between the dollar and the pound is $2.80 per pound, is simply a more complicated way of stating that the price of a pound is $2.80.

We have said that, with freely fluctuating exchange rates, the "price of pounds" is determined by demand and supply. Who makes up the demand for pounds and who provides the supply? If we oversimplify by assuming a two-country world for purposes of exposition, it is quite clear that the *demand for pounds comes from American importers* while the *supply of pounds comes from American exporters.* The point is quite simple. When Americans import goods, services, or securities they must purchase pounds owned by New York banks to make their payment to the British sellers. They, thus, "demand" the right to use the pound balances owned by the middlemen, U.S. banks. Similarly, when Americans export goods, services, or securities, they earn pound balances that they sell to U.S. banks for dollars. This action provides our middlemen with their "supply" of pounds.[3]

Under a system of freely fluctuating exchange rates, then, the price of foreign money can fluctuate without limit, being higher the more we import and lower, the more we export.

Full Gold Standard

The *full international gold-coin standard,* under which much of the world operated for many years, is a second possible structure. In this case, in order to comply with its requirements, the various nations

---

[3] It is, of course, true that, to the extent that different means of payment are used, a U.S. import may result in an increase in the dollar balances owned by British banks and a U.S. export might use up the dollar balan es owned by British banks. Since the effect of either of these on the exchange rate is precisely the same, we shall ignore the case of payment in dollars.

must: (1) define their monetary unit as being equivalent to a fixed amount of gold (e.g., one U.S. dollar = 23.22 grains of gold) and, (2) stand ready to exchange paper money (or gold coins) for gold, in unlimited amounts with anyone, at that price and/or exchange gold (or gold coins) for paper money in unlimited amounts with anyone at that price.

One of the important by-products of such a system is that exchange rates between the currencies of countries adhering to the standard are relatively stable. Let us refer to an example to see how this works out.

Suppose that the United States has defined the dollar as equivalent to 23.22 grains of gold and England has defined the pound as being the same as 113 grains of gold.[4] Now, since both moneys are defined in terms of a common substance, gold, they are related to one another. This relationship, called the *mint par of exchange,* is obtained by dividing the gold content of the dollar into the gold content of the pound. The result of this operation is approximately 4.87, indicating that the mint par of exchange between the pound and the dollar under those arrangements was $4.87 = £1.[5]

If, for purposes of furthering the example, we assume that the cost of transporting 113 grains of gold across the Atlantic in either direction is two cents, we can state definitely that the cost of British pounds can never exceed $4.89 per pound nor be less than $4.85 per pound. The exchange rate, in other words, can fluctuate only within the relatively narrow limits of $4.85 = £1 and $4.89 = £1.

The force that assures this high degree of exchange rate stability is the self-interest of traders. No American importer (needing pounds to make payment) will pay more than $4.89 to obtain a pound because he does not need to. Any tendency for the price of pounds to rise (as a result of a U.S. deficit that makes the U.S. demand for pounds exceed the supply) is limited by the gold standard mechanism itself. No American importer would be willing to pay more than $4.89 to get the pound he needs because he can always take (or, more likely, his bank will take for him) $4.87 to the U.S. Treasury and get 113 grains of gold, ship the gold to England, and exchange it at the British Treasury for one pound. The cost of shipment being two cents, our U.S. importer's total expense for his pound is $4.89. Under these gold standard arrangements, he need never pay more to get it.

---

[4] These are the actual relationships set by the two governments during much of the "heyday" of the international gold standard.

[5] It should be noted that this is not, in and of itself, an exchange rate, but simply the arithmetical result arrived at by dividing the statutory gold content of the dollar into the statutory gold content of the pound. It merely says that the British government has defined the pound as being worth as much gold as the American government has said $4.87 is worth.

Similarly, the British importer, if he is a profit maximizer, will never accept any less than $4.85 for his pound when he uses it to obtain the dollars he needs to make payment. For he too, has the option of taking his one pound to the British Treasury, exchanging it for 113 grains of gold, shipping the gold to the U.S. Treasury and swapping it there for $4.87. In this case, when the two-cent shipping cost is subtracted, he realizes a minimum of $4.85 for his pound. He need not accept less.

Thus, with the conditions as stated, the exchange rate between the dollar and the pound can only fluctuate between the narrow limits of $4.85 = £1 and $4.89 = £1. When a U.S. deficit raises our demand for pounds above our supply of them, the price of pounds can only rise to $4.89 per pound, at which point it will be cheaper for American importers to pay by shipping gold to England. The upper limit, $4.89 = £1 rate, is called the *U.S. gold export point.* On the other hand when a British deficit (necessarily a U.S. surplus in a two-country world) increases the U.S. supply of pounds above the U.S. demand for them, the price of pounds for Americans will fall toward $4.85 per pound (the cost of dollars to the British will rise to the point where they get only $4.85 for each pound) beyond which it becomes cheaper for British importers to obtain their dollars by shipping gold to the United States. The $4.85 = £1 rate is, thus, the *U.S. gold import point.*

Now this feature of the full international gold standard, the maintenance of stable exchange rates, is not inconsequential. In fact, it is alleged to be a major advantage of that time-honored set of arrangements. Stable exchange rates, it is argued, are important because they lessen the risk to traders and international investors, thereby encouraging more international transactions, and permitting a fuller exploitation of the advantages that accrue to all from greater world-wide specialization.

It is not difficult to understand the argument here. If an American importer should agree to pay £100,000 for British goods, 60 days from the date of sale, a sharp increase in the price of pounds during the 60-day period could turn a potentially profitable deal into a financial disaster. If the cost of pounds was $2.50 = £1 when he made the agreement, he expected his costs to be $250,000. But if the exchange rate should jump up to $3.50 = £1 at the end of 60 days, he will be required to pay $350,000, a figure that may do much more than wipe out his expected profit. Now if our importer is not a speculator, willing to gamble on the possible equal chance that he may gain by a reduction in the cost of pounds, as well as lose by a rise, he may simply shy away from international trading altogether, preferring to concentrate on less risky domestic trade. Consequently, the volume of international trade, and its important attendant advantage of fuller specialization, may be impeded.

Stable Exchange Rates via Exchange Stabilization Funds

But the international gold standard had some disadvantages to go along with its advantages and, in the post-World War II era, strenuous attempts have been made by Americans to "have their cake and eat it, too." They have come up with a system in which they have thrown off many of the fetters of the full international gold-coin standard while providing a different mechanism for retaining its advantage of stable exchange rates. This method, tried briefly during the 1930's, is to maintain *stable exchange rates via governmentally operated exchange stabilization funds.*

Under these arrangements, much of the old pre-World War I gold standard has disappeared. The link between the gold supply and the domestic money supply has, for most nations, been almost entirely broken. The fixed commitment to pay out gold for domestic currency in unlimited amounts to anyone has been universally eliminated. In short, much of the old gold standard has disappeared.

But, through the operation of exchange stabilization funds, reasonably stable exchange rates have been retained. These funds, at least in broad outline, operate very simply. They are equipped (by their governments) with supplies of gold, foreign exchange, and their own domestic money. When the exchange rate between theirs and another country's currency threatens to exceed the limits set,[6] it is the task of the stabilization fund to enter into the other side of the market and halt the undesired change. For example, if the cost of dollars to the British should threaten to rise beyond the agreed-upon top price, the British stabilization fund might hold down on the exchange rate movement by offering a supply of dollars from its own resources.

Floating Exchange Rates With Adjustable Pegs

The fourth type of international financial structure, *"floating" exchange rates with adjustable pegs,* might best be described as a combination of the first and third. Here, exchange rates are permitted to vary according to supply and demand within much wider limits than in the immediately preceding case where, for all practical purposes, the stabilization fund keeps them fixed. On the other hand, these fluctuations are not without limit as in the freely fluctuating exchange rate case discussed first. The limits to the allowable fluctuation may be determined by an absolute amount (such as 5 percent within a given time period) or on the basis of the cause of the fluctuation (whether it is caused by a temporary,

---

[6] For countries that are members of the International Monetary Fund, those tolerable limits are set by the Fund's requirements. See Chapter 16.

seasonal, or chronic deficit, for example) but, in any case, once the limits are reached the stabilization fund enters the market and stops their movement.

Exchange Controls

Finally, a nation may maintain stable exchange rates (and, indeed, avoid deficits altogether if carried far enough) via the technique of *exchange controls*. There are many varieties of exchange controls but in general, they are implemented by requiring that all foreign exchange earned by the nation's exporters be sold (usually at a fixed exchange rate for domestic currency) to a governmental agency which, in turn, "rations them out" to those importers whom it (or the law that governs it) deems most essential. In this way the excessive use of foreign exchange and pressure on exchange rates which are characteristic of deficits are controlled at the source by governmental authority.

So much for our discussion of alternative institutional structures. We are now prepared to see how deficits may be corrected or, at least, modified. This will be the subject of the two concluding sections of this chapter.

In the immediately following section, we shall take a look at a number of ways in which balance of payments deficits automatically set into motion forces that tend in the direction of correcting the deficit itself. Since these corrective forces differ depending upon the institutional set-up, we shall make use of the institutional breakdown just discussed to chart our way.

In the final section we shall turn to a consideration of the discretionary policy tools available to a nation wrestling with a deficit. The difference between the topics of the two sections is not unlike the difference between automatic and discretionary fiscal policy. The automatic corrective mechanism is set into play by the deficit itself and requires no specific discretionary act by the nation's policy makers. The discretionary policy tool, on the other hand, requires an act of Congress or a specific action by the executive intentionally aimed at dealing with the existing problem.

AUTOMATIC MECHANISMS TENDING TO CORRECT BALANCE OF PAYMENTS DEFICITS

It will greatly simplify the discussion in this section if we restrict ourselves to considering the correction of a deficit that has arisen because a country has begun importing more goods and services than it exports. This does not require that we assume no long-term capital movements or unilateral transfers; only that they offset one another and are not the cause of the deficit. In all cases, as we shall see, the deficit causes certain other variables in the economy to change, and the change in these other variables, in turn, tends to reduce the deficit itself.

Full International Gold-coin Standard

As we saw earlier, the excessive imports that create the deficit mean the demand for foreign money exceeds the supply, tending to drive up its price. Under the institutional arrangements of the full gold standard, however, the price can only rise slightly to the gold export point, after which gold will flow out to pay, in effect, for the deficit.

The Indirect Money-supply Effect

Now the loss of gold (if not offset by discretionary policy) must have some effects on the economy of the deficit country. It represents, after all, the base of its money supply. The discussion in Chapter 7 regarding the effects on the money supply and bank reserves of the sale of gold by the U.S. Treasury today gave a good idea of what these effects are. When the Treasury sells gold, not only the money supply but also member bank reserves go down by the amount of the sale. This means, in a fully loaned-up banking system, that the domestic money supply may be cut by several times the amount of the gold loss. Even though we are no longer on the full gold standard the effects of a sale of gold are similar.

But that is not all. The money supply reduction that results automatically from the gold loss must, in turn, other things being equal, raise the rate of interest and, in greater or less degree, cut down on aggregate demand.[7] And a reduction in aggregate demand must reflect itself in lowered prices and/or reduced employment, production, and income.

How does all this tend to reduce the deficit that started it all? Very simply. To the extent that the deficit country's prices are cut, it becomes a cheaper market for foreigners (as well as its own citizens) and it may therefore expand its exports. If, as is likely with the "sticky" prices with which we are familiar today, the cut in aggregate demand lowers incomes, the deficit country, having less to spend both at home and abroad, will import less. In either case, the effect is to lessen the deficit.

While all this is going on in the deficit country, the surplus country or countries are feeling the reverse effects. There, gold flows in, bank reserves and the money supply are increased, interest rates tend to be

---

[7] Indeed, under the unwritten but generally understood "rules of the game" of the gold standard, the central bank was expected to reinforce the effects of the gold loss by raising its discount rate to raise interest rates even more.

reduced, aggregate demand rises, and prices and/or incomes are raised. As a result of the price and/or income increases, the surplus countries' exports are cut and their imports raised, intensifying the corrective effects both there and in the deficit country.

Deficit Country	*Surplus Country or Countries*
1. Exports < Imports	1. Exports > Imports
2. Demand for foreign money > Supply of foreign money	2. Demand for foreign money < Supply of foreign money
3. Price of foreign money rises to gold export point	3. Price of foreign money falls to gold import point
4. Gold flows out	4. Gold flows in
5. Bank reserves and money supply cut	5. Bank reserves and money supply rise
6. Interest rates rise	6. Interest rates fall
7. Aggregate demand falls	7. Aggregate demand rises
8. Prices and/or incomes fall	8. Prices and/or incomes rise
9. To extent prices fall, exports rise; to extent incomes fall, imports fall	9. To extent prices rise, exports fall; to extent incomes rise, imports rise

What are the chances that this mechanism will completely eliminate the deficit? If we are realistic, none at all. The best that can be expected is that, because of it, the deficit will be somewhat less severe. But there is another, perhaps more potent, corrective mechanism working along with the *indirect, money-supply* effect described above. This may aptly be designated the *direct effects* on aggregate demand of the exports and imports of goods and services themselves. A careful look at these direct effects on aggregate demand seems in order.

The Direct Effects on Aggregate Demand

When foreigners spend money to buy currently produced goods and services from a nation's export industries, it is clear that they, no less than the domestic investors, government, and consumers, are adding to the demand for the output of its industry. For an open economy, then, aggregate demand equals not just $C + I + G$, as we assumed in Part II, but $C + I + G + X$, where X equals a nation's exports of newly produced goods and services.

As an element of aggregate demand, exports are very much like investment and government spending in the sense that their amount is largely unrelated to the domestic level of income. How much a nation is able to sell as exports is pretty much dependent on such "outside" factors as foreign tastes and incomes and relative prices and only slightly and indirectly influenced by the domestic income level. Consequently we shall treat it, as we do investment and government spending in the main, as an "autonomously" determined element of the demand for a nation's goods and services.[8]

A nation's imports of goods and services, on the other hand are, in most essential ways, like saving and taxes. Like saving and taxes they are an element of income earned from current production of the nation, which is not spent to buy its newly produced goods and services. They represent, that is, an additional "leakage." Consequently, when the theoretical material in Part II is modified to allow international trade into the picture, instead of saying that all income earned from production is split into three parts—C + S + T—we must recognize that it is divided into four parts—C + S + T + M, where M stands for imports.

Imports of goods and services are like saving and taxes in still another way. All three are directly related to the level of income.[9] This is especially true to the extent that a country's imported goods are consumer goods, because in this case, just as a country is able to spend more for domestically produced consumer goods when its incomes rise, it tends to spend more on foreign-produced items.[10]

When exports of goods and services are admitted as an element of aggregate demand for a nation's output, and imports of goods and services are recognized as a leakage from its incomes, we must amend the conditions for stable, rising, and falling production which were listed in Part II for a closed economy only. Now, we must say:

1. Condition for Stable Production (Equilibrium)—
    when C + I + G + X = C + S + T + M
2. Condition for Rising Production—
    when C + I + G + X > C + S + T + M
3. Condition for Falling Production—
    when C + I + G + X < C + S + T + M

It is these new conditions that reveal most clearly the second automatic corrective mechanism to which we referred above as the direct effects. A country that incurs a balance of payments deficit (where the deficit is

---

[8] It should be noted that the definitions used in this section differ somewhat from the conventional. In this chapter C, I, and G are defined as expenditures on newly produced *domestic* output only. Consequently, aggregate demand is C + I + G + (X − M). The latter would be the appropriate definition if, as in the national income accounts, C, I, and G were defined to include purchase of imports as well as domestic output.

[9] This, of course, is true of taxes when income taxes make up a significant part of the structure.

[10] Indeed, just as we were able earlier to talk about a marginal propensity to consume and a marginal propensity to save, we could now talk in terms of a marginal propensity to import, defined as $\triangle M / \triangle GNP$.

caused by an excess of goods and service imports) is, on that account, leaking more out of its income stream than foreigners are adding to it through their purchases. Consequently, *in addition to the corrective mechanism that works indirectly through affecting the money supply,* we have a direct cut in the nation's aggregate demand through its international trade. Whenever imports of goods and services exceeds exports of goods and services, the nation's involvement in international trade directly reduces its aggregate demand. Conversely, an excess of goods and service exports over imports adds to aggregate demand.

Now for our deficit country, this direct cut in aggregate demand puts further downward pressure on its prices and/or income, resulting in even greater increases in its exports and reductions in its imports than the indirect, money-supply corrective mechanism alone would produce.

It may be useful to refer back to the four-diagram framework used in Part II to illustrate the impact of these two corrective mechanisms on aggregate demand and the level of income. This is done in Figure 15-1.

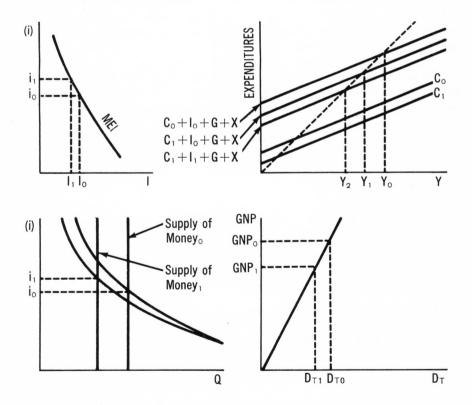

FIGURE 15-1

This framework, of course, does not show whether the downward movement of the Gross National Product is a result of production or price cuts, nor does it directly reveal the effect of either of these on the deficit but it should, nevertheless, help to reveal most of the story.

In Figure 15-1, we assume that the nation starts with equilibrium in its balance of payments and at an initial equilibrium level of output, Y_0. Then, a shift in consumer tastes away from domestically produced consumer goods toward foreign-produced goods creates a situation in which imports of goods and services rise (at the expense of domestic consumption) to exceed the constant level of exports. This change has two main effects.

First, the direct effect of it is to shift the consumption function down (from C_0 to C_1) thereby lowering aggregate demand to Y_1, in the first round. Secondly, assuming as we have been, a full gold standard, the outflow of gold in payment for the deficit cuts the money supply in the lower left-hand graph (from S of M_0 to S of M_1), raising the rate of interest (from i_0 to i_1), lowering domestic investment spending (from I_0 to I_1), which lowers aggregate demand and income even further. The result of all this is that aggregate demand is lowered to $C_1 + I_1 + G + X$, reducing GNP to GNP_2 in the second round. We need not trace through further rounds at this point.

The point is that two factors have simultaneously and automatically gone to work to lower aggregate demand and chip away at the deficit that initiated the change. These are the automatic corrective mechanisms available under the full gold standard.

How effective are the two combined? It is difficult to say except that it would require an extremely unusual set of circumstances for them to be adequate to completely eliminate the deficit. For this to happen the adjustment mechanism would have to lower the deficit country's income far enough so that its imports would be cut back by as much as they had originally risen. But this could only happen if neither taxes nor saving were reduced at all as income fell, which is an unlikely set of circumstances.[11] We are quite safe in proceeding on the assumption that the automatic mechanisms themselves will not be sufficient to restore balance of payments equilibrium completely.

Freely Fluctuating Exchange Rates

Let us jump now to a consideration of the corrective mechanisms available when there is no gold standard and exchange rates are allowed to fluctuate freely without artificial limit, according to supply

[11] While this is not the only circumstance under which the deficit could be completely eliminated, it is indicative of the extremely unusual conditions that would be necessary to accomplish it.

and demand. Once again, we shall assume that the deficit is caused by a sudden increase in imports of goods and services such that the country develops both a current account and balance of payments deficit.

As before, the deficit implies that the country's demand for foreign currency exceeds the supply being earned and that, consequently, its price tends to be increased. The difference between this and the gold standard case is that under these conditions there is no gold export point to stop the rise in exchange rates. They continue to climb as long as the excess demand resulting from the deficit remains.

Now in a frictionless world in which we could properly ignore the effects of expectations, any deficit would be immediately eliminated by such exchange rate changes. The price of foreign exchange would immediately rise to a new higher level that would "clear the market," leaving no excess of demand over supply. The deficit would disappear.

Unfortunately, however, we live in a world that is neither frictionless nor devoid of expectations. In the first place, friction in the form of institutional and other rigidities will keep the price of foreign exchange from rising immediately to a new equilibrium level. Until it does, the deficit, the using up of existing supplies of foreign exchange reserves, and the pressure on exchange rates continues.

During this interim of adjustment, the same "direct effects" on aggregate demand and the level of income as were described under the gold standard are in operation, for the same reasons. In addition, while imports still exceed exports, there is a modified version of the indirect money-supply corrective mechanism in force. While gold need not flow in this case, the mere payment for an excess of imports reduces a nation's domestic money supply by an equivalent amount, as we saw in the last chapter. While of lesser proportions than in the gold standard case, because of the fact that bank reserves are not reduced, this cut in the supply of money still plays some minor role in raising the interest rate and cutting back further on aggregate demand.

If the fluctuating exchange rate system works well, however, these corrective mechanisms are of minor significance. For this system has a mechanism of its own, the rise in exchange rates, which plays the main role in the restoration of equilibrium.

As the excessive demand for foreign exchange pushes up the cost of foreign money, citizens of the deficit nation will find that it now costs more to import goods. A 10 percent rise in the cost of pounds, after all, is just as effective in cutting back the quantity of British goods demanded by Americans as would be a 10 percent rise in the British domestic price level. The hope is, of course, that this exchange rate movement will indeed cut back on the deficit country's imports. And there is another side to it here too. If it takes more dollars to buy British pounds, then dollars have become cheaper to Englishmen. If everything works well this will lead the British to buy more American goods, thus raising U.S. exports. On both sides then, whether there is a cut in the deficit country's imports or a rise in their exports, the rise in the exchange rate has corrective effects.

This, it would seem, is ideal. There is an automatic mechanism working to correct a balance of payments deficit without requiring the domestic economy to suffer the stresses of deflation (and likely unemployment) which the gold standard's corrective mechanisms imply. Why not adopt it forthwith?

We shall devote a part of the following chapter to a discussion of just this question, so the bulk of the argument will have to wait. We can, however, make a few comments at this point. Those who oppose a freely fluctuating exchange rate system argue that the orderly developments we have traced through above may not be forthcoming and that, indeed, more harm than good might result. The main reasons for their scepticism are: (1) if elasticities of demand and supply are too low, the rise in the price of foreign money which results from a balance of payments deficit might be very large, inviting exchange speculation; (2) speculators, if they believe that the rise in the price of foreign money will continue, might act on their expectation by transferring short-term capital out of the deficit country, further complicating its problem and accelerating the exchange rate movement in a manner that may get out of control and lead to a breakdown of the system, and (3) both the first two reasons lead doubtors to expect wide exchange rate fluctuations that would, because of the risk factor, cut down on the volume of international trade. We shall return to these arguments in the following chapter.

Exchange Rates Held Stable by Exchange Stabilization Funds

The full gold standard has been gone from the scene since the 1930's and there is little likelihood of its reemergence. Freely fluctuating exchange rates have been employed only sporadically by isolated countries in the past and, at the moment, are used nowhere. We do have, however, a world in which essentially stable exchange rates, without the full gold standard's trappings, are the rule. This result is obtained by the action of national exchange stabilization funds that enter directly into foreign exchange markets, adding to the demand for foreign money when its price threatens to drop or supplementing the supply to forestall a price rise. What automatic corrective mechanisms remain under these conditions?

We still have the direct effects of the deficit on aggregate demand, with their attendant effects on the state of the domestic economy, to push us part way toward balance of payments equilibrium. And, as in the previous case, we retain a watered-down indirect money-supply effect also. Since paying for imports reduces our domestic money supply dollar-for-dollar and receiving payment for exports increases it in like amount, one result of our imports exceeding our exports must be a cut in our money supply. This has the same direction of effect on interest rates and aggregate demand as was evident in the gold standard situation, but is of lesser magnitude because bank reserves are not necessarily reduced thereby.[12]

Floating Exchange Rates With Limits Maintained by Exchange Stabilization Funds

Some experts feel that most of the advantages of freely fluctuating exchange rates could be obtained while its main disadvantage is avoided by adopting a system under which rates are permitted to vary within wider, but prescribed limits. For example, exchange rates might be permitted to vary by as much as 10 percent up or down from their present levels (rather than the existing practice of permitting only a 1 percent fluctuation) with the nation's exchange stabilization fund standing in the wings, ready to halt the fluctuation when an appreciation or depreciation of 10 percent has been realized.

Such a system, if it should be widely adopted, would provide the following automatic corrective mechanisms: (1) the exchange rate, within the area in which it is permitted to vary and (2) the same direct and indirect effects as were described in the preceding case when the limits are reached and stabilization funds step in to hold rates stable.

Thus we see that, whatever the institutional arrangement, international payments deficits generate some the seeds of their own destruction. Unfortunately, however, with the possible exception of the freely fluctuating exchange rate case, none of the automatic mechanisms are vigorous enough to go all the way and completely wipe out the deficit that triggered them, unless severe unemployment is passively accepted.[13]

For the nation with a chronic deficit and a limited supply of foreign exchange reserves this invariably means one thing—some positive action must be taken. If built-in, automatic forces cannot do the job, then

[12] This statement, of course, takes no account of the fact that the United States is still on a modified form of the gold standard and to the extent that it *does* lose gold as a result of its deficits, the corrective effects are essentially the same as they were under the old full gold standard.

[13] The fifth institutional arrangement described earlier, exchange controls, is not discussed in this section because (1) it is a *discretionary* policy tool and (2) it can keep a deficit from developing in the first place and so, requires no corrective mechanism.

authoritative, discretionary policy must take over. We turn now to a brief coverage of the discretionary policy measures available for dealing with a balance of payments deficit.

DISCRETIONARY POLICY MEASURES TO DEAL WITH A BALANCE OF PAYMENTS DEFICIT

No nation can allow a balance of payments deficit to continue indefinitely. Of course, one with a large stockpile of gold and foreign exchange reserves can put off discretionary action for quite a while in the fond hope that before the bottom of its international reserves barrel is reached, some fundamental change will occur which will solve its problem for it. Indeed, since the discretionary tools available are often painful, "sitting tight and hoping for good luck" may be the wisest of courses for a nation that has sufficient reserves to permit such luxury.

But, barring such fortuitous developments, a nation with a truly chronic deficit must, sooner or later, take positive action. What, specifically, can it do?

Basically, four lines of discretionary action are available. They are:

1. Raising of trade barriers to cut the spending by its citizens on foreign goods, services, and securities
2. Action by the government to reduce its own foreign purchases and gifts
3. Devaluation of its currency
4. Restrictive monetary and fiscal policy.

Let us consider these alternatives in turn.

The Use of Trade Barriers

Trade barriers are as old as nations themselves. They include, in addition to tariffs, such more completely restrictive devices as quotas and exchange controls. All such measures are aimed, in the aggregate, at reducing the volume of a nation's imports.[14]

Tariffs are really a special form of excise tax placed upon the importation of foreign goods and services and, in some cases, securities.[15] Quotas can be very much more restrictive in that they involve an absolute barrier to imports beyond a certain point rather than simply a hurdle

14 This is true with the single exception of subsidies to exporters, a measure we shall not discuss, which is aimed at raising exports rather than cutting imports.
15 A tax placed on the sale of foreign securities in the United States seems most appropriately classified as a special form of tariff.

that can be overcome. The case of exchange control can be the most extreme of all because, in this case, a governmental agency simply "takes over" all foreign exchange earned by the nation's exporters (by requiring its sale for domestic currency at a fixed exchange rate) and then rations it out to favored importers according to some scale of national priorities, thereby effectively eliminating "excessive" potential importers who would otherwise contribute to the deficit.

The trade barrier method of dealing with a balance of payments deficit is held in very low regard by most authorities. It should be, in the opinion of most, employed extensively only as a last resort. Its widespread unpopularity results from the fact that it impedes international specialization and that it is unlikely to succeed in its objective in any case. The more fundamental economic objection to a raising of trade barriers is clear cut. By interfering with the patterns of trade, such barriers limit the degree of international specialization and thereby lead to a misallocation of resources which reduces world production. On a more practical level it is even to be doubted whether these objectionable results will, to any significant degree, be counterbalanced by a "favorable" effect, on the nation's balance of payments. Because trade barriers that "work" by cutting down a nation's imports, necessarily reduce another nation's exports. It is extremely unlikely that the "injured" nation will simply sit there and take it; it will almost certainly retaliate quickly by raising its own trade barriers, thereby canceling out whatever balance of payments advantage the deficit nation had obtained from its own action. We must conclude that this course is, in general, to be avoided.

Cutting Foreign Spending by the Government

A second discretionary approach available to cut a balance of payments deficit is for the government itself to reduce its foreign spending. To the degree that it imports goods and services it could cut these, and to the degree that it makes gifts to foreigners it could reduce these.

But even this apparently more direct approach is not without its problems. In the first place, whatever good effect it would have on our balance of payments might come at quite a cost. If, to solve a balance of payments deficit, a nation should sacrifice programs of foreign spending which seem important to its own security, the remedy might well be worse than the disease. In any case a risk of undetermined magnitude exists.

In the second place, the good effects of this approach on the deficit country's balance of payments may be substantially less than would appear at first glance. When a government spends or gives its money to foreigners the complete effect of this action on its balance of payments depends partly on what foreigners do with the funds they receive. If foreigners use money acquired in this manner to buy goods and services, which they would not otherwise purchase, from the deficit country, eliminating the gifts and/or government foreign purchases will reduce the goods and service exports of the deficit country along with the reduction in import items. To the degree that this happens, the deficit would be unchanged and the action, ineffective.

Devaluation

Devaluation of a nation's currency consists of reducing its value relative to that of other countries. This can be done, for a gold standard country, by reducing the gold content of the currency, that is, raising the mint price of gold. Where a stabilization fund keeps exchange rates stable, all that is needed is a statement that the fund will permit its currency to depreciate to a designated new level.[16]

It is, of course, hoped that devaluation will work by reducing the nation's imports and raising its exports because foreign money is now more expensive for its citizens and its money is cheaper for foreigners.

There is, however, no guarantee that it will work this way. In the first place this action, like an increase in trade barriers, is subject to retaliation on the part of the nation's trading partners—a development that could render it totally ineffective. Nor is this the only problem. Even in the absence of retaliation, devaluation will only succeed in reducing the deficit if demand elasticities are favorable.[17]

The point here is complicated, but important. Assume that the United States has a deficit and that Great Britain represents its sole trading partner. If the United States devalues the dollar so that the exchange rate rises from $2.00 = £1 to $3.00 = £1, the action will certainly reduce the number of pounds Americans purchase to pay for imports from Britain. So long as the U.S. demand for British imports is anything other than *perfectly inelastic* (in which highly unlikely case, Americans would purchase the same number of pounds at the higher price) the devalution will reduce the quantity of pounds (and therefore, the quantity of imports) demanded by Americans and help reduce the U.S. deficit.

On the other side, however, things are not so clear-cut. American goods are now cheaper for Britons because dollars cost less. But whether this will lead them to spend more pounds on American goods depends upon the degree of elasticity of the British demand for U.S. goods.

16 It should, of course, be obvious that the country that permits freely fluctuating exchange rates does not have devaluation available as a *discretionary* tool because, under this institutional setup, the same effects are available automatically.

17 Elasticity of supply in the affected countries is also a factor that is relevant in determining the effectiveness of devaluation. In order to simplify as much as possible, we shall ignore this added complication in our discussion.

If their demand is of greater than unit elasticity, they will spend more pounds on U.S. goods than before and the U.S. deficit will be further reduced. If their demand is of unit elasticity, they will spend the same number of pounds as before the devaluation and, while this will not help cut the U.S. deficit, the fact that Americans are buying fewer pounds from the British will reduce it. If, however, the British demand for U.S. goods is of less than unit elasticity, the devaluation will lead them to spend fewer pounds to buy U.S. goods which will, in and of itself, tend to worsen the U.S. deficit.

Under circumstances of highly inelastic demands in both countries it is entirely possible for devaluation to worsen the U.S. deficit. Because, if the American demand is highly inelastic, the favorable effects of cutting the American demand for British goods would be small. If the British demand for U.S. goods is highly inelastic, the unfavorable effects of cutting their demand for U.S. goods would be large. In such a situation, devaluation would not only not work, but it would worsen the U.S. deficit.

Finally, there is one further hazard of devaluation—the problem of expectations. It is extremely difficult for a nation formally to consider such a step without the nature of its deliberations leaking to the general public. If advance information of an impending devaluation does leak out, it will be certain to lead to a mass withdrawal of short-term capital from the devaluing nation. It is only natural that those who hold short-term dollar assets will, faced with the knowledge that the dollar is to be devalued, desire to shift into gold or other currencies until after the devaluation takes place. And such action could markedly worsen the deficit country's problems.

Expectations may also complicate matters after the devaluation has been carried out, if speculators should decide that more devaluation will be forthcoming. Here again, their expectations will lead them to withdraw short-term capital, which will expand the deficit and, conceivably, force the further devaluation that they expected.

Restrictive Monetary and Fiscal Policy

Given the problems associated with the three discretionary policies already discussed, it would be ideal if the last remaining tool could represent all virtue and no vice. Such, however, is not the case for restrictive monetary and fiscal policy.

This *classical* medicine to cure a payments deficit works primarily by reinforcing the automatic mechanisms. It consists of a tight money policy and budget surpluses to raise a nation's interest rates and lower its prices and/or incomes. To the extent that short-term interest rates are raised, it is hoped that the nation will be the beneficiary of an inflow of short-term capital. To the extent that the nation's prices are reduced, it is expected that it will be able to sell more to foreigners. To the extent that its incomes are reduced, it is hoped that it will cut back on its imports.

There can be no doubt that sufficiently restrictive monetary and fiscal policies can eliminate a balance of payments deficit. But how this is accomplished is a matter of no little concern. If we lived in a world of very flexible prices—prices that would easily and quickly fall as a consequence of a cut in aggregate demand, this policy would have much to recommend it. But, unfortunately, that is not our world. A reduction in aggregate demand, resulting from restrictive monetary and fiscal policies would, given the downward inflexibility of prices in the modern world, almost certainly lower employment, production, and income in the deficit country.

Now let there be no mistake about this. If carried far enough there is no question but that such a policy could eliminate the deficit, even though the primary effect is not on prices. But the nation that uses this approach will have solved one problem by creating what may be a far more serious one. It will have restored international stability by sacrificing its domestic stability. It will have eliminated a balance of payments deficit by the dubious means of creating a recession.

Indeed, it was precisely this facet of the old full international gold standard which played an important role in the decision to abandon it. Under it, a balance of payments deficit meant automatic corrective effects, which tended to cause unemployment; in addition, the so-called "rules of the game" required a re-enforcing of these effects with restrictive discretionary monetary policy. International deficits, in other words, were eliminated by creating domestic recessions. Most nations of the world have made it clear that they long since have had quite enough of such arrangements. The unemployment seems worse than the deficit it cures. Not only would they not return to the old gold standard but they would refuse, except in the direst of emergencies, to use restrictive monetary and fiscal policy to right an errant balance of payments.[18]

Perhaps the best way to summarize the points made in this section is to restate the central lesson of economics. *As long as resources are scarce, getting more of one thing requires giving up something else.* The same general point can be made about economic policy measures. *As long as our economic goals are in partial conflict with one another, we may be able to achieve one only by losing some ground in our progress toward another.*

A balance of payments deficit may be ended by trade barriers, but to do so would impair the world-wide allocation of resources. It might

18 Note, however, that Great Britain, with a most serious international payments problem, has instituted such a policy in 1966.

be ended by reducing foreign spending by government, but to do so might jeopardize the national security. It might be countered by devaluation of the currency, but then again this may not work. Or, finally, it could be fought with restrictive monetary and fiscal policy, but only at the likely cost of increasing unemployment.

The economic arena, it seems, is not one of blacks and whites, but one of grays. Economic policy measures are not classifiable into good and bad in any absolute sense, but almost all require a delicate balancing of the good effects against the bad. We must recognize that there are few policy measures that advance us toward one of our goals without, to some degree, conflicting with another.

16 | Current Problems in International Finance

The problem of how a nation can deal with a balance of payments deficit is only one aspect of a much broader problem—the "proper" organization of the entire world's international monetary structure. We shall attempt to touch on both problems in this chapter as they apply to the United States specifically and to the entire free world.

To accomplish this, the chapter will contain three main sections. In the first we shall discuss very briefly the background and history of international financial developments that have led us up to the present situation. Then, we shall consider, in some detail, the recent U.S. balance of payments deficits, and what has been and might be done to eliminate them. Finally, we shall take a look at possible future problems and some proposals for dealing with them. In essence then, this chapter consists of a quick survey of the past, the present, and the future of international finance.

THE PAST—MID-NINETEENTH CENTURY THROUGH WORLD WAR II

The Golden Era—1870-1914

The period from about 1870 to 1914 has often been characterized as the *golden era*. During this time the world was untroubled by the vast upheavals associated with major wars and the full international gold standard held the center of the stage.

It was in many ways an idyllic era, and the gold standard seemed to many to be the ultimate in sane and stable economic arrangements.

Although such faith in the now-discarded system may seem, with the invaluable aid of hindsight, to have been overdone, one can hardly deny the inescapable fact that it worked amazingly well.

The unquestioned financial center of the world at the time was that staunch citadel of free trade, Great Britain. She played her key role well. As a developed industrial giant, Britain permitted less fully developed nations to finance trade deficits by making long-term loans abroad. As the heart of the financial world, she played an important role in fostering the development of freer trade with a minimum of trade barriers and restrictions. And, along with most other nations, her monetary authorities obeyed, reasonably faithfully, the so-called *rules* of the gold standard game whereby monetary policy was tightened in the face of a payments deficit and eased to combat a surplus.

But it took more than skillful management to make the system work so well. Other conditions favored it greatly. In the first place, wages and prices were considerably more flexible than they are today. This had the important effect of permitting the drop in demand associated with payments deficits to lower prices rather than income and employment—a much preferred result. In addition public and official attitudes had not yet reached the point where "doing something about unemployment" was considered a proper area for governmental action. Hence the policy conflict that has worried us so much since—between policy to deal with a payments deficit and policy to deal with unemployment—was largely absent.

One does less than justice to the international gold standard if one does not recognize its solid record of accomplishment prior to World War I. And yet one does a certain violence to history if one does not recognize that the "ideal" conditions for its efficient operation largely evaporated under the violently upsetting pressures of World War I and its aftermath.

The Unsettled Years—1918-1930

Not that an attempt was not made to return to the "good old days" of the prewar gold standard after the conflict. Most major countries went back "on gold" as soon as possible. But the conditions of the nineteenth century, fortunately or unfortunately, were gone forever. The institutional trappings of the gold standard were restored but the conditions necessary to make it a viable, efficient system of world financial order were gone for good.

A full explanation of the problems of the between-the-wars gold standard is not permitted by the scope of this book. We can, however, mention some of the chief causes of difficulty—unrealistic reparation demands imposed on vanquished Germany; an attempt by the British to reestablish their pound at the same relationship with gold as that maintained in prewar days—a clear overvaluation; excessive use of the protective tariff by the emerging industrial giant, the United States; and finally, the growing recognition, especially after the experience of mass unemployment in the twenties and thirties, of the fact that the strict discipline of the gold standard required the sacrifice of what was rapidly emerging as the major domestic policy goal—maintaining full employment with stable prices.

The combination of all these factors produced, if not a hostile climate, at least a less than ideal environment for a smoothly functioning gold standard. And when, in the early 1930's, the public's confidence in the ability of its governments to honor their pledge to pay gold on demand to all comers dipped sharply, country after country, drained of its gold supply through payments deficits, public hoarding demands, and speculative short-term capital movements, was forced to abandon the standard.[1]

The Chaotic Thirties

The 1930's was indeed a turbulent period in international finance. It was featured not only by the abandonment of the time-honored full gold standard by most nations but also by a wild scramble of unilateral devalutions, increased tariff barriers, and a whole range of actions calculated to impede the restoration of normal, free international exchange. It was an economically sick world that girded itself for the second all-out war of the century in 1939.

U.S. actions during the interwar period were, at times, deplorable, at other times, exemplary. The nation at first enabled the post-World War I reparations arrangements to work by, in essence, loaning Germany sufficient amounts to enable the Germans to pay reparations to England and France, which countries, in turn, used these proceeds to pay off part of their war debts to the United States. U.S. lending to permit this *triangular* deal, however, was made necessary partly by its own greatly increased tariff barriers in the 1920's which made it all but impossible for the Germans to earn the reparation payment through exports.

When the U.S. stock market crash in 1929 put a virtual end to longterm U.S. lending, and when the United States followed up this calamity with the new Smoot-Hawley tariff bill establishing the highest tariff rates in its history, the Germans were simply unable to meet their obligations. And, in turn, the British and French were unable to keep up with scheduled repayments on their war debts to the United States.

---

[1] It would be incorrect to say that the U.S. decision to go "off gold" was forced by any immediate shortage of gold reserves, however.

In the 1930's the United States had no choice but to declare a *moratorium* on payment of inter-Allied war debts and, of course, the Germans were forced to default on much of their reparation burdens. The stresses and strains of the depression-wracked world of the thirties then led to the mass withdrawal from the gold standard mentioned above. The U.S. went off in 1933 and returned to its present *modified* gold bullion standard in 1934. It did not, however, make this transition without one further, apparently ill-advised move. When it reestablished its present standard in 1934, it also devalued the dollar in terms of gold. This probably improved its balance of trade temporarily, but it not only failed miserably as an antidepression measure but also helped to trigger the destructive wave of competitive devaluation that followed.

Only in the latter thirties did the United States begin to demonstrate its awareness of the futility of unilateral competitive trade restrictions. During this period the historic Reciprocal Trade Agreements Act was passed, providing for substantial reductions in U.S. tariff barriers; the Tri-Partite Agreement with England and France was signed forming the basis for an end to competitive devaluation; and the Export-Import Bank was established to provide long-term loans to some of the trading partners of the United States.

These more enlightened, constructive policies were followed up during and after World War II with all-out efforts to avoid the mistakes of unilateralism of the twenties and thirties. No heavy reparations were demanded of the defeated Axis powers; no large inter-Allied debts were built up during the war, largely as a result of the U.S. Lend-Lease Program; the basis for large-scale international monetary cooperation after the war in the form of the International Monetary Fund was established in a historic conference at Bretton Woods; and the rebuilding of the economies of the war-ravaged western Allies was speeded up immeasurably by the unprecedented, far-sighted postwar Marshall Plan. The lessons learned at such heavy cost in the interwar period had provided the basis for the far more enlightened multilateral approach of the late 1940's and 1950's.

Probably the clearest examples of the changes in attitude were the American Marshall Plan and the establishment of the International Monetary Fund. Let us turn, in somewhat greater detail, to these two important postwar measures.

The Marshall Plan

The Marshall Plan will probably go down in history as one of the truly outstanding achievements of U.S. policy. Indeed, in light of the development of the Cold War, it would be difficult to overestimate

the importance of this vast and historic effort to nurse a devastated Western Europe back on the road to economic and military self-sufficiency.

It is certainly not difficult to understand the need for the Plan. The
ravages of a six-year war had all but demolished the productive potential of the Western European Allies, to say nothing of West Germany.
Their needs were great but their capacity for filling them had been deci-
mated by the devastation of war. They needed desperately, for purposes
of rebuilding their own economic strength, to import vast quantities of
crucial goods from the only major industrial nation whose productive
power had not been impaired by war—the United States. But their
inability to produce large quantities for export made it all but impossible for them, on their own, to earn the dollars required to import
those things that were so badly needed. There was, in short, an enormous *dollar shortage* to be dealt with.

The United States had at least two good reasons for responding
with its enlightened offer of Marshall Plan aid. In the first place it recognized that the devastation created by the common war against the
Axis powers was a cost that ought rightly to be shared by all freedom-
loving peoples, not just those unfortunate enough to be geographically
situated in the war zone. In the second place the growing menace of the
U.S.S.R., whose antagonistic policies were backed by a powerful Red
Army, seemed an immediate threat to the Western European democra-
cies. The United States felt that it was as much in its interest as in theirs
to take the necessary steps to restore them to economic vigor.

Though we cannot credit the remarkably rapid recovery of Western
Europe entirely to Marshall Plan aid—certainly, the efforts of the Western European countries, especially toward a unified economic community, played the major role—we should not minimize the contribution
made by the immediate postwar grants of the United States. European
recovery was, indeed, so rapid and the dollar shortage so short-lived a
phenomenon, that in less than a decade the huge balance of payments
surpluses of the United States had become deficits.

The International Monetary Fund

The establishment of an International Monetary Fund
(I.M.F.) was another major step toward mature international cooperation
in the postwar period. Established in 1944 at Bretton Woods, the I.M.F.
began operations in 1947.

It had two main initial purposes—to set up a system whereby reasonably stable exchange rates could be maintained without requiring a
deficit nation to undertake deflationary domestic policies and to move

towards elimination of the extensive network of exchange restrictions which characterized the post-World War II scene.

It required each member nation to set a relationship between its currency and gold (or the dollar, which was itself defined in terms of gold), an action that automatically established a set of postwar exchange rates between the currencies of member countries. They were then expected (through exchange stabilization funds) to take action to keep exchange rate fluctuation within 1 percent of the stated *pars*.

Devaluation of a member country's currency for purposes of dealing with a *fundamental disequilibrium* was permitted without Fund authorization if it amounted to less than 10 percent, but greater changes required I.M.F. approval.[2] This, of course, was an attempt to maintain reasonably stable rates and to forestall the type of competitive devaluation that had characterized the 1930's.

The main activity of the I.M.F. in addition to setting down the ground rules just discussed, was to be the provision of loans of gold and/or foreign exchange to member countries suffering temporary balance of payments disequilibriums. To provide the necessary funds each member country was required to pay in a quota, based on its economic capacity, 25 percent of which was to be in gold and the rest in its own currency. The total resources of the Fund, obtained from these national quotas, were $8 billion originally but have since been increased to about $15 billion.

Member countries suffering payments deficits could then borrow gold or needed foreign exchange from the Fund to the full amount of their own quota to tide them over a period of deficits. They did not, however, have the right automatically to borrow this amount within any given year. Only the first 25 percent of their quota was freely available for borrowing, with an additional 25 percent of their quota available, per year, as long as the lending country approved.

The ability of the I.M.F. to deal with payments imbalances is seriously limited, both by its own total resources and by the restrictions on borrowing rights. Since, in the world as a whole, deficits on the part of some countries must be matched by surpluses on the part of others, only half the $15 billion can be borrowed at any one time. The borrowing rights to the other $7.5 billion belong to the surplus countries who have no need for borrowing. But, since in any one year only 25 percent of a deficit country's quota may be borrowed (and even that may be subject to certain restrictions), the total amount available immediately from the Fund is less than $2 billion—an amount that, from past experience, can hardly be considered sufficient to handle all possible contingencies.

2 Despite this provision, however, several major postwar devaluations were carried out by the simple expedient of "informing" the I.M.F. of the action after it was taken.

The International Monetary Fund has represented a major milestone along the road to full international monetary cooperation. Yet it has not, and was never designed for, the solution to all the world's problems in this area. It has worked diligently for the reduction of exchange restrictions. It has provided some short-term funds to deficit nations in need. It has provided a vehicle within which problems may be discussed and constructive solutions worked out without immediate recourse to disastrously divisive unilateral action.

But there have been, since its inception, those who have felt that it is not equipped to do the job that is required. In the very Bretton Woods discussions that set it up, a distinguished British delegation, led by the late J. M. Keynes, argued for a much larger Fund with substantially greater lending powers than were finally given it. More recently, some recognized experts in the area of international finance have revived what was essentially the earlier British position of turning the I.M.F. into a true world central bank, thereby greatly enlarging its lending power. And, in addition, in recent years there appears to be growing support in some quarters for a move away from one of the Fund's main principles, toward more freely fluctuating exchange rates. Some of these proposals will be discussed briefly in the concluding section of this chapter.

THE PRESENT—U.S. BALANCE OF PAYMENTS DEFICITS AND THEIR POSSIBLE SOLUTIONS

In the immediate post-World War II years, the United States, already possessor of almost 70 percent of the free world's gold supply, ran heavy balance of payments surpluses while, of course, the leading nations of Western Europe had to contend with substantial deficits. It was a situation that seemed to many to be likely to continue indefinitely and, indeed, methods of dealing with what was assumed to be an almost perpetual dollar shortage dominated discussion.

A look back at the events of the late forties and early fifties, however, provides a much better perspective of what was happening than was possible at the time. The *dollar gap,* which was the cause of so much concern, was rapidly being bridged by developments all around. The role of Marshall Plan aid has already been mentioned in this regard. Not only did it permit a temporary bridging of Western Europe's balance of payments gap but it also aided the rebuilding and modernization of European industry to the point where it could better compete in world markets.

And, with the intensification of the cold war, what had originally been thought of as a temporary, balancing American foreign-aid program, became instead a semipermanent fixture qualifying it, in the terminology employed earlier, as an autonomous, rather than a balancing entry in the U.S. balance of payments.

In the meantime Western Europe was acting on its own to recover its share of world trade. Not only was it modernizing its productive equipment but it acted firmly and boldly to achieve a degree of economic integration through the Schuman Plan, the European Economic Community, and the Common Market which gave it trade advantages it had never before possessed. Finally, the nations of Western Europe acted, in 1948 and 1949, to devalue their currencies sharply with respect to the dollar to curtail their then heavy deficits.

While the United States was occupied with the Korean War and then, later, a postwar boom in the first half of the 1950's, vast changes in its international economic position were taking place almost without notice. What had been considered a dollar gap had already disappeared. But the relatively small U.S. payments deficits that had begun to show up caused no alarm whatsoever because foreigners were quite content to hold the bulk of their excess dollar earnings in dollar form. This, in turn, was a consequence of the rapid development of a gold-exchange standard for which the pound and the dollar were the *key currencies*.

Rise of the Gold Exchange Standard

This additional development of the post-World War II years deserves comment. A rapidly expanding volume of trade required drastically increased international reserves to finance it. And yet, the world supply of prime international reserves, gold, had increased only at a much slower pace. A method had to be found of making the too small and maldistributed world gold supply stretch further. One partial answer to the problem appeared to be a gold-exchange standard.

The rise of the gold-exchange standard was not the result of any worldwide planning. It spread as a result of individual national decisions to hold part of their monetary reserves in dollars (or in pounds, for the sterling bloc) as well as in gold. It was made possible by the oft-repeated promise of the United States to exchange gold for dollars (or dollars for gold) at the statutory price of $35 per ounce for any foreign holder of dollars.

The advantages to other countries from this arrangement are obvious. Instead of tying up all their monetary reserves in the nonincome earning form of gold, they can hold substantial portions in the form of short-term dollar assets, which not only earn interest but are, as long as the U.S. honors its promise to make them convertible into gold, "as good as gold" itself. For the United States, on the other hand, it meant that its

small deficits during the early and middle fifties, led only to a piling up
of more short-term dollar obligations to foreigners who were, in the main,
more desirous of expanding the dollar-asset portion of their monetary
reserves than of taking out gold.

The Development of Large U.S. Deficits

But the almost unnoticed deficits of the mid-fifties mushroomed suddenly in 1958 to a scale that seemed to demand not only attention but action from responsible authorities. It was a combination of two
developments that rang the warning bell.

In the first place the relatively small annual deficits of the earlier fifties
suddenly shot up to the truly significant $3 billion neighborhood. In the
second place, foreign nations that had been willing, in the past, to accept
the proceeds of their surpluses with the United States almost entirely in
the form of increased holdings of short-term dollar obligations suddenly
switched tactics and withdrew over $2 billion of gold. This sudden change
in foreign attitudes undoubtedly resulted from a combination of two
factors. On the one hand, some of them, having already built up their
dollar reserves to the tolerable limits, felt obliged to take gold to keep a
balanced proportion of gold and dollars in their monetary reserves.
Others, however, probably reacted to the sharply expanded U.S. deficit as
a danger sign and, on the chance that the United States might be forced
to devalue, took the defensive speculative action of withdrawing gold.

Nor was the experience of 1958 to be a random, isolated episode. Balance of payments deficits of roughly the same magnitude continued from
1959 through 1964 during which time the United States lost another
$5 billion worth of gold, while its short-term obligations to foreigners
jumped upward by over $10 billion.

It was clear that not only had U.S. payments deficits jumped per-
ceptibly but that they were leading to a loss of gold at a rate that not
even the huge stocks of the United States could support indefinitely. Indeed, by the end of 1964 the U.S. gold stock had fallen from the comfortable $22.9 billion level of 1957 to a mere $15.5 billion. There was ample
reason for concern.

But the seriousness of the problem is not indicated even by these
startling figures. While the gold stock of the United States still stood at
over $15 billion in 1964, the lion's share of it was not directly and freely
available to meet possible future deficits because U.S. laws at that time
required the Federal Reserve Banks to "back" their outstanding Federal
Reserve Notes and deposit liabilities by gold certificates equaling at least
25 percent of their total. Since each $1 gold certificate ties up $1 of gold,
the money supply outstanding as of the end of 1964 "used up," as backing

for required gold certificates, over $12 billion of the gold possessed by the United States. Consequently, less than $3 billion of the $15.5 billion it possessed at that time was available to settle, if need be, future payments deficits.

Nor does even this provide the full picture. For over a decade, as U.S. deficits continued and the gold-exchange standard spread, foreigners had been building up their ownership of short-term dollar assets. By the end of 1964, these bulked to about $24 billion. Now if the United States were to continue to make dollars held by foreigners convertible into gold, this entire $24 billion represented a potential further drain on its gold supply. Indeed, the dwindling gold supply of the United States was, under existing arrangements, threatened on three fronts. There was, first, the danger that future deficits would lead to further gold purchases by foreigners. There was, second, the ever-present possibility that even if future payments deficits could somehow be prevented, foreigners, who already held well over $24 billion of short-term dollar assets, could request that substantial portions be converted to gold. And, finally, there was the fact that even if future deficits and foreigners' requests to exchange dollars already held for gold could be forestalled, a growing U.S. economy would require a growing money supply, which, in turn, would tie up increasing amounts of the U.S. gold stock behind required gold certificates. It was a sobering picture that clearly seemed to require action.

The "Causes" of the U.S. Deficits

Before turning to the steps taken and available to deal with the deficit and gold drain, it will be useful to take a closer look at the nature of the U.S. deficits. For this purpose, we shall use data from the 1960 balance of payments as an example of the problem with which the United States has been faced in each year since 1957. Table 16-1 contains the figures.

The problem, if not the solution, is clearly apparent. While the United States was able to earn a substantial $3.8 billion current account surplus, its investments abroad and its gifts to foreigners were so far in excess of this total, that it ended up instead with a $3.9 balance of payments deficit. Foreigners, in 1960, chose to use $1.7 billion of this to withdraw gold and allow the other $2.2 billion to pile up in the form of short-term claims on the United States.

Which of the foreign transactions of the United States is the cause of its deficit? Though it is impossible to single out any one as the cause, it is quite clear that three activities play the major role. In the first place, if the United States did not feel it necessary to keep troops abroad and incur $3 billion of military expenditures, its current account surplus

TABLE 16-1   U.S. Balance of Payments, 1960 (billions of dollars)

Exports Transactions Requiring Payment to Americans		*Imports—Transactions Requiring Payment by Americans*	
Exports of Goods and Services	27.0	Imports of Goods and Services, Excluding Military	20.2
		Military Imports of Goods and Services	3.0
		Long-term Investment Abroad by Americans, Net	3.5[a]
		Unilateral Transfers, Net	3.4
		Unrecorded Transactions	.7[b]
Gold Exports	1.7		
Short-term Capital Movements (Increase in Foreign Ownership of Short-term Assets)	2.2		

[a] The $3.5 figure includes a $1.3 increase in short-term assets owned abroad by Americans, which are treated by the Department of Commerce as autonomous transactions.

[b] These are generally believed to consist of short-term capital movements, records of which are not completely available.

SOURCE: Department of Commerce.

would undoubtedly be noticeably larger. Secondly, if the United States were not investing abroad so heavily, its immediate problem would be less severe. Thirdly, if the United States felt justified in reducing its unilateral transfers, of which the foreign-aid program is a major component, the deficit could be reduced.

But one cannot, with justification, jump to the conclusion that the elimination of any one of these three types of foreign spending would "solve the problem," since the two sides of the balance of payments are intertwined in a manner that is very difficult to unravel. For example, the elimination of the United States' unilateral transfers would reduce its deficit, but by nowhere near the amount of $3.4 billion. This is because a substantial number of the dollars given to foreigners end up being spent on U.S. exports. Elimination of the United States' unilateral transfers, then, would, besides reducing the import-side total by $3.4 billion, also cut its exports of goods and services by an amount that might easily be over $2 billion.

And the same thing, perhaps to a lesser degree, would be true of efforts to cut U.S. military expenditures abroad or U.S. investment abroad. Programs under which the United States makes dollars available to foreigners may also permit them to buy U.S. goods and services they would not have purchased otherwise. Such cross-connections between the two sides of the balance of payments must be borne in mind whenever corrective action is considered.

U.S. Discretionary Policy to Combat Deficits

So much for the causes of the deficit. Given the nature of the problem, what has been done and what further steps might be appropriate?

The U.S. government has already taken a number of discretionary policy steps aimed at easing the problem. It has undertaken extensive measures to increase the sale of American goods and services abroad. It has placed greater restrictions on purchases abroad by American tourists. It has taken steps to further *tie* U.S. foreign aid grants, requiring that more of the money be spent on U.S. goods and services. It has attempted, in a variety of ways, to cut back on that portion of its military spending abroad which it considers not vital for national security. It has attempted to convince other free world nations of the justice and wisdom involved in their taking over a larger share of both the burden of maintaining U.S. forces abroad and of foreign aid. It has attempted, with considerable success, at least up to 1965, to keep U.S. prices and wages from rising as rapidly as are those of its trading partners. It has succeeded in raising U.S. short-term interest rates relative to those in other countries in the hope of attracting short-term capital to the United States, as well as forestalling a wholesale exodus of funds already held there.

But all this failed to keep the U.S. deficit below the $3 billion level through 1963, and when, in that year, a sharp upsurge of foreign-security sales in the United States seemed destined to make matters even worse, the President proposed to Congress a bill that would place a 15 percent tax on foreign stocks and bonds floated there. This so-called *interest equalization* tax was to be made effective as of July, 1963, and was to apply to all foreign-security sales except those of the underdeveloped nations and Canada. Although it was not finally passed until 1964, its bite was felt almost immediately because of the expectation that it would be made retroactive, as the President had suggested, to July, 1963.

For a while this action seemed to be paying off handsomely. Foreign security sales dropped off sharply in late 1963 and the U.S. balance of payments improved notably. But the end was not yet.

For, while the interest equalization tax did cut back sharply on foreign security sales in the United States, other forms of American lending to foreigners rose quickly to keep the U.S. outflow of private capital at record levels. In late 1964 and early 1965, direct bank loans to foreigners zoomed to record heights and the U.S. deficit turned up sharply once more. And on top of all this, the French government announced its intention of converting sizable portions of its short-term dollar assets to gold. The squeeze was on and, once again, the nation had to respond.

With the U.S. gold supply rapidly approaching the legal minimum required to back up Federal Reserve Notes and deposits at Federal Reserve banks, Congress acted in early 1965, as noted above, to eliminate the gold-certificate requirement behind Federal Reserve deposits. This eminently sensible action, while playing no direct role in the elimination of U.S. balance of payments deficit, did at least free over $5 billion of the remaining U.S. gold supply to support the dollar in international finance.

In addition, in February, 1965, President Johnson, making use of authority granted him in the interest equalization bill, applied the same 15 percent tax to long-term bank loans to foreigners. The President coupled this action with a request for voluntary cooperation by the financial community, to hold down extensions of loans to foreigners during 1965 and 1966. In essence, lenders were asked to keep the increase in foreign loans down to an annual rate of 5 percent.

For 1965, these new measures worked extremely well. The financial community cooperated with the government's program and the result, despite a reduction in the U.S. current account surplus, was a reduction in the overall payments deficit of the United States for 1965 to $1.3 billion. After seven years of deficits in the $3 billion neighborhood this was a notable improvement.

The United States did, however, lose $1.5 billion of gold during the year, much of it to France, and as of mid-1966 its gold stock had gone down to $13.6 billion. In addition, more storm clouds seemed to be gathering. Sharp U.S. price increases in 1965 and 1966, for the first time in many years, and a booming U.S. economy led to notable increases in U.S. imports. Major responsibilities in Viet Nam were putting more strain on the U.S. balance of payments. Despite the new pressures, however, the 1966 deficit appears to have been kept down to about the 1965 level.

THE FUTURE—POSSIBLE FUTURE PROBLEMS OF INTERNATIONAL FINANCE AND SOME SUGGESTED REFORMS

Further Methods of Dealing With the U.S. Deficit

If recent improvements in the U.S. balance of payments cannot be maintained in the future, further discretionary action to deal with the problem is absolutely essential. Within the present international institutional framework, continued U.S. deficits will almost certainly lead to continued gold losses. And although the amount of gold the United States has available to meet such drains was raised to about $7 billion by the elimination of the gold-certificate requirement behind deposits at the Federal Reserve, a continuation of deficits of the magnitude of recent years (coupled with a continuing growth in the quantity of gold certificate-backed Federal Reserve Notes) could, in not too many years, exhaust even this. Then what?

One action that many have favored for years would be to go all the way in the elimination of gold-certificate reserves behind domestic money by removing the requirement that remains behind Federal Reserve Notes. Such action would release the entire $13.6 billion of gold to meet future deficits and while it would not, in and of itself, eliminate the deficit it would certainly provide policy makers with needed time to find the solution. And time, in these matters, is not a subject for scorn.

For the uncomfortable fact, as pointed out in the previous chapter, is that most of the major discretionary actions still available come at a cost that most are not anxious to rush into paying.

The United States might, for example, attempt to improve its position via an expansion of trade barriers. Such a step, however, would not only run counter to its long-run policy of encouraging free, unobstructed world trade, but would also, because of almost certain retaliation, probably be doomed to failure. It should be considered, if at all, as only a last-ditch alternative after almost everything else has been tried.

The United States might choose to go further with its restrictions on foreign investment, but such a step would interfere further with the world allocation of resources, and would have the unfavorable long-run effect of reducing future interest and dividend payments from foreigners.

The problem might be attacked by a further paring of its military expenditures abroad or foreign aid payments, but in both cases whatever gain is made in the balance of payments must be balanced off against the sacrifice of other objectives, most specifically, the national security. This, too, would appear to be a high price to pay for balance of payments equilibrium.

Another possible approach would be the imposition of sufficiently restrictive monetary and fiscal policies to cut U.S. imports by the required amount. This policy could certainly do the necessary job on U.S. balance of payments if the United States were willing to pay the almost certainly high price that would come along with it in the form of a domestic recession. Once again such a balance of payments solution would probably be far too expensive. The United States is likely, quite properly it would seem, to reject this "intentional unemployment" approach.

If all the previous approaches are rejected and the U.S. deficit still continues, only one further course is available—devaluation of the dollar.

There are several means open for devaluing the dollar if the United States chose to do so:

1. Accomplish the devaluation by raising the dollar price of gold, thereby reducing the value of the dollar in terms of other currencies, as well as in terms of gold
2. Raise the price of gold indirectly by refusing to pay out any more gold for foreign-held dollars
3. Abandon the present system altogether by adopting a freely fluctuating exchange rate mechanism and permitting the value of the dollar to fall as far as supply and demand conditions dictate.

The alternative of raising the price of gold, say from the present $35 per ounce to $50 per ounce, would, so long as other nations take no action to offset its effects, have two possibly favorable effects. In the first place it is argued that by raising the value of the present gold stock and by encouraging a more rapid rate of gold production, it would expand the world's supply of prime international reserves. Secondly, to the extent that it results in a reduction in the value of the dollar relative to other currencies, it could reduce the U.S. payments deficit.

Powerful arguments on the other side exist, however. Among the objections to a rise in the gold price are:

1. To the extent that it results in more productive resources being devoted to the extraction of an essentially sterile object, it would promote economic waste.
2. It would provide windfall benefits to gold-producing nations, two of the largest of which, the Union of South Africa and the U.S.S.R., the United States does not desire to aid.
3. The mere consideration of such a step would trigger unfavorable speculation on the part of present holders of dollars and, after it was carried out those who had not already switched from holding dollars to holding gold would be unfairly penalized for holding onto their dollars.
4. It might lead to speculation that further gold price increases were imminent.
5. It may not solve U.S. deficit problem in any case.

Apparently impressed by the weight of these opposing arguments, the U.S. government has tried to make clear that it has no present intentions of taking this step.

Another way of achieving approximately the same results would be for the United States to renounce its promise to convert foreign-held dollars into gold. The present U.S. law, often characterized as a *24-hour gold standard,* permits the Secretary of the Treasury to refuse the payment of gold at any time. Consequently, if foreigners' demands to convert dollar holdings into gold should, at any time, become too large, the United States could simply refuse to do so.

The effects of such an action, however, may well be profound. In the first place, by cutting off the main source of gold supply, the United States would probably cause a rise in its dollar price, thus indirectly devaluing the dollar. In the second place, such action would amount to an abrogation of the promises under which the United States encouraged the development of the present gold-exchange standard with the dollar as a "key" reserve currency and would be tantamount to its renouncing its obligation to contribute to stable exchange rates under the I.M.F. charter. The United States will obviously think long and hard before taking such a step.

Finally, the United States could devalue the dollar by going all the way from the present stable exchange rate mechanism to a system of freely fluctuating exchanges. This action would permit the dollar to fall relative to other currencies according to the free play of supply and demand. We shall have more to say about this approach shortly but it should be recognized here that action of this sort would represent a major departure from the type of international monetary machinery envisaged by the International Monetary Fund and painstakingly put together over the years.

Devaluation, however carried out, would be a most serious step. In fact, in the words of the Council of Economic Advisors:

> While the Articles of Agreement of the IMF permit exchange rate adjustment in case of a 'fundamental disequilibrium'—an imbalance that is chronic and intractable at the existing exchange rate—most countries are reluctant to take this step. *For a reserve currency country, this alternative is not available.* For other major industrial countries even occasional recourse to such adjustments would induce serious speculative capital movements, thereby accentuating imbalances.[3]

It should be clear by now that dealing with persistent balance of payments deficits is anything but easy. The United States is indeed fortunate to have had a huge supply of gold at its disposal during the past decade, a luxury that has given it time to implement the less drastic policy tools available and time to wait for developments in other countries which will be favorable. As of mid-1966 it is still to be hoped that, long before some of the more "costly" policy moves might be forced upon the United States, a combination of moderate policy actions and "favorable" price movements abroad may save the day.

[3] *Economic Report of the President, 1964*, p. 139. The italics are the author's.

The Problems of a Gold-exchange Standard and Some Suggestions for Major Reform

The American deficit is, however, only a part of a much broader problem. Serious concern has been expressed recently regarding the stability and viability of the entire international monetary mechanism. It has been argued, for example, that a serious shortage of international reserves is almost certainly in the offing, especially if the United States is successful in eliminating its deficit. And even more disquieting is the viewpoint of some authorities that the present gold-exchange standard, based as it is on reserves held largely in the form of certain key currencies, is inherently unstable and peculiarly biased toward the generation of periodic liquidity crises, such as that which led to the devastating monetary upheavals that characterized the decade before World War II. Such fears, coming as they do from respected authorities in this area, are not to be taken lightly.

It is clear to all that the supply of international reserves in the form of gold is not likely to increase at the pace needed to finance the expanded volume of trade which a growing world economy can be expected to generate. Consequently there is no doubt that other sources of international reserves must be employed.

A thriving gold-exchange standard provides such a source in the form of the domestic currency issued by the so-called key currency countries. In today's world, nations freely accept and freely hold, not only gold but also dollars and pounds as a part of their international reserves. The "strong" currencies that serve as international reserves obtain their status of general acceptability from the industrial and financial strength of the nation issuing them, as well as from additional institutional features, such as the U.S. promise to pay gold on demand. They remain generally acceptable, however, only as long as they retain that strength.

The Alleged Inherent Instability of the Gold-exchange Standard

But this, unfortunately, is the problem. Other countries can obtain increasing supplies of the key currencies only as long as the key currency countries run balance of payments deficits that permit the accumulation of more short-term claims on them. And, indeed, this is the only way in which the gold-exchange standard can provide additional liquidity—additional international reserves to the world. But the very process whereby international reserves are thus increased is, at one and the same time, a process that "weakens" the key currencies.

The longer the United States runs balance of payments deficits, the proceeds of which surplus nations are willing to accept in the form of increased short-term dollar claims, the more it is contributing to the expansion of international liquidity. But the greater the build-up of short-term claims on the United States, relative to its gold supply, the less able it becomes to honor its promise to exchange gold for dollars. As this process continues, sooner or later other countries may come to question the strength of the dollar as a reserve currency, and, as one result, increase their requests that the United States convert their dollars to gold. When, finally, gold is withdrawn, not only are international reserves not increased but confidence in the key currency is further undermined. It is, in the opinion of some critics, a system that generates its own destruction.

Paradoxically, then, if the United States is successful in ending its payments deficits it will, at the same time, be shutting off the main source of increased international reserves that have been financing the expansion of world trade. If it does not end its deficits, on the other hand, the very process by which it increases world liquidity will, sooner or later, destroy the strength of the U.S. dollar as a key currency and help bring on a major liquidity crisis such as that which rocked the world in 1929. In this view the United States is caught on the horns of a dilemma which only an eventual overhaul of the international monetary mechanism can eradicate.

While the logic of the above arguments is apparent to all, there is by no means complete agreement on the best solution. Many authorities feel that the United States should retain the essence of its present system while amending it and supplementing it by international financial cooperation to overcome its most glaring weaknesses. Others, less convinced of the basic logic of the present mechanism, would prefer a thorough overhaul of the structure, including a major change in the role and nature of the International Monetary Fund. Finally, a third group would prefer sidestepping altogether the problem of adequate international reserves by adopting a system of freely fluctuating exchange rates. Let us take a closer look at these three proposals.

Proposals to Bolster the Present System

The more moderate approach would retain the essence of the present structure but would rely heavily on bilateral agreements and an expansion in I.M.F. lending power to deal with stubborn imbalances. To a degree this approach is already being followed. The United States has made arrangements with other governments for what have come to be called *swaps* of one another's currency. This is an arrangement whereby the monetary authorities of two nations exchange deposit balances of one another's currency to be used for stabilizing foreign exchange markets. In addition, ten of the leading industrial nations have signed an agreement to make available as much as $6 billion of their currencies to the International Monetary Fund, beyond their required quotas, in case of need. Similar awareness of the advantages of international cooperation is indicated by the willingness of certain Western European countries to pay off long-term debts owed to the United States ahead of schedule in recent years.

Those who feel that major surgery on the international monetary mechanism is not now needed point to acts such as these as evidences of the desire, willingness, and capacity of nations to cooperate today in a manner almost unheard of in the upheavals of the 1930's. They advocate giving such multilateral cooperation a chance to work before making any drastic changes in the system itself.

The Triffin Plan

A second approach, most clearly exemplified by the views of Professor Robert Triffin of Yale, would be to take the bull by the horns and change the essential nature of the I.M.F. itself in a way that would eventually eliminate the present dependence on the dollar and the pound as international reserve currencies. Triffin argues that the I.M.F. should be transformed into a true world central bank with the power to create international reserves as they are needed by deficit countries. This would be done by requiring member countries to hold a certain minimum percentage of their monetary reserves as deposits at the I.M.F. These deposits, not in the form of dollars or pounds or other national currencies, but in the form of the newly generalized claim on the I.M.F., would be freely and automatically available for use. The I.M.F., itself, would then be empowered to create additional international reserves (new claims on itself) by lending and investing in the same manner as does a national central bank. In this manner, Triffin believes, the pressure now placed on key currency countries would be removed and a new, truly elastic source of international reserves would be established.

Triffin's proposal has aroused considerable interest and no little controversy. The chief opposition to it has come from those who feel (1) that such a major change is not needed to deal with U.S. economic problems and (2) that his proposal contains an inflationary bias in the form of a new, and largely uncontrolled, creator of spending power. Triffin's response to the *inflationary bias* charge is that, while his plan is very similar to the *Keynes Plan* presented at the original deliberations of the Bretton Woods Conference, it differs from it substantially in detail in that it contains built-in defenses against inflationary credit expansion.

The Triffin approach and variants of it have already been the subject of considerable thoughtful discussion. In all likelihood it will be given careful consideration in the years ahead but, short of a major crisis demanding immediate attention, it does not appear probable that it will be adopted in the near future.

Freely Fluctuating Exchange Rates

A third major approach to substantive change in the world's monetary machinery would appear to be the old but increasingly popular plan of "letting the market do it," that is, shifting to a system of freely fluctuating exchange rates. Perhaps the outstanding American proponent of this approach is Professor Milton Friedman of the University of Chicago.

Friedman and those who are in agreement with him on this issue feel that the cost involved in the struggle to maintain stable exchange rates is substantially greater than their benefits. If exchange rates are allowed to adjust to the dictates of supply and demand, the need for the maintenance of a large volume of international reserves, to tide a nation over a deficit period, will be largely eliminated. In addition, some claim, the nation with a deficit in its balance of payments will be much freer to employ monetary and fiscal policy in the direction that is appropriate to its domestic economic circumstances, relying on exchange rate changes to take care of its international imbalance.

Any assessment of the merits of this argument is fraught with difficulties and a firm conclusion is all but impossible. Its advocates argue that the traditional defense of stable exchange rates, the claim that they encourage wider trade by eliminating the risks involved in exchange rate movements, is much overdone as far as trade in goods and services is concerned. As long as it is possible to hedge in the purchase of foreign exchange—to buy needed foreign currency at today's rate for delivery in the future—traders can shift the exchange risk onto the shoulders of professional speculators.

The real area of difference between the proponents and opponents of fluctuating exchange rates is in the nature of the speculation to be expected. If there is downward pressure on the value of a given currency, and its adjustment downward is expected to reach a new equilibrium level soon, then speculators will find it in their own interest to help stop the downward movement by bringing in short-term capital once the new equilibrium level has been reached. If, however, a downward movement, once started, triggers the expectation that it will continue, speculators will accentuate the downward movement by removing short-term capital. Such a development once started, could become an accelerating movement, feeding on itself, and possibly ending only in the complete destruction of the monetary system.

Those who oppose freely fluctuating exchange rates feel that, on the basis of brief past experiences with this system, the actions of speculators are as likely to be a destabilizing as they are to be stablizing, and that its adoption is as likely as not to lead to monetary chaos. Its defenders read the lessons of history differently. Noting that the system has only been tried in times of great world upheaval, and usually after other arrangements have already failed, they point out that employing these cases as evidence is about the same as citing the tuberculosis mortality statistics of Arizona as proof that its climate is unsuited for those afflicted with the disease.[4]

There is much to be said for this argument since it is quite true that, with one or two possible exceptions, most past experience with fluctuating exchange rates came at the most inopportune times. It is difficult, indeed impossible, to determine in advance how well a fluctuating exchange rate system would work. But it remains, like the Triffin proposal, a program for change buttressed by the support of a group of highly competent advocates, and merits careful consideration.

[4] This statement is a paraphrase of a comment by Professor Friedman before the Joint Economic Committee.

IV | *THE ROLE OF POLICY*

17

The Goals of Monetary Policy

THE EVOLUTION OF THE SYSTEM'S OBJECTIVES

The original Federal Reserve Act and the System it created had, as we have seen, a set of objectives that, by today's standards, could only be called extremely modest. Indeed it is probably fair to say that the intent of the framers of the Act was more to provide a means of *accommodating* the banking system and the business community than of *controlling* their actions.

Among the few explicitly stated objectives, it will be recalled, were the providing of an elastic currency supply and the establishing of a *lender of last resort*—the discount mechanism—for banks in need of aid. There can be no denying the fact that these were important and needed improvements in the U.S. monetary system. But it is equally clear that they are a far cry from the much more basic controlling functions with which the Federal Reserve of the 1960's is charged.

There were, of course, some fairly feeble semiautomatic control mechanisms built into the original act as a consequence of the commercial loan theory. It was (mistakenly) expected, for example, that both the volume and the quality of credit extended would be held to acceptable limits by the fact that discounts and note issues were linked, by law, to the volume of short-term, commercial loans. But the major functions of monetary policy with which we are all so familiar today were, in large part, glaringly absent from both the Act itself and the intentions of its creators.

Nor should this be very surprising. The economic responsibilities

assigned to the government in capitalistic America have always been limited by its citizens' faith in the capacity of the private market system
to serve their economic needs more than adequately. As long as economic
theory provided a deceptively comforting explanation of the self-adjust-
ing nature of a free enterprise system and as long as events did not go
sufficiently awry to call this theory into serious question, the Federal
Reserve System could be afforded the luxury of tending primarily to
"house-keeping" chores for the banking system. The issues of preventing
unemployment and spurring economic growth were simply not generally
thought of as major problems and were not, in any case, considered a
proper concern of government. Balance of payments equilibrium, now a
matter of considerable concern to the System, was an objective reasonably
simply attained by adherence to the "rules" of the world-wide gold standard "game," the very playing of which, incidentally, implied some considerable domestic price instability.

But the press of circumstances has changed all that. The strongly
laissez-faire philosophy that permitted the Federal Reserve System to begin operations with only modest, ill-defined objectives and responsibilities
has had to adjust to the problems created by a staggering depression in
the 1930's, a major war in the 1940's, and the alternately *hot* and *cold* war
in the 1950's and 1960's. Inevitably the responsibilities of government in
the economy—including, of course, the Federal Reserve System—have
mushroomed. As a corollary the objectives of government policy have
multiplied too.

The devastating impact of the Great Depression coupled with the
theoretical contributions of Keynes ended forever the philosophy that
government had no role to play in the *maintenance of full employment.*
Long before Congress officially declared, in the Employment Act of 1946,
that ". . . it is the continuing policy and responsibility of the Federal
Government to use all practicable means consistent with its needs and
obligations . . . to promote maximum employment, production and purchasing power," it had become generally understood that the federal government had undertaken the obligation of doing what it could about
unemployment and, as an agency in a position to execute economic
policy, the Federal Reserve System had inherited a new and far-reaching
task.

The commitment to some degree of *price stabilization,* though never
specifically written down into law, had always been more or less understood as one of the System's duties. It was not, however, until the excess
demand generated by World War II and its aftermath dramatized the
need for action in this area that it began to receive substantially equal
weight as an additional responsibility.

By about 1950 it had thus become popular to refer to the objectives of the Federal Reserve System as, in addition to its service functions, the maintenance of full employment and price stability. The textbooks of that day mentioned little else. And yet there was a third objective that tended to remain obscured until, once again, belated recognition of a current problem thrust it forward to full and widespread acceptance. This was the objective of *promoting economic growth*. While the virtues of growth for improving living standards and the key role of the Federal Reserve System in facilitating it had long been recognized, it had, for years tended to be shunted aside and ignored in deference to the agreed-upon primacy of preserving economic stability.

It seems clear that it was the attainment of some rather startling rates of growth for the Russian economy, especially in the 1950's, coupled with what appeared to be lagging U.S. growth rates that reawakened an interest in "doing something" about economic growth. As a consequence, the System had acquired a third major policy responsibility of pressing significance.

But the evolution in its list of policy obligations does not stop even there. In the late 1950's, the emergence of very large balance of payments deficits and the consequent alarming outflow of gold elevated still another Federal Reserve obligation, if not to the center of the stage, then certainly well out of the wings to which it had been relegated for so many years. This, as we have seen, consisted of an obligation to direct monetary policy in order to promote the restoration and *maintenance of balance of payments equilibrium*.

So the Federal Reserve has come a long way in a half century. A central bank, created primarily for the purpose of dealing with a few essentially institutional problems that were nagging the nation around the turn of the century, has had to adapt itself to tending to four far more fundamental objectives. By way of summary, these include:

1. The maintenance of *reasonably* full employment
2. The maintenance of *reasonably* stable prices
3. The maintenance of an *adequate* rate of economic growth
4. The restoration of balance of payments equilibrium

OTHER CONSTRAINTS UPON THE PURSUAL OF THESE FOUR OBJECTIVES

To pursue these four sometimes conflicting objectives at the same time would be a monumental task even if there were no restraints on the means used to achieve them. The fact is, however, that our policy makers are only free to pursue these objectives within the constraints set by the nation's other important economic goals.

Basic among these is our determination that these four economic goals shall only be pursued within the context of maximum personal economic freedom. There may be a number of means available for achieving faster growth or fuller employment which, because they would involve significant sacrifices in personal freedom, we would choose to bypass.

Another economic goal that may act as a constraint on the use of economic policy to achieve the four objectives of the Federal Reserve, is the desire for an equitable distribution of income. Although often (as, for example, in the case of price level stabilization) actions to promote one of the four Federal Reserve goals will also promote equity in income distribution, this is not always the case. Sometimes policies conducive to economic growth and balance of payments equilibrium may tend to alter the pattern of income distribution in a manner that, in the minds of many, may be considered inequitable.

Of course these matters are not so much the concern of the Board of Governors as of Congress. For it is Congress that must take the overall view concerned with the balancing of all economic objectives. It is Congress that, upon deciding whether or not to grant a given stabilization tool to the Federal Reserve, must decide whether its use will seriously compromise some other important objective, such as economic freedom. All that the System can do is accept the powers given it and pursue the objectives for which they are designed.

It is nevertheless not inappropriate for us to be mindful of this broader responsibility of the legislature. There may be, it is true, other weapons that might enable the Federal Reserve to pursue more effectively its four main objectives. But because they might conflict seriously with other equally important economic objectives, Congress may be eminently correct in withholding them.

THE PROBLEM OF DEFINING THE FOUR OBJECTIVES OF THE FEDERAL RESERVE

All four objectives have thus far been stated only in vague, ill-defined terms. For example, we aim for reasonably full employment, reasonably stable prices, and an adequate rate of economic growth. What do all these qualifying adjectives mean? Just how *full* and *stable* is "reasonable" and how *rapid* is "adequate"? If we are to use monetary policy measures to promote reasonably full employment, how do we know when we have got there? More concrete, specific definitions are clearly in order although, as we shall see, they may not be easy to come by.

The Objective of Reasonably Full Employment

Measuring Unemployment

The task of keeping the record on U.S. employment experience balance belongs jointly to the Bureau of Labor Statistics and the Census Bureau. The latter agency collects the basic data that guide U.S. policy makers through extensive monthly interviews with a massive 35,000 family sample of the population.

Their approach is to interview each family in the carefully selected sample each month to determine such important facts as the size of the labor force, the level of employment, and the level of unemployment.

Any person, fourteen years of age or over, who has worked as a paid employee or in his own business for as much as one hour during the week of the survey is considered employed.[1] All those who have not worked during the survey week but who are actively seeking work are considered in the labor force, but unemployed. In addition, those who did not work during the week and are not now actively seeking work are treated as a part of the labor force and unemployed if they (1) have been laid off from their regular job and are waiting to be called back, (2) are waiting to start a new job within the next thirty days, or (3) volunteer the information that the reason they are not actively seeking work is because they know that "no work is available in their area."

The sum of those out of jobs, but actively seeking them and those out of jobs who are not seeking them for the above reasons makes up the total unemployed. This total, added to those who reported some work during the survey week, makes up the total civilian labor force.

Much editorial ink has been spilled over the issue of whether this approach to measuring our unemployment rate is the proper one for policy purposes. Some have charged that by including teenagers down to fourteen years of age, by making no distinction between those who are the sole family breadwinners and those who are second or third income earners in the same family, and by including some who are not actively seeking work, unemployment figures tend to be inflated. Others have pointed out that, by counting a person as employed even though he or she may have worked only a few hours during the survey week, the extent of part-time employment (or, more pointedly, part-time *un*employment) is missed in the global figures.[2] And some have even gone so far as to

[1] Those who have worked for no direct compensation in a family-owned concern for as much as fifteen hours during the survey week are also considered employed.

[2] This, as well as much other detail, *is* available in the Census Reports in addition to the overall figures.

imply that the figures have been deliberately manipulated to "make things look worse than they are" in order to justify massive government action.

It seems clear that the latter charge is, at best, unwarranted and, at worst, downright malicious. But there is nevertheless, room for disagreement as to some of the details and definitions employed. Perhaps the core of the issue here is in deciding on the basic purpose of the employment data. What are U.S. unemployment figures expected to reveal?

If they are to be interpreted as an index of "economic hardship," then there is much to be said for concentrating on the unemployment rates of heads of households only. And such data is part of the current detail made available. On the other hand it can logically be argued that whenever our economy fails to provide employment for one who actively seeks it, regardless of his "need" for work, it is failing to operate efficiently. If we desire an unemployment figure to measure the effectiveness of the economy in using the resources available to it, the overall unemployment rate would appear to be the appropriate figure.

The Recent Record of Unemployment

There can be no doubt that many different breakdowns of the detail of unemployment are appropriate for different purposes. But it seems clear that, for purposes of determining the need for monetary-fiscal policies, the overall rate of unemployment is as good as any. What has our recent experience with unemployment been? Table 17-1 shows the record since 1929.

The figures in Table 17-1 provide a panoramic view of the ups-and-downs of the American economy since 1929. The last year of the roaring twenties, with its highly respectable 3.2 percent unemployment rate gave way, beginning in 1930 to the catastrophe now known as the Great Depression. For a twelve-year period unemployment stayed above 8 percent of the labor force and for ten of those years the rate was in excess of 14 percent! For those who enjoy frightening themselves 14 percent of today's labor force would amount to over 10 million unemployed workers! World War II, of course, with its tremendous deficits, quickly brought the rate down to below 2 percent. When the war ended, to the consternation of the many economists who had predicted a major postwar slump, the unemployment rate was held below 4 percent until the first U.S. postwar recession in 1949. Recovery from that recession plus the added impetus of the Korean War once again drove the rate down to the 3 percent level until the second U.S. postwar recession (and the end of the Korean War) saw it shoot up once again to over 5 percent. During the prosperity of the mid-1950's a level of 4 percent was approached again but, starting with

TABLE 17-1   Percent of Civilian Labor Force Unemployed,
1929-1966

Year	Percent Unemployed	Year	Percent Unemployed
1929	3.2	1948	3.8
1930	8.7	1949	5.9
1931	15.9	1950	5.3
1932	23.6	1951	3.3
1933	24.9	1952	3.1
1934	21.7	1953	2.9
1935	20.1	1954	5.6
1936	16.9	1955	4.4
1937	14.3	1956	4.2
1938	19.0	1957	4.3
1939	17.2	1958	6.8
1940	14.6	1959	5.5
1941	9.9	1960	5.6
1942	4.7	1961	6.7
1943	1.9	1962	5.6
1944	1.2	1963	5.7
1945	1.9	1964	5.2
1946	3.9	1965	4.6
1947	3.9	(April) 1966	3.7

SOURCE: Employment and Earnings, Bureau of Labor Statistics.

the third postwar recession in 1958, a significant and perplexing upward shift in the average level seemed to have befallen the economy. In an economy that had been able to hold unemployment well below the 5 percent level in nonrecession-nondepression periods for almost thirty years, the unemployment rate stayed well above that point for seven successive years. Clearly something of significance had happened.

Nor was the rise in the U.S. unemployment rate the only disquieting bit of evidence. Comparisons with unemployment rates in the other major industrialized countries revealed that, with the single exception of Canada, U.S. employment experience in the early sixties was among the worst in the industrialized world. These comparisons are shown in Table 17-2. The estimates in Table 17-2 do not represent the officially reported unemployment rates of these countries, since their definitions and methods of collecting unemployment data differ markedly from those of the United States. Instead, to enhance their comparability, they are the result of a careful study in which the official foreign data have been adjusted to approximate that which would have resulted from the use of U.S. methods.

TABLE 17-2   Estimated Unemployment Rates in Eight
Industrialized Nations, 1959-1964

Year	United States	Canada	France	West Germany	Great Britain	Italy	Japan	Sweden
1959	5.5%	6.0%	2.8%	1.6%	3.1%	5.7%	1.9%	N.A.
1960	5.6	7.0	2.7	.7	2.4	4.3	1.4	N.A.
1961	6.7	7.2	2.4	.4	2.3	3.7	1.3	1.5%
1962	5.6	5.9	2.5	.4	2.9	3.2	1.1	1.5
1963	5.7	5.5	3.1	.5	3.4	2.7	1.1	1.7
1964*	5.2	4.7	2.5	.4	2.5	2.9	1.0	1.6

* Estimates for 1964 are highly tentative.

SOURCE: Arthur F. Neef, "International Unemployment Rates," *Monthly Labor Review,* March, 1965.

All this, of course, raised some vitally important questions. Why did the U.S. unemployment rate remain at such high levels in recent years even in the absence of recession? Why has the U.S. unemployment experience been so unsatisfactory when compared with other industrialized nations? These questions, the answers to which we should seek in any case, are especially vital to the determination of the appropriate policy measures to employ.

It is not difficult to come up with a few reasons for the United States' lack-luster performance with respect to other countries. To begin with, of the U.S. work force only about 8 percent is in agriculture while some of the other nations in Table 17-2 use substantially larger proportions on the land. This makes a difference, since unemployment in agriculture is traditionally extremely low.[3] Then, too, it has been argued that because of institutional arrangements and social custom the foreign worker is less likely to leave his job and look for a different one than the American (mobility is higher in the United States) and, because of the generally higher level of living in the United States, the American worker out of a job is financially able to withstand the losses associated with unemployment for a longer period. Probably factors such as these do help explain some of the U.S. deficiency, but it is difficult to credit these differences with a full explanation.

What else may have caused them? And how might we explain the deterioration in the U.S. performance in the latter fifties and early sixties as compared with earlier years? Two partially opposing viewpoints have

[3] Unemployment figures, however, do not reflect the degree of *under*employment which may be involved in the agricultural sector.

been advanced. One group has argued that changes in the structure of demand and in the techniques of production have combined to widen the gap between the skills possessed by the American worker seeking a job and the skills demanded by the American employer seeking a worker. The expansion in unemployment is thus seen as a structural problem, responsive to policy measures such as retraining but not to those, such as monetary and fiscal policy, whose primary impact is simply the raising of aggregate demand.

Another group has insisted that the prime cause *has* been a deficiency of aggregate demand and that, therefore, expansive monetary and fiscal policies were quite in order.[4]

Frictional vs. Recession Unemployment

All this leads us to a classification of types of unemployment. It has become traditional in economics to recognize that not all unemployment is the result of a deficiency in aggregate demand. Some, that which we shall identify here as *frictional,* results from the freedom and dynamism of the U.S. economy and is not efficiently combatted by such measures as monetary and fiscal policy.[5]

Included in the category of frictionally unemployed are those temporarily out of a job because of such developments as:

1. Shifts in public taste from product A to product B
2. Shifts of industry location
3. Introduction of labor-saving equipment or of techniques requiring a different order of skill
4. Seasonal shifts in demand (or in supply conditions)
5. Voluntary resignation to seek a better job

Not even the most efficiently organized economy, so long as it views economic freedom, progress and adaptation to consumer desires as important matters, could eliminate frictional employment altogether. The crux of the issue is not its elimination but the irreducible minimum percent unemployed that we must accept as the price of a dynamic, free economy.

The dominant view regarding this irreducible minimum level of frictional unemployment appears to have altered in recent years. Whereas shortly after World War II a 3 percent unemployment level was generally considered a "satisfactory" performance, a combination of the logic involved in the structural unemployment argument and a considerable amount of frustration at the inability of the United States to approach

[4] In point of fact, the preponderant majority of U.S. economists probably grants some credence to both views.

[5] The *frictional* category employed here includes that unemployment which we have just identified as *structural.*

this goal in recent years has led many to revise their *target* goals upward. Many now accept 4 percent as a reasonable minimum; others, however, regard even this as unattainable without considerable inflation.

Unemployment over and above the irreducible frictional level, whether that figure is 3 percent or 5 percent, will be considered *recession* unemployment caused by *a general deficiency of aggregate demand.* The term is perhaps a bit misleading since recession unemployment as we have defined it can occur during the upswing of the business cycle as well as the recession phase. Witness 1937, for example, where a cyclical upswing still left over 14 percent of the labor force unemployed.

The crucial factor in this distinction between types of unemployment, for our purposes, is the appropriateness of monetary (and fiscal) policy to deal with it. In general, since monetary policy operates through affecting aggregate demand, it is appropriate to combat recession unemployment but not frictional. Consequently, reasonably full employment as a goal of monetary policy means the elimination of recession unemployment.

The use of the term *irreducible* to refer to frictional unemployment, incidentally should not be taken to mean that no government policy measures are available to deal with this type of unemployment. Certainly restraining, better employment information, etc., represents admirable and potentially fruitful attempts to do just that. We, however, are concerned with monetary policy's capabilities vis-à-vis employment and it seems quite clear that these lie almost exclusively in the area of combatting recession unemployment.[6]

The Objective of Reasonable Price Stability

The Measurement of Price Levels

The task of keeping the record for price levels in the U.S. economy is also primarily the responsibility of the Bureau of Labor Statistics, which regularly publishes both a *consumer's price index* and a *wholesale price index.*

The former, popularly known as the "cost of living" index, is intended to measure the percent change in the cost of a *basket* of approximately 400 representative consumer goods and services since the *base period* of 1957-1959. The goods that enter the basket and the weights attached to each of them are determined from a survey taken in 1960-

---

[6] Expansive monetary and fiscal policy can, however, albeit at the possible cost of some price inflation, produce such a bouyant demand that it will cut down the frictional unemployment level, also. This points up the fact that it is actually extremely difficult to separate the two types, since it can hardly be denied that the higher the level of aggregate demand the sooner even the frictionally unemployed worker is going to be able to land a new job.

1961 (and usually updated about every ten years) of actual consumer expenditures by a selected group of urban wage earners and clerical workers. Thus the index is really only directly applicable to middle income urban families. The relative weights applied to major categories of consumer goods in the present basket include 22 percent food, 33 percent housing, 11 percent apparel, 14 percent transportation, and 19 percent health and recreation.

The index itself, of course, measures only the percent change in the prices of these goods since the base period. That is, the price of the goods entering the basket in 1957-1959 represent an index number of 100—they are 100 percent of the prices in the base year. The 109.9 index for 1965, then, implies that it cost 9.9 percent more to buy that basket of goods in 1965, than in the 1957-1959 base period.

The wholesale price index, also published monthly, reflects the percent change in the wholesale prices of a basket of approximately 2,200 commodities selected (and appropriately weighted) to represent all commodities either produced here or imported for sale here.

The Recent Record of Prices in the United States

Table 17-3 reports the movement of both the consumer's and the wholesale price indexes since 1939, both on a base of 1957-1959. The 48.4 figure for the consumer price index in 1939 indicates that the market basket being priced would have cost only 48.4 percent as much in 1939 as it cost in 1957-1959.

The two indexes follow roughly similar paths, both showing a substantial reduction in the purchasing power of the dollar over twenty-five years. In both cases prices climbed by something over ten index points during the World War II years of 1941-1945, a record that is a bit deceiving since price controls were in effect during most of this period. The major inflationary binge, as revealed by both indexes, was during the 1946-1948 immediate postwar period when price controls were removed and the excess demand that had been suppressed by price controls during the war, made itself felt. Relative stability was again restored in the three years from 1948 to 1950. Another major spurt in both indexes can be seen in 1951, this one associated with the onset of the Korean War. Once again, by 1952, both indexes settled down to a period of stability through 1955 but inched up notably during the middle 1950's.

Then, from 1958 through 1964, the nation enjoyed remarkably stable prices. The consumer price index did rise by an amount that averaged 1.2 percent per year during the period, but increases of this magnitude are certainly moderate and must be considered well within the bounds of reasonable stability.

TABLE 17-3   Consumer and Wholesale Price Indexes,
1939-1966 (1957-1959 = 100)

Year	Consumer's Price Index	Wholesale Price Index
1939	48.4	42.2
1940	48.8	43.0
1941	51.3	47.8
1942	56.8	54.0
1943	60.3	56.5
1944	61.3	56.9
1945	62.7	57.9
1946	68.0	66.1
1947	77.8	81.2
1948	83.8	87.9
1949	83.0	83.5
1950	83.8	86.8
1951	90.5	96.7
1952	92.5	94.0
1953	93.2	92.7
1954	93.6	92.9
1955	93.3	93.2
1956	94.7	96.2
1957	98.0	99.0
1958	100.7	100.4
1959	101.5	100.6
1960	103.1	100.7
1961	104.2	100.3
1962	105.4	100.6
1963	106.7	100.3
1964	108.1	100.5
1965	109.9	102.5
(March) 1966	112.0	105.4

SOURCE: *Monthly Labor Review*, U.S. Department of Labor.

The behavior of the wholesale price index in the 1958-1964 period was even more remarkable. In six years the index rose by a total of one-tenth of 1 percent!

The difference in the two is probably largely accounted for by the fact that the wholesale price index does not include services, a category that has played a major role in raising the consumer index.

One conclusion seems inescapable. Whether it came as a result of judicious use of policy or more happenstance, the United States enjoyed reasonable price stability in the seven years preceding 1965.[7]

But 1965 seems to mark another turning point. Not only has the U.S. unemployment rate fallen once again to the 4 percent neighborhood but prices have once again started to rise notably. Policymakers, who for several years had concentrated on raising demand, began, once again, to consider means of restraining it.

What's Bad About Inflation?

The costs of unemployment seem so obvious that spelling them out in order to demonstrate the desirability of the full employment goal hardly seems necessary. The merits of price stability, however, are something else again.

In the first place, there is by no means unanimous agreement among economists that moderate price increases are an unmitigated evil. Some few, indeed, would argue that the benefits outweigh the costs. Secondly, even if all agreed with that preponderant majority who look upon even moderate inflation as, on balance, a bad thing, we need to be sure that we are in agreement as to what these bad effects are. In what ways does a moderate inflation hurt?

---

[7] This conclusion is strengthened even more when it is recognized that many experts believe that the process of constructing U.S. price indexes contains an *upward bias* that produces increases in the index that are not, in fact, rises in the cost of living. The biases are said to result from (1) inability to make adequate allowances for quality improvements and (2) the fact that a market basket of fixed proportions is maintained for ten-year periods making no allowance for the fact that consumer purchases may shift from the items rising most in price to those rising least.

This point is understood when the record on wholesale prices in the United States is compared with that of other industrial nations in recent years. The table below is made up from data taken from an article by Helen B. Junz and Rudolf R. Rhomberg entitled "Prices and Export Performance of Industrial Countries, 1953-63," reprinted in *Balance Payments—1965*, Hearings, Subcommittee of the Committee on Banking and Currency, U.S. Senate.

Wholesale Price Indexes for Selected Countries, 1958, 1963, and 1964 (1953 = 100)

Country	1958	1963	1964	Change from 1958 to 1964
United States	110.3	110.9	111.5	+ 1.2
Belgium	103.4	101.5	106.4	+ 3.0
Netherlands	105.3	113.8	120.0	+14.7
Germany	103.0	112.3	113.7	+10.7
France	92.7	94.3	N.A.	N.A.
Italy	99.1	104.6	N.A.	N.A.
United Kingdom	110.9	120.5	N.A.	N.A.
Sweden	109.1	118.5	121.6	+12.5
Canada	105.5	101.2	102.1	− 3.4
Japan	98.0	100.7	101.4	+ 3.4

Let us eliminate one issue at the outset. Our inflation discussion will be couched entirely in terms of the types of moderate inflation with which the United States has been faced, rather than in terms of runaway, hyper-inflation. The latter malady, wherein spenders' expectations of more inflation not only bring it about, but feed on themselves until prices are sky-rocketing upward at ever-increasing rates is, in the judgment of every-one, disastrous. But it is not a problem with which the United States has had to deal, nor is there any reason to expect it in the forseeable future. Consequently, except for noting the fears of some that sustained moderate inflation might degenerate into a hyperinflation, we shall not concern ourselves with it.

What are the real costs and dangers associated with a moderate infla-tion on the order of a 1 percent or 2 percent, or even 5 percent rate per year?[8] Undoubtedly the tendency to alter arbitrarily the distribution of income and wealth is both the best known and most important. A rise in the general average of all prices does not affect all prices equally and, hence, tends to reduce the "slice of the total pie" available to those with incomes (or wealth) which are relatively fixed in money terms, and to enlarge that which accrues to those whose dollar incomes (or dollar value of wealth) tends to rise more rapidly than the average of all prices.

More specifically this means, of course, that those whose money incomes are in a form that can only be raised very much more slowly than prices are rising or, worse, those whose money incomes are absolutely fixed, such as private pension recipients, tend to lose command over goods and services, while others, who are in the fortunate position of having money incomes go up by 10 percent while the average of all prices rises by 5 percent, gain. Similarly, those whose wealth is held in a form that is fixed in dollar terms (such as savings accounts, bonds, and life insurance) find the value of their wealth being eroded away, while debtors (those who owe fixed numbers of dollars) and those who hold their wealth in a form in which its dollar value may rise more rapidly than the price level (such as some land holders and some common stockholders) clearly are better off.

Such redistributions, being arbitrary and capricious, are clearly to be condemned and must be listed as a major cost of inflation. And they are, without doubt, the most important liability of moderate inflation. But there is more to the case against inflation than this.

Rising prices also affect the allocation of resources, and the rate of

8 The following discussion leans heavily on the excellent article by Tibor and Anne A. Scitovsky entitled "Inflation versus Unemployment: an Examination of Their Effects," in the Commission on Money and Credit volume entitled *Inflation, Growth and Employ-ment* (Englewood Cliffs, N.J., Prentice-Hall, Inc., 1964).

economic growth. When prices are rising, institutional differences between industries entirely unrelated to consumer desires may permit some prices to rise more rapidly than others, thereby distorting the efficiency of resource allocation. In addition, since inflation generally leads to a more pronounced rise in expected returns from investment than in the cost of credit, misdirected investment, which would not have taken place under other circumstances, may be the result. Such a development not only misallocates resources in the conventional sense but also hampers the nation's economic growth. A further problem is the uncertainty under which businessmen must function during inflation, another potential source of misallocation and misdirected investment.[9]

The potential effect of domestic inflation on a nation's balance of payments must be listed as an additional liability. If the prices of our export goods rise relative to those of competing nations, the likely result will be a cutback in our exports (coupled with some rise in our imports from the now relatively cheaper markets abroad) and a nudge toward a deficit in our balance of payments.

Finally, moderate inflation is feared by some to provide a psychological stepping stone to hyperinflation. The line of reasoning involved is simple. A rate of inflation of 3 percent per year, it is argued, may not be so terribly costly in and of itself, but it is difficult to hold it to that for any length of time. For when the public comes to expect such an increase in the future it will take such actions to protect itself from the effects of the expected inflation that it will speed it up. This process of: inflation—expectation of more inflation—action—more inflation thus becomes self-generating with a tendency to feed on itself until prices are rising at ever-faster rates. The end result of such an explosive cycle, it is argued, is very likely to be disastrous hyperinflation.

In summary then, moderate inflation involves the following potential costs and dangers:

1. Arbitrary redistribution of income and wealth
2. Misallocation of resources
3. Misdirection of investment and a consequent slowing of economic growth
4. Weakening the nation's balance of payments
5. Setting the stage for future hyperinflation

[9] There is, of course, another side to this argument. Some feel that, by widening profit margins, moderate inflation stimulates, rather than retards, growth. In addition, it has been argued that, given the built-in resistance to downward price adjustments so generally recognized today, rising price may be required to bring about the changes in relative prices which permit reallocation of resources according to consumer desires.

The Objective of Adequate Economic Growth

The economic growth objective, as noted earlier, acquired substantially greater emphasis in the 1950's as a result of two developments. First, production data from the leading industrial nations showed the growth rate of the United States to be lagging markedly behind most other nations for the post-World War II period. Secondly, the intensification of the cold war provided additional reasons for concern.

The Recent Record of Economic Growth

There is no one best measure for economic growth. Like so many other statistics the "proper" measure depends upon the purpose for which it is to be used. For some purposes the rate of increase in real GNP is the best measure. For others, the rate of increase in real GNP, per capita, is a sounder guide. And for other purposes, still different measures should be used. Fortunately for us, however, the recent record is sufficiently similar for all the most common measurements to permit us to use only one of them for purposes of illustration.

Table 17-4 shows the average annual rates of growth in real GNP for seven major industrial nations during the 1950's. It reveals clearly part of the reason for concern with recent American growth rates. With the single exception of the United Kingdom, the United States is at the bottom of the list. And, when the second half of the decade is compared with the first, we see an especially sharp decline in the American economy's performance.

TABLE 17-4   Average Annual Rates of Increase in Real
Production for Seven Industrialized Countries, 1950-1960

Country	Average Annual Percent Increase 1950-1955	Average Annual Percent Increase 1955-1960	Average Annual Percent Increase 1950-1960
France	4.5	4.2	4.3
West Germany	9.0	6.0	7.5
Italy	6.0	5.9	5.9
United Kingdom	2.6	2.7	2.6
Japan	7.1	9.4	8.8
U.S.S.R.	7.0	6.5	6.8
United States	4.3	2.3	3.3

SOURCE: Stanley H. Cohn, *Dimensions of Soviet Power*, Joint Economic Committee Hearings, December 10-11, 1962, Part II, pp. 69-89.

The Case for a More Rapid Rate of Growth

Taken by itself, without consideration of the costs involved in achieving it, more rapid economic growth is obviously desirable. This, after all, has always been the means by which man's standard of living has been raised.

But the recent intensification of concern with the growth rate in the United States can hardly be attributed solely to a rekindled American yearning for even higher living standards here. After all Americans are already the world's wealthiest people. As, each year, they become even more affluent one would expect the emphasis on economic growth to recede rather than intensify. Why then the sudden reemergence of economic growth as a major goal?

The answer, of course, is primarily political. The Soviet Union has publicly announced its intention of "burying" the United States economically and has backed its boast with an impressive postwar growth record. Despite the fact that it still lags far behind the United States in total production and notwithstanding legitimate reservations regarding the U.S.S.R.'s capacity to maintain its impressive growth record over the long run, its challenge and performance have been sufficient to arouse American concern with growth.

Nor is the direct economic challenge of the Soviet Union, with its ominous military overtones, the entire story. While the two industrial giants labor to demonstrate the superiority of their respective economic systems, the entire civilized world looks on in fascination. For among the many newly emerging, underdeveloped nations, economic development is the undisputed number one goal. Without the same intense commitment to economic freedom or the long heritage of democratic government to influence their course, these largely *uncommitted* nations will undoubtedly cast their lot with that type of economic system which seems most likely to provide the shortest route to development. The United States knows and the Soviet Union knows that the future course of many uncommitted nations depends heavily upon the apparent outcome of their current economic contest. Little wonder that the economic growth objective has gained stature in the last two decades.

The Balance of Payments Equilibrium Objective

Since it has received extensive coverage in Part III, there is little need to expound on the recent record of the U.S. balance of payments nor on the reasons for seeking equilibrium. Normally an objective that is subordinate to the other three, this one periodically emerges to a position of greater prominence whenever, as in recent years, a chronic balance of payments deficit develops.

CONFLICTS AMONG THE GOALS AND THE TRADE-OFF ISSUE

The real core of the policy problem is not in specifying the objectives nor even in deciding on the particular means with which to pursue them. Rather it is the exasperatingly difficult chore of promoting four potentially incompatible goals at the same time. For there is no natural law which guarantees that policy measures to promote full employment shall not impede price stability; nor that steps to eliminate a payments deficit shall not increase unemployment; nor, indeed, even that measures to eliminate moderate inflation shall not impede economic growth. In fact the longer we pursue our four objectives the more uncomfortably convincing becomes the proposition that, to some degree and in some circumstances, we cannot actively promote one goal without at the same time sacrificing another.

To the extent that this is true, economic policy must come to grips with some exceedingly difficult problems of choice. No longer is the problem the simpler one of "what to do about unemployment or about inflation or about lagging growth." Instead we must deal with the infinitely more complex questions: "If policy X is undertaken to achieve objective A, to what extent will it impede objectives B, C, or D? And if it does interfere with objectives B, C, or D while promoting A, at what rate are we willing to 'trade off' a loss towards B, C, or D, in order to obtain a gain towards A?"

Neither of these questions is really answerable in the current state of economic knowledge. However, we cannot escape the necessity of making the choices that determine our fates simply because completely reliable information is lacking. For the decision to do nothing is just as much a positive policy decision based on limited knowledge as is a faltering attempt to do something. What do we know about the answers to these questions? Let us take them one by one.

Under what circumstances are policy measures to pursue one objective compatible with the other goals and when are they in conflict? The picture is certainly not all black. In many situations action primarily aimed at one goal will either simultaneously promote another or, at least, not conflict. In general, for example, policy measures aimed at combatting inflation will, at the same time, help reduce a balance of payments deficit.

Similarly there is fairly general agreement that action to moderate a rapid inflation will aid in the process of long-run growth. And again, measures to raise aggregate demand to cut unemployment at the trough of a severe business cycle are not likely to have much, if any, undesirable price-level effects. Finally, many would argue, despite some distinguished dissenters and a lack of empirical evidence, that action to raise employment will be conducive to long-run growth at the same time.[10]

Although there are undoubtedly a number of conflict areas, we shall restrict our discussion here to the single, most important problem. This is, of course, the tendency for policy measures aimed at combatting unemployment through an increase in aggregate demand to spill over into increased prices, thereby also tending to cause deterioration in the balance of payments. Or alternatively, it is the tendency for measures intended to combat inflation (and to combat payments deficits) to increase the level of unemployment.

Unfortunately the elementary notion that aggregate demand should always be increased when there is excessive unemployment and always decreased when prices are rising is not of much practical use as a policy guide. Because, except for the depths of depression, increases in aggregate demand not only reduce unemployment but also tend to cause price increases. And, except for clearcut boom periods, measures to cut aggregate demand not only hold down prices but also hold down employment. The policy maker thus is often confronted with a difficult choice. If he takes steps to bring us closer to full employment, he may well be driving us away from price stability and balance of payments equilibrium. If he does what is necessary to hold down prices and combat payments deficits, he could be responsible, at the same time, for creating more unemployment.

Such dilemmas as these are, of course, unfortunate, but hardly unique to the student of economics. What is the essence of economics after all, if it is not the problems of choice? Since we cannot have everything we desire we must choose those things that satisfy as many desires as possible. This is the central problem of economics and the dilemma noted above is simply a different member of the same family.

If in many circumstances we cannot fully realize all our goals simultaneously, we must somehow make a choice about how much price stability we are willing to forego in order to reduce unemployment by X percent. Or, how much extra unemployment we are willing to endure as the price for achieving an X percent reduction in the rate of inflation.

[10] Among those who express doubt that a full-employment state necessarily produces the fastest growth rate are H. G. Johnson, "Objectives, Monetary Standards and Potentialities," *Review of Economics and Statistics* (February, 1963), and A. A. Phillips, "Employment, Inflation and Growth," *Economica* (February, 1962).

In order to make an intelligent choice between full employment and price stability, two types of information are essential. In the first place, if, for example, we are considering policy to raise aggregate demand, we should know something about how much extra inflation we will incur as a result of a sufficient boost in demand to cut unemployment by 1 percent. In point of fact, we know very little about this important matter but Professors Samuelson and Solow[11] have attempted a rough estimate. In the Samuelson-Solow view, the cost of complete price stability in the present U.S. economy would be in the neighborhood of 5 percent to 6 percent of the labor force unemployed. To get unemployment down to the level once considered *ideal*—3 percent of the labor force—the United States would, according to their estimates, have to employ such expansionary policies as will cause inflation at the rate of about 4.5 percent per year. If the United States were willing to settle for an unemployment rate of 4 percent, the cost in terms of price rise would be about a 2 percent rate of inflation, per year, and so on. We do not know whether the Samuelson-Solow estimates are the "correct" ones and they themselves take considerable pains to point out the tentative nature of their figures. They do, in any case, represent one effort to come up with data that are essential for informed policy.

But even if they knew exactly how much inflation to expect as a consequence of a 1 percent reduction in unemployment, U.S. policymakers would need still additional information to permit them to adopt the *optimum* policy. They would require some ideas about the community's value judgments regarding the relative merits of full employment and price stability. If prices are now stable and unemployment is at a 5½ percent rate, does the public desire to shoulder the costs of a 2 percent inflation rate in order to obtain the benefits a 1½ percent reduction in the unemployment rate? Does the gain in welfare that results from raising employment and production by a given amount exceed the loss in welfare from the inflation thereby incurred? Of course we have no ready-made answers to these questions but they are nonetheless issues that matter very greatly in the determination of economic policy.

One point stands out clearly in all this. We need not expect perfection in economic policy. Whatever steps are taken to improve our lot in these areas will cost us something in return. Intelligent policy consists not of vainly seeking cure-alls, but rather of facing up to the necessity of balancing potential gain against potential loss on the basis of the best (although highly imperfect) information available and acting accordingly.

[11] Paul A. Samuelson and Robert M. Solow, "Analytical Aspects of Anti-Inflation Policy," *American Economic Review*, May, 1960, pp. 177-194.

SOME CONCLUDING COMMENTS ON WAYS OF MINIMIZING THE PRICE STABILITY—FULL-EMPLOYMENT DILEMMA

To recognize that there is no choice but to face up to conflicts that exist is by no means to conclude that nothing can be done about the conditions that create them. Given the current state and structure of the U.S. economy it appears that reducing unemployment to a 3 percent level once again would bring about considerable inflation. For now Americans must accept what is, and make the best compromise they can among their conflicting objectives. That is about all that can be done with monetary-fiscal policy.

But, as controllers of their own destinies Americans may be able to make some structural and institutional changes that will, in the longer run, reduce the area of conflict. For example, anything in the way of improved education, job retraining, employment information, and the like which tends to reduce the number of *structurally* unemployed can do so without causing inflation. Similarly anything that can be done to reduce rigidities and monopoly elements in cost and price structures[12] may reduce the inflation cost of antiunemployment policy further.

And in addition certain steps might be considered to minimize the costs of stabilization policy after it is carried out. For example, it has been suggested that, since the main cost of inflation is the arbitrary redistribution of income and wealth which results, a monetary-fiscal policy might be considered which creates truly full employment (say the 3 percent level) and then those groups most harmed by the accompanying inflation could be recompensed by means of transfer payments. If such a scheme should be administratively feasible the conflict problem might well be substantially eliminated. The fact is, one cannot now "have one's cake and eat it too," but it would be very foolish to cease searching for a way.

[12] Such action is appropriate so long as it does not too seriously conflict with other public policy objectives. There are some potential conflicts here, too, which must concern us.

18 | How Monetary Policy "Works"

Monetary economics and opinion regarding the efficacy of monetary policy is presently in a state of flux. But this is hardly a novel situation. Indeed, it is no overstatement to describe the field as having been in such a state for the past half-century.

Time and again since the 1920's, students concerned with how monetary policy works and how well it works have had to reorient their thinking in response to new theoretical developments, new empirical evidence, and the hard facts of experience. The result has been a whole series of changes in attitude toward monetary policy, some of them approximating 180-degree turns.

Faith in the powers of the monetary authorities probably reached its zenith in the 1920's. In that period a near-hypnotic spell cast by a booming economy, along with a firm conviction that all that was required to keep things moving ever onward and upward was a reasonably intelligent handling of the discount rate, convinced many an observer that a new and permanent "plateau of prosperity" had been achieved. Fiscal policy was as yet unknown and, in any case, unneeded. Monetary policy—indeed a mere fraction of what we now call monetary policy—was sufficient to handle any problems that might crop up. Or, at least, so it was believed at the time.

The 1930's, of course, irreparably shattered the rose-tinted glasses. Not only had we fallen off the prosperity plateau but monetary policy seemed utterly incapable of doing anything whatever about it! Truly, a reassessment of the potentialities of monetary policy was in order.

As might have been expected the reaction went almost all the way.

The same monetary policy weapon that some had looked upon as a virtual panacea ten years earlier now appeared next to useless. Not only had the experience of the thirties shown it incapable of easing a depression but empirical evidence that began to appear regarding the lack of responsiveness of investors to interest rate changes seemed to cast serious doubt on its usefulness in either direction.

There the matter stood until after World War II. Monetary policy had reached its lowest ebb. To its opponents it represented an exercise in futility; and even its staunchest defenders admitted to very serious weaknesses.

But a revival was already underway. In the late 1940's and early 1950's the defenders of monetary policy developed a new thesis to explain how monetary restriction could achieve its objectives no matter how unresponsive investors might be to interest rate increases. This new approach, popularly entitled the *availability thesis*, focused on the effects of monetary restriction on lenders, rather than borrowers. And it was successful in restoring monetary policy, once again, if not to the giddy heights it enjoyed in the 1920's, at least once more to a position of respectability.

Buttressed by the theoretical support of the availability argument, monetary policy became the work horse of the U.S. stabilization arsenal during the 1950's. And its successes and failures since have stimulated still further debate. On the one hand a host of critics has arisen in recent years to point out more of its deficiencies, both of omission and commission. On the other hand, the impressive empirical data uncovered by the *new* quantity theorists has tended to reemphasize the importance of the supply of money as a determinant of economic activity.[1]

All this debate—this intellectual ferment—provides, of course, the clearest possible indication of the vigor of a healthy, dynamic discipline. We cannot hope to delve into it all in this text. However, we should be seriously remiss if we made no attempt to sketch in at least the broad outlines of the current policy debates. This is the purpose of the present and the following chapters.

We shall proceed in the following manner. In the next section a brief review of the monetary policy tools will be offered. Following this we shall trace through the various causal mechanisms that connect policy action with spending. That is, we shall discuss *how* monetary policy is supposed to "work." Finally, and at greater length, we shall turn in Chapter 19, to the arguments of the many critics of monetary policy. In order to keep

---

[1] To be more accurate, the quantity theorists have stressed changes in the rate of change in the money stock as the important causal variable. In addition it should be noted that their feeling that a long and variable lag separates changes in the money stock from its effect on economic activity has led them to oppose discretionary monetary policy in favor of a fixed rate of increase in the money stock each year.

the discussion within manageable proportions most of it will be couched in terms of the stabilization potential of monetary policy with only brief attention to the economic growth and balance of payments objectives.

THE MONETARY POLICY TOOLS: A REVIEW

It has, by now, been made clear that the powers of the Federal Reserve include three general credit controls. Let us briefly review each of these with a view to reasserting their initial impacts.

Altering the Discount Rate

An increase in the discount rate, it will be recalled, is intended to affect the banking system in three ways. First, because borrowed reserves now cost more it is hoped that fewer member banks will borrow them. Second, it is expected that a rise in this particular rate will tend to cause other short-term interest rates to rise. Third, it is hoped that the psychological effect of an increase will cause member banks to slow down in their current lending activities out of concern for a likely future shortage of reserves. In addition, it can be expected that, along with a rate increase, Federal Reserve officials will be increasing the intensity of their counsel to member banks to refrain from overuse of the discount facilities.

To the degree that they work, then, discount rate increases will:

1. Keep the total supply of member bank reserves from increasing as much as they might have
2. Force some increase in short-term interest rates
3. Possibly cause member banks to conserve, to some degree, the excess reserves they already have

A discount rate decrease, of course, would be aimed at the opposite effects.

Altering Required Reserve Ratios

An increase in required reserve ratios has a double, and quite direct effect. In the first place, it will convert some existing bank reserves from the category of excess reserves to that of required reserves, thereby reducing lending and money-creating potential. Secondly, it will lower the coefficient of money supply expansion, insuring that whatever excess reserves remain in the system can supply less added money and credit. A required reserve ratio decrease will have precisely the reverse effects.

Open-market Operations

The sale of U.S. securities by the Federal Reserve System will reduce member-bank reserves by the amount of the sale. The effects of this on the money and credit supply will depend, of course, on whether the reserves removed were excess or required. If they were required the money (and credit) supply will likely have to be reduced by some multiple of the reserve loss. If they were excess, the effect will be merely to keep money (and credit) expansion below the levels that otherwise might have been reached.

HOW MONETARY POLICY IS SUPPOSED TO WORK (THE CHAIN OF CAUSATION CONNECTING MONETARY POLICY TOOLS WITH AGGREGATE DEMAND)

Granting the initial effects of the monetary policy weapons, what can we say about the causal connections between them and their ultimate goal, aggregate demand? We must avoid jumping immediately to the superficial conclusion that "it is *obvious* that cutting the money supply will cut spending." We need to concern ourselves with the "hows" and the "whys" of this step of the analysis.

Let us take, for purposes of illustration, the case of an open-market sale by the Federal Reserve, aimed at a reduction in (or forestalling an increase in) aggregate demand. Through what channels does the policy work?

It seems clear that expenditures *could* be affected via the initial effects of the sale in four different (although not mutually exclusive) directions. Such a transaction may affect (1) expectations, (2) interest rates, (3) lenders' willingness and ability to expand loans, and (4) the banks' and the publics' liquidity. Although these effects are inherently intermingled, we shall attempt to consider them separately.

The Potential Effect via Expectations

To the extent that the operation is recognized as a specific anti-inflationary step it may well affect expenditures via the effect it has on the expectations of commercial bankers and of spenders.[2] It might, for ex-

---

[2] However, it should be remembered that one of the more important features of open-market operations, in contrast to discount rate and reserve requirement changes, is its smaller effect on expectations.

ample, cause banks to slow down their lending in anticipation of an upcoming reserve shortage. In a similar manner it may create an additional element of uncertainty for businessmen which will lead to a reassessment of their investment plans. However, it must be admitted that we know little about these effects. It is just as possible that the expectational effect could be perverse, causing a current increase rather than a reduction in demand. If this were the only effect of monetary restriction, monetary policy would be a slender, and indeed, potentially treacherous reed on which to depend.

The Potential Effect via Increased Interest Rates

The effect of the policy on interest rates is more clearly in the desired direction. The very act of selling the securities must, by lowering their market values, raise their yields. This in turn, through arbitrage, will tend to raise interest rates generally. And the rise in interest rates, in turn, may affect spending in a number of ways.

Interest as a Reward for Savers

To begin with, it has been argued that savers, seeing the reward for saving enhanced, may take advantage of its by saving more (thereby consuming less). This, of course, was a hypothesis important to the earlier classical economists' theories. Few, if any, would grant it much importance today. For it is pretty generally agreed that the rate of interest plays only a very minor role in the determination of the quantity saved.[3] While some few people may cut their consumer spending in order to take advantage of the higher interest return, this particular anti-inflationary effect is likely to be extremely moderate, at best.

Interest as a Cost to Borrowers

Somewhat greater favorable effects may, however, be expected as a result of the increase in the interest cost to borrowers. This, of course, is the monetary policy effect that was singled out in our four-diagram model in Part II. Some portion of the spending carried out by each of the three major expenditure groups is with borrowed funds. If a rise in the cost of these funds leads any of them to cut their spending plans, the policy has, to that extent, succeeded.

There is, however, little likelihood that credit spending by consumers or government will be much affected by small interest increases. The

[3] This, of course, is not to say that differing rates of interest (as, for example between commercial bank savings accounts and saving and loan deposits) may not be important determinants of the *form* in which savings are held.

credit demands of both are considered to be highly unresponsive to the rate of interest. But investment spending money may well be more vulnerable.

In the first place a larger proportion of investment expenditures are financed with borrowed money than is the case for the other two groups. This exposes it that much more to the effects of the interest rate increase. Then, too, for some investment projects, especially those on plant and equipment which must be financed over a long period of time, the interest cost is a very important element in the total cost of the project. It is entirely conceivable that, for those projects that would have been just barely feasible at an interest cost of 5 percent, an increase of 5½ percent may force cancellation or postponement. To the degree the interest rate increase accomplishes this, it is doing the job for which it was intended.

The reader will recognize, of course, that what we are really considering here is the slope of the MEI curve. If the curve is reasonably flat over the area of interest rate increase, many projects will be postponed and the restrictive monetary policy will have been highly effective. If, however, the curve is quite steep, the interest rate increase will not do much to cut aggregate demand.

Over the years a considerable amount of evidence has been amassed which seems to indicate that the MEI curve is, in fact, quite steep. This, as a matter of fact, was one of the more important reasons for the sharp reversal in attitude toward monetary policy in the 1930's and 1940's. Although some question the validity of much of this evidence, the majority of economists still seem prepared to accept the idea of a fairly steep MEI curve.

Now the implications of all this for the effectiveness of monetary policy were, and are, very important. If the main effect of a restrictive policy is via increases in interest rates, to say that the MEI curve is steep is tantamount to saying that monetary restriction does very little good. And that was precisely the dominant attitude until the so-called *availability* argument produced a change in vantage point.

The Effect on Lenders—The Availability Argument

To stop concentrating on the borrowers, and their reactions, and to take a long hard look at what a restrictive monetary policy does to the lenders was the objective of the availability advocates. For after all, no matter what borrowers would be willing to do with borrowed funds, they cannot do it unless the lenders make it available to them. How do the lenders react to monetary restriction?

To begin with it is perfectly obvious that if restrictive monetary policy is carried so far that the member banks actually lose some reserves that are now required to *back up* present outstanding deposits, the result eventually will have to be, not only a cessation of additional loans, but an elimination of some of those now outstanding. In the more usual case where only present excess reserves are removed it will still be true that the banks will have lost their capacity to grant additional credit. Now it is clear that in either one of these cases, the elasticity of the MEI curve is of little importance. For even if businessmen *are* willing to carry out almost as much investment at 5½ percent as at 5 percent, the banking system is, by law, unable to accommodate them.[4] The ability of lenders to finance credit spending has simply been reduced and that is the end of the matter.

There is, however, a good deal more to it than this rather obvious point. When reserves are reduced and the potential supply of credit thereby cut there are two ways in which the smaller amount available may be rationed out. One is to allow the market price to do the job. In this case, of course, the *price* is the rate of interest, which could rise to the point where the sufficient demanders are *rationed out* of the market so that the quantity demanded is reduced to equal the smaller quantity that can be supplied. If, however, the MEI curve is highly inelastic this implies a very sharp rise in interest rates.

There is, of course, another means of rationing out a smaller supply —authoritative rationing by the lenders. Instead of immediately raising interest rates by the amount necessary to clear the market, lenders might begin to screen loan applicants more carefully, turning down some *who would be willing to pay the going rate of interest* and granting others smaller loans than they had requested. Such credit rationing by lenders, of course, implies a certain degree of oligopolistic power. But it also implies that lenders are facilitating the restraint policy. In such a case the inelasticity of the MEI curve (the fact that borrowers would be willing to pay substantially increased interest costs rather than go without their loan) is of little moment, because the credit they need to finance their intended spending is simply denied them.

Nor, in the opinion of some, is this the only helpful way in which the credit restraint policy affects lenders. Even though excess reserves may be removed, banks with substantial portfolios of short-term U.S. securities may find it profitable to unload some of these low yield assets in order to permit the granting of more of the higher-income business loans in demand. Now such an activity may seem innocent enough on the surface, but for reasons we shall examine shortly, it almost certainly would permit an increase in aggregate demand. For it would very likely involve replacement of largely idle (zero velocity) money with active money. Conse-

---

[4] As we shall see shortly, however, bankers may find it worth their while to sell some of their government securities to the nonbank public, thereby enabling themselves to expand the loan portion of the earning assets at the expense of securities.

quently such portfolio readjustments by banks would work counter to the intent of the restrictive monetary policy.

But, it has been argued, this activity, too, is limited by a tight money policy, since monetary restraint, by raising short-term interest rates, guarantees that present holders of U.S. securities can only unload them at lower prices. The result is that banks that might otherwise sell securities in order to make loans will, because of unwillingness to realize capital losses on such sales, feel *locked in* to their present security holdings. If so, monetary policy is that much more effective. However, as we shall see shortly, many doubt the potency of the locked-in effect.

The Effect via Reduced Liquidity

Finally, it might be argued, as is increasingly the case in recent years, that the open-market sale ultimately affects aggregate demand as the end result of a long series of balance sheet adjustments by the banks and the public, triggered by the initial reduction in liquidity caused by the sale. The specifics of the transmission mechanism between the open-market operation with its attendant reduction in the banks' and/or the public's liquidity and decreased spending on new goods and services have not yet, if the truth be told, been adequately spelled out. However, in general the process envisaged goes something like this. When the Federal Reserve sells securities, the buyers, be they the banks or the public, have given up liquidity in payment. Their effort to reestablish a desired degree of liquidity among their bundle of assets—real and financial—will lead to sales of other assets, declines in their prices and consequent increases in interest yields (direct or implied) on them. This will happen not only in the bond market but also in the equities market and, eventually, will spill over into the market for goods and services. When it does, spending on goods and services (just as spending on bonds and equities) will be cut back.

19 | The Critics of Monetary Policy

Despite the recent resurgence of faith in monetary policy, doubts about its effectiveness and its incidence persist. The primary purpose of this chapter is to spell out, and where possible evaluate, some of these doubts.

Before we proceed, however, a few introductory words of caution may help the reader maintain his perspective. The list of criticism is long, the thrust of the arguments in some cases crucial, and the credentials of the critics themselves, for the most part, unimpeachable. They present, in its totality, an impressive "case" against monetary policy. Indeed the entire list is so lengthy and seemingly pervasive that there is some danger that the casual reader may obtain a deceptively and unnecessarily bleak picture of the potentialities of monetary policy. Without, in any way attempting to prejudge or to gloss over the very real and very important weaknesses that we shall be discussing, the reader will be wise to guard against unjustified magnification.

In the first place not all the alleged weaknesses are due to inherent defects in monetary policy, as such. Some are due to structural deficiencies in monetary policy weapons and, hence, more or less easily correctable; some are due to improper use or timing of existing tools; and some are the result of other structural features in the economy, such as authoritatively administered price ceilings or oligopolistic features that hamper or distort the efforts of the monetary authorities. While, in evaluating policy, we must consider the world that exists, with all its structural imperfections, it is important that the appropriate culprit be identified.[1]

[1] For an excellent discussion bearing on this point, see James R. Schlesinger, "Monetary Policy and Its Critics," *Journal of Political Economy* (December, 1960), pp. 601-616.

Secondly, it must be recognized that we shall be considering, in a single chapter, the particular criticisms of a large number of authorities. Not even the most "critical of the critics" is so disenchanted with monetary policy as to subscribe to them all. In fact the vast majority, even of the so-called critics, cannot accurately be referred to as *opponents* of monetary policy. In almost all cases their general view of monetary policy is "necessary and desirable but not perfect and sufficient." They see weaknesses that they feel require correction. They caution against overreliance on this particular policy tool to the exclusion of others. They point out limits to its effectiveness. But they are not embarked on a holy crusade to overthrow the Federal Reserve System and eliminate monetary policy. They seek, instead, to strengthen them both.

PROBLEMS WITH ANTIRECESSION MONETARY POLICY

There is considerably less controversy among economists regarding the degree of effectiveness of monetary policy to combat recession than is the case for a tight money policy. So we shall begin with the easier case.

For years it has been popular to sum up the relative effectiveness of monetary policy in recession and inflation with that overworked cliché: "You can pull on a string but you can't push on it." The obvious inference, of course, is that monetary restriction to counter inflation has more chance of success than monetary ease to combat recession.

Generally speaking, the vast majority of economists still appear to subscribe to this generality. The reason for this relatively pessimistic view regarding the capabilities of antirecession monetary policy is reasonably well illustrated by that other tired old saying: "You can lead a horse to water but you can't make him drink."

The problem during recession is a deficiency of aggregate demand. "Success," if it is to be achieved by monetary policy, consists of increasing someone's purchase of newly produced goods and services. But monetary policy is singularly unequipped for, single-handedly, accomplishing this. It can increase bank reserves, lower interest rates, and expand the money supply. And, to the extent that there exist some marginal investment projects that have been held up by too high interest costs or limited credit availability, these steps will help.

However not very much can be expected from this alone. At the height of recession the MEI curve is generally thought not only to shift to the left, as profit prospects dwindle, but also to steepen in response to increased uncertainty. Many projects that previously would have been undertaken at some low rate of interest now appear so risky that, at least in the short run, even a *zero* rate of interest will not call them forth. In these circumstances, monetary policy alone is nearly impotent. While the Federal Reserve can provide the banking system with adequate reserves and lending capacity, something else is required to convince potential spenders to take advantage of the improved borrowing opportunities.

Although this is the major problem with combatting unemployment of whatever magnitude there are some significant differences, both of degree and kind, between battling a minor recession of the postwar variety and a major depression like that of the 1930's.

In the case of a major depression that has been in existence for some time, monetary policy is at its weakest. Not only is the MEI curve likely to have fallen substantially, and possibly steepened to the point where it crosses the quantity axis at only a limited volume of investment (even a zero interest rate calls forth insufficient capital spending) but there may well be problems getting the interest rate down. It is at just such a time, that the liquidity trap barrier may be encountered. For at very low interest rates both the public and the banks may be satisfied to simply hoard increases in funds permitted by Federal Reserve action. In the 1930's not only was the business demand for borrowed funds low, but the banks themselves were satisfied (given the deplorable circumstances) to pile up and hold huge quantities of excess reserves. In this situation the Federal Reserve could not even be sure that the additional reserves it provided the banks would expand the *money supply,* let alone aggregate demand!

The situation is less desperate in a milder recession. In this case a liquidity trap is highly unlikely. The interest rate can be lowered. And although the MEI curve may have steepened somewhat, it will hardly become perfectly inelastic. Some degree of success, in other words, can be expected.

Nor is a large accumulation of excess reserves, so typical of a major depression, likely. For the situation must be very bad indeed to convince bankers that they will be best off earning no income at all on the excess reserves they have. Our experience in the postwar recessions to date has not revealed any great increase in excess reserves. Instead, banks have used the reserves provided them primarily for the purchase of U.S. securities. In the process, of course, new money has been created but, unlike money created in the process of making business loans, much of it has been used for purposes other than spending on newly produced goods and services.[2]

In summary, there is general agreement that monetary policy alone

---

[2] A large increase in excess reserves might not be encountered again even if we should have a major depression as serious as that of the 1930's. The existence of a large, diversified national debt today provides banks with a safe investment source of a kind and magnitude which simply did not exist in the 1930's.

is an ineffective means of combatting deficiencies of aggregate demand. Monetary ease at such a time is certainly not considered harmful; indeed it is approved by almost everyone.[3] Perhaps the prevailing attitude could best be summed up by calling it "necessary, but far from sufficient."

THE ALLEGED WEAKNESSES OF ANTI-INFLATION MONETARY POLICY

The real debate in the past decade or so has centered on the effectiveness of monetary restraint. Indeed, so many deficiencies have been suggested by the critics of so-called *tight money* policies that some degree of compartmentalization seems necessary to assure a manageable consideration of them all.

Four major categories of criticisms have been levied. These include the arguments that:

1. Conventional monetary policy does not work at all against certain types of inflation.
2. Discretionary monetary policy, as now applied, works perversely with respect to the business cycle, doing more harm than good.
3. Tightening of general credit controls works capriciously as between different groups of people.
4. To the extent that monetary restriction does work in the desired direction, it does so very weakly.

Let us consider each of these groups of criticisms in turn.

Conventional Tight Money Policies Are Inappropriate to Combat Certain Types of Inflation

It has become usual to identify two different types of inflation. So-called *demand-pull* inflation is a rise in the price level *caused by a prior rise in demand*. Prices are pulled up by a rising total demand for goods and services. *Cost-push* inflation, on the other hand, is a situation wherein prices are pushed up, *in the absence of a prior rise in demand*. This can result from either unions or management exercising their market power to simply push up prices. Or, in a development sometimes referred as *demand-shift* inflation, it may result from a shift in demand from product A to product B, with the price of B rising while rigidities and market imperfections prevent an offsetting decline in that of A.

---

[3] However, as we shall see in the next section, easy money policies in the recession may well complicate the problem of combatting the next boom.

Monetary policy (and fiscal policy also), designed as it is to work by altering aggregate demand seems, at least on the surface, quite appropriate for handling the demand-pull variety of inflation. Here the initiating cause of the problem is an excess of aggregate demand. What better way to deal with it than by removing its source?

But the several varieties of cost-push inflation present quite a different problem. Here, it is *not* excessive demand that is at the root of things. How then can a tool which can only cut demand do the job?

A simple numerical example might help the reader to see the nature of the policy dilemma caused by cost push inflation. Suppose, as of a given time, the money supply is $100, income velocity is 3, the average price of newly produced goods and services is $2.00 and the number of units being produced is 150. Therefore:

$$M \times V_y = P_y \times O$$
$$\$100 \times 3 = \$2 \times 150$$

Now suppose that without any increase in demand (MV_y), prices are simply marked up (either because higher wages forced the price increase or because sellers were attempting to increase their profits) to $3.00. When this happens to P_y, something else in the equation of exchange has to give. It is perfectly obvious that, *so long as spenders continue to spend only $300 (MV_y)*, 150 units (O) cannot be purchased at $3.00 per unit. Indeed, only 100 will be bought. And the result in that case can only be a rise in unemployment caused by undesired inventory increases.

Opposing this development, what "firepower" have the policymakers? Monetary and fiscal policy, used in the conventional (restrictive) direction to combat the price rise will very likely make matters worse, since if MV_y is now cut to, say, $240 (and if prices are rigid in a downward direction, as is generally the case), only 80 units can be sold! The government's policy, aimed at combatting inflation will only have made the unemployment more severe.

Of course, the reverse policy might be employed to avoid this calamity. Via easy money (or fiscal) policy, aggregate demand might be raised to $450, thereby ensuring that all 150 units would be bought and no unemployment result. But if this way out is chosen, what have the authorities really done? They have, contrary to one of their goals, taken the very steps that were necessary to sustain the price increase. Far from combatting inflation, they have been placed in a position of aiding and abetting it!

And the same kind of problem exists for demand-shift inflation. If the price level has risen because a shift in demand has raised the prices of the more favored items while rigidities have kept those now relatively less desired from falling in price, a monetary policy-induced cut in aggregate demand can only cut sales and, in the same manner as before, create unemployment.[4]

The conclusion from all this seems clear. Policy weapons designed to work through alterations in aggregate demand are simply not equipped to handle the several varieties of cost-push inflation. For, although a very sharp reduction in aggregate demand may eventually force producers to lower prices even in these cases, this can only come at a cost of increased unemployment in the interim. And this seems too big a price to pay.

So we must recognize control of cost push inflation as a clear-cut deficiency of monetary policy. How serious a breach in our defenses it is, is a question that has not yet been answered. Quite a few respected economists, however, have expressed the view that the danger of serious and sustained inflationary pressure from this source is minimal.

Discretionary Monetary Policy Makes the Business Cycle Worse; The Problem of Time Lags

Among the most serious of the attacks against monetary policy as it is now employed is the charge that, because of time lags involved in its operation, it actually reenforces the business cycle. That is, discretionary monetary policy, aimed at minimizing inflation and unemployment, misses the mark by such a margin that it makes them worse.

There is nothing complicated about the logic involved. It starts from the universally recognized fact that monetary policy measures do not affect aggregate demand instantaneously. There is a process involved which takes time to work through. Those who believe that discretionary monetary policy is positively destabilizing simply argue that the time required for this process to work itself out is very long—so long, indeed, that policy measures undertaken to combat on-going inflation will only come to fruition (cut aggregate demand) some months after the inflationary pressure has disappeared and the economy has turned to recession. In that case, of course, the monetary policy will only make the recession worse.

Similarly, in their view, monetary action undertaken to raise aggregate demand to combat recession can also be expected to make matters worse, because by the time aggregate demand is actually increased by monetary measures taken many months previously, the economy may have

---

4 Note another problem here. If, as tastes change, resources are reallocated via a mechanism that permits some prices to rise while others cannot fall, inflation of the demand-shift variety may be a price we must pay in order to obtain proper resource allocation. On this point see, Tibor and Anne A. Scitovsky, "Welfare Aspects of Economic Growth, High Level Employment, and Price Stability," *Inflation Growth and Employment*, Commission on Money and Credit (Englewood Cliffs, N.J., Prentice-Hall, Inc., 1964).

recovered and be well on the road to inflation. The antirecession measure would thus merely magnify the succeeding inflation.

The dispute here, between those who take this extremely pessimistic view and those who do not, has to do with different estimates regarding the actual length and variability of the policy time lags involved. There is no disagreement about the existence of these lags, only about their duration.

The relevant time lags have, for purposes of discussion, been broken into three types. The first, the *recognition lag*, is the time between the development of a need for action in the economy and recognition of that need by policy makers. Unless and until forecasting techniques provide very much more dependable results, this period will be, almost certainly, several months long. Second there is an *administrative lag*, the time between the recognition of need for action and its execution. For monetary policy with the seven-man, semi-independent Board of Governors in the driver's seat, this lag is probably very short.[5]

Finally, there is an additional period, which has been called the *operational lag*, between action by the policy agency and its final effect on demand in the economy. For monetary policy, for example, this would be the time between an actual sale of securities on the open market and its intended reduction in spending.

A number of pioneering efforts to shed some light on the length of these lags have been undertaken in recent years. One scholar, for example, finds that over 19 past business cycles, turning points in the rate of change in the money supply preceded turning points in the business cycle by periods of from 12 to 16 months.[6] Another investigation, centered on the length of the operational lag, turned up estimates of from several months to over a year, depending on the type of project being financed.[7] A third finds the relevant lag to average around six months.[8]

None of these studies claims to have the last word, the definitive answer, on the length of these lags. But elusive though it is, that answer is of crucial importance. For if the lag *is* relatively short, then discretionary monetary policy can be relied on to make some contribution toward business-cycle stabilization. If, on the other hand, it is as long and variable as some investigators believe, then it follows logically that discretionary monetary policy should be abandoned altogether.

[5] This is, as we shall see, somewhat in contrast to the situation for fiscal policy.

[6] See M. Friedman, "The Supply of Money and Changes in Prices and Output," in *The Relationship of Prices to Economic Stability and Growth*, Compendium, Joint Economic Committee (Washington, 1958).

[7] See Thomas Mayer, "The Inflexibility of Monetary Policy," *Review of Economics and Statistics*, November, 1958.

[8] See A. Ando, E. C. Brown, R. Solow, and J. Karaken, "Lags in Fiscal and Monetary Policy," *Stabilization Policies*, Commission on Money and Credit (Englewood Cliffs, N.J., Prentice-Hall, Inc., 1963).

Some of those who take the latter position have urged just that. Professors Friedman and Shaw, for example, have argued that, since their search of the record convinces them that the past efforts of the United States to achieve stability via discretion have had exactly the opposite effect, it should forthwith give up attempts to ease credit in recessions and tighten it in booms. Instead they feel the United States should content itself with an invariable policy of raising the money supply from 3 percent to 4 percent each year—a figure related to the expanding needs of the United States for long-run growth—whatever the phase of the business cycle.

Implementing the Friedman-Shaw proposal would, of course, require far-reaching changes in the U.S. monetary machinery. The present discretionary power of the Board of Governors to employ their tools as they see fit would be abolished in favor of a law requiring the Federal Reserve to take such action as would raise the money supply by 3 to 4 percent each year, come what may. The present *monetary managers* would thus become mere technicians instead of policy makers.

Such a change, if it were to be made, could be defended by its advocates as a purely pragmatic act, based solely on the evidence from the past that discretion has not done an adequate job. Yet it would not be without important philosophical overtones. Long before the Friedman evidence cited earlier was developed he and his illustrious predecessor at the University of Chicago, Professor Henry Simons, had argued for an end to discretion in economic policy on more fundamental and philosophical grounds.

For example, over thirty years ago Professor Simons said:

A democratic, free-enterprise system implies, and requires for its effective functioning and survival, a stable framework of definite rules, laid down in legislation and subject to change only gradually and with careful regard for the vested interests of participants in the economic game. It is peculiarly essential economically that there should be a minimum of uncertainty for enterprisers and investors as to monetary conditions in the future—and, politically that the plausible expedient of setting up "authorities" instead of rules, with respect to matters of such fundamental importance, be avoided, or accepted only as a very temporary arrangement. The most important objective of a sound liberal policy, apart from the establishment of highly competitive conditions in industry and the narrow limitations of political control over relative prices, should be that of securing a monetary system governed by definite rule.[9]

It thus seems evident that, while part of the steam behind the proposals to eliminate discretion in monetary policy comes from empirical

[9] Henry C. Simons, "Rules versus Authorities in Monetary Policy," *Journal of Political Economy* (February, 1936).

evidence that discretion has not worked well in the past, part of it is also based on a more fundamental distrust of discretionary policy, in principle.

As of the mid-1960's the case for eliminating discretion in monetary policy appears to have attracted only a minority of economists. Many doubt that the empirical evidence that has been thus far presented makes an adequate case against discretion. And as for the more fundamental case for *rules* instead of *discretion,* many would concur with the following view of Professor Samuelson:

> In principle, the choice has never been between discretionary and non-discretionary action; for when men set up a definitive mechanism which is to run forever afterward by itself, that involves a single act of discretion which transcends, in both its arrogance and its capacity for potential harm, any repeated acts of foolish discretion that can be imagined.

> *   *   *

> Specifically, consider the suggestion of a money supply which is to grow at exactly 3 per cent per year, a policy advocated by some who think no other actions would then be required. Suppose this had been enacted in the United States in a random recent year, without knowledge of the balance of payments problems just ahead, and without knowledge of the massive shift to time deposits such as we have been experiencing as a result of both raised interest rate ceilings on such deposits and the natural shift to such deposits as interest rates generally rise. The results could have been quite bad in comparison with what actually happened; and if the balance of payments situation had, for unpredictable reasons, been a great deal worse, the results could have been disastrous.[10]

General Credit Controls Apply Capriciously to Groups of Spenders; The Charge of Discrimination

A third major set of criticisms centers not on whether spending is cut or how much it is cut or when it is cut but rather on *whose* spending is deterred by monetary restraint. To state the issue directly, it is argued that tightening of general credit controls has a disproportionately severe effect on the spending plans of certain groups, while leaving other groups of spenders relatively unscathed. The result is, these critics argue, an unplanned, capricious, and in substantial degree, undesirable selectivity in the impact of general credit restraint.

Let us run through the essence of the argument from the beginning. Credit restraint, if it is to work at all, must have a bite. Some people who would have carried out added spending in the absence of the policy must now find it unwise or impossible to do so. The question with which we are concerned is the identity of those groups whose spending is inhibited.

[10] Paul A. Samuelson, "Reflections on Central Banking," *The National Banking Review* (September, 1963), p. 16.

In a first approximation this would not seem to be too difficult a problem. General credit restraint reduces the total supply of credit available. This tends to raise its price, in this case the rate of interest. The prime function of this higher interest rate is to ration out the smaller amount of credit available. If there is a perfect market, those who desire to use credit for purposes that will most satisfy consumer desires will be able to afford the higher interest cost, and still obtain it, while those who would have borrowed for less socially desirable purposes will be *rationed out* of the market. Consequently, so the argument runs, it is those who desired credit for the least socially desirable purposes who will find themselves unable to obtain it. And surely, since for the restrictive policy to work at all *someone*'s spending must be cut, this is the optimum result.

But, say the proponents of the *unplanned selectivity* thesis, this argument grossly oversimplifies the situation. To begin with the credit market is far from a *perfect* market. It is not just the rise in the price of credit that impersonally rations out the smaller supply but—and this comes from no less avid supporters of monetary policy than the developers of the availability argument themselves—also a significant amount of authoritative credit rationing by individual lenders. While both borrower A and borrower B may be willing and able to pay the higher interest rate required, the lender may now arbitrarily decide to grant the request of one and refuse that of the other. How can we be sure that this provides an optimum allocation? Then too are there not a number of structural imperfections that could have the effect of diverting credit from one sector to another to the detriment of the general welfare?

Specifically, it has been argued, at least three sectors tend to bear a disproportionately heavy burden from general credit controls. These include home construction especially that financed by government guaranteed mortgages, state and local governments, and small and new business. We shall consider each of these briefly.

Borrowing to Finance Home Construction

Because it was the first clear-cut sustained *tight money* period in recent years, data from 1955-1957 have been heavily relied upon for empirical evidence regarding the impact of credit restriction.[11] During that period single family dwellings starts fell off from 1,194,400 to 872,700. Almost the entire decrease was in homes financed by government guaranteed mortgages. For example, new home loans made with FHA and VA mortgages fell from almost $6 billion in 1955 to less than $4 billion in

[11] Credit ease was the rule for the bulk of the 1930's, while from 1941 to 1951, monetary policy was largely subservient to financing and refunding the national debt.

1957. During the same period housing starts under these government guaranteed mortgages were reduced from 51 percent of the total to only 30 percent. There could be little doubt that something was severely curtailing the purchase of homes under government guaranteed mortgages.

Nor is there much doubt about the reason for these sharp declines. During a period when credit was tight and interest rates generally were rising rapidly, government guaranteed mortgages carried with them an interest rate limitation that became more and more unrealistic the higher other rates rose. Lenders, who had more takers for the available credit than they could accommodate, quite naturally began to back away from taking mortgages on which they could charge only 4½ percent when alternative opportunities offered them 6 or 7 percent. The result, hardly surprising, was a dramatic cutback in housing starts financed with government guaranteed mortgages.

Whatever the cause, all this has some real social implications. Since generally government guaranteed loans have been relied upon to finance smaller homes while conventional mortgages traditionally have been used for larger ones, the tight money policy, *coupled with the interest rate limitation*, tended to fall with disproportionate weight on relatively lower income families.

It hardly seems necessary to point out that, to the degree this happens, it is not really an inherent weakness of monetary policy but rather an inevitable result of the interest rate limitation itself. Nevertheless it must be granted that, given the existing institutional framework, the impact of credit restriction appears to fall with special severity on medium and small-size home buyers.

This particular charge has arisen again with renewed vigor and, significantly, much more wide-spread public acceptance, during the intensely tight money year of 1966. As credit conditions have tightened, interest rates have risen markedly all around but the availability of credit for home mortgages has been especially severely restricted.

The recent experience has stimulated considerable publicity regarding the alleged discriminatory impact of monetary policy. Specifically it has become quite common to read in newspapers and magazines that a restraint policy, which relies almost exclusively on monetary policy, is likely to impinge with special severity on certain areas of the economy, especially home construction. Indeed, by early fall of 1966 this argument had amassed sufficient support to lead to the introduction of several special bills into Congress aimed at easing the credit squeeze in the mortgage market. And, it is worth noting, recent difficulties in financing home construction have not, as was the case in the mid-fifties, been concentrated almost exclusively in the government-guaranteed area.

State and Local Government Capital Expenditures

The experience of the mid-fifties also led to the suggestion that credit restriction may have disproportionate effects on capital expenditures by state and local governments. The immediate evidence cited in support of this charge was a marked decline in state-local borrowing from 1954 to 1956 and numerous reports of municipalities' canceling previously announced bond offerings or inability to sell some that were offered. In addition, there was evidence that the interest paid on municipal bonds rose relatively much more under credit restraint than did other interest rates. All this led to the hypothesis that the state and local government sector may be especially hard hit by credit restraint. If so, it was argued, the potential impact on the nation's economic growth should be given consideration since many of the capital expenditures of state and local governments were to provide social goods and services considered vital to growth.

Although we do not yet have sufficient information on this to permit a confident evaluation, we do know that actual capital expenditures for these governments during 1955 and 1956 were quite high despite the cut in new borrowings. This is the case even when one allows for the growing population and rising incomes of the period. In addition there is some reason for doubting the validity of the high level of 1954 borrowing as a base for comparison. Although this was an easy money year—a fact which, no doubt, stimulated borrowing somewhat—a more persuasive explanation would seem to be the fact that, for reasons other than credit policy, a large number of important toll highway bond offerings came onto the market that year.

Despite these reservations, however, there are some peculiarities of the state-local government sector which do seem to tend to magnify its susceptibility to credit restriction. In the first place some municipalities are restricted, by statute or constitutional limitation, in the amount of interest they may pay. When such limitations are unrealistically low, rising market rates may prevent such governments from finding a market for their bonds.

In addition the market for state and local government securities is shaped in a peculiar fashion by the fact that the income on the bonds is federal income tax-exempt. Because of the tax-exemption feature, municipal bonds can generally be sold, to those otherwise subject to federal income taxes, at rates below comparable taxable securities. The market for these bonds is dominated by high-income individuals and commercial banks, both of which are subject to heavy federal taxes. In a period of tight money, however, commercial banks usually withdraw almost completely from municipal bond buying in order to concentrate their dwindling credit capacity on higher income business loans. This means that, at such times, very many more state and local securities must be absorbed by individuals.[12] The market for state and local obligations is thus drastically narrowed as a result of credit restriction. The result is that, in order to entice enough lower-income individuals to purchase the municipal securities seeking placement, very sharp increases in interest yields are necessary. State and local governments, therefore, may find themselves paying rates that are up by 50 percent when other rates have only increased by 25 percent.

Borrowing by Small and New Business

Another sector said to be uniquely susceptible to the cutting edge of a tight money policy is that of new and small business. The argument here is intuitively appealing although, once again, we have no reliable quantitative evidence to document it.

When credit is restricted, it is argued, the market power of lenders permits them authoritatively to *ration* credit, granting the credit requests of some while refusing others. It is to be expected, when there is not enough to go around, that the large, well-known, long-established concern will have preference over the small, newly established credit applicant. Thus, in the view of the critics, the bigger, well-established firms will suffer little deprivation from credit rationing while the new, unknown firm will bear the burden. And to make matters worse, the newer firms, having little or no retained earnings, are the ones most urgently in need of external financing.

While this result may or may not be justifiable from the viewpoint of relative risks, its effect on the nation's economic growth could be undesirable, since new products and new ideas, as often as not, are introduced by new firms struggling to establish themselves. If a tight money policy shuts them out, the ultimate cost could be considerable.

The Implications of the Discrimination Charge

If the charge that general credit controls discriminate between groups of credit users in a manner that cannot be justified on grounds of consumer satisfaction or the general welfare could be proven, what would be the major implication?

Much of the ground would be cut from under the standard defense of general over selective controls. If general credit controls could be shown to exert a capricious, haphazard, pattern of impact on the economy the

---

[12] Many of the other financial institutions have little or no interest in state and local securities because, being subject to little or no federal income tax liability, they are unwilling to pay the necessary premium (in terms of lower yield) to purchase the feature of tax exemption.

otherwise strong a priori case for general controls over selective is seriously weakened. General credit controls, it might be argued, are selective too, but in an unplanned way. How much better to take specific cognizance of our goals and then set out with the clear-cut intent that selective controls imply, of reducing the credit available to those sectors that promote our goals least.

Such, at least, is an inference that a firm believer in the discrimination thesis might draw. Unfortunately we do not yet have sufficient facts to make a conclusive judgment. But few economists of today seem prepared to go as far as the argument in the preceding paragraph.

Monetary Restraint Does Cut Aggregate Demand but Its Effect Is Weak

The reputations of some of those who argue that monetary policy is destabilizing and some of those who argue that general credit controls are seriously discriminatory are such as to command solid respect and careful consideration. But respect and consideration do not necessarily imply agreement.

For the majority of economists in the 1960's are neither so pessimistic regarding the time lags involved as to be prepared to eliminate discretion nor so convinced of the capriciousness of quantitative controls as to be willing to abandon them. Judiciously administered monetary policy still seems capable, in the minds of most, of making positive contributions toward stabilization of economic activity.

But among this large group the degree of faith in monetary policy varies widely. At one end of the spectrum there are those whose confidence in the potency of credit control seems almost completely unshaken by the events of the past thirty years. Not so for many others, however. For them the record reveals too many disappointing experiences to justify implicit and unreserved faith. "Of course monetary restraint is helpful," they seem to say, "but we need to guard against expecting too much from it. The economy has changed over the years and in many ways these changes have weakened the effectiveness of monetary policy. Let us make use of monetary policy, by all means, but let us also be aware of its limitations."

We turn now to consider this viewpoint.

Lack of Responsiveness of Investors to Changes in Credit Conditions

One of the earliest sources of disillusionment regarding monetary policy was the results of surveys, both in England and the United States, which revealed the rate of interest as a relatively unimportant factor in the investment decision. More recent econometric studies have tended to reenforce this disturbing conclusion.

Many reasons have been advanced to explain this apparent insensitivity to interest rate changes. In the first place it has been pointed out that for many shorter-run investment projects the interest rate is only a minor cost consideration. Consequently, even significant interest rate changes have only a small effect on profit prospects. For longer-run projects, where the total interest cost bulks much larger, other complications enter. For these are the very undertakings that, because of the distant horizon involved, require very large risk allowances. If, for example, projects now under consideration are limited, because of large risk allowances, to those that (in the absence of risk allowance) are expected to earn a 20 percent return, one is entitled to wonder how many would be abandoned as a result of a 1 percent increase in interest rates.

Another possible reason for investors' seeming insensitivity to interest rate alteration is the large proportion of internal financing so characteristic of recent years. In 1964, for example, when gross private domestic investment totaled about $88 billion, capital consumption allowances and retained earnings combined provided over $65 billion of the needed funds. That is, only about one-quarter of the funds needed to finance investment expenditures had to be borrowed on the capital market.

In theory, at least, the interest cost is the same whether the funds had to be borrowed externally on the capital market (with a consequent out-of-pocket interest payment) or were provided internally through the firm's own saving. For in the latter case there is an implicit interest cost involved which is measured by the amount of interest return given up by committing the funds to finance capital expenditure directly rather than lending them out to someone else at the market rate of interest.

Despite the airtight logic involved in the above argument, there is considerable room for doubting that all firms do maximize profits in this way, since many firms' company policy bars investment outside their main line of business. Consequently funds raised internally from depreciation charges and retained earnings are not considered really eligible for financial investment elsewhere.

To the extent this outlook is taken, a rise in the market rate of interest from 4 to 5 percent, as a result of credit restriction, may not really be looked upon as an increase in investment cost. Certainly a firm which refuses to use internal funds for any purpose other than financing its own investment outlays and which possesses ample amounts for its needs, will be less responsive to market rate increases than one forced to rely solely on external funds. And the fact that a preponderance of investment is financed internally may add significantly to the alleged insensitivity to interest rate changes.

Finally, market power of some firms may also play a role in explaining borrower insensitivity to interest rate increases. To oligopolistic firms the rise in credit costs, not unlike a hike in taxes, may provide just the impetus needed to permit a comparable price increase. If this is the case the burden of the interest rate increase will fall on consumers rather than reducing investors' profit prospects. Such "shifting of the burden" to consumers is even easier for regulated public utilities selling a distinctive service subject to highly inelastic demand. Here the firms need merely show the regulatory agency evidence that their costs have been raised to justify a rate increase. And if consumer demand is sufficiently inelastic little, if any, cutback in expenditures would be expected.

Institutional and Structural Developments Permitting Velocity Increases

If aggregate demand is to be arrested or reduced by a policy of credit restriction, the target is not M alone, but MV_y. Obviously a 10 percent cut in the supply of money will accomplish nothing if it is accompanied by a 10 percent increase in income velocity.

Few will argue that velocity changes do completely offset money supply changes but there is a good deal of evidence that, for a variety of reasons, monetary authorities must be prepared for some weakening in their effects from this source. A restriction in the supply of money leads quite naturally to ingenious efforts on the part of the public and the financial community to make the smaller money supply "do more work" than before.

No better evidence of this ingenuity exists than the development of the Federal Funds market, which, after all, is little more than a device to make an existing supply of member bank reserves stretch a bit further. When the credit restraint screws are tightened, the banking system does not idly accept its fate but rather seeks to make the reserves it has go as far as possible. The effect is to lessen, to some degree, the impact of the restraint policy.

Of much greater quantitative importance, however, are the efforts of banks to rearrange their portfolios in response to tight money pressures. The bank with no excess reserves cannot increase the money supply. But it can, if it chooses, unload some of the U.S. securities it owns in order to permit an increase in its loans to business. And there is every reason for believing that such an act will, while leaving the supply of money unchanged, permit a rise in the velocity of spending. Let us see how it might work.

Suppose Bank A, with no excess reserves, decides to sell $500,000 of its portfolio of U.S. securities to the nonbank public. Since the tight money policy has raised interest rates, Bank A will have to face the fact that the market price of the securities will have fallen, perhaps to the point where a capital loss will be realized. According to the locking-in argument covered earlier this potential capital loss may give rise to some hesitation but for purposes of our illustration suppose Bank A goes ahead with the deal. If the purchaser of the securities banks at Bank A, the effect of the sale will be:[13]

Bank A

U.S. Securities	— $500,000	Demand Deposits	— $500,000

Now, while Bank A has no more reserves it has acquired an increase in its *excess* reserves. Consequently it has acquired the capacity to make added loans in the amount of $500,000.

Bank A

Loans	+ $500,000	Demand Deposits	+ $500,000

Once this step is completed it would seem that we are back where we started. Bank reserves are unchanged. The money supply is unchanged. All that has happened is that the banks have altered their portfolio of earning assets from securities toward more loans. But let us look at it a bit more closely.

What kind of money are the purchasers of the securities likely to have given up—funds that they had intended to spend on goods and services? Hardly. It seems very likely that the money that disappeared when the securities were purchased was idle money—money that had been held as an asset—money that, since it would not have been used to purchase goods and services, had an income velocity of zero.

And how about the new money created as a result of the new business loan? Almost certainly it is active money that the borrower intends to spend on newly produced goods and services. The result, therefore, will be a replacement of idle money with a zero income velocity by active money with a positive velocity. In the economy as a whole the money supply is the same but its velocity of spending on goods and services has increased. Aggregate demand has gone up despite the monetary authorities' success in holding bank reserves and the money supply constant.

[13] If the purchaser banks at another bank, clearance of his check in payment will, of course, give Bank A $500,000 of added reserves. The reserves, however, will simply come from another bank and represent no net addition to the system's reserves.

There can be no doubt that this can happen. But it is a question of fact whether it does happen to any significant degree. The locking-in thesis argues that the potential capital losses involved will help keep it within bounds. But the facts from past tight money periods are hardly reassuring, as Table 19-1 below reveals.

TABLE 19-1   Loans and U.S. Securities at Member Banks, 1953-1959 (billions)

Year	Loans	U.S. Securities	Change in Loans	Change in Securities
1953	$57.8	$52.6	—	—
1954	60.3	57.8	+ $ 2.5	+ $5.2
1955	71.0	50.7	+ 10.7	− 7.1
1956	78.0	47.6	+ 7.0	− 3.1
1957	81.0	47.1	+ 3.0	− 0.5
1958	84.1	54.3	+ 3.1	+ 7.2
1959	94.8	46.8	+ 10.7	− 7.5

SOURCE: *Federal Reserve Bulletin.*

As a recession year, 1954 was one of *easy money* conditions. Note that during the year while loans went up only $2.5 billion, banks used the reserves provided them to up their security ownership by more than $5 billion. During 1955, 1956, and part of 1957 very tight money conditions existed. This is evidenced by the fact that the public's ownership of demand deposits was almost constant from 1955 to 1957. But from 1954 to 1957 member banks expanded their loans by over $20 billion while unloading over $10 billion of their U.S. security holdings. If the locking-in device was working at all, it would seem that its effects were slight.

Recession again in 1958 dictated another period of monetary ease and member banks took advantage of it to expand their loans by about $3 billion. More to the point, however, they rebuilt their U.S. security holdings by the large figure of $7.2 billion. Consequently when the monetary brakes were slammed on again in 1959 the member banks were able to finance an over-$10 billion expansion in loans largely through selling off the securities purchased the previous year.

It is apparent that these member-bank portfolio rearrangements in response to changing monetary conditions have been of significant proportions and that they represent a potentially important weakness for monetary policy. How, the reader may wonder, can this be, in light of the locking-in thesis?

It is difficult to escape the conclusion that the locking-in effect from potential capital losses represents, at best, a minor obstacle to unloading

404   THE ROLE OF POLICY

securities. There are a number of reasons why this should be so. In the
first place banks, peculiarly, are permitted to deduct all their capital
losses from ordinary income in computing their corporate income tax
liability.[14] This means that about half the loss is compensated for by
decreased tax liability.

In the second place, commercial bank-held securities are generally
quite short-term so that the capital losses associated with usual interest
rate increases are likely to be quite moderate. Indeed only a slight increase
in the interest rate differential between securities and loans can make a
switch to the latter a paying proposition.

Finally, and more fundamentally, once interest rates have risen the
capital loss on securities held exists, whether realized or not. Rational
profit-maximizing behavior would seem to consist of accepting the fact
that the loss, even though unrealized, has already been made and making
current portfolio decisions on the basis of future expectations rather than
past history. The loss has already been incurred so that the banker has
little choice but to lick his wounds and carry on from there to do the
best he can. And this may very well consist of selling the securities, realiz-
ing the loss, and making new higher-yield loans.

Whatever the reasons, as we have seen, banks have seen fit to alter
their portfolios drastically in response to changing monetary conditions.
And their ability and continuing willingness to do so may be one of the
more important sources of frustration of monetary policy.

Increases in Velocity Facilitated by Nonbank Financial Intermediaries: The Gurley-Shaw Thesis

Another area of weakness of monetary policy, in the view
of some, is the absence of direct control over credit expansion by financial intermediaries other than commercial banks. Popularly entitled the
Gurley-Shaw thesis, after its best known proponents, this argument em-
phasizes the potential capacity of nonbank financial intermediaries
for undermining, through their credit expansion activities, a tight
money policy.[15]

In essence the Gurley-Shaw thesis argues that nonbank financial
intermediaries, such as those discussed in Chapter 1, can and do contribute to a rise in the velocity of spending which, despite the monetary

---

[14] This is unlike other taxpayers who are limited, for the most part, to deducting
capital losses from capital gain income.

[15] For the essence of the Gurley-Shaw thesis, see J. G. Gurley and E. S. Shaw, "Finan-
cial Aspects of Economic Development," *American Economic Review* (September, 1955);
Gurley and Shaw, *Money In a Theory of Finance* (The Brookings Institution, Washing-
ton, D.C., 1960); and John G. Gurley, Study Paper No. 14, "Liquidity and Financial
Institutions in the Postwar Economy," a part of the *Study of Employment Growth and
Price Levels* for the Joint Economic Committee, (Washington, D.C., 1960).

authorities' acknowledged ability to hold the money supply stable, permits potentially inflationary increases in effective demand.

Suppose, for example, that the Federal Reserve attempts to combat inflationary pressure by a contractionary monetary policy. This, along with the rising demand for loanable funds raises interest yields on securities issued by investors. Nonfinancial intermediaries—let us take a savings and loan association as an example—find that their income from financial investment into such direct securities is rising, permitting them to offer higher interest rates in order to attract savings from prospective shareholders.

Suppose now that a saver, who has been content to hold part of his savings in the form of a demand deposit at a commercial bank, finds that the higher return available on a savings and loan share just overcomes the advantage of higher liquidity of the demand deposit. He writes a check on his checking account and deposits it in a savings and loan association.

Note that the money supply is unchanged. The demand deposit that used to belong to our depositor now is an asset of the savings and loan association. Suppose now the savings and loan association uses this amount (the demand deposit) to purchase a mortgage. The home-builder now uses the previously idle demand deposit to purchase building materials and, without any change in the money supply, spending has risen.

The special role played by the financial intermediary, in this case, is in convincing the original owner of the idle deposit to give it up in return for an asset only slightly less liquid with an attractive return. He might not be willing, himself, to purchase the mortgage, but because the savings and loan association offers him a much more liquid alternative, he decides to accept the near money.

Still another way of looking at the influence of financial intermediaries in this respect is to consider the possible expansion of credit in two cases—one, where only commercial bank expansion is involved and the other, where a savings and loan association enters the picture. Suppose the commercial banking system has $100 of excess reserves, a required reserve ratio of 20 percent, and no other reserve leakage. If commercial banks alone expand to their legal limit, $500 of additional credit can be granted in the form of $500 of new demand deposits created.

But now let us suppose that along the way, perhaps at the Bank B level, one of the recipients of new demand deposits transfers them to a savings and loan association. What effect will this have?

If Bank A has all the excess reserves initially, it will lend $100:

Bank A

Loans + $100	Demand Deposits + $100

Then, as before, the borrower of the newly created money will write checks payable to his creditor, Mr. Jones, who, we assume, deposits them in Bank B. Bank B, in turn, collects them via the Federal Reserve.

Bank A		Bank B	
Federal Reserve Account − $100	Demand Deposit of Borrower − $100	Federal Reserve Account + $100	Demand Deposit of Mr. Jones + $100

At this point, let us assume that Mr. Jones succumbs to the attraction of the interest being paid by a savings and loan association and transfers his $100 there. The T-account effects on Bank B and the savings and loan association are:

Bank B		Savings and Loan Association	
	Demand Deposit of Mr. Jones − $100 Demand Deposit of Savings and Loan Association + $100	Demand Deposit at Bank B + $100	Deposit (Shares) of Mr. Jones + $100

Now the savings and loan association, finding itself with extra liquid funds, uses the $100 to purchase a mortgage:[16]

Bank B		Savings and Loan Association	
	Demand Deposit of Savings and Loan Association − $100 Demand Deposit of Mortgage Holder + $100	Demand Deposit − $100 Mortgage + $100	

Of course at this point we can expect the mortgage holder to spend his funds to purchase his home, a rise in aggregate demand. But what the reader should especially note is the fact that, throughout all this, the

[16] Although, in fact, the savings and loan association would probably find it necessary to withhold some small part of the $100 as a liquidity reserve against its increased liabilities, we ignore this in our example.

total reserves and demand deposits of the commercial banking system are unaffected. They are still in a position to (in total) extend $500 of credit, even though the savings and loan association has already lent $100. The result, then, is that financial intermediaries facilitate a larger supply of loanable funds (although not of money) than would have been possible in their absence.[17]

Nonbank financial intermediaries, like commercial banks, can also raise velocity via portfolio adjustments. If, for example, they can locate holders of idle money who are willing to purchase some of their more liquid assets, such as U.S. securities, intermediaries can use the proceeds to grant additional credit to spenders, thereby promoting a further rise in aggregate demand.

There has been, especially during the late 1950's, much debate over the validity of the Gurley-Shaw thesis, and the extent to which nonbank intermediaries weaken the effectiveness of a credit restraint policy. Some of those who see it as a significant limitation on the Federal Reserve's ability to combat inflationary pressure have advocated the application of compulsory cash reserve requirements to the nonbank intermediaries. Others, however, while granting much of the logic of the argument, find little evidence that, in the past at least, the activities of financial intermediaries have constituted a serious breech in U.S. defenses against inflation.[18]

The National Debt as a Potential Obstacle to Monetary Restriction

One further problem is the restraining influence sometimes imposed on monetary policy by the large U.S. national debt. The Federal Reserve, it will be remembered, in addition to its main role as stabilization agency, is charged with the responsibility of aiding the Treasury in its handling of the debt. Sometimes, unfortunately, these two duties seem to conflict.

In the years during and immediately following World War II this problem assumed such major proportions that monetary restraint was, for all intents and purposes, abandoned altogether in order to permit the

[17] Note, however, that aggregate demand would have been increased only if Mr. Jones had decided to save the $100 he received and had held it as an idle demand deposit if there had been no savings and loan association. If he had cut back his intended consumption spending by $100, in order to make his savings and loan deposit, the extra spending made possible by the mortgage purchase would have just canceled that which he chose to forego.

[18] See, for example, the excellent article by Warren L. Smith, "Financial Intermediaries and Monetary Controls," *Quarterly Journal of Economics* (November, 1959).

System to concentrate on aiding the Treasury in its task of financing and refinancing the national debt. What happened then should help clarify the nature of the problem.

It was necessary, during the war, that deficits of unprecedented size be financed by sale of new U.S. securities. The Federal Reserve unhesitatingly agreed to, in essence, underwrite this gigantic financing job by providing what amounted to an unlimited market for government securities. The technique employed was a guarantee by the System to purchase, at par and in unlimited amounts, any securities offered it. The effect, of course, was to immeasurably ease the Treasury's problems. U.S. securities became a virtually riskless investment—safe not only from risk of default but also from any temporary decline in market value. They were as liquid as money itself and paid interest in the bargain. The Treasury, quite naturally, found the arrangement more than satisfactory.

But, of course, all this ease in government financing could not be purchased without a price. And in this case the price was economic stability. At a time of full employment and rising prices the monetary policy obviously called for was restraint, especially open-market sales. But in its effort to aid the Treasury with its financing, the Federal Reserve System had committed itself to unlimited open-market purchases to keep bond prices up to par. Instead of restricting member-bank reserves it was pouring out more. Monetary restraint had given way completely to support of the bond market.

This policy was finally ended after bitter debate by an agreement in 1951 between the Federal Reserve and the Treasury which has since come to be known as the *Accord*. Under the terms of the agreement the Federal Reserve pledged itself to continue to aid the Treasury to the extent of preventing the development of "disorderly" conditions in the government bond market but withdrew altogether from any commitment to "peg" bond prices at fixed levels.

Barring a war of major scale it is unlikely that monetary policy will again be sacrificed so completely to support the government bond market. Nevertheless the existence of a large government debt plus a continuing responsibility to aid the Treasury in all new borrowing and refunding imply some restriction on the System's freedom of action.

When a new Treasury issue is being offered it becomes just a bit more difficult to continue an active policy of restraint. For the commitment to prevent disorderly bond market conditions may require a temporary cutback in open market sales to prevent sudden drastic (and perhaps disorderly) declines in government bond prices. At least it seems fair to say that the System's role as Treasury fiscal agent complicates a bit, its capacity to promote economic stability.

The Fear of Going Too Far

When prices are rising at full employment there is no difficulty in agreeing on the proper direction of monetary policy. Restraint is clearly called for.

But the degree of restraint is something else again. There can be little doubt that if the Federal Reserve pulled out all the stops, employing the full weight of its powers at once, most inflations could be stopped cold. The power is there and, used without caution, it could, in most cases, do the job. The real problem is finding, if it exists, just that degree of restraint which will stem the inflationary tide without forcing the economy over the precipice into recession.

In the minds of most, inflation is bad, but recession is worse. The monetary authorities can hardly be unaware of the very real possibility that too intense a dose of credit restraint, imposed on an economy in the last stages of an inflationary binge, may be just the push required to bring on the downturn. And, because some critics have charged them with just such overzealousness in the past, it is not difficult to visualize the Federal Reserve authorities' "foot on the brake" as a tentative, cautious one rather than a firm, overconfident one.

If this is the case the weakness is not that of monetary policy itself but of the authorities' reluctance to use it to the fullest extent. Such reluctance, let it be made clear, reflects the prudence of the monetary authorities, not a lack of decisiveness or courage. Federal Reserve officials must operate in the same murky jungle of uncertainty which plagues all economic policy makers. The continuing inability to forecast business cycle turning points and the inherent problem of partially conflicting goals require a not inconsiderable degree of restraint. It is all too easy, with the advantage of 100 percent hindsight, to look back from the comfortable vantage point of the classroom and criticize past policy decisions. It is quite another problem to be charged with making the decision in advance of the event. Restraint and caution in the use of monetary policy tools are essential ingredients of sound policy-making, whatever their cost.

CONCLUSION

Few economists today are so impressed by monetary policy's potency as to counsel reliance on it alone to carry out the task of economic stabilization. On the other hand, fewer still are so discouraged by its alleged weaknesses as to advocate throwing up our hands and abandoning it altogether. The preponderant majority view it as a useful, indeed, an indispensable, tool in our kit of stabilization weapons.

But as the imposing list of criticisms just completed would imply, many would support changes in the structure of the U.S. monetary mechanism to improve its effectiveness. We turn to some of the proposed structural changes in the next chapter before, in the final chapter, evaluating the alternative policy devices.

20

Proposed Changes in the Structure of U.S. Monetary Institutions

As we have seen, events of the past 50-odd years have given rise to significant changes in both the structure and the functions of the Federal Reserve System. In the process, what was originally a weak, decentralized "paper tiger" of a monetary authority has become a true central bank with all the powers typically assigned to such an important institution.

The dynamic nature of the economy of the United States, however, will undoubtedly not permit it to stand pat for long with a monetary structure the essence of which has remained basically unchanged since the major revisions of the 1930's. New problems as well as some reservations regarding the adequacy of some of the older solutions, have brought forth, as they must in a healthy society, a rash of proposals for change.

We turn, in this chapter, to look at some of these proposals. Before doing so, however, it may be helpful to review, in capsule form, some of the more important changes that have been made in the past.

MAJOR CHANGES IN MONETARY MECHANISM, 1913 TO THE PRESENT

As noted earlier, the Federal Reserve System had hardly been established before the *commercial loan* theory provisions that permeated much of it began to be modified—and eliminated. The most important changes, however, took place during the 1930's, in response to that period's unparalleled bank collapse. The following are some of the most significant of these changes.

1916   Member banks were permitted to borrow from the Reserve banks with notes secured by U.S. securities as collateral. The original act had required that all such borrowing be secured by *short-term commercial loans* from bank customers.

1917   Federal Reserve Notes could be issued with a backing composed of 40 percent gold and 60 percent short-term commercial loans rather than the original 40 percent gold plus 100 percent short-term commercial loans.

1932-1935[1] Federal Reserve banks were permitted to use U.S. securities as collateral to back Federal Reserve Notes.

1932-1935 Member banks were permitted to borrow from Federal Reserve banks using "any asset acceptable to the Reserve banks" as collateral. This markedly broadened the accessibility of the Federal Reserve discount facilities to banks with liquidity problems, but Federal Reserve loans secured by assets other than government securities or short-term commercial loans still carried a ½ percent higher discount rate.

1932-1935 Commercial banks were forbidden, for the first time, to pay interest on demand deposits. In addition, interest payable on time and savings deposits was made subject to maximums to be set by Federal Reserve authorities and the newly established Federal Deposit Insurance Corporation.

1932-1935 The Board of Governors was given authority, for the first time, to alter reserve requirements at their discretion from the levels set in the original act[2] to levels twice as high. This marked the introduction of one of the most powerful credit control weapons of the United States.

[1] Three significant pieces of banking legislation in the early 1930's changed the U.S. system markedly. These included an emergency act, the Glass-Steagall Act of 1932, and the Banking Acts of 1933 and 1935. Since all three were aimed at fundamental reform of a devastated banking system we shall lump them all together as reform measures without bothering to specify which action was taken in which particular act.

[2] Actually, the requirements set in the original Act were lowered by 5 percent for each category in 1917 when, for the first time, banks were required to hold all reserves on deposit at their Federal Reserve banks. This requirement continued in effect until 1959 when member banks were once again permitted to count vault cash as a part of their reserves.

1932-1935   The Open Market Committee as presently constituted, with the Board of Governors in a majority, was established. This replaced the more informal committee that had been operating for several years without specific legislative authorization.

1934   The Securities Exchange Act of 1934 authorized Federal Reserve authorities to restrict credit granted by any bank for the purpose of purchasing securities. As a result, the first *selective* credit control—the power to set margin requirements—was authorized.[3]

PROPOSED CHANGES IN THE COMPOSITION AND POWERS OF BOARD OF GOVERNORS

Geographical and Occupational Restriction on Board Members

According to current law the Board of Governors consists of seven members appointed by the President to fourteen-year terms. Despite the importance of their office, however, the President does not have a completely free hand in his choice of Board members. For the Federal Reserve Act itself imposes both geographical and occupational restrictions. "In selecting the members of the Board, not more than one of whom shall be selected from any one Federal Reserve district, the President shall have due regard to a fair representation of the financial, agricultural, industrial and commercial interests, and geographical divisions of the country."[4]

Students of the subject are almost unanimous in the view that these occupational and geographical restrictions on the selection of members of the Board of Governors serve no useful purpose and, indeed, may be an impediment to selecting the best men available. Any contemplated reform of the System should include their elimination.

Term of Chairman of Board of Governors

In addition to appointing Board members as openings occur, the President has the duty of selecting one member as chairman of the Board of Governors for a four-year term. This appointment is especially important because the chairman's role is a crucial one in the formation of monetary policy. Partly because of the strong personalities of recent chairmen and partly because of the unwieldy size of such crucial

[3] Control over credit granted by nonbank lenders for the purchase of securities was also instituted under this act.
[4] "The Federal Reserve Act," Section 10.

policy-making units as the Open Market Committee, the views of the chairman have tended to dominate policy.

Entirely aside from the more fundamental issue of whether the monetary structure should be such that it will provide the chairman with such disproportionate power, the present setup does not always guarantee that the incumbent chairman will be the choice of the incumbent President. Or, to put it the other way around, there is no guarantee that the four-year terms of the chairman of the board and of the President will coincide. Consequently it is entirely possible that an incoming President may "inherit" a Board of Governor's chairman appointed by his predecessor, whose term still has several years to run.

Now it might be argued that, in light of the desire of the framers of the act to make the Federal Reserve "independent" of the executive, this prospect need not be frightening. We shall have more to say about the independence issue shortly. For the moment, however, suffice it to say that few students of the matter believe that it is wise to continue the present arrangement in this respect. The large majority believe that the term of a chairman of the Board of Governors should be made coterminous with that of the President.[5]

Such a change would guarantee an incoming President the right to select a chairman whose policy views are, at the very least, not directly opposed to those of the Chief Executive. In other words whatever the merits of an independent Federal Reserve, it should not be carried to the point of saddling a newly elected President with a clearly hostile Federal Reserve Chairman.

Indeed, many would go a step further and have the chairman serve at the pleasure of the President, making him subject to dismissal (as chairman) whenever an irreconcilable clash of views arises. The effect of such a move, on the System's independence, of course, would depend partly on whether future chairmen continue to dominate the determination of monetary policy.

The Size and Composition of the Board

It has often been observed that a seven-man Board may not be the optimum-sized group for effective administration and policy determination. Under present regulations, a new member is appointed every other year to a fourteen-year, nonrenewable term.[6]

[5] See, for example, the testimony of expert witnesses in Volume 2 of *The Federal Reserve System After Fifty Years*, Hearings before the House Committee on Banking and Currency, 88th Congress, 2nd session, February and March, 1964.

[6] A Board member may, however, serve more than fourteen years if he is appointed to complete an unexpired term and then reappointed, in his own right, to a full fourteen-year term.

Suggstions for reform in this area center largely around reducing the number of Board members and shortening their terms.[7]

Reduction in the number of Governors to five or three, as has sometimes been recommended, would have several favorable effects. In the first place a three- or five-man group is probably a more efficient sized unit for determination of policy. Secondly, it seems reasonable to expect that the degree of Chairman-domination varies directly with the size of the Board. Thirdly, reducing the number may have the desirable effect of up-grading the status of the average Governor, thereby making the post more attractive to the ablest men available.

Shortening the appointment terms of the members would surely make the Board of Governors somewhat more responsive to the desires of the executive, if only by enabling any President to appoint a larger number of Governors in a four-year term. Whether this is desirable or not depends, once again, on one's views as to the "proper" degree of independence the System should have. One possible disadvantage of shorter terms is the difficulty this might create in attracting able men to Washington.

Eliminate Present Open Market Committee

Another proposal that seems to attract strong support from many experts is consolidating complete power for open-market policy into the hands of the Board of Governors. The present setup, whereby the Presidents of five Federal Reserve banks share membership on the Open Market Committee with the seven members of the Board of Governors has little to recommend it. The presidents of the Federal Reserve banks are (formally, at least) not public employees. On the face of it, it is difficult to see why they should participate directly in the determination of one of the most important arms of public policy.

It is true that, as representatives from different geographical areas of the nation, the Federal Reserve bank presidents may bring with them advice and information on happenings in their regions with which Board members may not be completely familiar. But there is no reason why such advice, information, and assistance, from all Reserve bank presidents, could not be forthcoming even if they were not voting members of the Open Market Committee. Logic, experience, and the preponderant majority of the experts all seem clearly in favor of abandoning the remnant of regionalism that the present Open Market Committee reflects and turning the full power to conduct open-market operations over to the Board of Governors alone.

[7] See *The Federal Reserve System After Fifty Years, op. cit.*

Proposed Changes in the Discount Mechanism

Technically speaking, the Board of Directors of each Federal Reserve bank sets its discount rate, subject to the *review and determination* of the Board of Governors. In fact, the System has long ago recognized that the nation is no longer a sufficiently isolated group of regions to permit, for any period of time, different discount rates in different regions. The result has been that for some time, discount rates for all Federal Reserve banks have been "set," in fact, by the Board of Governors. Although there would result no real change in practice, it has been suggested that the law be changed to state specifically that the Board of Governors not only reviews and determines but also *sets* discount rates for the Reserve banks.

A second issue in discount rate regulation has had to do with the fact, noted earlier, that the discount rate charged on notes from member banks secured by member-bank assets other than eligible paper[8] or government securities must be $\frac{1}{2}$ percent higher than that on eligible paper or governments. This $\frac{1}{2}$ percent penalty rate represents the last vestiges of the old, long-since-discredited *commercial loan* theory, and serves no useful purpose. Sentiment for its elimination is almost unanimous.

More controversial is the proposal by at least one eminent authority to eliminate the discount mechanism altogether.[9] It is argued that (1) open-market operations are adequate to carry out any desired monetary policy and (2) because the discount rate lags behind market rates it tends to provide a source for weakening the intended credit policy. For example when in a boom period, authorities want to restrict credit, not only is the discount window itself a source of added credit but it becomes relatively cheaper to obtain so long as the discount rate does not rise as rapidly as open-market rates. Opponents of this proposal, however, appear to be in the majority. Although many are prepared to grant that discount rate alterations represent at best, a weak credit control device, the importance of the discount window as an outside source of liquidity in cases of emergency still seems significant.

Another proposal that has attracted some interest is that the discount rate be tied to the rate on U.S. Treasury bills, thereby eliminating the possibility of discretionary changes. Such a proposal has the merit of keeping the discount rate in line with open-market rates (at least in greater degree then is true at present) thereby lessening the likelihood that the discount window might be used to circumvent policies of credit restriction.

[8] Commercial loans of 90 days or less to finance the purchase of inventories.
[9] See Milton Friedman, *A Program for Monetary Stability* (New York, Fordham University Press, 1960).

Member-bank borrowing from the Federal Reserve has always been advertised as a privilege rather than a right. That is, any Federal Reserve bank has the power to refuse loans requested whenever, in its judgment, refusal is warranted.

Federal Reserve practice, however, is not to refuse loans, when requested.[10] Instead, Reserve authorities concentrate on discouraging member banks that appear to be abusing the facilities of the discount window from asking for a loan in the first place. The result is that, in fact, a bank that has not first been warned by Reserve authorities can expect always to be accommodated. For the vast majority of member banks, then, the facilities of the discount window amount to a right that they can freely avail themselves of, so long as they receive no prior warning that they are abusing the privilege.

If banks whose borrowing practices are not in accord with an existing policy of general credit restraint are the ones who receive these "prior warnings" then the discount window does not provide a means of evading credit restriction. In fact, however, in the words of one distinguished Federal Reserve official, "The stress is on good banking practices; no attempt is made to orient each borrowing bank's position into the broader policy aims of current Federal Reserve credit control. Moreover, any bank with a good record can be virtually certain . . . that it will get a loan."[11] In other words, the Fed makes no attempt to use its power to refuse access to the discount window in a manner that will supplement its existing general credit policy. More pointedly, the member bank that is able to overcome its "reluctance" to borrowing from the central bank may do so, even if its action undercuts a policy of credit restraint, with impunity.

All of this would seem to indicate that those who feel that the discount facility has the potential of frustrating, to some degree, a policy of general credit restraint, are correct. However, only a few consider this threat a sufficiently clear and present danger to necessitate the recommendation of shutting the window altogether.

Proposed Changes in Reserve Requirement Regulations

As we have seen, the National Banking System's arrangement of dividing member banks into three groups, according to size of city was carried over into the original Federal Reserve Act. As a result, until 1962, three different sets of reserve requirements were applied to the three different groups of member banks. In 1962, the category *Central*

---

[10] For an excellent statement on this issue see Charles R. Whittlesey, "Credit Policy at the Discount Window," *Quarterly Journal of Economics*, May, 1959.

[11] Robert V. Roosa, "Credit Policy at the Discount Window: Comment," *Quarterly Journal of Economics*, May, 1959.

Reserve City Banks was abolished, leaving only *Reserve City* and *Country* bank categories, for whom reserve requirements behind demand deposits could be varied from 10 to 22 percent and from 7 to 14 percent, respectively.

There is little to be said in defense of this arrangement. Different reserve requirements for member banks in cities of different sizes made some sense a century ago under the National Banking Act. They have nothing to recommend them now. Up to 1960, when vault cash was made a part of the legal reserve there was some logic in the arrangement of lower required reserves for country banks because typically, these banks find it necessary, due to the nature of their business, to carry relatively more vault cash than their big-city counterparts. Today, however, even that justification is eliminated. Logic, justice, and more effective control of the money supply all argue for the elimination of the two-group breakdown and the application of the same reserve requirements to all member banks.

Proposed Changes in Interest Rate Limitations

In the general overhaul of U.S. banking legislation in the 1930's, the Board of Governors was given the power to set a maximum on the interest that could be paid on time and savings deposits. At the same time, member banks were forbidden to pay any interest on balances in checking accounts. Both measures were motivated by the experience of the thirties, when it was felt that, in their zeal to attract deposits, banks committed themselves to such high interest obligations that they were forced to grant relatively high-risk loans in order to earn sufficient income.

Among economists there is a strong majority view that the limitation on time and saving deposit interest rates should be abolished.[12] If banking authorities do an adequate job in their supervisory capacities, there would seem to be no reason to worry about the quality of their assets. On the other hand, the interest rate limitation, if it is set low enough to have any effect at all (that is, at a level below that which the banks would voluntarily pay in the absence of the regulation) can only hamper commercial banks in their efforts to compete for savings with the rapidly growing nonbank financial institutions.

In addition to the solid opposition to savings deposit interest rate maximas, there is a not inconsiderable number of economists who would favor eliminating the current prohibition of interest on demand de-

[12] See, for example, the views expressed in *The Federal Reserve System After Fifty Years, op. cit.*

posits.[13] This, like the limit on savings deposit rates, is viewed as an un-necessary and improper interference with competition which distorts the free flow of funds, and penalizes commercial banks without sound reason.

Although, as noted, the majority of economists appear to favor elimi-nation of the power to set interest rate ceilings on commercial bank time and savings deposits, Congress, as recently as late September, 1966, has taken a step in the opposite direction. Moved by the competition among savings institutions for the limited funds that have been available during this period of severe credit restriction, Congress has passed and the Presi-dent has signed into law, a new bill, which extends the authority to regu-late interest rates payable on savings by several lending institutions other than commercial banks. According to some of the bill's proponents, its purpose is to forestall potentially dangerous competition for funds among lending institutions which might have the effect of endangering the sol-vency of important segments of the financial community.

PROPOSED CHANGES IN THE STRUCTURE AND POWERS OF THE FEDERAL RESERVE BANKS

Proposal to Retire Federal Reserve Bank Stock

The unique feature of the Federal Reserve banks—private ownership coupled with public control—does not appear to have led to any real conflicts in practice. The public responsibilities of the System have, as they must, always taken precedence over any formal obligation the Reserve banks might seem to have to their private owners, the mem-ber banks. To put the issue bluntly, any potential conflicts between the private interests of their owners and the public interests of the United States, have been decided on the side of the latter. And there can be no question but that this is how it should be.

Why then, some ask, should the legal fiction of private ownership be continued? If, as owners, the member banks do not and should not have any right to control policy, why not eliminate the ambiguities by making the Reserve banks publicly owned as well as publicly controlled?

Following this line of reasoning bills have been introduced in Con-gress in recent years to amend the Federal Reserve Act in order to retire present outstanding Federal Reserve bank stock. The member banks hold-

[13] Indeed, one distinguished authority would go further than this and require that the Federal Reserve pay interest to the member banks on their excess reserves. See James Tobin, "Towards Improving the Efficiency of the Monetary Mechanism," *Review of Economics and Statistics* (August, 1960).

ing such stock would be reimbursed at its par value and would receive in its place, a simple *certificate of membership*. If such legislation were passed the Federal Reserve banks would become publicly owned as well as publicly controlled institutions and the current anomalous arrangement would be ended.

Such a change would probably be advisable if only to clear the air and formalize that which has been the case in practice for many years. The effect, however, would be strictly a formality.

Proposal to Eliminate Gold-certificate Requirement Behind Federal Reserve Notes

Another relic for the distant past, the formal connection between U.S. gold stock and member-bank reserves, has recently been abandoned. As we have seen pressure on our balance of payments has forced Congress to take a step that would have been sensible whatever the balance of payments situation—elimination of the required gold-certificate reserve behind member-bank reserves.

This leaves the United States with one last formal tie between its gold and money supply—the requirement of 25 percent in gold certificates behind Federal Reserve Notes outstanding. Since the United States has long ago wisely abandoned the formal, *full* gold standard in favor of an authoritatively determined money supply, there is no real case for any such link, formal or otherwise. The 25 percent gold-certificate requirement for Federal Reserve Notes should be eliminated as soon as possible.

The Question of the Use of Federal Reserve Bank Earnings

A long time critic of the Federal Reserve System, Congressman Wright Patman, Chairman of the House Committee on Banking and Currency, has argued persuasively for stricter Congressional control over Federal Reserve bank earnings and their disposition.

As of the present Federal Reserve bank earnings are used to pay (1) their own expenses, (2) their share of the Board of Governors' expenses, (3) a 6 percent dividend on their stock to member banks, and (4) an amount necessary to bring their surplus up to twice their paid-in capital. Earnings in excess of these amounts, totaling many times the size of the dividend payment in recent years, are turned back to the U.S. Treasury.

Congressman Patman has argued that in the area of use of earnings, the peculiar "privately owned, publicly controlled" characteristic of the Reserve banks has had significant effects. Unlike formally public institutions, the Federal Reserve does not have to come to Congress for appropriations to pay its bills. It has enough earnings of its own, primarily earned via its ownership of U.S. securities, to far more than pay its bills. Indeed, it faces neither the normal test of the market nor the usual careful scrutiny of Congressional appropriations as a restraining influence on its spending. Patman feels that the result has been wasteful expenditures that would not have been made under other circumstances.

It is doubtful whether many would agree that the System has been guilty of any serious waste. There is, however, this significant point. Representative Patman points out that the salaries paid high officials of Federal Reserve banks are generally substantially higher than those of most of the highest governmental officials of the United States. The figures, as of January, 1964, are shown in Table 20-1.

TABLE 20-1   Annual Salaries of the Principal Federal Officials, Including the Highest Paid Officials of the Federal Reserve System, January 5, 1964

President of the United States	$100,000
President, Federal Reserve Bank, New York	70,000
President, Federal Reserve Bank, Chicago	55,000
President, Federal Reserve Bank, Philadelphia	40,000
President, Federal Reserve Bank, Cleveland	40,000
President, Federal Reserve Bank, Richmond	40,000
President, Federal Reserve Bank, Atlanta	40,000
President, Federal Reserve Bank, Minneapolis	40,000
President, Federal Reserve Bank, Dallas	40,000
President, Federal Reserve Bank, San Francisco	40,000
First Vice-president, Federal Reserve Bank, New York	40,000
President, Federal Reserve Bank, Kansas City	37,500
Vice-president and Senior Adviser, Federal Reserve Bank, New York	37,500
Chief Justice of the United States	35,500
President, Federal Reserve Bank, Boston	35,000
President, Federal Reserve Bank, St. Louis	35,000
Vice-president, Federal Reserve Bank, New York	35,000
Vice-president of the United States	35,000
President of the Senate Pro Tempore, when there is no Vice-president of the United States	35,000
Speaker of the House of Representatives	35,000
Associate Justices of the Supreme Court	35,000
Vice-president, Federal Reserve Bank, New York	32,500
Vice-president, Federal Reserve Bank, New York	31,500
First Vice-president, Federal Reserve Bank, Kansas City	30,000
Vice-president, Federal Reserve Bank, New York	29,000

TABLE 20-1 (Cont'd)

Vice-president and General Counsel, Federal Reserve Bank, New York	$28,500
Vice-president, Federal Reserve Bank, New York	28,000
Adviser to the Board, Board of Governors of the Federal Reserve System	27,500
First Vice-presidents, Federal Reserve Banks: Boston, Philadelphia, Richmond, Chicago, St. Louis, and San Francisco	27,500
First Vice-president and General Counsel, Federal Reserve Bank, Atlanta	27,500
Vice-presidents (2), Federal Reserve Bank, New York	27,500
U.S. Representative to the United Nations and Representative in the Security Council	27,500
U.S. Permanent Representative to NATO	27,500
Ambassador at Large	27,500
Chiefs of Mission, Class 1, Foreign Service	27,500
Vice-president, Federal Reserve Bank, San Francisco	26,500
Adviser to the Board, Board of Governors of the Federal Reserve System	26,000
Secretary of the Board, Board of Governors, Federal Reserve System	26,000
General Counsel, Board of Governors, Federal Reserve System	26,000
Vice-president, Federal Reserve Bank, New York	26,000
Assistant Vice-president, Federal Reserve Bank, New York	25,500
Circuit Judges, U.S. Courts of Appeals	25,500
Chief Judge and Associate Judges, U.S. Court of Claims	25,500
Chief Judge and Associate Judges, U.S. Court of Customs and Patent Appeals	25,500
Judges, U.S. Court of Military Appeals	25,500
Director, Division of Research and Statistics, Board of Governors of the Federal Reserve System	25,000
Director, Division of Examinations, Board of Governors of the Federal Reserve System	25,000
First Vice-presidents, Federal Reserve Banks: Cleveland, Minneapolis, and Dallas	25,000
Vice-president and Senior Adviser, Federal Reserve Bank, Richmond	25,000
Vice-president and Cashier, Federal Reserve Bank, Philadelphia	25,000
Assistant General Counsel, Federal Reserve Bank, New York	25,000
Secretary of State	25,000
Secretary of the Treasury	25,000
Secretary of Defense	25,000
Attorney General	25,000
Postmaster General	25,000
Secretary of the Interior	25,000
Secretary of Agriculture	25,000
Secretary of Commerce	25,000
Secretary of Labor	25,000

TABLE 20-1 (Cont'd)

Secretary of Health, Education and Welfare	$25,000
Deputy U.S. Representative to the United Nations and Deputy Representative in the Security Council	25,000
Chiefs of Missions, Class 2, Foreign Service	25,000
U.S. Representative to the Organization for Economic Cooperation and Development	25,000
U.S. Representative, European Communities	25,000
U.S. Representative on the Council of the Organization of American States	25,000
Special Representative for Trade Negotiations	25,000
Director, Office of Emergency Planning	25,000

SOURCE: *The Federal Reserve System After Fifty Years,* Hearings before the House Committee on Banking and Currency, 88th Congress, second session, February and March, 1964.

The facts are clear. Ten of the twelve Federal Reserve bank presidents and two of their vice-presidents are paid more than the Vice-president of the United States and the Chief Justice of the United States Supreme Court. Eleven vice-presidents of the New York Federal Reserve bank alone receive higher salaries than any member of the President's Cabinet.

Of course, there is nothing particularly surprising about officials of privately owned firms earning larger salaries than government officials— even those at the highest levels. But surely the case for higher earnings for a Federal Reserve bank official rests on much different grounds than that which justifies high salaries in other private financial corporations.

For if the Federal Reserve banks really are "public" institutions it is difficult to justify paying their officials as though they were not. Among the prime policy decisions that top executives in ordinary private banks must make (for successful determination of which they presumably earn their attractive salaries) are their interest-rate policy and their securities-portfolio policy. In the case of Federal Reserve banks both these strategic decisions are made for them, for all practical purposes, by the Board of Governors.

The above is in no way intended to question the truly high quality of many of the officials of Federal Reserve banks nor even to argue that they are, as might be implied, overpaid. It does however seem that the Congressman has a solid point when he argues that if Federal Reserve officials really are public officials the source of the Reserve banks' income is a matter of legitimate public concern.

PROPOSED CHANGES IN REGULATIONS GOVERNING THE MEMBER BANKS

Submitting All Commercial Banks to the Same Regulations

Enforcing high banking standards, payment of checks at par and rigorous reserve requirements are difficult enough in their own right. But applying such standards to a group of banks which is not really compelled to submit to them is infinitely more so.

National banks, of course, have no alternative to Federal Reserve regulations. But state banks are free to choose between these and the sometimes far more liberal standards enforced by state regulatory bodies. If they consider existing Federal Reserve requirements too confining, they need not join the System in the first place. If, having once joined, state banks find changes such as a rise in reserve requirements too unpalatable, they are free to withdraw at their option.

There can be no doubt that System authorities are alert to the possible effects of tightened regulations on the number of state member banks. Indeed, there is little question that the risk of forcing existing members to withdraw from the System acts as a constraint, of indeterminate significance, on the use of such monetary policy weapons as increased reserve requirements.

In light of problems such as these it has been suggested that our laws should be changed to require all commercial banks, national or state, to join the Federal Reserve System.[14]

Such a step would provide at least two major benefits. First, it would free Federal Reserve authorities to employ whatever regulations they find appropriate, without fear of forcing banks from the System. Secondly, by compelling all banks to observe the same reserve requirements, it would not only permit fairer competition among banks but would give the authorities more accurate control over the money-supply and credit conditions. As it is now a shift of deposits from member to nonmember banks will usually, because of differing reserve requirements, permit an alteration in the money and credit supply.

On the other hand, disadvantages in such a change are difficult to uncover. It is true that those banks that now benefit by staying out of the System would protest. No doubt, also, there would be those who would

---

[14] A variant to this which might be more palatable but would have essentially the same effect would be to require all banks subscribing to the F.D.I.C. to join the Federal Reserve. This would bring in all but about 250.

object that such legislation had irreparably damaged the long-established concept of a dual banking system. But such complaints carry little weight unless it can be shown that there are some real benefits for society from a dual system or from permitting some banks to operate under more favorable legal conditions than others. Evidence of any such benefit is certainly not obvious.

Altering Reserve Requirements for Savings Deposits at Member Banks

The rapid growth of nonbank financial institutions relative to commercial banks has drawn some attention to the differences in the regulations governing them. With respect to reserve requirements behind savings accounts it has been pointed out that commercial banks operate at a competitive disadvantage. Two suggestions have been put forth to deal with this problem.

The Commission on Money and Credit has come out for elimination of the reserve requirements on member-bank savings accounts.[15] The Commission argues that adequate supervision of member-bank portfolios should be adequate to maintain needed levels of liquidity and solvency so that reserve requirements, as such, are unnecessary. Such a step would undoubtedly aid commercial banks in their competition with nonbank savings institutions.

But, opponents argue, could not the same advantage be obtained with better control by retaining present reserve requirements for savings deposits at member banks while passing new legislation to extend these controls to competing thrift institutions not now subject to them. We shall not attempt to choose between these two alternatives. Both would enhance the competitive position of banks relative to their rivals.

Proposal to Broaden the Authority for Branch Banking

As noted earlier federal law permits national banks to operate branches only to the same extent as state banks located in the same state. This has meant no interstate branch banking, no branches at all within some states, and only limited branching in many others. While historically the aim of these restrictions has been to promote competition, there is some evidence that, by keeping branches of larger city banks out of smaller one or two bank communities, it may have accomplished the opposite.

[15] See *Money and Credit,* The Report of the Commission on Money and Credit (Englewood Cliffs, N.J., Prentice-Hall, Inc., 1961), p. 69.

Many authorities are of the opinion that a more liberal policy regarding branch banking would accomplish the twin objectives of providing more efficient banking facilities for many smaller communities as well as increasing the degree of competition.

Once again liberalization of branch bank regulations for national banks would likely lead to charges of undercutting the dual banking system. If, for example, national banks should be accorded state-wide branching permission in a state that prohibits branches for its own state-chartered banks, the national banks would have such a decided advantage that the state law might have to be changed. Whether this possibility provides sufficient grounds for continuing the present branching restrictions is a question that is not readily answerable.[16]

THE TRANSITIONAL COSTS

If the United States were starting out fresh to form a new banking system, most of the improvements we have considered thus far would, in all probability, be incorporated. It has, however, a going and reasonably successful monetary system. Whatever benefits the United States may acquire from changing it will have to be netted out against the transitional costs of change itself.

This point is often illustrated with regard to the tax structure by the old saying: "An old tax is a good tax." The point, of course, is that once a tax has been in effect for some time people and institutions and the price structure have had a chance to react fully to it until a new equilibrium situation has been achieved. It may have been a "bad" tax when it was first levied, it may have inflicted much cost in adjusting to it, but now that all adjustments have been made to it, *there may be more cost involved in readjusting to a new "better" tax*, than in sticking with the old "worse," but "accustomed" one.

The same general point can be made about any proposed institutional change—the monetary sphere not excepted.[17] While the elimination of the Open Market Committee, clarification of the public nature of Federal Reserve banks, extension of the same reserve requirements to all commercial banks, and the like are all solid, worthwhile suggestions that would probably improve the U.S. monetary system in the long run, the benefits would be tempered by the costs of the change.

[16] If branching regulations should be liberalized for commercial banks there seems to be no reason why the same conditions should not be applied in the case of savings and loan associations and mutual savings banks.

[17] For an excellent statement on this point see G. L. Bach, "Economics, Politics and the Fed," *Harvard Business Review* (January-February, 1962).

One can quite reasonably argue that despite the fact that many of the monetary institutions of the United States were conceived a half-century ago under conditions vastly different from those facing it today, the United States has managed to make them work tolerably well. True, many of these characteristics are illogical, but unless as a practical matter they seriously hinder the nation from reaching its goals, little (other than intellectual satisfaction with a logical structure) is to be gained from changing them.

Such an argument has much to recommend it. This is not to say that so long as the system does not collapse no institutional changes should be made. It is only to point out that before one plunges enthusiastically into remaking the system into a classroom "ideal," it is well to consider carefully whether the future benefit justifies the present cost.

THE ISSUE OF FEDERAL RESERVE INDEPENDENCE

Debate over the proper relationship between the monetary authority and the rest of government is almost as old as the nation itself. Long before the Federal Reserve System was conceived the administration of Andrew Jackson battled with the Second Bank of the United States over the question of whether or not the executive should control the monetary system. The same battle, in much altered form and intensity, continues to the present.

As a public agency, the Federal Reserve System today does possess a unique degree of insularity from both the executive and the legislature. As we have seen, members of the Board of Governors, once appointed, serve fourteen-year, nonrenewable terms. A President who is displeased with a Board member may not remove him from office nor can he elicit obedience to his views by a promise of reappointment. Similarly, the System is insulated from one of the most potent of the legislature's control techniques, the Congressional appropriation. Because the System earns its own income it need not appear annually before Congress requesting funds. This certainly does provide the Federal Reserve with a degree of freedom of action not possessed by the ordinary government agency. But a word of caution is in order lest the reader jump to unwarranted conclusions. The Federal Reserve System is not and cannot be, *completely* independent of the legislature. Congress created it through legislation and can, of course, change it or abolish it at its pleasure.

Despite this important reservation, however, the Federal Reserve System does possess a degree of independence within the government which is unique. It seems in order to ask "Why?" What is there about the monetary authority and its responsibilities which has seemed to justify giving it such special treatment? Why, in other words, *should* it be "independent"?

According to no less interested a party than the United States Treasury Department, the degree of independence from the legislature which exists ". . . is based upon the simple and convincing proposition that monetary management, involving as it does highly technical operations, should be handled by independent experts. Moreover experience in this country and in many foreign countries indicates strongly that the highly important task of monetary management, if it is to be impartially and effectively handled, must be divorced from the 'politics of the day,' "[18] In other words the Federal Reserve must be partially independent of the Congress because (1) monetary policy is a technical task and (2) Congress is too responsive to the "politics of the day" to maintain the required long run perspective monetary managers must have.

In addition, the Treasury department supports substantial independence from the executive as follows: "If the Executive were to possess the power over the creation of money (which is the prerogative of Congress and has been delegated to the Federal Reserve), while at the same time bearing the responsibility to borrow to meet the government's fiscal requirements as cheaply as possible, there might be considerable danger of reliance on unsound monetary policies to minimize (in the short run) government borrowing costs, at the expense of encouraging inflationary pressures. This is no idle academic theory; it has happened in this and other countries."[19] In other words, the Executive, if it had responsibility both for debt management and monetary policy, might be guilty of placing the former duty ahead of the latter—keeping interest rates down to lower debt financing costs when economic conditions call for higher interest rates.

Now there is much to this case for independence—enough, indeed, to have impressed legislators in the United States for over a century. Yet we must be careful not to overstate it. We must, for example, guard against seeming to imply that monetary authorities alone possess unbiased wisdom and objectivity; that monetary policy contains some special power to affect the economy in ways no other policy weapon can; that it would be somehow proper and right for the monetary managers to attempt to effectuate their views no matter what the desires of the majority of the populace. The case for independence is a strong one, but carried to extremes, it can become indefensible.

This theme appears over and over again in testimony by monetary

---

[18] *The Federal Reserve and the Treasury: Answers to Questions from the Commission on Money and Credit,* U.S. Treasury Department (Englewood Cliffs, N.J., Prentice-Hall, Inc., 1963).

[19] *Ibid.*

experts on the subject. Perhaps the best way to bring out the flavor of these views is to reproduce a few quotations.

Professor J. Gurley, for example, says:

The independence of the Federal Reserve has been defended on the grounds that anti-inflationary policies are unpopular and so should be carried out by an independent agency removed from immediate political pressures. This seems to mean that even though the majority of people are against these tight monetary policies, the action should still be carried out because some independent agency knows what is best for the people. Fiscal policies have their unpopular features, too, the same as monetary policies, but there is no reason why an agency, independent of the administration, should levy and collect our taxes.[20]

Professor Dudley Johnson holds that ". . . to argue that the control over the money supply should be independent of the values of certain representatives of the citizenry in a democracy strikes me as ludicrous."[21]

And again, Professor H. Scott Gordon says:

The view that operating independence is desirable springs largely from the fear that the executive branch may be tempted to misuse the great financial powers of the central bank by perverting it to partisan or even personal ends. To my mind, such evils are possible in all spheres of governmental operations, and the real guarantee against them is the light of public knowledge. The sphere of finance does not inherently contain greater dangers of this sort than those of, say, defense or public works.[22]

Clearly these and other experts are simply making explicit reference to the fact that independence, carried to extreme, is unworkable and indefensible. As a restraining influence—as a check or balance—it is probably useful to have a Federal Reserve with sufficient independence to oppose the executive's policy once in a while. But it would be unthinkable to have a popularly elected executive who favors an expansionary policy totally frustrated by a permanently entrenched and completely independent monetary authority that sees things differently. In any such all-out confrontation, the two arms of government would simply have to come together and work out their differences or the nation would be the loser. Independence carried to such extreme would be the height of folly.

The Federal Reserve and the Treasury, of course, recognize this fact. That is why the Chairman of the Board of Governors and the Secretary of the Treasury meet, at least weekly, to coordinate policy. That is why the President periodically confers with the chairman of the Board.

[20] J. G. Gurley, Testimony before the House Banking and Currency Committee, published in *The Federal Reserve System After Fifty Years,* Hearings (January-February, 1964), p. 1310.

[21] Dudley Johnson, *ibid.,* p. 1444.

[22] H. Scott Gordon, *ibid.,* p. 944.

Monetary and fiscal policy represent different means of striving for essentially the same ends. Monetary managers probably will feel somewhat more keenly their responsibility for maintaining stability in prices. Fiscal policy framers may well be just a bit more sensitive to the problems of unemployment. The result may be some differences of opinion on the direction of policy at certain points in the business cycle. This is to be expected and is probably healthy.

Such differences however cannot be allowed to develop into an all-out battle with fiscal policy working in one direction and monetary policy in the other. Effective coordination is an absolute essential to prevent independence from doing more harm than good. Perhaps Professor Lerner said it best when he observed, "We need enough separateness between the monetary authority and the fiscal authorities for there to be some sense in saying they have to be coordinated. They should be neither completely independent or completely integrated into a single unit."[23]

[23] A. Lerner, *ibid.*, p. 1409.

21

The Policy Alternatives

Even the most sanguine of monetary policy adherents recognizes that it alone would be an inadequate bulwark against the persistent threats of inflation, unemployment, lagging growth, and the balance of payments disequilibrium. If U.S. goals are to be even roughly approximated, monetary policy clearly needs help. We turn in this chapter to a brief consideration of the major policy alternatives.

FISCAL POLICY

The prime complement to monetary policy is fiscal policy. Let us define fiscal policy as alterations in tax revenue and/or government expenditures which are intended to affect the level of aggregate demand.

This definition is sufficiently broad to cover both discretionary fiscal policy and the nondiscretionary variety, popularly known as the *automatic stabilizers*. Discretionary fiscal policy consists of action by the legislature to change tax laws or government expenditure programs with the intent of altering aggregate demand.[1] The automatic stabilizers, on the other hand, consist of changes in the amount of tax revenue collected from existing tax laws or changes in the amount spent under existing government expenditure programs which require no new legislation but come about automatically as a result of changes in the level of income itself. In what follows we shall concern ourselves primarily with discretionary policy although we shall not ignore the automatic stabilizers altogether.

[1] Properly speaking discretionary fiscal policy also encompasses action by the executive to speed up or slow down the completion of already authorized programs.

What Is, and What Is Not Fiscal Policy

It is important that the student see clearly the distinction between fiscal policy and other activities of government. One source of confusion which sometimes arises is a failure to recognize that while discretionary fiscal policy does entail alterations in tax laws or expenditure programs, not every tax or expenditure change should be considered a fiscal policy action.

Discretionary fiscal policy, per se, should be thought of as changes in taxes or government expenditures *which are undertaken primarily for their effect on aggregate demand.* It is entirely possible, for example, for government to launch a new program calling for increased spending, providing at the same time for sufficient added tax revenue to forestall any rise in aggregate demand. Such action would simply represent an attempt to increase the size of the public sector rather than a fiscal policy measure as the term is customarily used.

In this connection, it is useful to keep in mind the distinction between different economic activities of government drawn by Musgrave.[2] There is the allocation branch that uses taxes, expenditures, and other devices to reallocate resources, both between the public and private sectors and within the private sector itself. Secondly, there is a distribution branch that may use taxes and expenditures to alter the distribution of income. Finally, there is the stabilization branch the function of which is to use taxes and expenditures in order to achieve the "proper" level of aggregate demand. Fiscal policy, as we are using the term, consists of the activities of the stabilization branch alone.

Another distinction that should be drawn here is that between fiscal and monetary policy. Since many activities involve them both and since the aims of both are the same—the pursuit of main economic goals via alterations in aggregate demand—there is sometimes a tendency to confuse them. For purposes of this text we shall define a "pure" monetary policy measure as Federal Reserve alteration in aggregate demand via changes in the liquidity of the community's wealth alone. Hence, an open-market purchase from the public which simply exchanges money for U.S. securities, would be an example of pure monetary policy.[3] On the other hand, simply "giving" the public more money by, as has sometimes been whimsically suggested, "dumping it out of airplanes," would be a combination of monetary and fiscal policy. For in this hypothetical case not only is the liquidity of people's wealth increased but its amount is

[2] R. A. Musgrave, *The Theory of Public Finance* (New York, McGraw-Hill Book Company, 1959).

[3] Of course, such a policy would affect aggregate demand through its effects on the rate of interest.

also increased. In effect, this consists not only of creating more money but of paying it out in the form of an increase in (randomly distributed) government transfer payments.

On the other hand, a pure fiscal policy measure would involve altering taxes or expenditures, without changing the money supply. A reduction in taxes, with the resulting budget deficit financed by sale of securities to the public, would be an example since there is no change in the money supply. If the deficit were financed by sale of securities to the banks, however, the measure combines elements of monetary *and* fiscal policy, since in addition to the tax cut, the money supply is increased.

How Discretionary Fiscal Policy Works

The potential role of fiscal policy should be clear from the material covered in Part II. If the requirement is to raise production and employment, aggregate demand must be increased. Fiscal authorities can choose any of three methods.[4] They may raise government spending on goods and services without altering taxes; raise government transfer payments without changing taxes; or lower taxes without reducing government spending.

The first approach will raise aggregate demand directly, since government spending on goods and services is a part of aggregate demand. The other two alternatives work (raise aggregate demand) only slightly less directly. In both cases disposable income (plus perhaps business saving) is directly increased with the expectation that a rise in private spending, C and/or I, will be forthcoming.

In all three cases, the initial rise in demand will trigger a multiplier, which will magnify the final effect. On the other hand, if we assume no increase in the supply of money (deficit raised by sale of bonds to the public) the expansionary effects of all three will be tempered somewhat by the rise in the rate of interest which must be induced by the increased transactions demand for money.

Let us turn now to a brief consideration of the chief characteristics of each fiscal device.

Raising Government Spending on Goods and Services, Taxes Unchanged

This approach has an initial advantage over the other two in that aggregate demand must first go up by the full amount of the increase in government spending. Raising transfer payments or lowering

4 Or, of course, they can choose any desired combination of the three.

taxes merely gives private spenders more to spend. If their marginal propensity to spend is less than one, the initial rise in aggregate demand will be less than the amount of the tax cut (or transfer increase).

On the other hand, the time lag involved in this case may be a serious detriment in comparison with the other two. It takes time to organize public work projects (even after Congress has acted) while tax cuts and/or transfer payment programs can be instituted and affect the spending stream almost immediately. Another potential problem with raising government spending is the fact that most of the initial effects fall on the construction industry and its suppliers. Now if this is one of the industries suffering with excess capacity, the effect is good. If, however, the unemployment is more widespread and the construction industry is near capacity, the initial effects of the government spending may be partly dissipated through raising construction prices and costs.

Raising Transfer Payments, Taxes Unchanged

As just noted, unless the recipients of increased transfer payments happen to have a marginal propensity to spend of one, $1 billion of added transfers will raise aggregate demand initially (before the multiplier effects are considered) by something less than $1 billion. However, since the average transfer payment recipient is generally in the lower part of the income scale, there is a good likelihood that his MPC will be quite high. If so, the initial effect on demand will be only slightly less favorable than is the case for goods and service expenditures.

To the degree that the added transfer payments are designed as additions to unemployment compensation, this approach has the additional virtue of reaching, reasonably quickly, those in most need of aid.

On the other hand, depending upon the extent and duration of the program, one might object to the possible incentive effects of transfer payments. Public works projects, it might be argued, possess the advantage of requiring the recipient of government paychecks to work for them, thereby avoiding the risk that the government's fiscal policy action will undercut the incentive to work.

Reducing Taxes, Government Expenditures Unchanged

Lowered taxes, by providing households and businesses with enlarged *disposable* incomes, lead to increased private spending. Of course, the amount of increase depends heavily on whose taxes are cut. If the beneficiaries of tax relief are heavy marginal spenders, the boost given aggregate demand will be significant. If, however, individuals with low MPC's or businesses with little incentive to invest are the affected parties, the fiscal action will be less successful.

One criticism often made of this variant of fiscal policy is that, if it is the income tax that is cut, the only immediate beneficiaries are those who are still employed and earning sufficient income to benefit from the reduction. The unemployed, on the other hand, currently earning little or no income, derive little or no immediate relief.[5] In addition, as noted above, it is likely that it will affect aggregate demand less, per dollar of fiscal action, than would increased expenditures on goods and services.[6]

The Determinants of the Degree of Effectiveness of Fiscal Policy

Few deny that intelligently administered fiscal policy can play a significant role in achieving economic stability. In fact, as a stabilization tool it undoubtedly receives more widespread support than monetary policy. But we must be on guard against allowing oversimplification to distort our evaluation.

As a first approximation it is often argued that the effects of fiscal policy on the equilibrium level of production and income can be read off from the following simple expressions:

$$\frac{1}{1\text{-MPC}} \times \triangle \; \begin{array}{l}\text{Level of Govern-}\\ \text{ment Spending on}\\ \text{Goods and Services}\end{array} \;=\; \triangle \; \begin{array}{l}\text{Equilibrium Level}\\ \text{of Production}\\ \text{and Income}\end{array}$$

or

$$\frac{1}{1\text{-MPC}} \times \left[\text{MPC} \times \triangle \; \begin{array}{l}\text{Level of}\\ \text{Tax Revenue}\end{array} \right] = \triangle \; \begin{array}{l}\text{Equilibrium Level}\\ \text{of Production}\\ \text{and Income}\end{array}$$

or

$$\frac{1}{1\text{-MPC}} \times \left[\text{MPC} \times \triangle \; \begin{array}{l}\text{Level of}\\ \text{Government}\\ \text{Transfers}\end{array} \right] = \triangle \; \begin{array}{l}\text{Equilibrium}\\ \text{Level of Produc-}\\ \text{tion and Income}\end{array}$$

[5] They do, of course, benefit indirectly via the multiplier effects if the measure has its desired effect.

[6] As long as transfer payment programs are concentrated among the unemployed and lower-income groups, where MPC's can be expected to be high, they too probably raise demand more than tax cuts.

Now there is nothing wrong with putting it this way as a simplified first approximation but the alert student will recognize that this does involve considerable abstraction from reality. While we cannot, within the scope of this book, exhaustively treat fiscal policy, it does seem in order to carry it a bit further than these expressions permit. What are the determinants of the degree of effectiveness of fiscal policy?

To keep the discussion within manageable proportions, we shall consider only the stabilization objective of fiscal policy. Indeed, in order to avoid unnecessary duplication, let us concentrate on only one side of the stabilization task—fiscal action to deal with unemployment. What will determine how effective a given fiscal program will be, in its goal of raising employment?

As the list below indicates, it is convenient to break the discussion down into two major categories. Since the aim is to raise employment through the medium of increases in aggregate demand, we must first consider the factors that determine the effect of the fiscal policy on total spending. Then, since the increase in demand is means rather than end, we must go on to discuss the circumstances under which demand increases are, indeed, likely to cut unemployment.

Factors Determining the Degree of Effectiveness of Antirecession Fiscal Policy

I. Determinants of the effect of the fiscal policy on aggregate demand
   A. How does the government spend its funds?
      1. On goods and services or transfers?
      2. In an area where the initial recipients of funds spent by government have a higher or lower MPC than the average for the community?
   B. How does the government raise the funds it spends?
      1. By taxing or borrowing?
      2. If by taxing what is the MPC of the particular taxpayers affected?
      3. If by borrowing:
         a. To what exent, if any, do the lenders cut their consumer spending in order to lend to government?
         b. To what extent does the government's added use of loanable funds raise the rate of interest and, thereby, indirectly cut private spending?
      4. If the fiscal action took the form of tax cuts, what is the MPC of the taxpayers affected?
   C. Does the fiscal policy itself cause offsetting cuts in private spending for any other reasons?

II. Given the rise in aggregate demand, what determines its effectiveness in eliminating unemployment without raising prices?

  A. How near to full employment are we?
  B. How near to full employment are the industries most directly affected by the government policy?
  C. How closely do the areas of unemployment and added government spending coincide geographically?
  D. How long does it take for aggregate demand to be affected?
  E. To what extent does the unemployment result from deficient aggregate demand rather than from structural factors in the economy?

Regarding the first question—the effect on aggregate demand—the variables are numerous. A given-sized fiscal program will raise demand more, other things being equal, the more government spending is devoted to goods-and-services expenditures rather than transfers where there is a possible leakage resulting from the MPS of transfer recipients. In addition, the second round of the multiplier effect may differ somewhat depending on the particular MPC's of those paid by the government. For example, a $10 billion rise in government spending on goods and services raises demand by a full $10 billion in the first instance. Even if the MPC for the "average" citizen is $\frac{4}{5}$, however, there is no guarantee that the rise in consumer spending which results next period will be $8 billion. For the recipients of the money spent by government may not be average. They could conceivably be well-paid contractors and construction workers with an MPC well below the average for the community. If so, the full effect on aggregate demand will be less than the $50 billion that the simple formula would predict.[7]

If the fiscal action takes the form of added government spending, the ultimate effect on demand depends heavily on the method used to finance the added expenditures. If taxes are increased to pay the tab, the expansionary influence of the rise in government spending will be in large measure (but not entirely) offset by the contractionary effect on private

---

[7] If the MPC for the average member of the community is $\frac{9}{10}$, but that of the group which initially receives the $10 billion extra spent by government is only $\frac{1}{2}$, the ultimate rise in the equilibrium income level would be $35 billion rather than $50 billion. Looking at it on a period by period basis, we would expect:

Period 1	Period 2	Period 3	Period 4	Period 5	
+ $10 billion	+ $5 billion	+ $4 billion	+ $3.2 billion	+ $2.56 billion	etc.

The increase in period 1 is the rise in government spending, while that in period 2 is the added consumer spending done by the group that initially receives the funds spent by government. From period 3 on, it is assumed that new income is dispersed to the community at large, where the average MPC, $\frac{9}{10}$, applies.

consumer spending of the tax hike. Only if the MPC of the taxpayers were one, implying that all of the tax increase (reduction in disposable income) would come out of consumer spending and none of it out of saving, would such a *balanced budget* increase fail to raise aggregate demand. Nevertheless, financing the government spending by taxes would almost certainly mean a smaller net rise in demand than if the funds were borrowed.

If the government borrows the funds via sale of securities, we must first consider the remote possibility that those who lend the money (buy the securities) may cut their consumer spending in order to do so. This hardly seems likely. Unlike taxpayers, whose incomes and private wealth positions are cut when the government takes more, bond buyers simply agree voluntarily to accept government securities for their loanable funds. Neither their incomes nor their wealth positions are cut so that there is no obvious reason to expect them to reduce their consumption. To argue otherwise is to imply that bond buyers decide voluntarily to save more (consume less) and lend the funds to the government simply because the government is trying to borrow. What seems very much more likely is that the bond buyers decide to divert funds that they had already decided to save away from private borrowers to the government.

But this too has its implications for aggregate demand. Even if we agree that those who lend to the government will not directly cut their spending in order to do so, the fact that government borrowing may reduce the funds available for business may indirectly cut private spending. If, for example, the government finances deficit spending by sale of securities to the nonbank public the increased demand for loanable funds —with no rise in the supply—will be likely to raise interest rates, cutting back investment spending somewhat. The reader will remember from the theory section that the expansionary effects of a rise in government spending will, assuming no rise in the money supply, be somewhat tempered by a rise in interest rates.

As we noted then, this need not happen if the deficit is financed by sale of securities to the banks. For in that case the increase in the demand for money (or for loanable funds) may be just offset by the rise in the supply of money (or loanable funds) so that the interest rate need not rise. The conclusion from all this is that the net increase in aggregate demand will be greatest if increased government spending is financed by borrowing from the banks, less if the funds are borrowed from the non-bank public; and least of all if they are raised via taxation.

Finally, we must recognize the possibility that the expansionary effects of fiscal action could be partially offset by the direct reactions of private spenders to the fiscal policy. For example, if there are investors who (rationally or not) are sufficiently fearful of a rise in the national debt to cut their outlays because of it, their doing so will certainly nullify part of the beneficial effects on aggregate demand.

It does not seem likely however, that such a negative response to fiscal action would amount to very much. In the first place, the modern business community is, in the main, too knowledgeable to react in this way. Secondly, there must be set off against such a response, the favorable effects of the fiscal policy on the expectations of those investors who understand its purposes and believe in its effectiveness. Those who expect the policy to succeed in raising demand would, on that account, probably increase their investment spending, reinforcing the policy.

So much for the determinants of the effect of the policy on aggregate demand. This takes us half the way. But if our objective is to raise employment we must go on to consider the conditions under which increased demand will accomplish the objective, instead of spilling over into such undesired results as price increases. This, of course, will depend, in the first place, on the phase of the business cycle. If there is substantial unemployment and unused capacity generally, increased demand is most likely to raise employment and real output with little pressure on prices. However the distribution of the unemployment matters too. If the industries most immediately affected by the fiscal action (for example, the construction industry) are near capacity, prices there may well be driven up even though there is considerable unemployment in the rest of the economy. Similarly, if the unemployment is geographically concentrated and the fiscal policy raises demand more generally throughout the economy, part of the added spending will be dissipated via undesirable price increases.

The time factor also matters. There is little benefit to demonstrating that, *if other things remain the same,* a given fiscal policy measure will ultimately raise aggregate demand by X billion dollars if that result would only be achieved after five years. If we are attempting to combat the business cycle, it matters little that aggregate demand could be raised by X billion dollars in five years, other things being equal, if there is good reason to expect the "other things" to change markedly long before five years. Perhaps, for policy purposes, we should concentrate our attention more on the expected rise in demand within a twelve-to-eighteen-month period rather than on an equilibrium result, which will never be realized anyway.

Finally, we must consider the possibility that the unemployment is not of the sort which a rise in demand can easily eliminate. If the unemployment is structural in nature, resulting, for example, from a work force whose training and skills simply does not meet the needs of employers with job openings, increased aggregate demand alone may do little to solve the problem.

The Weaknesses of Fiscal Policy Relative to Monetary Policy

Fiscal policy, whatever its strengths, is no panacea. Even its most enthusiastic adherents acknowledge that it has weaknesses, although there is, of course, disagreement regarding their severity.

One of the most serious drawbacks to discretionary fiscal policy, given the present institutional structure in the United States, is the time lag involved between the recognition of the need for action and the time when action can be taken. Because discretionary fiscal policy is entirely up to Congress to enact, delays of many months can be expected while the legislature considers action.

In this respect, fiscal policy contrasts sharply with monetary policy. Because monetary policy is in the hands of the seven-man Board of Governors it can be initiated with dispatch once the need for action has been determined. Clearly, with the existing U.S. governmental structure, monetary policy is superior to fiscal policy in terms of this particular time lag.[8]

Another disadvantage of the fiscal arm relative to its monetary counterpart is its inflexibility. Monetary policy, especially open-market operations can easily be reversed when conditions dictate. Fiscal policy, while not totally inflexible, is substantially more difficult to reverse. This is especially true of the public works variant of fiscal policy which, once turned on, is particularly difficult to stop before completion of the project.

A third problem with fiscal policy appears to be the political problem involved with its use to combat excessive demand. Fortunately, good economics coincides with good politics in a recession. A tax cut or an increase in government expenditure projects makes economic sense as well as being attractive politically. Unhappily this is not so in the inflation phase. In this case, good economics—a tax increase or reduction of government services—may be political poison. The result may well be that fiscal action to combat excessive demand may only be taken after even longer lags and in the most extreme cases.

Monetary policy once again has a relative advantage. While so-called tight money policies are by no means free of opposition and political pressures, the policy makers, the Federal Reserve Board, are far better insulated from the immediate threat of political retribution than are their fiscal counterparts. The result, almost certainly, is a speedier initial response to inflationary tendencies.

A majority of economists, while granting these deficiencies of dis-

---

[8] It should be noted that this advantage of monetary policy is not an inherent one. It exists because we have chosen to place the administration of monetary policy with a seven-man Board, rather than directly with Congress. If fiscal policy should ever be similarly administered, as has been suggested, its time lag problem would be markedly lessened.

cretionary fiscal policy, still feel that it can play a significant and, in some cases, dominant, role in the nation's stabilization policy. Some others, however, have become so impressed with the problems that they advocate abandoning discretionary fiscal policy altogether, relying only on the so-called automatic fiscal stabilizers to supplement monetary policy. It is their feeling that the lags involved in discretionary policy are so long and variable that fiscal action is more likely to reinforce the cycle than to combat it. In general, also, these opponents of discretionary fiscal policy appear to have more faith in the stabilizating potentialities of changes in money and credit conditions than some of their contemporaries.

Defenders of discretionary fiscal policy, on the other hand, might argue that its significant limitation is structural. Let Congress enact legislation to delegate a portion of their tax-setting power to an administrative agency not unlike the Board of Governors, they would argue, and much of the time lag problem would disappear.

DEBT MANAGEMENT

It has become traditional to refer to debt management as a third policy alternative, to be used along with monetary and fiscal policy. Although we shall abide by the strictures of tradition, there is room for questioning the validity of a treatment of debt management as an activity entirely distinct from monetary and fiscal policy. For debt management activities are so closely intertwined with monetary and fiscal actions that they often seem to merge.

Debt Management Defined

For our discussion we shall accept the definition of debt management employed by one authority in the field. Debt management includes "all actions of the government, including both the Treasury and the Federal Reserve, which affect the composition of the publicly held debt."[9]

Under this definition, the amount of new debt to be sold by the Treasury is in the fiscal policy province. Only the determination of its composition (the types of securities to be sold) involves debt management. Similarly the amount of securities to be sold (or bought) by the Federal Reserve is a monetary policy decision; the decision about the type of security to be sold (or bought) is one of debt management.

The lion's share of debt management decisions, however, are involved in the Treasury's efforts to refund the national debt. As outstanding

[9] Warren L. Smith, "Debt Management in the United States," Study Paper Number 19, *Study of Employment, Growth and Price Levels*, Joint Economic Committee (Washington, D.C., 1960), p. 2.

securities mature, the Treasury (assuming no tax surplus exists) must sell new ones to raise the money to pay off the holders of those coming due.[10] The choice of the type of new issue is, once again, a debt management decision. Some sense of the enormity of this refunding responsibility can be obtained from the fact that, as of February, 1966, over $94 billion of federal securities outstanding were within a year of maturity.

One further comment regarding our definition of debt management appears to be in order before we proceed. We are concerned only with changes in the composition of the publicly held debt. Publicly held debt should be taken to mean federal obligations owned by anyone other than the U.S. government investment accounts and the Federal Reserve Banks. As Table 21-1 indicates only a little over two-thirds of the total outstanding federal debt is publicly held.

TABLE 21-1 Estimated Ownership of Federal Securities, December, 1965 (billions of dollars)

U.S. Government Investment Accounts	61.9
Federal Reserve Banks	40.8
Individuals	72.2
Commercial Banks	60.9
State and Local Governments	22.8
Nonfinancial Corporations	15.7
Insurance Companies	10.4
Mutual Savings Banks	5.4
Foreigners	16.7
Miscellaneous and All Other	14.7
Total Federal Debt	321.4
Total Public Held Debt	218.7

SOURCE: *Federal Reserve Bulletin.*

The Objectives of Debt Management

What can and what should be accomplished via debt management? Opinions on this question have varied widely over the years.[11] In the years prior to the 1930's, the major aim of debt management

---

[10] In fact, refunding usually consists of an "exchange offering" of new securities to the holders of maturing obligations, rather than a sale for cash and then use of the cash to retire the old securities. Since the effect is the same in either case, we shall ignore the distinction.

[11] For a good discussion of these changing attitudes see the article by William E. Laird, "The Changing Views on Debt Management," *Quarterly Review of Economics and Business* (Autumn, 1963).

appears to have been simply to keep the then-small federal debt in as long-term a form as possible, thereby minimizing the Treasury's refunding difficulties. Of course, then, as now, the prime consideration was protection of the government's credit. Long-term debt, it was felt, was the "soundest" means of accomplishing this end.

The Great Depression and World War II changed all this. The former experience markedly intensified concern for economic stabilization while the latter, of course, gave us a truly large federal debt to manage. Debt management had become a major activity and considerable interest developed in employing it contracyclically, as a stabilization weapon to supplement monetary and fiscal policy.

In general terms, the idea was to shift (in refunding) toward long-term securities in periods of excess demand and then back toward short-term obligations during recessions. Lengthening the maturity of the debt structure during cyclical upswings was expected to help in at least two ways. In the first place, selling more long-term debt would tend to raise long-term interest rates. This, it was hoped, would hold down on investment expenditures somewhat. Secondly, by replacing highly liquid short-term obligations with less liquid long-term securities, the total liquidity of the public's wealth would be reduced so that, hopefully, further restrictions on demand would be forthcoming. The reverse, of course, follows in recession.

In recent years, however, the notion that debt management should be employed as a third stabilization weapon, has encountered increasing opposition.[12] Considerable doubt has been expressed regarding the magnitude of the effect on demand of such cyclical switches in the debt's maturity structure. In addition it has been pointed out that whatever can be accomplished through these means, to combat the business cycle, can probably be done more efficiently through intensification of monetary policy itself. Thirdly, the attempt to lengthen the maturity of the debt during booms runs some risk of undermining Federal Reserve policy since the Treasury sometimes requires support from the Federal Reserve when it attempts to place long-term issues. Such support, taking as it must the form of Federal Reserve open-market purchases, could require (at least temporarily) abandonment of a policy of restraint. Finally, borrowing long during booms when interest rates are typically high, and short during recessions when they are usually low, implies higher borrowing costs to the Treasury.

In the light of all these problems with a contracyclical debt management policy more and more economists appear to be moving toward the view that it does not really constitute an effective stabilization weapon.

12 See, for example, Warren Smith, *op. cit.*

There is widespread agreement that the maturity of the debt should be lengthened but not just during the boom phase of the cycle. Indeed, some would argue that the bulk of the long-term securities should be sold during the recessions, thereby taking advantage of the generally easier market conditions prevailing, and short terms during the booms. This would reduce the cost of servicing the debt, while generally easing the Treasury's refunding task. It would then be left entirely to the monetary and fiscal policy makers to take whatever action is needed to modify business cycle swings.

PRICE AND WAGE CONTROL VIA OTHER MEANS

When the problem is unemployment caused by deficient aggregate demand, fiscal and monetary policy stand virtually alone as the bulwarks of government policy. This need cause us little concern, however, for there is every indication that, given timely, skillful, and vigorous application, they will be adequate to meet the challenge. Moreover, the governmental assault on unemployment need not stop there. When the unemployment is of a structural nature, retraining, reschooling, and relocation programs may well pay large dividends in the form of further reducing the "irreducible" level of unemployment. The United States is far from solving all the problems connected with unemployment but most certainly it has come a long way since the bleak and desperate days of the Great Depression.

But the inflation problem represents a different kind of challenge. True, we think we know what to do about a moderate, well-behaved inflation caused by excessive demand, that is, with classical demand pull inflation. Here, too, monetary and fiscal policy are in order, in this case, to eliminate the excess demand. But here we encounter some problems. Not all inflations, even of the demand pull variety, are "well enough behaved" to permit the use of a sufficiently contractionary monetary-fiscal policy to do the job without risking serious conflict with other important national objectives. And worse still, other types of inflation, cost push and demand shift for example, may be largely beyond the effective reach of such aggregate tools as monetary and fiscal policy. What other defenses are there for such problems?

Authoritative Price and Wage Controls

Several times in the past the United States has found it necessary to resort to direct controls of prices and wages in order to handle the economic stresses of all-out war. These have always been considered temporary emergency measures to be abandoned as soon as possible after cessation of hostilities. Few economists concerned with maintenance of a dynamic and vigorous free enterprise system would consider them an appropriate element in the nation's peacetime stabilization arsenal.

It is not difficult to see why general price and wage controls on a permanent basis are so roundly deplored for the U.S. type of system. Generally they involve freezing wages and prices as of a given date, with later adjustments being available only through authoritative decision of a governmental body. Such an arrangement not only threatens individual initiative and personal economic freedom but also seriously impedes the very changes in relative prices upon which the economy depends so heavily for an optimum allocation of resources. There can be no doubt that long-run price-wage controls would drastically alter the nature of the U.S. economic system in a direction that few Americans would find acceptable.

In short-run emergency situations, however, the situation is different. An all-out war effort places demands on the economy which may not be handleable with ordinary peacetime methods. The tremendous increase in government spending normally called for can be counted on to spur a major inflationary surge unless it is offset by sufficient cuts in private spending.

The government, in such a situation, is faced with a choice among three unpleasant alternatives. First, it could leave taxes where they are, guaranteeing a huge government deficit, major inflation, and the massive and arbitrary redistributions of income and wealth which this implies. Equity consideration alone make this an unacceptable solution.

Secondly, it could raise taxes by an amount sufficient to cut private expenditures by the amount that government spending is increased. This approach seems, on first glance, to be eminently sensible and straightforward. However it is not all quite that simple. If such a massive tax increase could be carried out without serious interference with productive incentives, it would have much to recommend it. But that is exactly the problem. No one really knows to what degree such drastic tax hikes would hamper the incentive to produce and, faced with all-out war, past Congresses have not been of a mind to experiment and find out. Top priority at such a time must be assigned to high production for the nation's defense and any fiscal measures that might conceivably jeopardize this objective have been, quite understandably, shunned. Taxes were raised during World War II of course, and quite sharply. But the United States stopped far short of raising them by the amount necessary to forestall increased aggregate demand. A major inflationary gap thus existed which we chose to combat with the third alternative, authoritative price and wage controls.

These controls, necessarily accompanied by extensive authoritative rationing devices, have done their job during national emergencies but the United States has never accepted them as anything other than temporary emergency devices to be discarded as soon as circumstances permit. There is no reason to expect a change in this attitude in the future.

The Problems of Cost-push and Demand-shift Inflation

Demand-pull inflation, except for the case of wartime excesses, can be adequately combatted with monetary-fiscal measures. Unfortunately, however, no similar confidence exists in the government's ability to handle what have come to be called *cost-push* and *demand-shift* inflation.

Cost-push inflation is a rise in prices which occurs, not because of excess aggregate demand, but because businesses and unions possess the market power to simply mark up wages and prices, even when there is no excess demand for their product or service. Economists are in wide disagreement about the extent and seriousness of this phenomenon but all are agreed that, to the extent it exists, monetary and fiscal policy are not well equipped to handle it. For these two policy tools, as we have seen, operate through altering aggregate demand. If excessive demand is not the cause of the price increase, then, cutting demand may do little to help.

Demand-shift inflation can also exist without any excess of aggregate demand.[13] It arises as a direct result of the downward rigidity of prices in the United States. When consumer demand shifts from product A to product B (without any increase or excess of total demand), there is a tendency for prices in industry B to rise, reflecting the increase in demand, but, in most cases, no offsetting decline in prices in industry A where demand has declined. This latter results, of course, from built-in rigidities in industry A, which all but bar price cuts. With stable prices in A and rising prices in B the result is a rise in the average of both prices, or, in a word, inflation. Once again policy tools that simply cut aggregate demand are poorly designed to deal with the problem.

Voluntary Price Controls and the Council's Guidelines

Recognizing, among other matters, the problems just discussed, the President's Council of Economic Advisers unveiled, first in

[13] For an excellent discussion of this and the entire inflation issue see Charles I. Schultze, "Recent Inflation in the United States," Study Paper Number 1, *Study of Employment, Growth and Price Levels*, Joint Economic Committee, 1960.

1962, an essentially new, voluntary approach to price stabilization. In the words of the Council:

There are important segments of the economy where firms are large or employees well organized, or both. In these sectors private parties may exercise considerable discretion over the terms of wage bargains and price decisions. Thus, at least in the short run, there is considerable room for the exercise of private power and a parallel need for the assumption of private responsibility.

Individual wage and price decisions assume national importance when they involve large numbers of workers and large amounts of output directly, or when they are regarded by large segments of the economy as setting a pattern. Because such decisions affect the progress of the whole economy, there is legitimate reason for public interest in their content and consequences.

... Mandatory controls in peacetime over the outcomes of wage negotiations and over individual price decisions are neither desirable in the American tradition nor practical in a diffuse and decentralized continental economy. . . . It is, however, both desirable and practical that discretionary decisions on wages and prices recognize the national interest in the results.

... What are the guideposts which may be used in judging whether a particular price or wage decision may be inflationary?

... The general guide for noninflationary wage behavior is that the rate of increase in wage rates (including fringe benefits) in each industry be equal to the trend rate of over-all productivity increase. General acceptance of this guide would maintain stability of labor cost per unit of output for the economy as a whole—though not of course for individual industries.

The general guide for noninflationary price behavior calls for price reduction if the industry's rate of productivity increase exceeds the over-all rate—for this would mean declining unit labor costs; it calls for an appropriate increase in price if the opposite relationship prevails; and it calls for stable prices if the two rates of productivity increase are equal.[14]

Subsequently *Economic Reports* have repeated the wage-price guidelines in essentially similar form. How can we characterize this new approach to price stabilization? Basically it is an attempt to supplement, through voluntary means, the stabilizing potentialities of monetary and fiscal policy.

Critics, however, find much in the attempt which is objectionable. To begin with there is considerable doubt whether a truly voluntary appeal for restraint within the guidelines can work in a market-oriented economy. It seems to many to run counter to the very essence of the U.S. type economy.

Secondly, there is much concern with the possibility that, to the

[14] *Economic Report of the President* (January, 1962), pp. 185, 188-189.

degree it does work, it will do so capriciously, restraining some industries without affecting others, or holding down prices but not wages. In this connection there are those who argue that, however administered, the guideline policies are more likely to affect those large industries most exposed to the glare of publicity while leaving unscathed those less well publicized. Indeed, the Council itself lends some credence to this charge when it says, "These standards or 'guideposts' were also designed to permit the public to reach its own conclusions concerning the degree of responsibility exercised by leaders of business and labor."[15]

Thirdly there have been objections to the manner in which the government has responded to proposed price increases that appeared to exceed the guidelines. The power of the President to influence public opinion and the awesome economic power of the government as purchaser and as stockpiler have been cited as evidence that, at least in some cases, perhaps the guidelines are not truly voluntary.

As one critic has put it:

There is something distinctly wrong going on here. There are spasmodic and capricious interferences, by hazy formula, with market mechanisms which must be responsive to the constantly changing forces of supply and demand to retain their competitive vigor. There is a lack of precision as to when and how and to whom the controls or guidelines will be applied, which creates inequities that can lead to an erosion of good economic relations between government, industry and labor. There is the danger that the executive will be tempted to use these non-statutory powers which the government possesses. And, finally, the coercive methods and threats of reprisals which are being used to obtain compliance with executive edicts are creating a troublesome odor of punishment without legal sanction and without orderly procedures for redress of grievances.[16]

In essence, the critics seem to argue that if the guideposts were truly voluntary they would not help but that, since they are not really voluntary in practice, they are dangerously capricious.

Only time will reveal the effectiveness of this experiment. It does seem, however, that some of the critics miss one vital point, whatever the merits of their arguments in total. We do have means to deal with clear-cut demand-pull inflation but their use to deal with other types of inflation may not only fail to halt the price increases, but create unemployment and possible misallocation as well.[17] This, presumably, is the point of the Council of Economic Advisers when it says: "Both unions and manage-

[15] *Economic Report of the President* (January, 1966), p. 88.
[16] This quotation is from a speech by Allen Sproul, entitled *Perils of Personal Government*, circulated in mimeographed form.
[17] The rise in prices in the demand-shift case is essential, assuming other prices cannot fall, to reallocate resources according to consumer desires.

ment should reflect on the fact that if their actions create an inflationary spiral, the most likely outcome will be restrictive fiscal and monetary policies which will aim to stop further price increases but will in the process also reduce ouput, cut back profits, and reduce employment."[18]

[18] *Economic Report of the President* (January, 1966), p. 93.

INDEX